# Rural Education

## Also of Interest

† Available in hardcover and paperback.

# Westview Special Studies in Education

## Rural Education: In Search of a Better Way
### edited by Paul M. Nachtigal

The close-knit, personal nature of small rural communities results in school and community operating as a single integrated social structure. Useful rural school improvement strategies must, therefore, address needs that are recognized by both the local school and the community and must operate in a style congruent with the local setting. Although outside ideas and resources may contribute greatly to successful plans to improve rural schools, a high level of local involvement is essential in determining the specifics of those plans. This is clearly demonstrated by the thirteen case studies presented in this book, in which the strategies that have been effective over time in resolving rural school problems are distinguished by a high degree of local participation.

The cases—chosen to provide good examples of particular strategies and also to represent the diversity that characterizes rural America—cover centrally designed, heavily funded programs as well as small-scale, locally initiated efforts in such areas as teacher training, the introduction of new curricula, and community participation in education decision making and political action. The final chapters analyze the case studies in practical terms and recommend policy and practice for future rural school improvement.

Paul M. Nachtigal is director of the Rural Education Project at the Mid-continent Regional Education Laboratory. Prior to working on the study encompassed by this book, he was a project specialist with the Ford Foundation and served as superintendent of schools in several Colorado communities.

# Rural Education:
# In Search of a Better Way

edited by Paul M. Nachtigal

Westview Press / Boulder, Colorado

*Westview Special Studies in Education*

Published in 1982 in the United States of America by
  Westview Press, Inc.
  5500 Central Avenue
  Boulder, Colorado 80301
  Frederick A. Praeger, President and Publisher

Library of Congress Cataloging in Publication Data
Rural education.
    (Westview special studies in education)
    Includes index.
    1. Education,  Rural—United  States—Addresses,  essays,  lectures.  I. Nachtigal,
Paul M.  II. Series.
LC5146.R83    1982              370.19'346'0973            82-8368
ISBN 0-86531-323-7
ISBN 0-86531-324-5 (pbk.)                                  AACR2

Printed and bound in the United States of America

# Contents

**Part 3**
**Interpreting the Montage**

# Preface

This book reports on the findings of a national study of efforts to improve rural education. Given the diversity of rural education and the general lack of information about programs in small rural schools, however, it would be presumptuous to claim that what is presented here represents a definitive study of rural school improvement. Many good things have happened and continue to happen that could not be included because of the restraints of time and money. By including a wide range of strategies implemented in settings representative of the diversity of rural America this study has tried to capture the essence of rural school improvement.

I would like to express my appreciation to the authors of the case studies, who also assisted in the design of the study. Their varied backgrounds and multiple perspectives contributed much to the richness of the material. In a number of instances the team members were deliberately selected because they had been involved in the program they wrote about. The case studies were meant to be descriptive rather than evaluative; insights into the dynamics of rural school improvement efforts were deemed a higher priority than "objective" data about program outcomes.

I would also like to acknowledge the assistance of Dr. Robert Herriott, who, because of his experience in evaluating the Experimental Schools Program, contributed significantly to the practicality of the research design. And finally, considerable credit for the success of the study must go to Charles Thompson and Thomas Schultz, program officers at the National Institute of Education. Their active role in raising critical questions and ironing out bureaucratic problems was much appreciated.

The real substance of the study came from the site visits to observe the rural school improvement programs. I wish to acknowledge the fine cooperation we received and thank the many local program participants for their time and their openness in responding to our inquiry. It should also be said that local program participants have not always agreed with our descriptions of their efforts. Admittedly, a snapshot composed of data taken from documents and a few days on site can never do justice to a complex, long-term program.

The readability of the book has been greatly enhanced by the fine editorial work of Leslie Burger. Hers was the task of melding eight different authors into a coherent package without losing the unique flavor of each.

*Paul M. Nachtigal*

# Part 1

## Rural Education in America: Some Background

# 1
# Education in Rural America: An Overview

*Paul Nachtigal*

A three-story red brick elementary school, vintage 1900, dominates the highest point in Fort Gay, West Virginia, population 792. Its elevation belies the poor educational opportunities available to the thousand or so students drawn from a twenty-five-square-mile area where presidential candidate John F. Kennedy learned the meaning of Appalachian poverty. Across a dirt playground to the south is a prefabricated metal structure where the elementary school children and then the high school students of the neighboring Works Progress Administration–built high school file through to eat a hot lunch. Many students opt for hotdogs and soda pop dispensed from a crackerbox-size restaurant that fronts on school property and serves only students. The school in Fort Gay—as far west as you can get in West Virginia—is noted for its student-operated FM radio station; the community is known for its beer parlors that serve the suds-dry town of Louisa, Kentucky, just across the Tug River.

South Umpqua Consolidated School District 19 in southwest Oregon serves Canyonville (population 1,100), Myrtle Creek (population 3,000), the sprawling unincorporated town of Tri-City, the outlying rural population in the lush green valleys of Douglas fir country. South Umpqua High, a small-town version of big-city "suburban high," is located in Tri-City just off Interstate 5, the main north/south highway of the three Pacific states. Reflecting the national consolidation movement, the old high schools in Canyonville and Myrtle Creek are now junior high schools making room at the elementary level for more students. Not atypically, there was a long battle over the consolidation move, which resulted in removing the two high schools from their respective communities and the building of South Umpqua High. To add fuel to community dissension, there was a heavy snow on the day of the election, which prevented the more isolated populace from being a part of the decision making.

The San Juan County, Utah, school district sprawls in seemingly endless fashion across the northwest corner of Four Corners, the only place in the United States where four states meet (Colorado, New Mexico, Arizona, and Utah). The district's 7,799 square miles include wide open spaces, the beautiful vistas of Monument Valley, and a population of 10,000 souls about evenly divided between Navajos and Anglos. An old two-story elementary school flanked by a new high school with a new vocational school across the street serve the Blanding community, which sits in the middle of the district. Until recently it also served most of the Indian population farther south. A new high school for the vegetation-poor but resource-rich Navajo reservation just completed at Montezuma Creek, twenty-four miles to the southeast, serves the white energy-company employees and the surrounding Navajo community. Indian communities in the extreme southwest corner of the district, reachable only by traveling through neighboring Arizona, are still waiting for a school to serve their area. An all-Indian elementary school at Bluff, which serves a traditional Navajo community, and a predominantly Anglo K–12 system in Monticello at the opposite (northern) end of the system complete the physical facilities of the San Juan County school district, the largest geographically in the nation. As is traditional in dominantly Mormon (Latter Day Saints) communities of Utah, LDS "seminaries"—a kind of chapel to offset the ban on religion in public schools—have been built adjacent to most attendance centers.

The Alden, Iowa, Community School enrollment of 400 in K–12 is the product of a school consolidation in 1958 that educationally married the two small farm communities of Buckeye and Popejoy. A middle school attendance center is maintained in Popejoy eight miles to the northwest, and the remainder of the students are bused to Alden (population 876). In middle American fashion, the well-kept school shares the center of the community with an equally well-spruced Methodist church across the street.

The superintendent in Alden has held his position for eighteen years and teacher tenure averages ten years. These figures are above the national rural average, perhaps in part because the school has one of the highest salary schedules in the state for schools its size. This commitment has added up to excellence in teaching; for example, the high school science teacher has received the Iowa Academy of Science Award on two different occasions, and the home economics teacher has been recognized as outstanding teacher of the year by peers across the state. Community support of the schools is reflected in the recent approval of an $850,000 bond issue, an increasingly rare event in both urban and rural America. The Iowa Department of Public Instruction officially speculates that the move was "protective building," designed to ward off pressures to consolidate with Iowa Falls (population 6,654), six miles to the east.

The Fort Gays, Aldens, Blandings, and Canyonvilles of this country are home for the 54 million individuals who live outside America's designated urban areas. The 12,000 school districts in these communities constitute 75 percent of the operating school systems of the nation, educating approximately one-third of all students attending public schools.

The misperceptions about life in rural America are many. There are those, perhaps the majority, who feel that because of improved transportation and instant communication rural America will/has become just a more sparsely populated version of urban America. Sociologists John Friedman and John Miller represented this view when they wrote in 1965, "From a sociological and indeed economic standpoint what is properly urban and properly rural can no longer be distinguished. The United States is becoming a thoroughly urbanized society, perhaps the first such society in history."[1] Educational policymakers, apparently agreeing with this perspective, have pursued what David Tyack has described as a one-best-system model of education, which not only fails to recognize urban/suburban/rural differences, but ignores the needs of unique populations as well.[2]

An opposing perspective sees rural America as "the people left behind"—a part of the country where 14 million Americans live in poverty.[3] This perspective, updated by Frank Fratoe, describes rural America as being behind its metropolitan counterparts in terms of wage levels, family income, adequate housing, and access to education and health care. Rural school systems have relatively fewer support staff and services, less revenue, and lower per-pupil expenditures. Children in rural America begin school later, progress more slowly, and attain fewer years of education than their urban/suburban counterparts. In addition, rural residents are less likely to enter college, receive vocational training, or enroll in adult education programs.[4]

The communities of Mileston, Tchula, Lexington, Durant, Goodman, and Pickens are all served by the Holmes County, Mississippi, school system. They also have in common the characteristics of being rural, poor, and predominantly black. Remnants of the civil rights movement that made this a target county still remain. In Lexington, the United League has organized an unsuccessful attempt to boycott white-owned businesses to get better jobs. The sharecropper system has virtually disappeared; yet 800 blacks in Holmes County still live on plantations, where for three months of the year they chop and pack cotton for minimum wages or less, depending on what the landowners negotiate. During the other nine months they survive on their meager wages, government assistance checks, and whatever food they may have grown.

County schools were desegregated more than a decade ago, resulting in a black-controlled school system composed of 99.5 percent black students. The 1,350 white students attend the five private academies in the county. Blacks may run the schools, but the economy, dominated by operations like the 2,000-acre Egypt plantation, is firmly controlled by whites. The abandonment of the public schools by whites has eroded local financial support to the point that 40 percent of the operating budget comes from the federal government, according to the assistant school superintendent.

Another view sees rural America as a place where the good life can still be lived. Freshly painted farmsteads and neat, well-kept towns appear in orderly section-line fashion throughout the rich farmland of the Midwest. Devil's Lake, North Dakota, is a farming community and trade center an hour and a half drive west of Grand Forks. Located within the watershed of the Red River, the area around Devil's Lake is some of the richest farmland of the country. Huge $60,000 tractors, with air-conditioned cabs, stereo music, and two-way radios, till the soil. Commercials on local TV stations show such rigs driving off into the sunset, reminding third-generation farmers, who know only the tales of eating dirt behind a team of horses, that a Monrow plow can be folded up to meet the width requirements of the highway and headed home without the farmer ever leaving the comfort of the cab.

It is not too unusual, observers claim, for farmers with large spreads to work an average of eight to ten weeks out of the year—four or five weeks to get the crops in the ground, and four or five weeks to harvest. With no cows to milk and chickens to feed—those necessities being supplied by the giant grocery chains that hire people to shovel the manure and tend the hens and cows daily—they are free to travel and enjoy the good things in life during the long, hard North Dakota winters.

Although some are poorer than others in Devil's Lake, poverty is not obvious. The political process is relatively open and no one "owns" the area, residents claim. The schools are new or well-kept and the most modern equipment and progressive educational programs are in evidence, largely because of the close ties to the university in Grand Forks. The educators complain of the inevitable tight budgets, but they acknowledge that discipline problems are manageable. Devil's Lake is a good place to live, its residents insist.

A rapidly growing perspective views rural America as a place where city folks go to play, relax, and "drop out." It is a place where one can escape the intensity, stress, and noise of the city to fish, ski, boat, breathe fresh air, and enjoy the scenery. With greater and greater frequency urban dwellers are making the decision to opt for a more relaxing life-style on a small acreage or in a rural village.

James and Carolyn Robertson, who are part of this movement, argue in *The Small Towns Book* that with this renewed interest lies the possible extinction of the rural culture.

> Lacking knowledge of [rural culture's] workings, we tend to regard it with indifference while we absorb its virtues. Like a less "developed" society, it is

largely passive. Unaware of our effect, we damn it for being backward and then for being corrupted. . . . Continued migration of urban populations to rural communities will speed the process of suburbanization, for acculturation takes place in any instance in which new residents make demands on their new surroundings that require the establishment of services or facilities not demanded by previous residents and not indigenous to the prevailing occupational and social patterns.[5]

Wilmington, Vermont (population 1,586), lies on the eastern border of the Green Mountain National Forest. Just north of the Massachusetts line, the adjacent ski areas of Haystack, Hogback, and Mount Snow have turned the once-declining agricultural community into a booming recreational area. Swiss chalets and A-frames now share the valleys with the traditional white clapboard Vermont farmhouses. Main-street businesses, once abandoned, have been refurbished. One such establishment, Pancho's, caters to the American skiing craze with Mexican food and an Australian folk singer, who entertains with ballads of sailing the seven seas.

Wilmington is rural America in transition. Its once commonly held values are being challenged by the new ideas of "flatlanders," as the tourists are termed. Accustomed to urban amenities, the flatlanders are demanding new services of the schools and community. The children of more liberal, often one-parent families exhibit behavior different from that of local youth. Wilmington schools, because of their centrality to the community, have become one of the primary battlegrounds on which these cultural differences are played out.

The study team's travels in rural America suggest that the Friedman-Miller view of urbanization is too limited. We found a diversity that cannot be captured by a single perspective. Our travels to Lakota, Westbend, Fort Gay, Myrtle Creek, and other communities have convinced us that rural America is very much with us. The fact that it has largely been ignored in public policy has not made it go away.

In general, the layers of bureaucracy found in large urban/suburban communities are lacking in small communities. Communication can, therefore, be more direct, and verbal transactions can be substituted for written communiques. The validity of information is likely to be based as much on who said it as on what was said. Social relationships are more personal and tightly knit; people are known as individuals, not just statistics. Small-town rural society is generally more integrated, with individuals performing multiple roles. Running the town's business is a part-time job; construction workers still have multiple skills; doctors, when available, are general practitioners, not specialists; businesspeople tend to be entrepreneurs, not employees of large retail chains. Values tend to be more traditional, with more family structure intact, although this is changing in communities where in-migration is taking place. Traditionally, rural communities are more homogeneous in terms of race and socioeconomic status. Time is still measured by the seasons of the year rather than the ticking of a time clock. In rural areas, a man's word is still likely to be a binding agreement; trust is not yet a thing of the past.

Obviously the characteristics distinguishing rural communities from urban communities are not clear cut; rather, they form a continuum of rural to urban, with communities falling at different points depending on their size, location, and cultural history.

Schools serving small rural communities at the time of this study are the products of at least one round of school consolidation, a movement begun around the turn of the century. The movement resulted in the closing of most small country schools and the busing of children to the central school in town. Some parts of rural America have now completed a second round of consolidation. Interestingly enough, the new structures built as a result of the reorganization have often ended up not in town but out in the country. The rivalry of the neighboring towns involved in such mergers is sufficiently intense to rule out locating the new building in any one of the affected communities. With consolidation, busing has become an accepted part of rural education. Children in some of the large western school districts ride an hour or more one way. Problems related to busing—who gets picked up, where, and when; discipline; the purchase and maintenance of equipment—often consume more time for local boards and administrators than instructional matters.

The design of rural schools has been dictated by the prominent educational architectural style of the time rather than by any unique needs or opportunities inherent in rural communities. The oldest buildings still in use (circa 1900) are generally of the square two- or three-story brick construction design. The typical interior is noted for dark, squeaky wood flooring that has taken on the permanent smell of the "burnt cylinder" oil used for maintenance. Because the school was built before it was deemed necessary to have a full-time administrator, the principal's office is tucked into that nonusable space at the head of the stairs.

The next era of construction, the 1930s, was influenced by the austerity of the times and the need for a straightforward design that could be built by the Works Progress Administration (WPA), the New Deal's contribution to employment and public education. The two-story brick factorylike appearance was consistent with the uniform educational process that characterized both urban and rural education.

In the 1940s classrooms were placed end to end with long hallways on one side and an abundance of glass brick on the other, discouraging the use of the newly heralded audiovisual teaching techniques. The most recent era of construction incorporates large open spaces, movable walls, and carpeting (sold to the public as acoustical floor covering) to accommodate open education and flexible scheduling, which education innovators have been promoting as the education of the future. Urban schools of any given era look the same; rural schools are just smaller versions of "what's best."

The curriculum of rural education, with the possible exception of vocational agriculture and vocational home economics, is also a carbon copy of the larger school systems—or at least as much of a carbon copy as can be provided with limited staff and limited resources. The same textbooks used in urban schools are found in rural areas. The accepted standards of excellence created by state education agencies and regional accrediting agencies are the same in rural areas, including teacher certification standards, number of course offerings (measured in Carnegie units or equivalent timework measures), number of volumes in the library, and dollars spent per student. By almost any of these urban measures, rural schools come out looking second best. Analysis of data on whether or not they turn out a less well-educated adult is as yet inconclusive.

The teaching staff of small rural schools is generally a mix of long-tenured locals—housewives or part-time farmer/rancher/loggers who are credentialed, like to teach, and need the additional income—and outsiders who are working their way up in the profession. Because positions in rural schools are not considered to be the best jobs, outsiders' tenure is likely to be short. Generally there are more outsiders on the high school staff, and therefore high schools have a higher rate of turnover than the elementary schools.

This rather clear dichotomy between locals and outsiders—a distinction not found in the anonymity of an urban or suburban system—creates interesting problems for rural school reform efforts. The locals, because they are established community members, have as a first priority maintaining the ties that make them part of the community fabric. The outsider, on the other hand, wants to secure a future in the teaching profession. When a school improvement effort is introduced that requires a shift in the status quo, locals are likely to take their behavior cues from the community social structure, while outsiders are more likely to look to the profession for theirs.

The celebrated teacher surplus of recent years has yet to reach the more isolated school systems of the country. It is not unusual for rural school districts to still be looking for teachers, particularly in the more specialized subject areas (music and art), after the school term is under way and the accreditation teams are breathing down their necks.

Although the stringent codes of social conduct once imposed on rural schoolmarms and schoolmasters have gone the way of the one-room school, teachers in small communities continue to be more vulnerable to community pressures than those who teach in larger systems. They are known and constantly observed by the school patrons. If things are not going according to custom, they will surely hear about it, if not at school then in conversation at the local grocery store. Once teachers have established their reputations and created the necessary trust relationships with parents, the close school-community linkages have much to contribute to the quality of the children's education.

Administration, in the sense we now interpret it in urban systems, is limited in most small school districts. In the smaller districts principals either carry a teaching responsibility (part-time or even full-time in some cases) or serve as principal for more than one building. If they are teaching principals, they are likely to be teaching in one of the upper grades where special-subjects teachers can relieve them for a period or two to take care of their administrative duties. Support personnel, i.e., guidance counselors and reading specialists, are part-time or provided by a regional service agency—if available at all.

The most crucial person in a small school system, the superintendent, appears also to be the most problematic. Small schools, unlike large systems, are relatively free of bureaucratic inertia. As a result, a good leader can create a positive climate and institute educational improvements in rather short order. Likewise, a poor superintendent can arrive on the scene and destroy a program equally as fast. The qualifications of a good rural school superintendent cannot be quantified. One of the prime criteria appears to be the ability to get along in the community—more specifically, to stay in harmony with the school board.

Because of this need to be in tune with the community and because there is no bureaucratic buffer to protect the superintendent when relationships begin to wear, those with long tenure are in the minority. By far the majority of small-school superintendents are short termers, either using the small-school experience as a stepping stone to a better position or, outlasting their welcome in one small school, moving on to another until things get too uncomfortable there. It is not unusual to find situations in which the custodian, because he cleaned the building when the present community leaders were in school, has more political influence than the chief administrator.

The small rural school is likely to be one of the biggest (if not the biggest) businesses in town. School board membership is therefore of greater importance than in urban areas. In depressed communities, where control of jobs means political power, positions on the board may be hotly contested. Board membership is likely to include the town doctor, if there is one, one or two prominent businesspeople, and representation from the larger landholders of the area. Board meetings held in the evening after the day's work is done are seldom attended by members of the community. When a delegation does show up, a significant problem is afoot, one that could not be resolved by direct contact with school personnel or by the member of the board whose constituency is involved.

To break down by size the operating school districts in the country, the

National Center for Education Statistics uses the following categories: fewer than 300 students; 300 to 999; 1,000 to 2,499; 2,500 to 4,999; and 5,000 or more. These are useful divisions because the kinds of problems experienced by rural schools in trying to implement what is basically an urban school system are to a large degree related to size. A K–12 school system of fewer than 300 students means at the elementary level some teachers will have multigrade assignments. And in spite of the claims for nongraded/cross-grade groupings, the accepted, preferred standard assignment is one grade. A 300-student school system will have a high school of 100 or fewer. To offer the necessary (i.e., state approved) course of study requires a teaching staff that can teach in more than one content area, resulting in four, five, or six preparations for the teachers each day.

School systems in the 300 to 999 enrollment category have more than one section of each grade in the elementary level, thus offering some options if certain students cannot get along with certain teachers, as is often the case. At the high school level, teachers are much more likely to be able to teach in their major field. In school districts of fewer than a thousand, support personnel, curriculum specialists, and the administrative staff required by the ever-expanding state and federal programs are usually not affordable until the system gets into the larger enrollment brackets.

Again these limitations are predicated on the urbanized one-best-system model of education. If communities were given the opportunity to pursue some other models, the problems related to size might not be problems at all. The present rules of the game, however, place small rural schools at a distinct disadvantage.

To describe only the instructional side of a small rural school does not do it justice, for much of what is cherished by rural communities happens outside the classroom in so-called extracurricular activities. In larger school systems extracurricular activities are just that —a small part of the total program involving a relatively small percentage of the student body. In the small rural school the rate of participation in extracurricular activities is much higher. The leadership, character building, and socialization skills that come from activity trips, Future Farmers of America judging competitions, and other events are in fact an integral part of the school program. The role that athletic contests and musical and dramatic presentations serve in linking rural schools and rural communities is extremely important, because unlike the case in cities such events may be the primary, if not the only, source of public entertainment and public pride. The function of a rural school goes far beyond that of educating children; it is not only a piece of the local social structure, it is often the hub that holds the community together.

The small rural school increasingly is finding itself between a rock and a hard place. It clearly gets its support from and is expected to serve at least in part a rural community culture. It is also inextricably a part of an urbanized, one-best-system structure. From the local community perspective, the school that was once "theirs" is seen more and more as an outsider as more rules of the game are determined by state and federal mandates.

Programs are now required for special populations of which a rural community may have only a handful of representatives; legislation requires modification of building facilities for physically handicapped, when the community may have never had such students enrolled; accountability structures are such that $700 in clerical help may be necessary to administer a $2,000 milk program. Teachers must now do a better job of teaching the basics and also carry out a comprehensive program of career education. All of these special concerns must be administered by an administration consisting of one person, who also carries the instructional leadership responsibilities of a building princpal and, if the district is small enough, may have to double as nurse and janitor when those part-time people are not around.

It is difficult to argue against legislative mandates for special populations. Minority groups and the handicapped have too long been ill served. These special populations should not be penalized for where they live. There are reasons, however, to question some of the mandates on *how* programs are delivered. Within the personalized social milieu of the small community, intangible benefits should not be traded off too readily for more specialized programs. Classes are likely to be smaller, so teachers know their students and the students' parents. School personnel are accessible to the community (perhaps, from their perspective, too accessible). The close linkages between teachers and parents provide a level of accountability not found in larger systems. Lacking the bureaucratic superstructure of larger districts, rural schools have an inherent flexibility, which for the most part goes unused because of the one-best-system standard that has been imposed on them. Because of school size, teachers know their peers, the administration, and even the governing board. They thereby maintain a sense of control that is lost in larger systems.

Rural communities and rural schools continue to exist with their unique qualities in spite of the country's preoccupation with urbanization and attempts to overlay rural America with urban policies and urban structures. Rural communities are not miniature versions of the cities; they have different characteristics and different needs. Small rural schools that have traditionally been considered the weakest link in the public school system are now being hit the hardest by the triple threats of declining enrollment, limited resources, and increasing demands for program accountability. A model of schooling that was only marginally appropriate for rural communities under the best of conditions is rapidly becoming untenable as conditions become more difficult.

## Notes

1. John Friedman and John Miller, "The Urban Field," *Journal of the American Institute of Planners* 31 (November 1965), pp. 312–320.

2. David B. Tyack, *The One Best System: A History of American Urban Education* (Cambridge, Mass.: Harvard University Press, 1974).

3. President's National Advisory Commission on Rural Poverty, *The People Left Behind* (Washington, D.C.: Government Printing Office, 1967).

4. Frank Fratoe, *Rural Education and Rural Labor Force in the Seventies* (Washington, D.C.: Department of Agriculture, 1978).

5. James Robertson and Carolyn Robertson, *The Small Towns Book* (New York: Anchor Press/Doubleday, 1978).

# 2
# Rural School Improvement Efforts: An Interpretive History

*Paul Nachtigal*

Before presenting selected examples of recent rural education improvement activities, a brief review of past efforts is useful in establishing a historical perspective on rural school improvement. The commonly held view of professional leadership through the years depicts rural education as the poor country cousin of the public school system. By accepted standards rural schooling has been backward, poorly financed, and poorly staffed; it has offered fewer educational opportunities and turned out students less well equipped to cope with an industrialized urban society. Efforts to resolve these deficiencies fall into four themes of rural school reform based on different assumptions about the nature of the problem.

## Theme I: The Rural School Problem

As late as 1820 only 13 cities of over 8,000 people existed in the twenty-three states that composed the Union. American education *was* rural education. By 1860, the number of cities had increased to 141, marking the beginning of an urbanization trend that continued unabated until the 1970s.[1] With this surge of urbanization the critical problems for an emerging education system appeared in the cities, and it was here that the shape of American schooling evolved. With the modus operandi and standards of excellence established in the cities, it is little wonder that rural schools were seen as inferior simply because they were rural.

Convinced that within the techniques of industrialization—bigger is better, specialization, proper supervision—lies the secret for efficiency and effectiveness in education, reformers molded rural education into a likeness of urban education. Even before the twentieth century (and paralleling the industrial development of the country), efforts were made to systematize rural schools. The best professional thinking was that even the smallest one-room school could be given a graded structure with the stuff of learning broken down into discreet subject-matter courses. This provided some order for schools having all age levels in one room under the tutelage of highly transient schoolmarms or schoolmasters whose success was measured by whether or not they could manage the students.

In the 1890s the National Education Association Committee of Twelve on Rural Schools took steps to prescribe remedies for the rural school problem, many of which are still being applied today: "consolidation of schools and transportation of pupils, expert supervision by county superintendents, taking the schools out of politics, professionally-trained teachers." The rural school would teach country children sound values and vocational skills; the result was to be a standardized, modernized "community" in which leadership came from professionals.

"Don't underestimate the problem of school reform," Ellwood P. Cubberly wrote in 1914, "because the rural school is today in a state of arrested development, burdened by education traditions, lacking in effective supervision, controlled largely by rural people, who, too often, do not realize either their own needs or the possibilities of rural education, and taught by teachers who, generally speaking, have but little comprehension of the rural-life problem. . . . the task of reorganizing and redirecting rural education is difficult and will necessarily be slow."[2]

In the eyes of early reformers, opportunity for rural youth meant uniform regulations—as it does today. David Tyack, in *The One Best System*, described the extent to which such regulations were spelled out, down to the size and kind of pictures to be hung on the wall of the school. The ultimate goal of these reform efforts, according to Tyack, was the deliberate shifting of power from lay people to professionals.[3] The completeness of this shift of power is reflected in the successful implementation of school consolidation policies through the years. One can find few communities that have willingly given up their schools; the pressures for consolidation have almost always come from the outside by professionals. Armed with their rational arguments for efficiency and effectiveness, these professionals have reduced the number of school districts to some 16,000 during the last seventy-five years. And although few would argue that we still need the 200,000 one-room schools that existed in 1910, it is clear that the one-best-system approach exemplified by consolidation, standardization of educational practice, and centralization of decision making still pervades public policy today.

## Theme II: The Necessarily Existent Small School

The second theme did not emerge until the late 1950s. Basically agreeing with the one-best-system philosophy of Theme I, the necessarily existent small school concept was a by-product of the last major wave of school consolidation. In Colorado, the School District Reorganization Act of 1949 had reduced the number of districts from 2,222 to approximately 900. Eight years later the legislature passed the Reorganization Act of 1957 to finish the job of eliminating small, inefficient districts. This act reduced the number of districts to 184, just 3 more than now exist. What became clear even with this drastic reduction of school districts was that because of population sparsity some schools would continue to enroll small numbers of children. One third of the state's school districts still enroll fewer than 300 students, K–12, and over half (114 districts) enroll fewer than 1,000.

Against this backdrop, the Rocky Mountain Area Project for Small High Schools (RMAP) was developed. Its origins date back to 1954 when the superintendent of schools, the school board, and a selected citizens' committee in Aspen, Colorado, voiced the feeling that America's small rural high schools have inherent strengths that are not being fully recognized or utilized. Three years later the Rocky Mountain Area Project was funded by the Ford Foundation's Fund for the Advancement of Education as a companion to school district reorganization. The project would explore the "modification of methods of instruction" to improve instruction in the necessarily existent small high school.

Housed in the state department of education, the four-year effort focused on twenty schools scattered across Colorado. Attempting to capitalize on the strengths of smallness to overcome the limited and often weak programs found in such schools, RMAP explored the use of multiple-class teaching and small-group techniques. Technological aides were employed, including the Encyclopedia Britannica and the Harvey White physics and Frank Baxter chemistry film series; correspondence courses were offered when qualified teachers were not available; neighboring schools joined together for gifted-student seminars; and efforts were made to build flexibility into class scheduling. Week-long summer workshops held in a resort location, nationally known consultants, and two full-time project personnel provided what has now become known as networking and technical assistance for the participating schools.

As a state education agency–based improvement strategy, RMAP served as both carrot and stick. To be a part of the program, the school had to be "necessarily existent"; schools that had not yet reorganized and needed to could not participate. If they were reorganized they could receive the support of RMAP and be excused from accreditation standards, which in turn might stand in the way of exploring more suitable instructional processes.

The Rocky Mountain Area Project was one of a number of small-school improvement efforts supported by the Fund for the Advancement of Education and later by the Ford Foundation. Another such effort, the Rural School Improvement Program sponsored by Berea College, trained teachers to work with the small schools in the back hollows of eastern Kentucky. The Berea Program, sensitive to the cultural differences of these small communities, trained teachers to work with parents on locally perceived problems, which generally included physical renovation of school plants. As with RMAP, much of the assistance was taken to the community rather than expecting the participants to come to a central location for help.

The Alaska Rural School Project, also Ford Foundation financed, was based at the University of Alaska in Fairbanks. It established extensive training sessions for teachers bound for native village schools. Most of these schools were accessible only by bush plane and even then weather might prohibit travel for weeks or even months. Yearly supplies for school and personal use had to be shipped in during the summer. A young teacher fresh from the "lower forty-eight" had neither the teaching skills nor the physical and psychological survival skills for such an assignment. Summer sessions for new (and later experienced) bush teachers addressed these problems, in most cases even taking prospective teachers to the villages for a number of days prior to the beginning of school to orient them to the new environment. Two such teachers who taught in Huslia and Hughes, neighboring villages fifty air miles apart on the Koyukuk River, solved part of their isolation problem by buying small airplanes and learning to fly. When weather permitted they could get together and share mutual problems of teaching in the bush.

Other programs spawned by the "necessarily existent" rural school concept included the Rural Education Improvement Program of the Southern Association of Colleges and Schools, a regional accreditation agency (funded by the Danforth Foundation); the Oregon Small Schools Project; the Texas Small Schools Project; and the Upper Midwest Small Schools Project in North Dakota. It is interesting to note that the latter three organizations, which did not receive substantial foundation funding, are still in existence; the foundation-supported efforts ceased to exist soon after the funding ran out.

This era of small-school improvement efforts was capped by the Western States Small Schools Project, a $1.5 million, five-state program funded by the Ford Foundation and designed to seek solutions to common problems related to small and rural schools. The Western States Small Schools Project carried on some of the strategies of RMAP and explored many others, including the installation of new curricula, computer-based modular scheduling, telephone teaching, programmed materials, nongraded organization, bilingual and career exploration education, and the use of teacher aides.

The concept of the necessarily existent small schools was put into law in twenty-two states, some of which also provided supplemental funding. Although it is clear that many of the strategies implemented by these projects did in fact make sense for small schools, only in isolated instances have the practices continued. Personnel changes, the disappearance of project support systems, and the continual pressures of one-best-system standards have erased almost all vestiges.

### Theme III: The Strengths of Smallness

Theme III emerged about the same time as Theme II: the late 1950s. Its principal spokesman was Dr. Frank Cyr of Columbia Teachers College and the Catskill Area Project in Small School Design. Free from the political pressures of school consolidation within which RMAP operated, Cyr argued that not only were small schools necessary, they were desirable. Using an automobile/train analogy to contrast the potential flexibility and responsiveness of small schools versus the rigid efficiency of large systems, Cyr proposed that one could take advantage of the inherent strengths of smallness and offer a quality of education that even urban schools might emulate.

> The train is a series of specialized units—locomotive, baggage car, express car, day coaches, diner, parlor car, sleeping car—loosely coupled together. . . . A big school is a series of specialized units, too. The elementary pupils are segregated by age; the secondary pupils are segregated according to specialized subjects taught in classes of 20 to 40 students. There all pupils study the same subject under the same teacher at the same time. The large school is built, with this specialization in mind, as a series of specialized units. Teachers are trained and certified according to this same principle of standardized "subjects" taught.
>
> The small school should be as utilitarian as the automobile. The small school, like the automobile should be designed as a self-contained unit. It should not be designed as a series of specialized units, as is the railroad train. Like the automobile, the small school should be designed to serve the varied needs and interests of small groups of students. This means there is need for a new design of small schools, a design that will replace the rigidity of the specialized big-school pattern with a more flexible pattern. This design rests on several related characteristics.
>
> - The small school serves small groups.
> - Human relations are basic.
> - Organization and operation are articulated.
> - Operation must be flexible.
> - Personnel must be versatile.
> - Facilities must serve multiple purposes.
> - Pupils participate in policy and planning.
> - The school is an integral part of the community.[4]

What Cyr argued intuitively others have since supported with research. In 1964, Barker and Gump presented evidence in *Big School, Small School* that small schools indeed have a number of strengths not shared by large schools. For instance, the proportion of students who participated in district music festivals and dramatic, journalistic, and student government competitions was highest in high schools with enrollments between 61 and 150, with participation being three to twenty times as great as in schools of 2,000 or more. Academically, small-school students took more courses, with greater variety (many being "nonacademic"), than urban students, who tended toward more specialized programs even though large schools in fact offer a greater range of courses. The authors concluded that "it may be easier to bring specialized and varied behavior settings to small schools than to raise the level of individual participation in large schools."[5]

Jonathan Sher and Rachel Tompkins, in *Economy, Efficiency and Equality: The Myths of Rural School and District Consolidation*, have taken on the ultimate argument against small schools: that they are more expensive and less efficient than large schools. After reviewing the data on school economy/efficiency studies they concluded, "The point is not that economies of scale are nonexistent in rural education, but rather that they must be considered in conjunction with existing diseconomies." The savings incurred by larger classes and having one top administrator when small school districts are combined into a larger unit may be more than offset by higher transportation costs. Further, there is little evidence that consolidation has resulted in lower per-pupil cost or lower taxes.[6]

James Guthrie, in looking at the consequences of school consolidation, examined questions of "economic efficiency," "instructional outcomes," and "participation outcomes."[7] After reviewing studies on school size he concluded that "Evidence in favor of cost savings associated with larger size school and school districts is at best ambiguous. In the instance of rural schools, the setting where consolidation has been most dramatic, it is exceedingly unclear that efficiency favors larger organizations. Transportation appears to make the difference."

Establishing cause and effect relationships between instructional outcome and school size or any other single variable is very tenuous. Guthrie has concluded that with the exception of the badly handicapped, who do require the special teachers and equipment that only larger schools can provide, "There is sufficient evidence to suggest that the quality of school life is not always made better by attending schools that are bigger." On the matter of public participation in school organization, Guthrie points out that prior to the consolidation movement each school board member represented 250 constituents; now that number averages in excess of 2,000.

## Theme IV: The Problems of Education Are Generic

By the mid-1960s, attempts to differentiate rural school problems from urban problems as expressed in Themes II and III were lost in the massive federal interventions of the Great Society programs. The world of education was broken down into the "disadvantaged" and the "nondisadvantaged," and because there were poor minorities in rural areas as well as urban the same solutions were imposed. The Elementary and Secondary Education Act of 1965 with its Title I programs for children of low income families (e.g., Urban/Rural of the Education Professions Development Act and Teacher Corps) was designed to address the public schools' inability to adequately serve the low socioeconomic/minority population. More recent legislation for other special populations (e.g., the handicapped and migrant education programs) is based on these same generic assumptions: The problems with the education system are the same regardless of where the schools are located and the solutions are equally appropriate for cities and small towns.

The decline of a rural education organization within the National Education Association and the American Association of School Administrators is a further indication of the demise of rural education as a special area of concern and reflects the extent to which educators perceive themselves as part of a generic school system. In the late 1960s key personnel from the school improvement efforts of Themes II and III attempted to reverse this decline by creating a new professional organization for rural educators, the National Federation for Improvement of Rural Education (NFIRE), which failed to survive under the pressures of Theme IV. In 1975 the Rural Education Association evolved into the Rural/Regional Education Association to attract a broader clientele. However, not all regional service agencies were rural and the organization lost much of its rural focus. Five years later the RREA voted to leave the NEA sponsorship and reorganize once again as the Rural Education Association to better serve rural educators. In spite of these organizational changes, membership remains small. The absence of a rural education professional organization is no doubt related to the fact that few educators anticipate making a career of rural education; even if they did, they would not consider such a career unique enough to need a separate professional organization.

Although the four themes of rural school improvement emerged sequentially over time, the later themes have not replaced the earlier. Indeed, the consolidation thinking of Theme I along with the generic assumptions of Theme IV continue to dominate current policy with regard to rural education. Because of this domination of the one-best-system mind set, Theme II is tolerated only where no other options exist and Theme III (the strengths of smallness) has yet to have an opportunity to test its viability. Education policymakers and the profession itself have been sufficiently urbanized in their thinking to be insensitive to the possible problems of implementing generic solutions in small rural schools.

## Rural School Improvement: The Recent Past

In order to better understand the current state of rural education improvement efforts, thirteen projects were selected for more intensive study. Program sites were chosen that represented the diversity of rural America. Recognizing the fact that improving education takes place in many different ways, the study selected strategies that addressed different definitions of the problems of rural education. Programs selected ranged from heavily funded, centrally designed strategies to locally conceived and operated projects with limited funds.

Most of the school programs studied were based on generic assumptions about educational improvement. Only a few recent and locally initiated projects tended to reflect a more differentiated view of rural education. Eight programs studied dealt with school improvement variables within the educational system, and the majority of these were clearly based on generic assumptions about school improvement. Three of the projects were based on the assumption that rural schools would be improved if teachers were better prepared: the North Dakota New School of Behavioral Studies in Education; the Mountain Towns Teacher Center in Wilmington, Vermont; and the Teacher Corps Program in Holmes County, Mississippi. The Holmes County project held to the model prescribed by the National Teacher Corps office; the New School and the Mountain Towns Center modified the delivery, if not the content, of teacher training to accommodate the problems of bringing inservice education to rural areas.

The Experimental Schools Program in South Umpqua, Oregon; the Regional Education Service Center in San Angelo, Texas; and the National Diffusion Network/State Facilitator project in Maine all addressed the problems of rural school improvement more broadly—through curriculum development, access to outside resources, and staff development. Again, the basic assumptions about education were generic in nature. The guidelines for Experimental Schools were identical for rural and urban systems. The Texas service center's theme of "services available anywhere, available everywhere" and its funding structure place that organization in the mainstream of one-best-system thinking. Almost all of the National Diffusion Network programs have been developed in urban and suburban settings and are deemed by program officials to be applicable anywhere. Elk River, Idaho, has been designated by that state as a "necessarily existent" small school for funding purposes, yet program requirements for state approval remain the same as for larger schools. Only in the *Loblolly* project in Gary, Texas, did the nature of the program reflect local conditions.

The remaining six programs dealt with school improvement variables outside the system. The designs for two of the programs were based on generic assumptions about education. The purpose of the Urban/Rural Program in Fort Gay, West Virginia, was to shift control from central administration and professionals to teachers and community. The project strategy derived at least in part from the Ocean Hill-Brownsville struggle for community control in New York City. Program designers reasoned that if it was a good strategy for poor minorities in urban areas, it was also a good strategy for poor minorities in rural areas. The Rural Futures Development Program in San Juan County, Utah, which formed school-community groups for rational problem solving, is considered to be a neutral process applicable to schools of any size.

The Leadership Development Program, although drawing on some fairly universal notions of developing leadership (e.g., internships, travel, and independent study), did recognize regional differences in rural areas and was organized accordingly. One of the programs that most clearly departed from mainstream thinking, People United for Rural Education (PURE) in Iowa, was clearly in opposition to the first theme in its strong resistance to wholesale consolidation of small schools. The Staples, Minnesota, School/Community Development effort was designed specifically to address a local set of circumstances.

In this group of thirteen programs, there is some evidence that the generally accepted assumptions that rural schools are the problem and/or that schooling is a generic proposition are being questioned. In a few communities, new thinking and new strategies are beginning to emerge. As is obvious from the brief description of rural communities in Chapter 1 and the array of school improvement efforts outlined in the study, rural America's efforts to improve education resemble a montage more than a coherent portrait. Many different messages come through, some of which we try to interpret in the final chapters. Others you will discover as you read the stories.

The following chapters are not intended to be formal evaluations of any given programs; they are stories of how a particular strategy occurred in a particular setting at a given point in time. If any of the variables were changed, the story would be somewhat different.

## Notes

1. Ellwood P. Cubberly, *A Brief History of Education* (Boston: Houghton Mifflin, 1922), p. 363.

2. Ellwood P. Cubberly, *Rural Life and Education: A Study of the Rural-School Problem as a Phase of the Rural-Life Problem* (Boston: Houghton Mifflin, 1914), pp. 105–106.

3. David Tyack, *The One Best System: A History of American Urban Education* (Cambridge, Mass.: Harvard University Press, 1974).

4. Frank Cyr, *Catskill Area Project In Small School Design* (Oneonta, N.Y.: State University Teachers College, 1959).

5. Roger G. Barker and Paul V. Gump, *Big School, Small School* (Stanford, Calif.: Stanford University Press, 1964), p. 196.

6. Jonathan P. Sher and Rachel B. Tompkins, *Economy, Efficiency and Equality: The Myths of Rural School and District Consolidation* (Washington, D.C.: National Institute of Education, 1976).

7. James Guthrie, *Education Finance and Organization Research Perspectives for the Future* (Washington, D.C.: National Institute of Education, 1980), chap. 5.

# Part 2

## A Montage of Rural Education Improvement Efforts

# 3
# "Going Open" in North Dakota: The New School for Behavioral Studies in Education

*Faith Dunne*

In 1965, the North Dakota legislature authorized the expenditure of $20,000 (matched by $70,000 in federal funds) to sponsor a study of public education in the state. Spurred by increasing professional concern about the quality of education, the two-year Statewide Study found the North Dakota schools "ineffective, inefficient, and inequitable" and recommended comprehensive reform. The committee, composed of members of the Legislative Research Committee, the Department of Public Instruction, and the University of North Dakota faculty, was especially concerned about the condition of the small rural schools. They made two recommendations for improvement: first, school districts should be consolidated into K–12 units whose high schools served no fewer than 200 pupils each; and second, the 1,834 teachers who did not hold bachelor's degrees (59 percent of the elementary teaching force) should be induced to complete their college education.

Further, the committee felt, the educational upgrading program designed for these teachers should be used as a means of changing the mode of instruction in North Dakota. Inspired by the Joseph Featherstone articles on English informal education, which had just appeared in *The New Republic*, the committee declared that the teacher retraining program should prepare "the desired new kind of elementary teacher—one who views, accepts, and skillfully pursues teaching as clinical method" through an experimental program emphasizing individualized instruction, continuous progress, close faculty-student relationships, and a great deal of clinical practice.

To achieve these goals, the New School for Behavioral Studies, an experimental college, was established at the University of North Dakota. It existed for four years (1968–1972) with a program based on teacher exchange. A less-than-degree teacher would take a year's leave of absence from the classroom to attend the New School in Grand Forks and would be replaced by a master's degree candidate, who would serve as an intern in the local school for that year. Interns were prepared in an eight-week summer program and were supervised and supported in their field placements by regional clinical professors hired by the university. The less-than-degree teachers spent a full nine-month academic year in the New School program. Both interns and less-than-degree teachers were trained in open classroom philosophy and methods; both were specifically expected, as the Statewide Study Committee put it, "to develop and introduce the style of instruction that should be utilized—with appropriate modifications—in the elementary schools in the State."

### Babe Sampson: Looking For Something Different

Edmore, North Dakota, is a small town, typical of the farm communities scattered across the broad, flat, incredibly fertile plain that stretches from the Minnesota border to the badlands at the western edge of the state. The 400-person town is a compact island in a sea of wheat fields. The one main street offers unadorned stores and civic services to the townspeople and to families from the surrounding farms. Edmore's resources are basic to life in North Dakota: a grain elevator (a social as well as a commercial center), a grocery store, a post office, three bars, two churches, a bank, a farm implement dealer, a dentist, a senior citizens' center, and a one-building school serving the area's 450 children in twelve grades.

Delores Sampson, called "Babe" by her friends and colleagues, lives on an 850-acre farm near Edmore. She and her husband, Ole, have lived for thirty-five years on this farm and have rebuilt every structure, from the tidy, modern house to the flat, metal grain storage sheds. They have prospered on crops of wheat, barley, sunflowers, and flax. In addition, Babe Sampson has been an Edmore teacher and a North Dakota rural educator most of her adult life.

Born and raised on a farm near tiny Starkweather, North Dakota (population 350), Mrs. Sampson graduated from high school at sixteen and enrolled in nearby Minot State Teachers' College. Her decision to teach was dictated by circumstances as much as desire. She started college during World War II, when certified teachers were in short supply everywhere and almost nonexistent in sparsely populated areas. "All the men were at war and a lot of the women were in the women's services," Sampson recalls. "There were girls right out of high school who took a test and became teachers. I wanted to go to college, but my rural elementary school begged me to get the sixty-hour certificate and come back and teach. So I did." At that time, a school the size of Victoria was lucky to get a teacher with the one-summer-plus-one-year "rural certificate." And, Sampson says, Minot managed to pack a lot of training into the twelve months they were given to turn young high school girls into teachers capable of holding their own in mixed-grade rural schools.

Sampson taught at the Starkweather school for a year and a half, until she married Ole Sampson and moved to their Edmore farm. Then, following the pattern of the time, she left teaching to devote her time to child rearing and helping her husband on the farm. In the normal course of life in North Dakota, that would have been the end of her career—at least until her children were grown. But Sampson was restless. "The exchange of recipes and news about babies just didn't do enough for me," she remembers, nor did her civic involvements in the church Ladies Aid Society and the 4-H Club. When her youngest daughter was three, Sampson decided to redirect her energies into education.

This was not an easy step in Edmore. Her certificate was not adequate for the Edmore School in the 1950s, and the courses she needed were not offered within commuting distance. That meant she had to move to Minot for a summer to take classes at the college. Ole supported Babe's desire to get her credentials, but many Edmore people disapproved. "'What is Babe doing to poor Ole?' people said," she recalls. "But there was no other way I could do it."

Sampson got her certificate and a job in the Edmore School in the fall of 1958. She loved being back in the classroom and quickly learned to run an orderly, quiet room. "But after a couple of years I started feeling that I had to go back to school again," she says. This time, she began to spend her summers taking courses at the University of North Dakota in Grand Forks, living with her widowed mother while her older daughters ran the household. But the courses she found at the College of Education did not satisfy her growing need to find something really different to do with her classroom. "I was frustrated," she recalls. "I remember one day I was handing out twenty-five fifth-grade spellers to my class and I said to myself, 'This is dumb, Babe. For five of these kids this is no challenge at all, and three of them can't even read the book. There must be something else you can do.'"

Nothing in her training told her how to resolve this problem. "I started experimenting on my own," she recalls. "I once gave a test on fifth-grade history—match the explorer to the place he discovered—and then gave it again six weeks later. Of course they didn't remember anything. But it was the only way I knew to teach." At a workshop in a nearby town, Sampson heard a teacher from California talk about "individualizing instruction." It was the first time she had ever heard the term. "She got me thinking about how I could meet individual needs. I went back to Edmore and got the spellers, took them home and made kits out of them—like SRA [Scientific Research Associates, a publisher of individualized instruction materials]."

Several schools in the surrounding area heard about her kits, and teachers came to Edmore to see what she was doing.

Sampson liked the way her students responded to the spelling kits, and she enjoyed meeting other rural teachers who were looking around for new ways to teach. But she wanted more. "I started talking to Dick Kunkel, the superintendent," she says. "He knew my frustrations. I didn't know what to try next, and he didn't know what to tell me." Then, in 1968, Kunkel heard about a new program that seemed ideal for teachers like Babe Sampson. The New School for Behavioral Studies at the University of North Dakota (UND) was being organized and would accept its first group of less-than-degree teachers in September. At Kunkel's suggestion, a university representative, retired school superintendent "Mac" McRae, came to the Edmore school to tell the staff about the New School's offerings.

According to McRae, the New School wanted to teach just what Sampson wanted to learn: how to capitalize on the differences between children's learning patterns rather than ignoring them; how to use the resources of the community to improve education; how to enable children to work responsibly on their own. McRae was vague about the details of the program—it was so new that many of them had yet to be worked out—but what he said made sense to Sampson. Always the adventurer on the Edmore faculty, she was ready to sign up for the New School's first year.

The Edmore school board was ready to let her go, partly because they had confidence in her professional judgment (and in Kunkel's) and partly because the plan appeared to work to their advantage. When Sampson went to UND, the board would send 90 percent of her year's salary to the New School. This money was used to pay university tuition, fees, and a $3,600 stipend for her. In return, Edmore would get a trained (if inexperienced) teacher, a master's degree candidate whose program consisted of an intensive summer course, a year's supervised internship in Sampson's classroom, and another summer session to complete degree requirements. The intern would be paid $4,000 for the year—money raised from Edmore's contribution and federal funds. Further, the two stipends would be tax free, making them worth more than many rural teachers' salaries. A year after Sampson began the program, she would have her B.Ed., the intern would have his or her master's degree, Edmore would have an upgraded teacher, and everyone would have gained, both educationally and financially.

Although the financial arrangements were spelled out in great detail, the nature of the New School program was not clear to Sampson until she got to Grand Forks for the beginning of the fall term. She remembers that she was "excited about going to a school where they didn't even have names on the courses yet." But she could not have imagined what she would encounter there. She knew little about the open-education movement but a lot about college courses in North Dakota. The New School violated all of her expectations. One of the basic tenets of the program, the faculty explained, was that it would model what it taught. They believed in individualized instruction: every New School student would have an individualized program. They believed in freedom of choice and personal responsibility: students at the New School would attend class or not as they saw fit, and there would be no grades, no required reading lists, no tests, and few lectures. These practices were philosophically consistent but somewhat unnerving to some of the older teachers who, like Sampson, had been strictly and traditionally educated and who believed, by and large, in externally imposed discipline.

Some of the less-than-degree teachers adapted quickly, but others were outraged. Many felt that they were able to handle the freedom the New School provided but that the undergraduates in the program were not. "We didn't think they would be ready to be interns if they didn't study," one teacher from that first group recalls. "We thought they should be punished if they didn't come to class or didn't prepare."

The response of the New School staff was to hold meetings in which grievances were aired and issues debated. "I still thrill when I remember some of those meetings where we tried to work out our differences," Sampson recalls. "There we were—all ages, all speaking out. Many of the women who were my age say they learned to speak out at the New School. They knew their opinion would be respected." Not all the teachers were won over, "but we reached a point where we could talk comfortably."

New School classes were as unfamiliar as the policies. Teachers accustomed to courses such as Mathematics Methods were instead confronted with Creative Expression, for which they had to write poetry, create skits and plays, and draw and paint. More traditional-sounding courses, such as Nature and Conditions of Learning, included "clinical experiences" in a demonstration room equipped with all the paraphernalia of an English open classroom. But in spite of the unusual titles and activities, many of the "innovations" presented to the group had a familiar ring. According to Sampson, "it was strange—most of the people who went in the first year had been testing out things the way I was. They'd tell us about some new innovation and we'd look sideways at each other and laugh and say, 'We've been doing that.' We were really surprised to find that we had done those open classroom things in our one-room rural schools. We just didn't have the fancy names for them. We always had the older kids helping the younger ones. We just didn't call it 'cross-age teaching.'"

While Sampson and her classmates were grappling with the New School's unexpected program, the first interns were out in the field, dealing with some unanticipated problems of their own. Like the less-than-degree teachers, the interns had been plunged into a program that resembled nothing they had ever done in college before. Many were very enthusiastic about the central concepts of open education and eager to implement them in classrooms. But, for the inexperienced teachers, fresh out of college, implementation was not as easy as it had sounded in Grand Forks.

Jim Cox, Sampson's replacement intern in Edmore, was one of the enthusiastic ones—and more successful than many. A clean-cut, charming young man (and the only male teacher in the elementary school), Cox was able to reorganize Sampson's room, restructure her curriculum, and begin the process of introducing concepts of individualization and child-centered instruction to the rest of the staff. This process was not without problems, however, as Sampson learned whenever she came home for a weekend. "Some parents were concerned because Jim didn't know exactly how far to let the kids go," Sampson recalls. "They weren't concerned about what the children were learning, but, as the year went along, a lot of parents got less supportive of the behavior in the classroom."

Everyone liked Jim Cox, Sampson says, so he was able to do a lot of things that would have raised a furor elsewhere. In fact, she feels that he was able to use more informal methods and materials than she was when she returned to Edmore School. "They knew that Jim was only there a year. When I came back, people watched my classroom a lot more carefully than they watched Jim. I did a lot of inservice training that first year back—there was a lot more going on in other classrooms than in mine. I had to be extra careful what I did because everyone was watching me."

But neither Sampson's caution nor her position in the Edmore community could completely ward off trouble when she returned home. A local woman launched an attack on Jim Cox, Babe Sampson, and the New School program in general. She accused Cox of being a Communist tool, if not an active Communist himself. She declared that Sampson had been lured into cooperation with a Communist plot that was trying to take over the minds of young North Dakotans by consolidating schools into units so large that children would need to board away from home in order to attend high school, away from the moral influence of family and community.

Some Edmore citizens believed the woman's story. The New School was a significant educational innovation in education-conscious North Dakota, and the newspapers had covered the first year of the exchange program thoroughly—and not always sympathetically. One intern was withdrawn from a school after he was arrested for possession of marijuana, confirming in the minds of the many that the New School was a haven for "hippy addicts." Citizens in Bismarck circulated a petition asking that New School interns be barred from the elementary schools. According to Jim Cox, rumors were rampant throughout the state: New School–trained teachers were encouraging "children to urinate in corners and telling kids that they ought to take off their clothes and probe each other's bodies," and New School staff were running naked in the corridors at UND. In this anxious context, scare stories made sense to some people in Edmore.

But most of the Edmore community were reluctant to accept the notion that Babe Sampson, lifelong resident of northeastern North Dakota, pillar of the church Ladies Aid Society, had overnight become a Communist or a Communist dupe. Babe's first year back in Edmore required a good deal of diplomacy, but it was manageable. "I was a good person for the New School program," she says. "I had done all the right things in Edmore for years and years—in church, 4-H—and never made a ripple. They watched me, but most of them trusted me."

Like many of the less-than-degree teachers who came through the New School program, Sampson returned to Edmore as an intern and a master's degree candidate, completing her master's work in time to graduate from the New School with one of her daughters. Unlike the majority of her classmates, however, she left her school to be a "resource colleague" for the New School program, giving workshops and helping interns adapt open-classroom practices to the needs of schools in the region around Edmore.

## The Program: Juxtaposing Alternatives

In 1967, when the Statewide Study Committee was drafting its report and Babe Sampson was experimenting with her spelling kits, Vito Perrone was dean of the interdisciplinary undergraduate program at Northern Michigan University on Michigan's remote Upper Peninsula. Perrone was interested both in interdisciplinary studies and in the burgeoning open-classroom movement, which made him a natural choice as a reviewer for the Statewide Study draft materials. Later, when the plan for the experimental school had been completed, Perrone's name came up again. He had administrative experience, an appropriate range of interests, and the kind of imagination that would make it unlikely that the New School would fall into the traditional mold of the old College of Education. In fact, Perrone expressed little interest in the conventional constraints of most education programs, saying that his desire was to "develop programs in teacher education that had none of the characteristics of teacher education programs."

This iconoclastic attitude appealed to the selection committee, and Perrone was invited to become director in January 1968. He had precisely six months to recruit students (less-than-degree, master's level, and undergraduate, to give the program its full mix), hire a staff, design a program, and plan the intensive summer program. Student recruitment was an early hurdle. Interested undergraduates were comparatively easy to find among the student population at the university. But less-than-degree students and master's candidates who were also experienced teachers were more difficult to locate and to enroll. Perrone's use of men like McRae—solid, familiar, North Dakota school people, with good connections among the superintendents—was deliberately intended to promote trust. McRae "didn't do any active recruiting," Perrone says. "He would just go out to the schools and give information—no pressure." The information McRae gave was general and vague. "We always started with what we could agree on," Perrone recalls. "The districts knew that the New School was a different kind of program. But a lack of labels meant that different people could interpret what we were planning differently. Who knows what language means for different people? We were better off without labels." McRae's unpressured, label-free information was evidently trusted by superintendents, teachers, and school boards: it produced a group of sixty less-than-degree teachers for the first round of the program.

Faculty recruitment was no easy task, either. Perrone set out to pull together a "single, unified faculty with no departments isolating them from each other, no divergent purposes dividing them." A number of liberal arts professors were interested in this concept of teacher education but had no experience in working in a nonspecialized environment and little background in working with prospective and active teachers. The College of Education faculty, understandably unhappy about the very existence of a teacher-training facility not under their jurisdiction, was not made happier by Perrone's manifest attitude toward traditional programs such as theirs. Only one faculty member, Clara Pedersen, transferred to the New School. Picking his way through these problems, Perrone chose his staff carefully, selecting people he thought would work well together in the kind of open program he envisioned. This took more time than he had and left the first year's summer program in a precarious position. "Those who began in June met as a staff for the first time on a Sunday night," Perrone recalls. "Monday morning we had sixty students. More staff came in August which meant yet new beginnings."

The New School staff spent the first summer session working through one crisis after another. "But we worked on consensus building all the time," Perrone says. "We talked all the time. So enormous problems never developed." It is difficult to understand how they were avoided. The eight-week summer program, put together in haste, had two major purposes. First, Perrone wanted to prepare interns (many of whom had never been in a classroom) to run informal classes successfully. This was challenge enough. In addition, Perrone wanted the exchange program to encourage "local school districts to reexamine their educational efforts by placing alternative patterns of thought and action into juxtaposition with their more established ways." That meant that the interns had to run their classrooms as models of informal education, encouraging other teachers in the building to come to them to learn techniques. This was a substantial burden to place on novice teachers, especially since it was part of the program's hidden agenda and not always part of the information McRae provided to the local schools.

The first year began with that hectic summer, and the pace never really died down. Once the summer program was finished and the first group of interns was out in the field, the faculty had to readjust their teaching to the needs of a new clientele—Sampson and the rest of the less-than-degree teachers—who had far more experience and considerably less flexibility than the younger group of interns. Further, the staff now had added burdens: troubleshooting for interns who ran afoul of administrators, community members, or their own classes; providing resources and materials for classrooms that were inadequately equipped for informal techniques; and supervising and evaluating interns. There was a cadre of "clinical professors" who filled those roles in certain parts of the state, but they were not enough that first year; New School staff people were constantly on the road. "If we had hidden back here, it would have been tough," Perrone says. "But we got out, all the time. I remember driving 600–700 miles in a single day to go to an hour-and-a-half meeting."

National press coverage provided another drain on New School time and energy. New School staff, already working to cool down rumors circulating in the North Dakota press, found themselves inundated with reporters from national news magazines, wire services, and popular education journals. Interest in the English open-classroom movement was at its peak in 1969, and the notion that conservative, rural North Dakota was "going open" suddenly appealed to reporters' sense of the novel. As the word spread, nationally and internationally, North Dakota began to draw a steady stream of visitors, many of them interested in seeing the New School interns in action. The exchange schools in rural towns within one hundred miles of Grand Forks received a steady stream of foundation officials, network television crews, English educators, and American writers all year long. "The kids got used to it," one principal says, "but it was hard on the teachers."

National publicity had a side effect. The University of North Dakota had never drawn large numbers of students from outside the state. Suddenly the New School became a national center for the study of open education, and applications began to pour in from all over the country. This was flattering, but it brought problems. The first set of interns had been young, and many were inexperienced, but virtually all of them were native North Dakotans like Jim Cox, familiar with North Dakota lifeways. The second-year interns in that turn-of-the-decade period included long-haired, bead-wearing young people whose looks and manners startled and often offended local citizens.

The New School program weathered its first two years in spite of the rushed planning period, the anxious students, rumors, bead wearers, and reporters. By the beginning of the 1971-72 school year there were still North

Dakotans who were concerned about what the university was doing, but the most difficult time had passed. The first sets of less-than-degree teachers were back in their classrooms, the initial internship groups had gone on to schools of their own (mostly in North Dakota), and the sky had not fallen. Like Babe Sampson, most of the experienced teachers knew how to strengthen (or resurrect) relationships with their own communities, and rumors—at least of the wilder, running-naked-in-the-hall variety—began to wane.

During the two remaining years of the New School's existence, the basic teacher-training program remained essentially the same. There were inevitable variations, year by year, as the staff and the needs of students changed, but the focus and philosophy were stable. The major changes came in the form of carefully selected additions to the basic program, each chosen to fill a particular niche in North Dakota education, and each calculated to spread the word about the value of informal teaching techniques to a new target population.

The Future Indian Teachers (FIT) program is typical of these added programs. Indian women, working as aides in reservation schools, wanted to complete their certification requirements so they could join the thin ranks of Indian teachers. But it seemed impossible for them to do so: many of these women could not afford—practically or psychologically—to spend extended periods of time in Grand Forks. Further, most of them needed long-term education; unlike the less-than-degree group, most of the aides had no college experience at all. Finally, they needed money. They could not afford tuition, and most needed to continue earning money while attending school.

Perceiving this as an appropriate target population, the New School staff set about creating a program that would meet the women's needs. They found federal Career Opportunities Program money to pay tuitions and replace the aides' salaries. Then they established a program that would allow the Indian students to complete their degrees without spending all their time at the university. Students in the FIT program worked for six weeks in their reservation school, under New School staff supervision, and then went to Grand Forks for six weeks of more formal study. This cycle was repeated until the students were prepared for the bachelor's degree and certification. There were seventy-five students enrolled in 1972, the program's first year. That was ten times the entire Indian teaching force in North Dakota. Enough FIT students ultimately finished the program to make New School graduates the dominant group among Indian teachers. "Before the FIT program," one reservation teacher recalls, "there was one Indian teacher at my school. Now there are thirty. It's all because of the program. They took us out of the woods and into the light."

Both the Follow Through and Teachers' Centers programs were developed along similar lines. A problem was identified and a solution was developed that would spread New School practices to a different teacher population while fitting into the educational jigsaw puzzle that Perrone and his staff were putting together. UND Follow Through, for example, is being used in a number of school districts in North Dakota, Washington, Montana, and New Mexico. It also serves a clear function for the university's students. As Perrone has pointed out:

> The Follow Through and the FIT program did not . . . operate in isolation from the "regular" teacher preparation program. The programs overlapped in many ways both on campus and off. For example, at Fort Yates, a master's degree candidate served her internship in a Follow Through classroom and had an FIT student as a teacher aide. And, of course, faculty and doctoral students conducted workshops and classes for participants in all the programs. Also, when they became juniors, FIT students joined the regular undergraduate program while on campus.

The programs added after 1970 did more to spread New School philosophy and practices across the state (and beyond it) than to reduce the number of less-than-degree teachers in North Dakota. As time went on, that task was farmed out to other programs. "We never wanted a monopoly on the less-than-degree teachers," Perrone says. "Part of what we tried to do was not to say 'You ought to come back to the University,' but to help teachers consider what was easiest for them in terms of their family situations." To make this work, the university encouraged the development of multiple ways for less-than-degree teachers to finish their certification requirements, preferably in a program developed by a New School graduate. New School doctoral candidates started less-than-degree programs at Mayville State College and in Valley City, and the university readily agreed not to compete for those students. In addition, the New School encouraged the development of summer programs at various state colleges as well as at the university. Staff members and graduates mounted credit-bearing workshops in various parts of the state. Centralization was not considered important; accessibility was. Ultimately, only 240 less-than-degree teachers graduated from the New School; twice as many got their credentials elsewhere.

By the summer of 1972, a variety of efforts had solved the problem of less-than-degree teachers. Only 13 percent of the state's teaching force was still without a four-year degree, and, as Perrone puts it, "The ones who were left were not in the high interest group." Thus, the need for an ad hoc school to meet a specific goal had come to an end. The New School, however, was well established and successful. At that point, Perrone and the College of Education began to discuss a merger. "Within three years, the New School had demonstrated that it could do what it set out to do," Perrone says. "We had altered the composition of the education faculty with good results, and we had developed the possibility of working productively with school districts and the state. It didn't make sense to run parallel programs. I thought, 'Can't we take what we've learned and coalesce with the College of Education to the advantage of all?'" There were people in the College of Education who did not see it that way, but, after a predictable amount of maneuvering, a good deal of bitter argument, and the early (and angry) retirement of the College of Education's dean, the Center for Teaching and Learning was created, with Perrone at its head. The center, which now runs the state's major elementary and secondary programs, resembles the New School far more than the College of Education, and it continues the work of spreading informal philosophy and practice across the state.

## The View of the Communities

The first year of the New School was filled with confusion and challenge for both the staff and the participants. But they, at least, were on the spot, talking through problems, seeing the program take shape. For the citizens and school professionals of the rural districts, there were too few reassurances and many distracting stories about what the New School for Behavioral Studies was trying to do to the children of North Dakota. The name itself raised immediate questions. Why did we need a "new" school? What was the matter with the old one? Why were they studying behavior? Didn't our children behave as well as anyone else? And each question bred new ones. "They should never have called it the New School," observes one of its graduates, now the director of a teachers' center. "It only made people nervous. When you are doing something new, in a conservative state like this, you have to justify it all the time. That's what happened with the New School."

When Ray Pelton came to Velva as its new superintendent in the fall of 1968, justification was precisely what he wanted. Velva is a small, prosperous, conservative central North Dakota town, a cattle-producing community ("The Charolais Capital of America"), whose citizens went to the school their children now attend. Velva demands order and discipline in its classrooms, and the superintendent is expected to enforce it. Pelton arrived on the job to discover that two of his experienced teachers were on their way to Grand Forks; their replacements were two inexperienced master's degree candidates with unusual ideas about how to set up a classroom. "I had just finished my doctoral program at the University of Wyoming," Pelton recalls, "and I had never heard about all these techniques. If they were so good, why hadn't I heard about them in Wyoming, I wanted to know." Unlike Jim Cox, whose personality helped redeem his classroom practices, the Velva interns got into deep trouble almost immediately and never got out. "There was one who just spoiled it for the rest of us," says a teacher who was part of the first year program. "She was inexperienced and just let it all hang out. It was too bad. When I got back, the teachers said, 'Well, I suppose the walls will come down now.' The interns gave the New School a bad name."

Pelton, suspicious of the program to begin with, suspended the Velva participation after the first year. Looking back, he admits that the program had a good long-term effect on the school as a whole. "The teachers who went to the New School really spread good ideas when they came back here," he says. "They went from being just good to being great." But he expresses no regret that the program ended after one year; he feels that Velva got all it needed (or could stand) from the participation of its two teachers.

Velva had only two interns, so the controversy about their classroom practices was largely confined to the school. But in other communities the New School presence was more visible and attracted more local concern. In Starkweather, where Babe Sampson grew up, the entire elementary program was turned over to interns during the first year of the program. The Starkweather School became a focus of national attention as it was transformed, overnight, into one of the most innovative open-classroom elementary schools in the country. This delighted reporters and education writers but not Starkweather. "A lot of people were pretty unhappy," says a Starkweather teacher who was part of the first group of exchange teachers. "Some practices that look good on paper don't work out so well in the classroom. We had to sell the program—I called in all the mothers to tell them about it before I went. Maybe we oversold it. When I came back they really jumped on me."

Part of the problem in the communities seemed to stem from a confusion about who was in charge of the interns. The rural principals and superintendents tended to supervise their classrooms rather closely, and they were held accountable for close supervision by their boards. The interns, however, felt primarily responsible to their university supervisors and sometimes ignored local expectations and standards. In one school, an intern and his class decided that the back wall of their classroom needed a mural. Without consulting the principal, the teacher bought the paint and had completed most of the project before informing anyone. His response to the principal's displeasure was surprise: Whose classroom was it, anyway? In another school, where the principal prided himself on orderly classrooms and empty, silent corridors, a pair of interns decided to use the hallway as a laboratory for demonstrations of aerodynamic concepts. The principal emerged from his office to find two young teachers and their classes flying paper airplanes in the hall. He was not amused, and his desire to allay community concerns about the New School did not increase after that incident.

The teacher-exchange program fared best in towns where the superintendent understood what was going on and was able to communicate his understanding to a trusting community. In Towner, for example, where Robert Muhs has been superintendent of the 420-pupil school for more than twenty years, the New School program continued, with reasonable community support, for years. "Some people talked about Communist infiltration," he says, "but most of it was hogwash, and I told them so. There never was a written contract between me and Dean Perrone. All he ever asked us to do was to try the program without any obligation to continue it past the first year." By the end of the New School program, most of Towner's teachers had been trained or retrained at the university. Evidently, when Superintendent Muhs tells Towner that something is hogwash, Towner is ready to believe him.

In fact, where there was administrative support, the New School program ultimately gained considerable support. "We had five or six who were deathly against it," remembers one former intern. "We were called Communists and I don't know what. But 60–70 percent were really for it." His perceptions are backed up by a 1972 study of the program done by a New School graduate, Sister Karen Craig. Sister Craig's questionnaire and interview-based evaluation of the program found fully 76 percent of the mothers in her sample either "favorable" or "somewhat favorable" in their feelings about the program. Given the swift implementation of the program and the startling contrast between open classrooms and the strictly ordered, silent schoolrooms that preceded them, this is a very high level of acceptance. Perrone attributes this adaptability to a willingness of North Dakotans to take risks. "If you look at North Dakota history," he says, "it indicates that people here have historically been willing to risk a lot for what they thought would benefit their families and communities. The New School was part of that."

### Looking Back: How Well Did it Work?

It is more than a decade since Babe Sampson went to Grand Forks to begin the program that "sounded exciting and challenging because I wasn't sure what it would be." Enough time has elapsed to make it possible to look at the achievements of the New School in terms of its original goals. Some of these objectives have obviously been achieved. The Statewide Study Committee wanted elementary school teachers "upgraded." Today, more than 90 percent of North Dakota's elementary teachers are fully certified, most of them through programs influenced, if not mounted, by the New School. The Statewide Study Committee wanted the graduates of their new program to remain in the state, even though that was not traditionally the pattern for teachers who acquired four-year certificates. Sister Craig's 1973 study of New School graduates showed that a substantial majority (85–90 percent) are still teaching in North Dakota, many of them at the schools in which they interned or originally taught.

It is less clear whether the New School achieved its central philosophical goal—the transformation of North Dakota's elementary classrooms from teacher centered to pupil centered, from group oriented to individualized, from structured to informal and open practices. The 1973 study of New School graduates found that these teachers were not as "open" as the New School staff would have liked, and former interns and less-than-degree teachers have shifted back to more traditional methods as the years have passed. Some classrooms (and some schools), however, remain very activity centered—personal versions of the New School's open-classroom ideal. Small groups of children cluster around science tables, lie on rugs to read library books, respond to large poster/collages with questions on them ("This is Durum Wheat  Can You Tell What is Made From It?"), or build towers out of cuisenaire rods. Most of these rooms are informal but very well controlled, clearly the domain of experienced open-classroom teachers.

Other rooms are hybrids, combining selected New School practices with more traditional modes of instruction. One young woman, an intern in the first year of the program, has noticed that her room represents the changes in her attitude over the years. When she began teaching, she says, her room was "all interest centers—no desks at all—lots of projects, puppet shows and plays." Now a sign hangs next to her desk—"If you Learn To Follow Orders Exactly, You May Someday be Able to Give Them"—and the children's tables and chairs are in neat rows facing front. But there is still a reading corner, near the windows, lined with a rug and piled with pillows, and a math center, well-stocked with math games and worksheets, occupies another corner. "You had to pick and choose the things that were right for you," the teacher says. "I'm kind of conservative by nature, so I had some questions about the program from the beginning  Some of those people were pretty idealistic. Many of the approaches were impractical—like letting the kids choose what they want to do. First graders need a definite pattern of growth and development, and the teacher needs to set it."

This teacher expresses very positive feelings about the New School program. She feels that the things she learned there have contributed significantly to her teaching style, even though she rejected much of what she was taught. "They helped me realize about individual needs. Now, I believe that teachers need to be in charge of a classroom—they were a little loose about discipline—but I realize that each child works at a different level, and I'm doing that in reading and math. That's the kind of thing that's left after ten years."

Finally, there are rooms that cannot even be called hybrids, because the original concepts taught by the New School have been altered almost beyond recognition. One teacher, a member of Babe Sampson's class at the New School, considers her experience in the program one of the best things that ever happened to her. She says that her room meshes all the things she learned in the New School with new concepts acquired during her master's degree program emphasizing behavioral modification techniques. This teacher has an "activity center" in a curtained-off corner at the back of her fifth-grade classroom, behind the straight rows of desks. The center is used as a reward for students who show the kind of behavior she wants to reinforce. "I give my children slips of paper when they do things I am trying to teach them," she says. "Right now, I'm working on getting them to wait until lunch to ask to go to the bathroom. They get a white slip for every day they don't ask to be excused. When they get twenty slips, they can go to the activity center. If they lose their slips, though, they have to start all over again. That teaches them personal responsibility—we learned how important that is at the New School."

It is doubtful that the New School faculty would cheer this definition of "personal responsibility" or use of activity centers. But the teachers' wide range of interpretations of the open-classroom doctrine is the product of one of their most deliberate strategies. "The New School taught me to find out what is me and to do that," one graduate says, echoing the sentiments of many others. "I'm always looking for change now—we're so much freer than we used to be. I want to find my own way now." According to Clara Pedersen, who has been with the program since its inception, the development of teachers' ability to make choices was a major goal of the New School. It was assumed that, ultimately, choice would lead to acceptance of more open practices. The New School faculty, said Pedersen, believed that teachers, like children, have to mature through developmental stages, from traditional conservatism to fully developed informal teaching. The job of the New School, she felt, was to foster natural growth. If some teachers haven't reached the point where they can have open classrooms, they need more time, more choices, more facilitation. The intention of the New School faculty was to model mature teaching and to encourage students to choose those mature techniques. But the rate of maturation was expected to differ from teacher to teacher.

This does not mean that Perrone and his staff must embrace all the translations of New School practices that exist in North Dakota classrooms. But it does give them the capacity to deal with that range. "We remain pretty responsive," Perrone says, "which means we deal with students who are so conservative it hurts. They aren't interested in alternatives, and we have to respond to their interests. We start with structures people can deal with and work from there." A belief in the continuing possibility of growth and change and a willingness to take pleasure in small gains keeps Perrone and his colleagues going. "My sense is that schools are different from the way they were in 1968," Perrone says. "When I went out in the schools then, they were pretty bleak. They aren't just what we'd want now, but they are changed."

### Analysis: What is Success?

The most remarkable quality of the New School program is its endurance. Rural school improvement programs, especially comprehensive ones, tend to die quickly—usually vanishing with the funds that support them. Ten years later, all recognizable traces of the reform have usually vanished. But in North Dakota, much has changed in ten years. The New School has become the Center for Teaching and Learning, with the modifications required for the absorption of much of the old College of Education. New programs have been added, and the staff has learned to respond to a new, more conservative group of young teacher candidates and a back-to-basics trend in instructional fashion. But the fundamental philosophy and program of the New School persists. New School graduates form the largest coherent group of educators in North Dakota. Former interns, less-than-degree teachers, and undergraduates trained in the New School program have become principals and superintendents and directors of teachers' centers and teacher-training programs throughout the state. The root concepts of informal instruction have become part of the fabric of North Dakota education.

Why has this happened? In spite of the carefully (and deliberately) drawn parallels between open-classroom teaching and certain one-room rural school practices, there is no reason to believe that open education was uniquely suited to the state. In fact, there was considerable evidence during the first two years of the program that some teachers and many community people considered it a significant departure from traditional practice. The success of the New School program lies not in its content, but in its strategy. Essentially, its history is the story of people who knew how to create—and institutionalize—change in conservative rural communities.

The strategy has several components. First, the program was a state-initiated, state-controlled effort from its inception. The legislature sponsored the Statewide Study, and the committee members were known and respected professionals in North Dakota. The recommendations in the Statewide Study Report were based on local information and an assessment of local needs. When the committee decided to promote open education, they talked about individualization and peer tutoring in one-room North Dakota schools, not about the British informal classroom movement, even though many of the committee members had originally been inspired by Joseph Featherstone's reports on the Leicestershire schools. Thus, there was never a sense in North Dakota that the New School had been forced upon the state in response to outside pressures or distant mandates. It was a state effort, worthy of state commitment. This made it comparatively easy for Perrone to build relationships with school people and with state officials, relationships that probably made it possible for the New School to weather the initial storm of criticism during the first two years.

Second, the program was designed to be decentralized. Within the exchange program, the teacher was expected to be the chief agent of dissemination of informal teaching methods. This inevitably limited the degree of change that would take place in some schools, but it also virtually guaranteed that the changes that were adopted would last. Making the local schools the arena for educational reform had its costs, as all the mistakes were very visible, but the successes were equally apparent and immediately available for implementation.

Perrone is committed to decentralization and to the use of trusted people as implementers of change. He actively encourages diffusion of power and responsibility rather than trying to maintain a center of control in Grand Forks. His style is to offer assistance to people who are trying to start their own programs and then to fade into the background, leaving the sense of ownership to those who will have to take the responsibility for the program. He has been very successful in that effort. One woman, trained at North Dakota State University in Fargo, now works in a small teachers' center directed by a New School graduate. The state Teachers' Center proposal was put together by Perrone and his staff, and he is active in that program. But this teacher has no sense that Perrone has had any impact on her work; she says, in fact, that she had never heard of him until she left the state to go to a Teachers' Center conference. This seems a good indication of the level of independence and self-determination encouraged by Perrone.

Similarly, the Mayville State College teacher-training program, which is run by New School graduates, and which is part of the new statewide (and Perrone-structured) Teachers' Center network, is considered entirely free from university influence. Faculty members admire the Center for Teaching and Learning and respect Perrone and his staff, but they feel that they have discovered their own direction and are pursuing their own paths. Nevertheless, their Teachers' Center appears to be focused toward encouraging small-group and individualized instruction, and their administrative concerns include the establishment of a financial structure that will culminate in support of their center by local school districts. They are going their own way, but much of the route has been paved by Perrone.

Third, the New School developed under conditions that Perrone claims are critical to success in programs of educational reform: more than enough time and less than enough money. This combination is usually reversed, he says, by foundations and the government, thus guaranteeing failure. "The federal government always wants a time limit," Perrone says. "What will you do in three years? In five? I never know how long it is going to take, so I don't tell them I do. You need to have no sense of constraint." Perrone feels that the time constraint placed by most federal and foundation grants forces the administrator to focus on quick measurable results, which are, in the long run, the least likely to last. If that pressure is removed, the program leaders can focus on the process and on the people involved in the process. This is more likely to lead to long-range commitment and long-term effects.

The issue of money is usually crucial, Perrone feels. Program designers generally assume that more money is better than less. More money allows room to deal with the unexpected, buys more talent, and enhances school districts' desire to participate. Perrone says that this approach is all wrong, especially if the objective of the program is long-term, institutionalized results. "Programs have to have the potential for self-support," he says, and that means they cannot be so heavily endowed from the outside that local institutions could not possibly afford to carry them on at the end of the funding period. Further, Perrone feels that the local contribution of funds builds a sense of ownership among the clientele. In the original New School exchange program, the school district contribution paid for part of the less-than-degree teachers' costs. This was not a great deal of money, and it probably could have been funded by the Office of Education grant. But Perrone feels that much of the district-level support for the program in its early years came from school boards that had invested district money in the program and thus had a stake in seeing it turn out well.

Finally, the New School had Vito Perrone, a considerable asset. Perrone came to North Dakota knowing what was necessary to make a school improvement program work in a rural state. First, he made a long-term commitment to stay on the job until the program was well established. Second, he spent endless hours building trust, with New School staff, with school people, with the State Department of Education. "An enormous amount of trust has developed over the years among people I work with," he says. "We're all in it for the long haul and we all know it." Third, he has an unusual ability to maintain a clear and focused vision of a distant goal, without losing patience with the very slow, incremental rate of change characteristic of rural areas. "We wanted to build systems that can continue," Perrone says, and that sentiment has dominated most of the major decisions the New School has made.

Compared to most visions of educational change, the New School program has had very modest effects. But in the context of rural school improvement efforts it has been a substantial success. The program tried to solve a problem that rural teachers and communities perceived as important, using a process that kept a considerable amount of power in the hands of the teacher and the district. The program did not push teachers out of rural education, nor did it send in teams of university experts to tell rural people how backward they were. And, ultimately, the program became part of the structure of education in the state. Rural school life in North Dakota may not have changed radically, but it has changed. As Perrone once said, "Most efforts to change the behavior of teachers have failed utterly. So people are coming from everywhere to see great and wonderful things and worship at the font of change. But this is no Mecca. We're just struggling to do some very difficult things." In North Dakota, the struggle seems likely to continue.

4

# The Teacher Corps
# in Mississippi:
# Washington Strategy
# Against Delta Dilemmas

*James Branscome*

From a few thousand feet in the air, Holmes County, Mississippi, where the rich black earth of the delta meets the hill country, looks as green as the Ozarks and as prosperous as Kansas. From the ground, however, it does not take a discerning eye to perceive that the county's political, social, and economic life is scorched and singed by racism. By any standard the country is rural and poor. Longtime followers of the county's battles between black sharecroppers and the white plantation establishment readily admit that it is only on the most narrowly defined scale of political relativity that dramatic progress can be claimed for the county's majority black population.

"The black man's water supply still begins where the white man's sewer stops," says Howard Taft Bailey, a black county supervisor who has been active for two decades in the poverty and civil rights movement in the county. Despite increasing black control of some county institutions in the state, "the only way we can get anything here is with federal dollars," he says. "The local and state judges are all white, and if you can't get into federal courts, you'd just as well forget justice." Bailey is one of 17 black supervisors of a total 410 in the state.

In Holmes County, where the schools were desegregated a decade ago, public school enrollment is 99.5 percent black and 0.5 percent white. Of 6,000 school-age children, the 1,350 white students attend five private academies ("segacademies") and the blacks attend the public schools ("attendance centers," as black schools are still called to differentiate between them and white schools).

Although blacks now control the Holmes school system, the whites control the economic system and see to it that the state legislature does not raise the property tax limits so that black officials can further tax white land. As a result, the local nonfederal expenditures per child in the county are only $730.83 per year. Were it not for a frenzied effort by the county school administration to apply for federal funds, its operating budget would not be met. In 1978 the county applied for thirty-two different federal education programs. Title I of ESEA (the Elementary and Secondary Education Act), for which 81 percent of the public school students qualify, provided over $886,000 per year—about $200 per child—and paid the salaries of nearly 100 school personnel.

"We can't let any possible opportunity go by because our need is so great," says Dr. David Jones, federal programs officer for the Holmes County Unified School District. "But on the other hand," he admits candidly, "we can't gear up over the summer to properly staff and manage the projects that do come through." Jones estimates that 40 percent of the entire district's budget comes through federal funding. With state minimum foundation funds barely covering teacher salaries, federal funds—aggressively sought and usually reaped—enable the system to maintain what most of the nation's educators would consider a minimal operation. "Since the local tax rate is zero, we look to indirect cost rates of federal programs to do things like building maintenance and mainline instructional activities. I know it is not what the feds intend, but it is the only way we can survive," explains Dr. Jones.

For both Mr. Bailey, the community leader, and Dr. Jones, the proposal writer, the overwhelming issue is the same: survival. And that's not easy. In 1978 blacks were arrested en masse in Lexington, the Holmes County seat, after protesting the refusal of white merchants to give anything but the most menial jobs to blacks. In February 1979 *Ebony* magazine showed photographs of a local doctor's office with waiting rooms still marked "white" and "colored." The magazine quoted a local leader as saying the so-called New South is a myth: "It's the old South with a smile," he said. Not until the signs in the doctor's office were featured on a CBS documentary about the twenty-fifth anniversary of the 1955 Brown decision ordering desegregation, and reporter Ed Bradley personally called the matter to the attention of HEW, did the signs finally come down.

Somewhere along the line, the economic system smiled—or at least grinned slightly—on the parents who send their children to Goodman-Pickens Elementary School, a depressingly overcrowded and deteriorating structure that packs 500 black children into space for 300. At the school, which is better than most in the county, only 76 percent of its students are qualified for Title I, the lowest figure in the district. Under USDA guidelines 95 percent of the students qualify for free lunches. Thirty-five percent of the parents of the student body are unemployed. The mean educational attainment level for male parents is 5.7 years; for female parents, 7.9 years. Seventy-two percent of those over the age of 25 in the Goodman-Pickens community do not hold a high school diploma. Such are the kinds of microscopic measurements that separate "better" from worse in Holmes County.

## Enter the Teacher Corps

Holmes County is the kind of place the Teacher Corps (TC) was made for. President Lyndon Johnson, himself a former teacher, said so on July 2, 1965, when he surprised the annual convention of the National Education Association in Atlantic City with the announcement that the administration was launching the program "to enlist thousands of dedicated teachers to work alongside of local teachers in city slums and in areas of rural poverty, where they can really serve their nation. They will be young people, preparing for teaching careers. They will be experienced teachers, willing to give a year to the places in their country that need them the most. They can bring out the best in our nation to help the poorest of children."

Reflection forces one to admit that in 1965 the Teacher Corps was as inevitable as the flowing of the Potomac. President Kennedy had already electrified the nation's pride by creating the Peace Corps. President Johnson followed quickly with the "domestic Peace Corps," Vista. John Kenneth Galbraith, the liberal economist, had written in *Harper's* magazine in 1964 that teachers needed to be enlisted in the war on poverty. "There is no place in the world where a well-educated population is really poor," he wrote. With Senators Edward Kennedy and Gaylord Nelson sponsoring the legislation, the Teacher Corps was soon off and running.

If President Kennedy had announced that Peace Corps volunteers were to be "agents of change," half of the nations in the world would probably have cut diplomatic relations. It was best left unsaid; they would be servants. In the first years of Teacher Corps, no one was that diplomatic. Even if they had been, the least discerning school administrator or college education department head could sense that sending thousands of idealistic young talents into schools presupposed that there were some nonidealistic old curmudgeons in the system who had not learned how to teach poor children. It was not surprising that *Nation's Schools*'s 1967 poll found that less than half of the nation's school administrators wanted the Teacher Corps program expanded and a third wanted it abolished.[1]

In all the volumes of material that have been written on Teacher Corps, no one has ever claimed it was an idea that bubbled up from the grasslands of Texas or the ghettos of Trenton.[2] It was Washington at its top-down best. The program was destined for political battles that significantly changed its mission while its mentor, the Peace Corps, forged ahead unchanged, worried only that American idealism might wane. To add to their miseries,

Teacher Corps directors would soon confront an unexpected engine chugging in the opposite direction on the same track: a teacher surplus.[3]

The Higher Education Act of 1965 created the Teacher Corps "to strengthen the educational opportunities available to children in areas having concentrations of low-income families and to encourage colleges and universities to broaden their programs of teacher preparation." The initial strategy centered on recruiting and training new teachers for low-income schools and recruiting and training interns who would work as part of teams headed by experienced teachers. Grants could go to institutions of higher learning or to local education agencies to carry out the strategy. Corps terms were set at two years.

Targeted schools and communities were not long in surmising that—at least for some areas—Teacher Corps was a liberal end run bent on battle with the perceived conservative tradition of the public school system. Data collected by Ronald Corwin on the early Corps members found that one-third of the interns classified themselves as "very liberal" and only 4 percent believed themselves "highly conservative."[4] "Politically and socially they were more liberal than other teachers; they exhibited little sense of loyalty to the school administration and to school rules but instead were inclined to be rebellious. They tended to view the solution of poverty to be in the structure of society rather than in personal drive."[5]

And as if to disprove the notion that a few days on bus duty will make all pedagogues right wingers, over half—54 percent—of the Corps members decided they had become more liberal after being exposed to the system. Perhaps that is explained by the fact that the philosophy of program directors and university faculty "in the highest category of liberalism was equal to or exceeded that of the interns."[6]

While Corps members were busy taking new vigor and the best education ideas of the 1960s to America's poorest schools, Congress was busy amending the Higher Education Act. By 1972, recruitment, selection, and training of volunteers was in the hands of local projects. In 1974 Congress added a key amendment calling for "training and retraining for teachers" and shifted the focus from the Peace Corps model to the "demonstration" model. In 1976 Congress (and Office of Education [OE] regulations) further changed the program by extending it to five years, mandating an elected community council to plan and supervise it[7] (including all education staff), setting a limit of four interns for each project, and directing that the first year of the program be a planning year. (This amendment resulted from OE experience in the Urban/Rural program. See Chapter 9.)

Thus, in a decade plus one year Congress had remade the Teacher Corps. The intern concept continued to exist, but the numbers greatly reduced (from 933 per year in the early years to an average of 324 a year in the late seventies), and the emphasis changed over to inservice education for existing teachers in cooperating schools. The number of experienced personnel participating in the program has risen from an average of 190 per year in the sixties to 16,200 per year in the late seventies. The small cadre of interns now serves primarily as a reason for making graduate courses readily available to established teachers who want additional training or master's degrees. The number of participating higher education institutions has risen from an average of forty-three per year in the early years to eighty-one today, and the number of participating school districts has risen from an average of seventy-six to eighty-one. Meanwhile, the budget of $37.5 million has remained constant from 1972 to 1979.

By 1978, after thirteen years of experience, the Teacher Corps had learned two important lessons:

> First, change is a slow process. Diffusion of change from one institution to another is a function of the acceptance and credibility of both the practices and products developed. . . . Training . . . must focus on the schools and staffs as they exist.
> The second conclusion is that schools are social systems—formal organizations. Therefore, systems theory and organizational behavior theory must be used in the conceptualization of preservice and inservice training.[8]

No critic of Teacher Corps has ever accused it of having a rural bias. It claims to have no specific rural policies or models. Rather, as program director William L. Smith explained in an interview,

> there is no explicit urban/rural policy breakdown, nor is there a conscious effort to set up a certain ratio of rural sites. There is an effort to get geographic distribution of funds on an equitable basis, and the urban/rural breakdown falls naturally because some geographic areas are rural, others urban. The Teacher Corps design centers on localistic programs with heavy community input in the planning and implementation: the model takes care of itself. There is no need for a specific rural model to be differentiated.

The national office lists five major objectives around which all sites structure their programs:

1. improved school/learning climate for children of low-income families
2. improved development systems for educational personnel development
3. institutionalization of objectives 1 and 2
4. adaptation and dissemination of objectives 1 and 2
5. development of a national body of knowledge about what works and what doesn't work in objectives 1, 2, and 3

"These objectives," Smith says, "all hold true regardless of the site: urban or rural, it doesn't matter." Nationally, Smith says the program had set priorities for programs that are multicultural and that lead to formulation of diagnostic and prescriptive methods of teaching. The Teacher Corps suggested the Holmes County, Mississippi, project be examined as an exemplary rural program.

### The Holmes County Teacher Corps Project

Mississippi Valley State University (MVSU), a predominantly black institution of 2,500 students, is located in Itta Bena approximately forty-five miles northwest of the Goodman-Pickens school. Through the years it has been primarily a teacher-training institution preparing a majority of the black teachers in Holmes County and the surrounding region. The idea for the Teacher Corps (TC) project came about when the Holmes County school superintendent William Dean and district federal programs officer Jones went to MVSU with a list of pressing district needs. These included higher student achievement, curriculum change in the schools, and the addressing of community problems and concerns.

To the university staff this request came at an opportune time. The School of Education had just gone through its own needs assessment as part of an effort to chart new directions for its programs. In addition, the new Graduate School of Education (offering an M.A. in elementary education) was seeking accreditation from the National Council for Accreditation of Teacher Education. Faculty members saw the TC project as a way to give the school respectability, make it more up to date, and provide additional money with which to fill deficiencies in staffing and curriculum as it approached review for accreditation. Not insignificant was also the fact that "the surplus of teachers nationwide turned our attention to inservice education," according to one university official. The Teacher Corps appeared to be the "best source of funds to meet our particular needs."

Under the leadership of Dr. Willie Epps, a faculty member and Holmes County native who had federal grantsmanship experience from a job in Washington, a proposal was developed with "input from the faculty, community, and the central office." The application was completed in December 1976 and funded in April 1977. The study team was told that the National Teacher Corps office played a major role in developing the final proposal. We were also told that the proposal went through thirty-three revisions and that the final proposal "was written after we already had the money." Epps was designated director of the project.

Teacher Corps brought $207,808 to the MVSU/Goodman-Pickens effort each year for two years, matched by $178,079 in local district monies. The money paid for TC personnel (a director and program development specialist at the university and a community coordinator, inservice coordinator, and team leader at the school), stipends and related expenses for four interns, salaries for teacher aides and student tutors, and other program-related expenses. Parents were paid travel expenses to pick up students who stayed for tutoring sessions, and parents who were trained to work with other parents in teaching their own children were paid $2.30 per hour to attend training sessions.

The money and staffing were directed at addressing "the overriding need to improve the overall achievement of children at Goodman-Pickens." The program proposed to do that through "a systematic replicable approach to staff development that is based on the converging interests, needs, and priorities of pre-service, inservice professionals, and lay personnel as they relate to effective instructional power and to accelerated growth on the part of children from low income families." To accomplish this the proposal provided for nothing less than a major attack on the educational system in Holmes County, excepting only the central office, the principals, and the participation of MVSU. Eleven specific objectives were listed, each with a number of subobjectives and all in some way related to the general focus of diagnostic/prescriptive teaching, competency-based instruction, and a better understanding of learning disabilities. The diagnostic/prescriptive process was to be applied to teachers' as well as students' needs. The objectives were:

- To develop a model training program for Teacher Corps interns, professional teachers, teacher aides, student teachers, and community leaders.
- To initiate collaboration among university administration, school district administration, college professors, district teachers, TC interns, teacher aides, student teachers, school board members, and local and state educational personnel.
- To diagnose the academic and social needs of the elementary students of the project school and analyze the needs of all instructional personnel so that a prescriptive training program can be applied to the teachers as well as to the students.
- To identify learning problems of teachers, teacher aides, Teacher Corps members, and parents.
- To promote the use of competency-based instruction, especially in teaching children with learning and behavioral difficulties.
- To provide a quality training program for community people in analyzing and assessing the needs of schools.
- To recruit and train parents to be a part of the instructional process at home and in the school.
- To disseminate information regarding the project.
- To establish and maintain open lines of communication.
- To provide TC interns the opportunity to observe and participate in

a number of different kinds of life-styles that make up our culturally
pluralistic society.
- To provide interns with experiences that will augment their knowledge
  and understanding of values, mores, social interaction, and economic
  factors affecting the culture of Holmes County, Mississippi.

To carry out these objectives, the program provided teachers with on-site
workshops and formal course work leading to a master's degree. The four
interns recruited by the local project also attended the courses in addition to
their other activities in the school and community. In an effort to get the
MVSU professors to teach as they would like their students to teach, the
project provided inservice workshops using such techniques as
microteaching and Flanders interaction analysis procedures (systematic
analyses of teacher-student interactions). Ten high school students were
paid to tutor low achievers after school. And, most importantly according
to most observers, the project started a community outreach program that
sent counselors to the homes of low achievers and organized programs to
get the parents into the schools.

Though MVSU staff made a great effort to accommodate the needs of
Holmes County teachers in terms of course location and staff availability,
the program actually offered was essentially the standard master's in education (Ed.M.) course format. Little or no curricular modifications were made
in light of the special needs of Holmes County teachers. For example, the
first course in the Ed.M. sequence was a course in research methods—an
area of little apparent relevance to the day-to-day needs of teachers working
with extremely poor minority rural students. The lack of curricular
modification probably reflected the background of the MVSU staff. It may
also have stemmed from a concern on the part of university officials that the
new graduate school meet professional standards. The traditional "second-
rate" status relegated to black institutions coupled with their eagerness to be
as good as other institutions probably precluded much in the way of innovative—and thus not easily defensible—programming.

Community activities ran the gamut from potluck suppers at the school
to a workshop on how to complete tax forms, a driver education class for
adults, sewing and macramé classes, nutrition classes, and training for
parents on how to help their children achieve in school. The community
council also helped nineteen local adults get their high school equivalency
diplomas the first year. A fashion show grew out of the sewing classes, PTA
membership rose, and there was an improvement in relations between the
white sheriff and the community.

While the community outreach program under the direction of Edna
Bates, a former lunchroom worker, was winning plaudits, the program
headquarters at MVSU was having problems. During the two-year period
the program had two directors, three program developers, and two inser-

vice coordinators. The interns, the principal, and the teachers in Holmes County all complained in unison about "communication problems": unclear guidelines, lack of authority, poor administration, political infighting in the school, and so on. No one involved in the project denies that serious problems plagued it throughout the two years or that all of the problems were ever addressed, let alone solved. As many of the problems that arose were "start-up problems" experienced previously by dozens of other TC projects, it is natural to ask what resources the program provided to the project nationally and regionally.

Diane Young, an education program specialist with the National Teacher Corps office, made trips to Holmes County in February 1978 and again in January 1979. In her reports she noted, "The university, new to TC, has experienced start-up problems—lack of a stable staff, insufficient staffing, lack of a clear understanding of project purpose and intent in the development of education beyond the project staff, field-based activity coordination difficulties and inadequate housing facilities for staff members. The project has overcome all of these problems and is making great strides in accomplishing its goals and objectives during its second year of operations." There is no evidence in TC files in Washington that Young's memo set off any alarms warning that the Holmes County project was in trouble.

In September 1977, when Holmes County was first beginning the Teacher Corps project, a team of resource people visited the project site as part of an experimental technical assistance activity requested by the Teacher Corps Washington office. Four regional Recruitment and Community Technical Resource (RCTR) centers, funded by TC since 1969, planned, coordinated, and implemented this Site Specific Orientation Program (SSOP) for all new projects in the nation. The southeastern RCTR center sent a resource team made up of two content consultants, an RCTR staff member, and Diane Young (the project's Washington monitor) to the site for three days to help clarify the TC program objectives, policy concerns, and involvement expectancies. After the two-year experimental SSOP through the RCTR centers ended, Florida State University received a contract from Teacher Corps in 1978 to launch a formal Site Specific Technical Assistance (SSTA) program. Therefore, the original SSOP team never went back to Holmes County.

Nancy Bonney, the director of the southeastern RCTR center, has a thin file on Holmes County. She explains, "It is our job to sell ourselves so that projects will want to use us. We operate on a request/response system. If projects perceive a need for our services, they request and we respond to their needs." Holmes County simply "did not call and request specific technical assistance services. However, we did maintain an informal communication system with them (through area workshops and meetings) and they received all the dissemination materials and regional workshop experiences the same as all other projects in the Southeastern region." No request ever came from Washington for specific help for Holmes County, Bon-

ney said. "The Washington program specialist could call and say that they
needed help or could strongly suggest to the project director that they request services of the RCTR Center. We couldn't call up a project and say
we're going to help you because that's not the way we work."

Told that Sylvester Williams had saluted Holmes County as one of the
best rural Teacher Corps projects in the country, a staff member of the
RCTR center said, "What criteria was that statement based upon?" There is
little doubt that the southeastern RCTR center is well-equipped with
voluminous technical assistance material and talent to help projects with a
number of problems, but they are isolated from the other Teacher Corps
technical assistance programs and they work on-site only on a request basis.

It is equally perplexing to try to determine what role the national office
sees itself playing in guiding local projects. Clearly in the case of Holmes
County they helped with the initial proposal, sent a specialist in twice to
write optimistic reports, and herded through an SSOP team. But when the
MVSU staff applied for a five-year program in 1979 and abandoned Holmes
County in favor of nearby Humphreys County, the national office reacted
by routinely approving the change. Asked why the national office did not
question the move, as it was our impression that much work would go for
naught in Holmes, Diane Young told us, "That is a local decision. We don't
get into that."

## Impact of the Program

Goodman-Pickens is a fairly traditional, tightly run school. The commonly held perception among local educators is that there is relatively little
structure in the homes of students, so the school should be tightly structured
to compensate. Students for the most part still sit in straight rows and line
up and walk single file to the lunch room. Principal Judge Nelson is proud
of the structure; he wishes there had been a similar structure to the TC project. "Teacher Corps was an opportunity for us to do those things that we
did not have the personnel to do," Nelson says, but he admits candidly that
the program needed more time to accomplish its goals. "By the time you get
going, the second year is almost gone. We need a third year to test the program." Although he is proud of the improved community relationship and
has praised the interns for making lasting contributions by organizing
school clubs and a physical education program, he admits that the program
did deliver its share of frustrations: "Lots of times they [MVSU-TC] did not
follow through, especially the first year."

Nelson cited the tutorial program as one of the best accomplishments in
terms of raising student achievement levels. He also credited the interns
with improving the skills of the "average" teacher in the school. Like nearly
everyone else, he singled out the community outreach program as having
the greatest overall impact on education. The school may be able to main-

tain some of the in-school programs without TC aid, but it definitely will not be able to keep the community program alive, he said. Nelson believes the TC experience made him a more sensitive administrator, but, "If I'd had $200,000 to spend myself, I'd have added three rooms first."

Although the teachers complained about the interns having too much free time and about having to attend sessions after school, they generally responded favorably regarding the program's accomplishments. They singled out individualized instruction and learning centers as educational techniques they would continue to employ. They agreed with Nelson that the best efforts had gone into community work.

The four interns, on the other hand, were not as enthusiastic. In our interviews only one stated that she would participate in the program again. "Communication, planning, clarity—somewhere it all went wrong," said one. "We'd get to the point that things were going smooth, and then somebody [at MVSU] would resign and we would have to start all over again," another said. And there were other frustrations: "If you tell the students you're a teacher, they don't believe you. They think you're an aide or something. The kids got the idea we were not teachers because of the way the teachers treated us. The teachers were resentful at first. They thought we were spying. The teachers knew we were coming about a week before we got here."

The interns were equally unimpressed by TC efforts to prepare them for the two-year experience. "When we read the TC brochures, we read of one program. They gave us something called 'What Every Intern Should Know.' What every intern should know is not in there." The interns said the first year was particularly frustrating because "it was never clear what we were supposed to do." None of them in May 1979 indicated an interest in remaining at Goodman-Pickens, although one has since changed her mind and been hired by the school.

The TC staff at MVSU differed in its interpretation of the results of the two-year experience in Holmes County. Staff member Perry Washington, a former Corps member at Peabody College, said, "TC has done them [Holmes County] a lot of good—more than they appreciate." He defended the program but said, "I'm not sure TC as it is in Holmes County now could last three more years." Washington blamed conservative teachers and political domination of the schools for many of the problems confronted by MVSU. "The teachers at Goodman-Pickens think tests are sacred," he said. "When we tried to introduce new stuff on testing, it was like we were tampering with their religion." He noted that TC created conflict and jealousies in the county educational establishment by concentrating on one site school and one satellite school. "Lexington never understood that they were a satellite school. They wanted interns and aides and all the same workshops like G-P had. If it had been county-wide, G-P would have taken TC more seriously—less for granted."

Washington said if he had been directing the program, he would have placed more emphasis on changing teacher behavior. "The teachers can get an M.A. [only two at Goodman-Pickens did], but if they still teach the same way, what's been accomplished?" Washington said he believes part of the MVSU problem in working with Holmes County stemmed from the local perception of the university. "MVSU sits in a field; Peabody is in a city. Peabody is a well-known school—when you go into a school with a new idea, they are more apt to accept it than they would if you were from MVSU." Washington set a minimum standard by which to evaluate the success of the program: "If anything changed at the schools in Holmes County, that says a lot. People now might be more willing to question school policy, the budget, etc."

Other MVSU-TC staff privately expressed disappointment with the project. "It's a highly political structure down there [Holmes County]. You would have to be involved in county planning to change things. The strategy would have to be more political than educational," one staffer said. Another blamed the disorganization on the program's administration at MVSU. "The roles were well defined, but the people did not assume the roles." The same staffer said he did not believe the interns were as well prepared by the program as they would have been in a regular M.A. program.

Dr. Dorothy Leflore, who has been project director since the second year, said the major impact of the program on MVSU to date is that the dean of the School of Education is looking at the program as a model for a multicultural education curriculum and field-based teaching. She claimed the major reason for pulling out of Holmes County was "the one-and-a-half hour drive for staff," and the reason for going to Humphreys County was that it was "very convenient." By not being close to the school and community in Holmes County, Leflore said, MVSU found it difficult to control rumors and the direction of communication. Putting out fires, she said, took time away from the progress of the project.

## Conclusions

The fact that the national TC office—alone among the many observers of the program—cited Holmes County as exemplifying the best of Teacher Corps in rural areas raises serious doubts about the extent to which it takes seriously its own mandate to follow "a rigorous selection procedure which provides for the accumulation of solid success/failure data." We are convinced that no objective observers of the Holmes County experience could see it as anything more than a mixed bag of results.

The shortcomings were due to both the strategy's design and its implementation. Teacher Corps did accomplish some important tasks:

- It paid for master's degrees for four interns (only one of whom is likely to stay in the system)
- It provided a free M.A. for two other Goodman-Pickens staff
- It offered graduate courses for another thirty to fifty teachers from both Goodman-Pickens and Lexington (the designated satellite school in the Teacher Corps proposal)
- It conducted workshops on a variety of topics
- It initiated a tutorial program that gave selected students badly needed assistance and tutors a bit of additional income
- It began a community outreach program that helped to reestablish school-community ties, which had been badly strained by the desegregation struggles

The six additional staff members supported by Teacher Corps funds were obviously welcomed at both the university and local school levels, where tight budgets prevented hiring additional personnel. Principal Judge Nelson and other staff, however, would probably have preferred lowering the forty-to-one student-teacher ratio rather than having a "team leader," "program developer," and other Teacher Corps personnel.

The teachers in general appreciated the assistance provided by Teacher Corps through workshops and home courses. Being able to take courses at home rather than driving the hour and a half to MVSU was a welcome change, even though the content was not always seen as beneficial. Traditional research courses and workshops on talented and gifted students would have been traded willingly for some practical help on teaching the basics to large numbers of students.

So, although assistance of any kind is welcomed by personnel in rural schools located beyond the usual outreach of service agencies, it is clear that the multiple objectives of Teacher Corps ("developing a model training program for professional teachers, teacher's aides, student teachers and community leaders"; and initiating collaboration among university personnel, local teachers and administration, school board members, and state educational personnel) were clearly beyond the feasibility of the two-year Teacher Corps funding cycle, even if the best and most imaginative higher-education resources had been available. Such expectations go far beyond what we now know to be possible with the best strategies for change. Further, the national objectives calling for multicultural diagnostic and prescriptive teaching simply did not strike a responsive chord in a school that is essentially all black and faced with the problem of trying to keep students in school when there is not enough space for those who do attend. The game of including in the proposal what the funding agent is willing to fund, however, continues to be played, and Holmes County secures the necessary money to hold school in the only way that it can, given the level of local and state support.

Implementing collaborative efforts between higher education and the public schools is difficult under the best of conditions. Although professors traditionally study the problems that teachers have to deal with daily, theory does not easily translate into practice. Bridging these gaps requires the building of long-term trusted relationships. The high turnover of Teacher Corps personnel literally guaranteed that these lasting collaborative relations would not be established. The optimism and the anticipation that good things would happen, which characterized relationships in the beginning, eroded during the two years until at the end both parties seemed relieved it was over. For the teachers, there were no more requirements to attend workshops after teaching all day; for the professor, there was no longer a need to leave the university and drive out to Goodman-Pickens to hold classes in the evening.

The educational problems of Holmes County are firmly rooted in the long-standing racial-social problems of the Deep South. Proposing to make even a dent in those problems in two years, especially with inservice education programs provided by the same institutions that originally trained the teachers, is at best wishful thinking.

Teacher Corps will continue to work with Humphreys County at least through the end of the next funding cycle. The fact that it is a five-year rather than a two-year cycle is a step in the right direction. Whether or not anything will be different at MVSU at the end of the five years is yet to be determined. For Holmes County the increment of improvement from the two-year effort appears to be small indeed. In the words of Rims Barber, a civil rights activist who stayed on in Mississippi to work on the problems of education, "Fresh eggs are better than rotten eggs . . . that ain't steak, but it's something . . . it's not talk about excellence, it's talk about improvement."

### Notes

1. Ronald B. Corwin, *Reform and Organizational Survival: The Teacher Corps as an Instrument of Educational Change* (New York: John Wiley and Sons, 1973), p. 4.
2. Ibid.
3. Ibid.
4. Ibid., p. 89.
5. Ibid., p. 113.
6. Ibid., p. 89.
7. Ibid.
8. "Teacher Corps Briefing Materials," brochure (Washington, D.C.: Office of Education, 1978).

# Natives and Newcomers: Vermont's Mountain Towns Teachers' Center

*Faith Dunne*

Wilmington, Vermont, is a crossroads, in many senses of the word. It is the village where Route 9, which runs along the bottom of Vermont from Brattleboro to Bennington, meets Route 100, which threads through the narrow mountain valleys up the center of the state. For more than a century it has been a focal point for tourism—a natural starting point for skiers, autumn "leaf-peepers," and summer campers or climbers fleeing the urban heat and crush. Most recently it has become an exurban frontier, home of the sophisticated, demanding "city people" who are moving to Vermont in increasing numbers, lured by ready access to ski slopes and the vague promise of a "good life."

The village of Wilmington has the uneasy look of a cultural crossroads. A sandwich shop sporting a large "Deli" sign sits across the street from an old-fashioned drug store whose sign announces that it has been "In the family since 1888." The old, rambling Crafts Inn still stands, even if its function as a ski dorm and tourist haven has been taken over by the modern ski lodges clustered at the foot of Mt. Snow in nearby West Dover. Along the roads leading into town, craft shops and mock-Swiss chalets jockey for space with falling-down maple-sugar houses and the weathered clapboard homes of the remaining native population.

There is little overt tension between the old-timers and the "flatlanders," as out-of-state people are contemptuously called by Vermonters. Like their buildings, they seem to live side by side in a state of guarded truce. Only a few issues will bring out the latent suspicion and defensiveness that run under the surface. One of these issues is schooling.

Much of the information about the period 1974–1976 was derived from John Watt's "The Rural Teacher Center: A Response to Rural Educational Change," report, Brattleboro, Vermont, 1979.

Schooling in Wilmington, as in most of Vermont, has changed enormously over the last eighty years. The old, one-room "district" schools, which augmented the fundamental education of the farm with basic literacy skills, have been replaced by a consolidated school providing a wider range of resources, a more complex curriculum, and up-to-date facilities. The teachers, once selected from the normal school graduates who lived in town, are now chosen for their professional credentials. The overwhelming majority (95 percent, the superintendent estimates), were raised in the suburbs of other states and trained outside of Vermont. Most insure their privacy (and their remoteness from community life) by living outside of Wilmington.

The student body has changed as well. As recently as 1970, six of twenty-seven students in one class were Boyds, all cousins. Today, the class full of interrelated Boyds has been replaced by the children of a more mobile, metropolitan population. By 1978, only three of the twenty-two second graders had lived in Wilmington from birth, and only one of those seven-year-olds had lived in the same house all her life.

The changes in Wilmington seem epitomized by the Deerfield Valley Elementary School (DVES), which serves the more than 200 first through sixth graders who live in the town. Constructed in 1970, the low, gray-shingled building sits next to a brook in a former cow pasture, three miles from the central village. It has an "adventure playground," full of challenging climbing equipment built from railroad ties and old tires, a multipurpose room decorated with murals of gigantic animals, and a carefully constructed nature trail. The interior is designed according to the "open concept" formula popular in the early seventies: a large library/media area occupies the center of the building, with classroom spaces around the periphery. Of the interior spaces, only the multipurpose room has walls. The rest of the carpeted areas are kept separate only by portable partitions, most of them heavily hung with childrens' drawings and stories.

This facility, built at a cost of more than $1 million, would be the pride of any suburb. So would the Mountain Towns Teachers' Center (MTTC)—an inspiration of Wilmington faculty—lodged in a comfortable space next to the DVES library. MTTC is a hospitable place; its couch and chairs are shabby but comfortable, and the partitions separating it from the rest of the school are covered with program announcements, samples of local crafts, and examples of children's writing and art. The space is clearly designed to encourage sharing. "Nicki," a teacher asks of an MTTC staff member, "do you know if anyone can give a course in Chisanbop [a method of fast mathematical computation that uses finger manipulation as its basis for calculation]?" "Connie is doing it with her kids," the staff member responds. "When they get good enough, she promises that she and her kids will teach other people how to do it." "Okay," the teacher says, "let me know when she's ready." This kind of interaction, repeated over and over in the course of the year, is typical of the life of the Center.

But southern Vermont is not suburban Westchester County, and both DVES and the Mountain Towns Teachers' Center arouse feelings other than pride in the hearts of many Wilmington residents and their neighbors. To some, the school's cost and luxury are wildly extravagant; to others, the open-space plan and carpeted floors invite poor discipline and general laxity. The Teachers' Center, perceived as part of DVES, shares the burden of these concerns. In addition, it is the target of other suspicions—that it is a flatlander enterprise; that it is typical of the kind of indulgence teachers demand nowadays (along with the classroom aides and special-subject teachers that the old district schoolmistresses never seemed to require); that it advocates a philosophy of education that leads to children chasing each other around with gerbils and calling teachers by their first names.

When DVES was first built, four years before MTTC was founded, the native town residents, who then dominated civic life, expressed these concerns with great vigor. Within weeks of the school's opening, petitions were circulating as fast as rumors, requesting that the principal be fired and that "open education" be eradicated from the Wilmington schools. That crisis was defused, according to a former teacher, by the school's first principal, a man who had "brilliant skill at handling parents. He would spend five hours a day drinking coffee with parents and listening to them. He had a real talent for helping community members to relax." Subsequently, the changing population of the town brought parents from metropolitan regions who were far more likely to look positively at the use of informal methods, which were becoming increasingly popular in the suburbs.

Public clamor rarely erupts now in Wilmington, but concern about "what's going on down there to the school" has not vanished from the minds of the remaining native residents of the town. Neighboring communities are equally concerned. The ski boom did not hit all of southern Vermont evenly. Wilmington got rich and cosmopolitan, but adjacent Wardsboro remained the province of hard-working, conservative locals. Dover, split in two by a mountain, was invaded by lodge owners and other suburban out-migrants on the ski-area side but remained virtually untouched on the undeveloped slope. Halifax, too far from the ski areas for resort prosperity, is still dominated by what one of the teachers calls "woodchucks"—a flatlander term for the poor, native residents who eke out a living logging or farming or doing factory work.

To the surrounding towns, Wilmington represents wealth, change, and metropolitan influences. Wilmington's neighbors view the town and its school with a combination of suspicion, hostility, and envy; they also see it as the harbinger of what the future may bring to them. This perception has had a significant effect on the development of Mountain Towns Teachers' Center. It may also have had a strong influence on its fate.

## The Creation of MTTC

MTTC was founded in 1974. Casey Murrow, who had come to Wilmington to teach in the new elementary school, and Sid Dupont, the school's second principal, had offered a course called The Open Classroom to area teachers in the fall of 1973. "It wasn't a very good course," Murrow says. "It was just an overview of informal classroom methods, gimmicks, that kind of thing. But it was an eye-opener for me—I couldn't believe that people would drive such a long way to come." But in southern Vermont and northwestern Massachusetts, teacher-oriented courses were not readily available, and those professionals who were hungry for both information and contact with others like themselves were ready to travel to get what they wanted.

By the end of the course it was obvious to many of the participants that they had common problems and common interests that stemmed from a mutual interest in the British open-classroom techniques but were not restricted to that interest. All of them worked in the region and all of them wanted to adapt new educational ideas to the exigencies of New England rural school life. From this common concern emerged the concept of developing a cooperative, multidistrict teachers' center, following the British teachers' centre model but altered to suit the New England administrative structure.

In 1974 there was still a fair amount of money around to fund educational innovations, and Murrow knew how to get access to it. He had just written a successful grant proposal for an environmental education program and knew that the state had some Title III money available. So he and a small group of teachers from the open-classroom course developed a proposal for a teachers' center that would serve Wilmington and several of its surrounding towns.

It was an ambitious proposal. For $25,000, plus in-kind contributions from local people, the prospective center promised everything from graduate courses to scrounge materials, from formal communications networks among teachers and schools to individual, nonevaluative, classroom support efforts. DVES offered to house the new center, providing it with meeting space as well as a place to put its professional library, its borrowable curriculum materials and resources, its catalog of equipment and materials owned by each of the member schools, and the equipment needed to publish its community resources directory and its regular newsletter.

Each of these elements was intended to meet a particular need of the now-typical southern Vermont teacher. Eight to 90 percent of these teachers, even outside Wilmington, are transplanted urbanites, accustomed to frequent interaction with other professionals and used to the easy availability of educational and cultural resources. Cut off from these amenities, and often uninvolved with the complex personal interrelationships that are the foundation of small-town life, these teachers feel keenly the professional isolation endemic in rural education. As Heidi Watts, the present director of MTTC points out, "If you are one of three teachers in a school in a small town and you don't like the other two, you're really in trouble." Further, she adds, professional isolation also involves "isolation from new ideas and from the need to think about new ideas. The need for continuous self-evaluation and reappraisal isn't felt—probably because there are fewer people to bump against, to make teachers feel the need."

MTTC proposed to create a professional community in this environment where one was unlikely to grow on its own. The Center was intended to attract teachers during after-school hours to a comfortable place where they could find and create classroom materials, exchange ideas, and engage in discussion of educational philosophy. In a more formal way, the governing board, which was to consist of one voting member of the faculty from each participating school, would be the basis of a communications network that would permit sharing of ideas, equipment, and materials throughout the region.

In addition to alleviating professional isolation, the Center planned to help compensate for the lack of urban resources. A library and resource center would provide the kinds of books and materials metropolitan teachers acquire from district centers. It would put together graduate-level courses for teachers who had no access to master's-level institutions in southern Vermont. As Mary Ann Abarno, one of the Center's originators and a teacher at the Dover Elementary School, puts it, "In Vermont, most teachers aren't natives. We're used to things being right around the corner. We're used to being pampered, maybe—and that's why we like the Teachers' Center."

In April 1974, the Title III proposal was funded and MTTC was officially born. From its inception it had been a child of DVES: Murrow and Dupont had done most of the writing and negotiation, the Center was physically located in DVES, and the only people who seemed to have a reasonably clear understanding of what a teachers' center could do were members of the DVES faculty. "I had support of some teachers from other schools in writing the proposal," Murrow recalls, "but they didn't really know what services a teachers' center could offer." Murrow was very much aware of the ambivalence with which Wilmington was regarded by other communities in the region and briefly considered trying to locate the Center somewhere else. "In a way it was too bad," he says. "We could have put it someplace else, I suppose, but no other town offered space and Wilmington was central and accessible. The trouble was that Wilmington was considered super-fancy, and MTTC didn't help that image."

To counter the "rich hippy" image of Wilmington, the search committee, composed of teachers appointed by the new governing board, looked deliberately for someone who would understand and implement the British-based, child-centered philosophy, but who could also impress older teachers and community members as a respectable professional. They found someone who appeared to be the perfect director. Dorothy Schubert, a Rowe, Massachusetts, elementary principal, had been a participant in Murrow and Dupont's original course. Schubert had a long-standing interest in British elementary teaching innovations and had, in fact, attended seminars in England, one of which included a round of visits to the teachers' centres in Oxfordshire. She had brought a number of English practices back to the Rowe school, where they had been successfully implemented. She was nearing retirement age and could afford to work for the small salary the Center offered. And, as Murrow puts it, "Dorothy was an older woman who had a calming image. She would make MTTC seem less like a crazy, radical Wilmington place. We needed that."

### The Trial Period

Dorothy Schubert was appointed in mid-June of 1974 and quickly began to put the Center together. First she hired Nicki Steel, a young woman with substantial knowledge of the arts and crafts skills considered important in many informal classroom curricula. Steel had lived in the Wilmington area for several years and knew people in both the schools and the communities MTTC would serve. Not incidentally, she also was willing to work long hours for minimal pay. Schubert and Steel, with the help of the governing board and assorted friends of the Center, began to set up the space donated by DVES. They got a second-hand couch, some chairs, a used refrigerator, a typewriter, and a substantial amount of barnboard, which they set up to use for displays. By the end of July, the physical shape of the Center had been established—a flexible, comfortable, attractive place, ready to be filled with materials and people sharing and learning from one another.

The structure of the Center reflected the philosophy of its initiators. Physically, and in terms of the resources it intended to provide, it was firmly rooted in the British open-classroom movement. But the founders, including Schubert, wanted to avoid total identification with one mode of teaching or with one age group. "When I thought of it in idealistic terms," Murrow says, "I saw it as a means of promoting more child-centered methods." He and Schubert both knew, however, that it was important to tread carefully in Vermont, a state where traditional practices die hard.

Schubert was ready to encourage and facilitate informal approaches rather than advocate them with the "missionary zeal" she felt.

The Center officially opened with an August curriculum workshop in arts and crafts designed for elementary-age children. Thirty-two teachers and parents attended the workshop, which featured a hands-on approach to curriculum development and displays of crafts produced by English children. It was run by two experienced English open-classroom teachers, and it was a great success. The workshop participants expressed strong approval for the Center and for the quality of the four-day course. By the time school opened, the future of MTTC seemed bright.

Schubert and Steel, with the active support of the governing board, threw themselves into an exhausting round of activity. They began to acquire materials and equipment: a Xerox machine, books, MACOS (*Man: A Course of Study*) films, curriculum kits from the New Hampshire Regional Center for Educational Training, animals, plant cuttings, learning games, and assorted free "stuff" from which teachers could create their own curriculum. All of these things had to be acquired, cataloged, circulated, fed, watered, and/or stored. In addition, the Center sponsored workshops and meetings, at the request of teachers or parents, on topics that ranged from reading disabilities to Words in Color, from tie-dyeing techniques to behavior problems. Finally, the two-person staff spent many hours arranging and rearranging furniture in an effort to make the Center a more welcoming and productive place for teachers to meet and work.

Some of these ideas worked, some did not. Formal meetings were generally well attended, but the workshops, even those designed in response to teacher requests, drew only a sprinkling of teachers. "We were organizing two workshops a week," Steel recalls, "but people weren't coming. It was kind of pompous of us to assume that people would drive ten or fifteen miles—in the snow—after teaching all day long to have us do things with them that might or might not work in their classrooms." For the same reasons, the Center never worked as a "drop-in" facility; in rural Vermont, especially in the winter, people rarely have the time or the energy—or the willingness to risk getting stuck in a drift after dark—to "drop in" anywhere.

Further, some teachers and community people from neighboring towns were suspicious of the Center. Dorothy Schubert or no Dorothy Schubert, the Center was in Wilmington and thus suspect. In addition to the perception of Wilmington as a rich resort town, the longstanding rivalries and hostilities that characterize New England small-town life stood in the way of easy interaction among communities. If the Center was in Wilmington, then it belonged to Wilmington; there was no reason for other towns to take a serious interest in it.

Others were hostile toward the Center because they associated it with the controversial Vermont Design for Education. The Vermont Design, an open-classroom–oriented philosophy for educational planning, had been implemented in Vermont by Harvey Scribner, state commissioner of education in the late sixties. The Vermont Design was greeted with great delight by liberal teachers (most from out of state) who felt that most of Vermont education was hopelessly backward, but it aroused substantial hostility among more traditional teachers and communities who saw the new state requirements as unwarranted interference with local educational control. As the Center quickly gained a reputation as a promoter of informal practices, it was identified with the pro-Scribner forces and was thus rejected by those who had rejected the Vermont Design. As the Center's 1975 Title III evaluation suggests, the MTTC biases were "probably more obvious than we realized."

MTTC staff and supporters recognized these problems but did not feel they were insurmountable obstacles. The Center had a small, intensely loyal cadre of supporters who used its facilities well. By early 1975, the physical operation was under control: materials had been gathered and means had been devised of getting them out to schools and keeping track of them. Participants considered the quality of workshops and meetings excellent, even if the attendance was not great. It seemed clear to the MTTC staff and governing board that the basic concept had great promise, but the means of linking the Center and its potential clientele needed to be changed. As Dorothy Schubert wrote in the 1975 annual report of the Center: "By the end of December, it seemed obvious that the 'workshops approach' was not the way to meet teachers' real needs; that coming to the Center . . . was not yet an attractive possibility to very many teachers. . . . Placing ourselves in their position, we could not help seeing that we needed to re-think our basic premises on 'delivery of services.'"

## Modifications in MTTC: Developing Rural Outreach

Rethinking produced a number of changes. Informal, "drop-in" workshops were replaced by more structured programs. A special-interest group in early childhood education, formed by Schubert in December 1974, generated an extensive schedule of meetings. The Center provided meeting space for this group and helped with scheduling and locating outside experts, but the interest group itself chose the topics and made the commitment to attend the sessions.

Formal course offerings also became a major part of the Center's services. Anne Watt, a Wilmington-based graduate student at the University of Massachusetts, offered an eleven-week, credit-bearing course, Education of the Self, in the spring of 1975, and the Murrow/Dupont seminar was recycled for a new group of teachers.

Graduate courses were most popular, especially with high school teachers, because they were credit bearing. Schubert recognized this as an unmet need of the teacher population in southern Vermont and set about formalizing the process. By the end of 1976, she had established the Five-College Consortium, a group of institutions that agreed, under a variety of criteria (all worked out in a precise and painstaking fashion), to grant credit for the Center's course offerings. In terms of breadth of impact, this was one of the Center's most successful efforts. The lack of any institution of graduate study in the southern Vermont area made the MTTC courses attractive to practitioners in that part of the state and spread the reputation of the Center far beyond its self-defined borders.

The most important change was in the Center's general attitude toward delivery of services. Not only did the staff drop the notion that teachers would make MTTC a routine stop in their weekly round, it also adopted the idea of bringing the Center to teachers, as the teachers evidently would not come to the Center. Starting in early 1976, the Center began running workshops in local schools, taking advantage of staff development days and responding to locally identified problems. Further, the Center began to turn its attention to the needs of teachers in the higher grade levels: the Murrow/Dupont seminar's second round was offered at a local high school; and a Right to Read workshop, held in the Readsboro school, had a special session for teachers of junior high students. "We started with an early childhood and elementary focus and a lot of people continued to see us that way," says Steel, so the shift to a higher grade emphasis was an important part of the Center's effort to expand its sphere of influence.

Finally, Schubert and Steel decided to try to export the informal interaction they had originally hoped to draw to the Center. They set up a schedule of twice-monthly visits to member schools during which any teacher could ask for a classroom observation, a demonstration of some technique or skill, a consultation on materials, or just a chat. "I do all kinds of things on school visits," Steel says. "I collect and return materials, work with kids in small groups—with and without the teacher—and I talk to teachers." The school visits were popular with the teachers who requested them. At Dover, a teacher said that faculty members especially liked having Center staff willing "to bring things to us, to do things in our classes."

The school visits solved some of the Center's physical and psychological accessibility problems but created some touchy situations. Although classroom visits were kept very informal, depending on teacher initiation and request, a number of local administrators were uneasy about non-staff people working in classrooms. Some saw the Teachers' Center as a threat to their own supervisory control. "You're constantly walking a tightrope," Steel says, "trying to please all different kinds of people. It is hard not to be threatening. I will stop by the principal's office to tell him what I did in a class so he doesn't worry about it."

By summer 1976, the Center had been oriented, reoriented, and was moving nicely in its new, service-outreach direction. But Dorothy Schubert was exhausted, frustrated by the multiple demands on her time, and ready to turn over the Center leadership to someone with fresh energies and different talents. "It was very difficult for Dorothy," says one of her former associates. "She would call me and say, 'I have such ups and downs with the Center. It's such a burden sometimes and such a joy sometimes.'" Finally, in August, Schubert decided to resign, and the governing board appointed a selection committee to begin the process of hiring a replacement.

## Changes in Leadership and Focus

Anne Watt, who had been associated with the Center since 1975 when she taught the Education of the Self course, applied for the job. "I was interested in getting more Center focus on classrooms and schools," she says. "That's what I stressed in my interview." The governing board liked Watt's vision of the Center's future direction, but the participatory decision-making process took a long time, and it was November before Watt assumed the directorship. "I felt overwhelmed by the job at first," Watt recalls. "The first week I had to go to every school board and tell them why they should give some money to MTTC. I didn't really know why they *should* support the Center—I was just walking in myself. But we had to do it, and do it right away, for the Title IV-C [formerly Title III] funding renewal."

Watt ran into problems immediately. If Schubert's soothing, almost grandmotherly personality had minimized the potential threat of MTTC intervention in inservice education, Watt's direct approach seemed to bring out the worst administrative fears of loss of control. David Morse, superintendent of Windham Central, one of MTTC's two participating supervisory unions, remembers, "When I first got here I was bombarded by a packet of materials from Anne Watt telling me all the things the Center was going to do for my teachers. Now, according to law, I have responsibility for supervision in my districts. They brought in a lot of courses—good ones, sometimes—but they didn't consult me about them. Anne Watt antagonized me—she was pushy."

Ralph McLean, superintendent of the Windham Southwest Supervisory Union (which includes the Wilmington schools) feels that this response was characteristic of district administrators. "A lot of the principals were not receptive to the Center because of the director," he says. "They were all men, and they saw Anne Watt as a pushy dame. She was very smart and better educated than most of them. That frightened some of them." McLean himself recalls a period when he—a new superintendent, fresh from Massachusetts—shared those concerns. "In the beginning," he says, "I thought Anne Watt was pushy—she seemed to be trying to take over the supervision of my teachers." McLean's concern was heightened to the point that he threatened to hold up the Center's Title IV-C renewal application. Watt was astonished by McLean's reaction to her inservice initiatives. She had no prior experience with teachers' centers and was unprepared to recognize or to deal with the territorial instincts of principals and superintendents. She knew that "principals were not on a par with me, educationally," but saw this as an opportunity for productive partnership, not for competition. She quickly learned otherwise. "One principal told me that he really respected the work I did, but he couldn't ask me to work with his faculty," Watt recalls. "He needed all the credit he could get for working with his teachers—he was on the firing line with the school board, not I."

Watt feels that the sense of the Center as a threat came when she tried to expand the range of service. "As long as the Center gave individual assistance to individual teachers, we were okay," she says. "But when I asked, 'What can I do for your whole faculty together?' they'd be threatened." The conflict with McLean was resolved with the help of a visiting team from the Vermont Department of Education. And McLean, once won over, became one of Watt's most ardent supporters. "Anne Watt is dynamic, a go-getter, full of ideas," he says now. "She threatens some administrators because they are always afraid of losing their power to someone else. But Anne sold the idea to schools—did all she could to get people to attend meetings, use the Center. The success the Center has achieved belongs to Anne Watt. I feel that the Teachers' Center has been a valuable tool in helping my teachers."

The entente with McLean ushered in the Center's most productive period, Watt says. "For five months, from August to December 1977, there was a time of peak functioning of the Center. I had the least financial pressure then and I was learning things." During this period Watt worked on her special interest, whole-school inservice programs, while Steel developed an informal networking program linking teachers with one another and students with other teachers. "One strength of the Center," Watt says, "was that Nicki and I had very different skills. She would take a very shy boy, for example, who had a hobby of snakes, and take him around to the different elementary schools to talk about his snakes. Or she would take three kindergarten teachers to another district to watch a famous kindergarten teacher in her classroom. The teachers would talk all the way up and all the way back. It was good for all of them. The teachers needed a linking person to get it together for them."

While Steel was working on linkages between individuals, Watt was forging connections at another level. "My biggest success was at the Rowe school," she says. "I began to work with the principal there—she began to call on me for advice. We brainstormed all the things I could do with the teachers and then they picked what they wanted me to do. I did a Magic Circle workshop, a workshop on the gifted, and facilitated the rewriting of their entire curriculum. I went down there to do a workshop once a month with lots of personal follow-through in between." In addition, Watt did a great deal of in-class work with teachers, "offering an empathic ear, sorting through instructional problems, asking the next question. I logged 200 hours one year on this kind of individual work."

This sort of activity fulfilled Watt's vision of what a teachers' center could do. "A teachers' center can be a source of professional support for both teachers and principals. It can personalize servicing each teacher's and principal's needs. It can do it if it has a professional linker—and the more skills that person has, the more levels of linking and support can be achieved."

Unfortunately, the success at the Rowe school was not repeated elsewhere. "Winning with principals would have been the way to success," Watt says now. "But I won only with one. It's a poor track record." The Rowe school appreciated Watt's efforts to mobilize school-wide staff development, but in the Wardsboro school, staffed by newcomers but run by a conservative, native-dominated board, the story was different. Watt says, "Everything I represented was anathema to the Wardsboro school board. I went to give a slide presentation to the board and they hated it. They were angry because I referred to them as 'isolated.' They knew I was an outsider."

But if whole-school inservice work was never widespread, the Center did have an impact on many of the area's teachers in a variety of ways. Heidi Watts, the Center's present director, says, "I can't think of a teacher in any of our schools who hasn't voluntarily participated in some activity of the Center." The level of participation has varied widely, however. Some teachers have taken a single course or have called upon Steel's field services occasionally. Others, primarily those from Wilmington or nearby schools, have used the Center intensively. "I use the Center most as a resource center," a long-time teacher from Marlboro says. "The Center helps find materials for me; Nicki always came out to help with field work. I have never called the Center and gotten anything but a positive response." Another teacher, from the four-teacher Halifax school, says that MTTC's most important contribution to her professional life has been "communication with other teachers. Nicki has made arrangements for me to visit other schools, talk to other teachers. The Center gives me a place to blow off steam, to get help." And a Dover teacher adds, "MTTC is our link to the outside—to quality ideas. They get people to open themselves to new ideas."

Many teachers responded with enthusiasm to the Center's willingness to provide intensive, personalized service, especially in the classroom, and wanted more and more of it. But for a two-person staff, working with a large number of schools scattered unevenly across difficult terrain, this kind of service was not easy to provide. In December 1977, when new demands began to encroach, expanded direct service became more and more difficult to achieve.

"That December we had to begin our proposal for federal funding for the Center," Watt recalls. "It was a real crisis at the door." The Title IV-C renewal option had run out and the Center had to find another source of money. Watt had convinced member schools in both supervisory unions to contribute small sums to the Center, but the money provided by individual districts would not begin to cover the costs of running the Center. Thus, many hopes rested on the success of three proposals: two for FIPSE (the Fund for the Improvement of Post-Secondary Education), and one for federal teachers' centers funding. Watt says she worked on the proposals continually—nights, weekends, spare moments at the Center—for three months. Casey Murrow, whose original proposal had been so successful, helped in the process, as did Watt's husband. Steel, who says she loathes writing, stayed out of the proposal-generating process and continued with her regular route of school visits and teacher-linking activities. According to Watt, "Nicki thought I was taking too much time on the proposals, being too much of a perfectionist. I resented her unwillingness to have anything to do with them."

Inevitably, the tensions between the two staff members had an impact on the Center's functioning. There were some complaints from teachers that they were being overlooked or underserved. The teaching principal at the Wardsboro school says that the Center, when pressed for time, favored the teachers who had adopted the open-classroom orientation. "Someone would drop by on the way back from Townshend, which is a more liberal community," he says. "Or one of them would stop in and I would have something for her to do, but she'd look at her watch and say, 'Well, I have to get to Townshend by 1:00.'" This principal felt that that kind of practice put him in an untenable position with his board. "Wardsboro is a very conservative community," he says, "and the board constantly wants to know what they are getting for their money. If I can't justify what I'm spending, I'm really out on a limb."

Limited services were only a part of the problem for Wardsboro and similarly conservative towns. The Wardsboro principal lives in Wilmington and drives past DVES every day. He says that he could use the Center facilities and materials, but doesn't feel they meet his needs. "I've moved away from the Center, philosophically," he says. "They have to recognize that Wardsboro will never be Wilmington, no matter how hard the staff works." And his mixture of resentment and jealousy toward the Center seems characteristic of the negative feelings that were increasingly directed at MTTC during this period. The fragile coalition among school people in very different communities began to break down, leaving the Center split between strong partisans and suspicious, even hostile, members.

In an effort to rekindle the sense of MTTC as a group effort, Anne Watt decided to sponsor a national event. The Teachers' Center Exchange, with offices in California and Washington, D.C., is a national organization that facilitates communications among teachers' centers. Among its other activities, it coordinates "Workparties"—conferences for teachers' center personnel. In the spring of 1978, Anne Watt convinced the east coast coordinator for the exchange "that there ought to be a Workparty for rural centers, and that we ought to have it at MTTC." The Rural Workparty in July drew teachers' center personnel from as far away as North Dakota, Texas, and California. Most of the people who attended were, like MTTC, waiting for the funding decision to come down from the states, and the discussions were filled with questions about whether rural centers would have their sparse population taken into consideration when decisions were made, and about what other directors planned to do if federal aid were not forthcoming.

## The Funding Crisis

The decisions on federal funding were supposed to be announced immediately after the Workparty. But the final process dragged on for weeks past the deadline, while the MTTC staff and governing board grew increasingly tense. Finally, on July 24, the day that Anne Watt began her Summer Institute course, Humanistic Skills for the Experienced Teacher, the announcement came through. As the August newsletter announced: "The news is not good. We were not awarded a federal grant for the coming year, but despite this sad news, much effort and energy has already gone into reorganizing for continuation of many aspects of the program." The newsletter called for volunteer effort to help make staffing decisions, raise funds, locate members, and organize adult education programs. Finally, it announced a Teachers' Center Rally at a local restaurant, which was intended to be a combination morale booster and mobilizer of local support.

It was a very difficult time for the Center. Various ad hoc committees organized to try to raise money through teacher pledges and a variety of fund-raising activities. McLean and Watt looked for other means of acquiring federal funds. Ultimately, they decided to apply for CETA funds with which to hire a coordinator of inservice programs, a public relations director/grant writer, and a clerk/typist. During this period Nicki Steel was running the center virtually single-handedly. Watt had resigned in September in order to work on her doctoral thesis, although she remained on the MTTC executive board to help with the CETA proposal and the hiring process. Casey Murrow, who had always been part of the Center's hard core of active volunteer workers, left for a year in Los Angeles. The school visitation schedule was cut back and countless hours were spent in what the MTTC newsletter referred to as "what-do-we-do-now" meetings. In the turmoil, some people, especially school board members, began to feel that the Center was doomed. "There's been a reluctance to provide any money for the Center," McLean said. "A lot of schools cut their Center money out of the budget because the federal program went down the drain. And, if you talk to them about it, they say, 'Oh, are they still going?'" During the period from August to December 1978, even the Center's staunchest supporters were unsure that it could survive on any functional basis.

New hope came in December 1978, when the CETA funding was at last approved and the governing board was able to hire Heidi Watts, a teacher educator who has lived in southern Vermont for more than eighteen years. Watts and Steel, with some clerical assistance, slowly began to try to put the Mountain Towns coalition back together again. Steel returned her full attention to direct service to teachers in the classrooms and to fostering communications among teachers, the only two Center activities, she says, that she ever really enjoyed. Watts took on the administrative tasks, the formal course offerings and coordination, and the mammoth job of rebuilding the fragile links between the Center and the districts beyond Wilmington.

This was not an easy task. In spite of her long residence in southern Vermont, Watts is female, an obvious flatlander, and a well-educated, clearly intelligent person. None of these qualities (nor the similarity in their names) made her readily distinguishable from Anne Watt to those who found Watt threatening. But Watts says that she tried hard to reduce administrators' fears by devoting much of her time to communication. "I spend a lot of time on the balancing act," she said in spring 1979. "I make sure I get in touch with each superintendent at least once a week. A lot of that time is 'wasted' in a practical sense. But it would be difficult to survive without the superintendent's support, and a great deal can be done if he is on our side. The same is true with principals. I try not to frighten them. I have to sound as non-Harvard as possible."

This appears to have been easier for Watts than it was for her predecessor. As Anne Watt says, "Heidi is better than I at organizing something and then fading into the background. That's very important. One thing that is required for a teachers' center leader is not to want control—we can't afford ever to think of ourselves as leaders." Watt's perceptions are apparently accurate. Superintendent Morse, who disliked Anne Watt, calls Heidi Watts "an organizer. She's intelligent, but low-key. I don't always know if I'll like the programs she develops, but at least I know she'll consult me." And Superintendent McLean, one of Anne Watt's great admirers, is equally positive. "We've been really lucky," he says, "because Heidi Watts is cut out of the same cloth as Anne. They're both real workers."

But hard work, even combined with diplomacy, was not enough to solve MTTC's basic problems. Money, as always, was the most pressing issue—and the one on which Heidi Watts was most reluctant to spend her limited time. But the CETA contract was due to end in early 1980, leaving the Center with only a year to find alternative funding or prepare to close. According to Watts and Steel, about $40,000 per year would be required to fund most of the Center's activities, assuming barely adequate staff salaries and some continuing CETA-paid assistance. Logically, the bulk of this support should have come from the consumers: the Mountain Towns districts the Center had served for five years. But there was general agreement that this level of funding was virtually inconceivable. It is difficult enough, McLean says, to convince local boards "to feel a sense of responsibility for the inservice training of teachers. They feel that teachers should be responsible for their own education." Governing board member (and Dover teacher) Mary Ann Abarno agrees. "If the towns had the money," she says, "they would want to spend it on something in town. More workbooks or something. Professional development is a pretty nebulous concept." It took several years to convince the local boards to fund this "nebulous concept" with as much as $300 or $400 a year. To expect them to raise their contribution to $2,000 or $3,000 per year was unrealistic in the extreme.

But if adequate support was not forthcoming locally, where was it to come from? Watts planned to rework the federal teachers' center proposal for the second round of funding. Some Wilmington supporters of the Center were working on a special town meeting to try to get $15,000 in leftover revenue-sharing money diverted to MTTC. In the meantime, a series of small-scale programs augmented the CETA money. "They may be able to make it from shoestring budget to shoestring budget for a while," Anne Watt predicted in the summer of 1979—and that is just what the Center tried to do. Heidi Watts got state funds for a Health Resources Center and set up master's level courses for local teachers. Steel expanded the program of adult education courses at a member high school. A small student-exchange program between Wilmington and New York City added a little to the budget, as did small individual pledges from teachers and from some of the district boards.

But a delicate issue arose here: If the Center diversified its activities in order to raise the money it needed to survive, how would it maintain its level of service to the local teachers without increasing its staff? Watts considered each new project carefully, trying to balance a desire to survive against an unwillingness to cripple the Center's primary functions. But the conflict inevitably remained. By spring 1979, Superintendent Morse felt that the money-raising issue had already cut too far into the Center's most important services. "The Center has spent most of its energies lately scrounging around for money to keep the Center idea alive," he noted. "If you're into that all the time, you can't do what you're supposed to do."

Further, there were differences in philosophy among the central people involved in the Center, differences that might have been manageable in affluent times but were too apparent when a tight budget made strict priorities necessary. Superintendent McLean wanted the Center to focus primarily on formal, credit-bearing courses. "I tried to get them to be more flexible," he says of the MTTC staff. "If a new teacher comes to my school and wants to get a master's degree, I want MTTC to be able to set it up. Work in classrooms and schools is fine, but we need to provide both services. And I think we can. Setting up programs wouldn't take all that much time." He adds that formal course offerings provide the best access to local funds, as most districts have money set aside to reimburse teachers for course tuition.

Neither Watts nor Steel, however, saw courses as a Center priority. Steel wanted to work in classrooms with teachers. "I like it when teachers call me and say, 'What do you have on Indians?' And I spend a half an hour getting posters, books, and materials together. Is that less valuable than talking about teaching philosophy? Many teachers' centers people look down their noses at providing materials. But it's more important to teachers." Watts disagreed—both with Steel and McLean. "Too many people see MTTC as a place where you can get Nicki to come and do something for fifteen minutes in an art class," she says. "I'd like to see it used for discussion of more philosophical issues. We should help teachers learn to do a better job of teaching children. We shouldn't be working with small groups of children, but rather getting teachers to ask the next-level question."

Those most involved in the Center—Watts, McLean, the governing board—tried to compromise, to manage a bit of what everyone wanted while raising money at the same time. But each of the functions was cut back, bit by bit, as the money began to run out. In the summer of 1979, Steel took a leave of absence while MTTC waited to hear the results of the second round of federal funding. This left the Center activities in the hands of Watts and a part-time typist. "You call down there sometimes, and no one answers the phone," McLean says sadly. "It's hard to keep going like that."

## MTTC's Demise

In the fall of 1979, two debilitating blows struck the already weakened Center. In September, the Office of Education announced its choices for federally funded centers; once again, MTTC was not on the list. The government does not specify its reason for negative choices, but the long-time supporters of the Center feel that the reasons are primarily political. "We have no political clout down here," McLean says. "The state department doesn't pay any attention to us." Anne Watt's feelings on the subject are even stronger. "The state thinks MTTC is too far from Montpelier to make it worth their effort. We've never been successful in getting money for southern Vermont." Then, in December, Wilmington held the long-awaited special town meeting on the extra revenue-sharing funds. The town voted not to give that money to the Center.

McLean sees little prospect of getting additional support from other superintendents, even to get the Center through to another funding cycle. "The superintendents around me see the Center as my Center," he says. "David Morse is setting up inservice programs in his district; a group of superintendents are getting together to talk about staff development. They're just reinventing the wheel. But they won't support MTTC. If I didn't fight, the thing would go down the drain—but every time I do fight, it solidifies their idea that the Center is mine."

McLean now feels that support for the Center is missing among teachers as well as administrators. "I feel the Center dispenses extremely valuable services," he says. "But it's rough. I guess nobody is really interested. Services are cut back and the teachers don't seem to mind." Heidi Watts thinks that power, not interest, is the issue. "I feel supported by many of the teachers and principals," she says. "They invite me to do workshops, they take courses. We have some good things going. But there's a lot of caution around. Principals are afraid they will offend their boards. And teachers have no conception of what it means to have power and wield it. They don't know how to use clout. Nobody thinks they are entitled."

### The Future of Rural Teachers' Centers

By June 1980, the Mountain Towns Teachers' Center had lost its battle for survival. What are the implications of its demise? It cannot be argued that the Center staff and governing board failed to do everything possible to keep it alive. Most of the people associated with the Center tell stories of the countless hours of volunteered time and effort expended on behalf of the Center. They also enumerate the resources offered: the comfortable meeting place for teachers from all over the area; the courses that would not otherwise have been available; the materials acquired and circulated that many schools would never have been able to buy on their own; the fat catalog of community people willing to share their knowledge with school children; the regular site visits and workshops. But none of this seems to have been enough.

Why? Some of the reasons stem from the basic nature of teachers' centers and have implications for the future of this mode of staff development in rural areas. Funding is a primary issue: even modest teachers' centers require large sums of money not presently built into most rural school district budgets. Many districts, hard pressed to meet the most basic schooling needs of their children, could not afford to contribute adequately to a teachers' center budget.

Others, who could afford it, find the concept unappealing. Staff development appears, to the lay person, to be something that benefits teachers, not children, and the links to actual classroom practice are often vague. Heidi Watts's desire to get the teacher to ask the next level of the educational question does not have any apparent connection to the improvement of sixth-grade spelling. Parents' concerns are quickly and effectively relayed to local school board members. As a teacher in Halifax—one of the less affluent of the MTTC towns—puts it, "My town supports education. If I wanted workbooks, I'd get them right away, no problem. To the school board, that's what education is all about."

It may be that larger communities recognize the generalized benefits of staff development. More likely, school boards in metropolitan areas have less to say about such issues, as teachers' unions and administrators have more power over budget allocations in larger places. Wherever the truth lies, it is obvious that rural Vermont communities can translate their educational beliefs into action with considerable speed, as the Wardsboro school board made clear to Anne Watt.

If local boards are unable or unlikely to support teachers' centers, where will the money come from? State and federal sources are possible, but there is fierce competition for rural-allocated money, and most of the general funding formulae favor programs that serve large numbers of children rather than small numbers scattered over a sparsely populated region. The most promising model may well be one joining local, state, and university funding to provide a center that can serve a rural region without overtaxing anyone's budget.

A second major problem is allocation of power. According to Heidi Watts, rural teachers centers, by their nature, present a potential threat to administrators. "Part of the problem with the teachers' center movement," she says, "is that it has given a growing illusion of control to the least powerful people in the schools—the teachers." This may be excellent for teachers, but it inevitably makes cautious the administrators who must satisfy their superiors and school boards. But if the administrator feels that he or she has ultimate control over the teachers' center, the threat can be defused. When McLean and Anne Watt had their head-on collision over the Title IV-C renewal proposal, the superintendent made it clear that he could ultimately determine the fate of MTTC. Once that was established, he became its primary administrative supporter. But few rural communities can support teachers' centers on their own, and that leaves administrators outside the primary district without a feeling of ownership and control. As Superintendent Morse says, "I feel a strong responsibility to provide things for my own district. I don't want to rely on an outside organization." As much as McLean might want to spread the sense of ownership among the other superintendents, the fact of unshared power limits the desire to share responsibility.

The problem of power is exacerbated when, as was true in Vermont, the teachers' center movement begins to gain momentum at the same time as teachers begin to organize and negotiate. In many rural communities, especially those unaccustomed to the widespread unionization of labor, teachers' unions are widely loathed, and school boards are accustomed to uncontested control over both budget and policies. If teachers' centers in such communities are associated with the unionization movement, they are likely to be viewed with strong suspicion. Morse makes this clear, pointing to the National Education Association/Vermont Education Association support of teachers' centers as one of his primary problems with the MTTC. "First thing you know, they will be wanting to negotiate inservice," he says, "and I won't stand for that."

A third problem is one of philosophical focus. The British teachers' centres were an outgrowth of the informal-education movement, and the early advocates of teachers' centers in America tended also to link them to open educational practices. That identification, even when modified by the staff of a center, tends to stick in the minds of local people and to carry with it many of the negative associations connected with "open classrooms." According to Casey Murrow, Dorothy Schubert began MTTC quite deliberately as a "vehicle for the dissemination of open-classroom methods," but soon decided that "she was pushing too hard," and broadened her focus. By the time Anne Watt assumed the directorship, she had decided that "you have to be eclectic to survive in a rural area because teachers are at so many different places." Heidi Watts clearly espouses a philosophy of individual teacher growth and development. But the reputation of MTTC as an advocate of open education has remained, according to Superintendent McLean, and makes some school boards, principals, and many secondary teachers uneasy about becoming involved in its activities.

Finally, the constraints of sparsely populated areas make rural teachers' centers difficult to run. Easy access is crucial to a drop-in center and travel time is a major limitation to site visits. As Superintendent Morse points out, many of his teachers do not use MTTC because of geography. "No teacher is going to teach until 3:15 and then drive an hour and a half because the Center has a new book." Rural teachers' centers must serve a broad geographic area, and the breadth of the area necessarily limits the efficacy of their service. Differences in access dictate differences in utility and thus differences in levels of support. If a teacher's contact with the Center is one visit from Nicki Steel every three weeks and an occasional summer course, that teacher is unlikely to fight for the existence of the Center. As long as population sparsity is a defining characteristic of rural life, this problem is likely to be a continuing one.

The problems of funding, power, philosophy, and geography helped to shape the fate of Mountain Towns Teachers' Center. But certain characteristics of southern Vermont played their part as well. MTTC was perceived as (and was) a flatlander operation in a region experiencing a tide of in-migration from the southern New England states. Steel says that this caused no problems, as "most teachers are not natives," but she ignores the fact that there are still many native residents who elect school boards for districts with predominantly Vermont-born children. Wilmington and West Dover are primarily in-migrant now, but in Halifax, Wardsboro, and Townshend, most of the children are related to each other and to the long-time residents of the community. Years of parallel living in southern Vermont have allowed some newcomers to forget that native Vermonters are accustomed to running the local schools according to their own views of what is right for children and have little use for innovation for its own sake or for outside expertise.

Innovation, in rural communities, tends to follow the recommendation of a trusted, long-time resident whose authority resides in proven reliability over the years. The typical transient teacher (or principal) in southern Vermont, who has little stake in the school's community, is not likely to stay around long enough to achieve this level of trust. Thus, support for MTTC was not likely to be generated by the direct consumers of its services, as it could be in more stable rural places.

In addition, it is not clear that MTTC focused its efforts on defining the educational interests and needs of the communities it served. Although both Watt and Watts argue that they put great emphasis on rurally oriented curriculum—developing materials on energy, on local community study, producing a major catalog of community resources in the Wilmington area—this is not what the teachers talk about when they discuss the Center. Steel, the only long-term in-school representative of the Center, did not see responsiveness to rural concerns as a priority issue. Asked to what extent she helped teachers design and implement specifically rural curriculum, she found the question surprising. "I've done some Foxfire stuff," she says. "What other rural curriculum is there?" As the Center staff was oriented toward the larger educational community and as the teachers they served were primarily newcomers, this lack of perceived focus is perhaps not surprising. But it can only have increased the sense of division between native residents and newcomer teachers in the towns beyond Wilmington.

Ultimately, MTTC appears to have died because it could not make its services seem sufficiently valuable to those who would have to support it—primarily school boards and superintendents. As long as the Center existed, as long as it was funded from outside the region, teachers were happy to use its circuit riders, take its courses, participate in its workshops. But beyond the small group of hard-core, passionate supporters, there was not enough feeling that a teachers' center was critical to the improvement of education in southern Vermont. And the development of that sense of importance among teachers, administrators, and community members seems to be necessary to the success of independent teachers' centers in rural communities.

# 6
# Holistic Change: The Experimental Schools Program in Oregon

*Faith Dunne*

The Experimental Schools Program (ES), initiated in 1971, represented an important change in the federal strategy of stimulating educational reform through the use of categorical grants to state and local educational agencies. Such piecemeal efforts were not producing the desired results. Experimental Schools, conceived as an applied research program, would explore a "holistic" strategy in which many aspects of a local educational system would undergo simultaneous change.

To satisfy the five "facets of comprehensiveness" underlying the five year program, projects had to include:

- A fresh approach to the nature and substance of the total curriculum in light of local needs and goals;
- Reorganization and training of staff to meet particular project goals;
- Innovative use of time, space, and facilities;
- Active community involvement in developing, operating, and evaluating the proposed project; and
- An administrative and organizational structure to support the project and to take into account local strengths and needs.

Each Experimental Schools project was to serve the entire enrollment of the school district, kindergarten through grade twelve.[1]

Much of the background material and some of the history of the South Umpqua Experimental Schools Program comes from an extended case study prepared by Lawrence Hennigh for the evaluation of the rural Experimental Schools Program. Readers who want a more complete history of South Umpqua and its ES Project should request copies of Hennigh's "Cooperation and Conflict in Long-Term Educational Change: South Umpqua, Oregon," from Abt Associates, Cambridge, Massachusetts.

## ES: One District's Experience

To understand what happened when the Experimental Schools Program came to the South Umpqua School District, one must first recognize that South Umpqua does not exist. There are three distinctive communities along that particular stretch of the South Umpqua River: Myrtle Creek (including Myrtle Creek Rural, which considers itself a separate entity), Canyonville, and Tri-City. They are joined into a single unit only by the superintendent's offices and the contested location of a shared high school. This is not simply a technical point. The tradition of independence and competition among the three communities is older and more powerful than recent efforts to encourage coordination and articulation of resources and facilities.

The communities that make up the South Umpqua School District are lodged in one of the narrow valleys of Douglas County, among the thickly forested hills of southern Oregon. A brief shoreline connects the county to the ocean, but the tall stands of Douglas fir dominate both the landscape and the economy. The deep green hills form an exquisite background for the pastures and flower gardens surrounding the small frame dwellings typical of the region. The South Umpqua district communities are relatively poor; lumbering and wood processing are the major occupations, augmented by jobs in a waning nickel mine, a little sheep farming, and some tourist traffic. But the standard of living is decent, and a sense of adequate time for relaxation and community affairs seems to compensate for a lack of great affluence. The three towns in the district have a general air of neighborliness and calm. Some of this sense is real; some is strictly illusion.

Several factors—going well beyond issues of school consolidation—have broken into the homogeneous peace of the area. Interstate 5, which runs up the valley from the California border, makes the communities readily accessible to each other and to the larger commercial and industrial centers of Roseburg and Riddle. The new propensity of suburbanites to seek the "good life" in rural America has had its impact on this lovely region; so has the steadily increasing tourist interest in outdoor pursuits. The influx of in-migrants and the shift in employment patterns have intensified old community loyalties in some residents while creating new sources of tension among neighbors and between towns.

As often happens in rural communities, these tensions tend to surface around issues concerning the schools. Myrtle Creek, Canyonville, and Tri-City reluctantly consolidated in 1964, after two previous efforts. The final vote was taken on the day of a serious snowstorm that kept many of the rural citizens from the polls. The positive margin was small, and the bitter feelings that marred the merger have persisted for years. Although both Myrtle Creek and Canyonville were allowed to retain their elementary and junior high schools after consolidation, the choice of Tri-City as the site of the common high school was enough to kindle conflict. Canyonville and Myrtle Creek were traditional football rivals, and one Myrtle Creek principal resigned his post when Canyonville coaches were assigned to positions in the new high school. Everyone except the citizens of Myrtle Creek resented the fact that the sports stadium remained at the old Myrtle Creek High School. Voters began to attack the school budget, which was defeated in 1967 and again in 1968.

The day the 1968 budget finally passed (on its third try, with more than $97,000 cut from the administration's $1,800,000 proposal), Dealous Cox assumed the superintendency. Cox was an Oregonian and an experienced administrator, although he had spent the previous years working at some distance from the daily functions of a school district. He had been a supervisor in an Intermediate Education Agency and a Title III officer for the U.S. Office of Education. But by 1968, he had tired of the Washington bureaucracy and wanted to take on something new. "I wanted to stop advising," he says, " and do something instead. I took the job in South Umpqua because there were lots of problems in that district. Maybe that was arrogant, but I wanted a district with many problems."

From the first, Cox had no intention of staying in South Umpqua for a long time. He was looking for a challenge, not a career. He says that he always felt the pressure of time, the desire to get things moving before it was time to move on. His original plan was to stay for five years, long enough to get a troubled district on its feet, and then go on to something else. "I wouldn't have stayed as long as I did if it hadn't been for Experimental Schools," he says.

Because he had a sense that there were many problems to solve in a limited period of time, Cox began to move quickly. The school board, a group Cox describes as "a traditional kind—local people, professionals mostly," wanted a dynamic superintendent who would accomplish enough to bury the conflicts of the past. They gave him four mandates: improve the faculty (many were teaching on emergency certificates with minimal academic background), improve the curriculum, build a new cafeteria at the high school, and get every federal dollar he could lay his hands on.

Upgrading the faculty was the first priority, and his strategy was typical of Cox's approach to reform. There were thirty uncertified teachers in the district (28 percent of the teaching staff), many of whom had been hired by an earlier superintendent in an effort to save money. Most had been in the schools for several years, long enough to build friendships and alliances in the community, some in the powerful fundamentalist churches of the area. Cox gave these teachers a choice: get certified or get out. The board offered to pay tuition for summer courses or evening classes. Cox went out of his way to set up special arrangements with Southern Oregon College to facilitate the effort. But his position on noncertified teachers remained firm. Many of the nondegree teachers went through the process and got their certificates. Others left the district. Some of those who remained felt that they had been unduly pressured and developed a distinct lack of enthusiasm for the future projects of Dea Cox and his staff.

The next step in this effort was to recruit the very best teachers obtainable to replace those who left— a considerable number in those days, when the district had a 32 percent yearly turnover. He launched a nationwide recruitment effort to identify what he calls "the educational leaders of the future" and to bring them to the district. The new teachers were very different from the old-timers: they were young, they were non-Oregonians, and they were highly educated and very ambitious. They came to South Umpqua because Dea Cox made it sound like an exciting place to be. They were committed to change, reform, and educational growth, not to the political and social intricacies of small-town life in southern Oregon.

By 1972, Cox felt ready for a new challenge. The staff had been radically changed, the old high school English and Social Studies course had been redesigned, both the athletic teams and the budget were winning year after year. Cox had acquired some federal funding in a low-key, not remarkably visible way. In a district that had been plagued by problems from its inception, things seemed to be under control at last. As Doyle McCaslin, assistant superintendent under Cox, puts it: "We were getting things moving—hiring teachers brighter than we were. It was Camelot."

### Enter the Experimental Schools Program

The new challenge came in the form of a brochure describing the Experimental Schools Program. ES seemed a perfect opportunity to Cox. The program offered money for locally designed comprehensive school improvement, and Cox felt ready to meet the board's mandate to redesign the curriculum. He intended to coordinate the academic offerings of the district, moving away from the custom of allowing each teacher to choose books. ES also appealed to Cox's research interests. "They were trying to find national answers to educational problems," Cox says. "We had the chance to find out some answers about the process of change." The opportunity seemed sufficiently attractive that Cox gathered up his assistant superintendent and the district coordinator of federal programs and went off to spend several days in isolation, generating a proposal that promised the U.S. Office of Education sweeping changes in the South Umpqua schools.

The proposal was a success. Robert Herriott, director of evaluation for all of the Experimental Schools Program's rural projects, says, "Cox and McCaslin knew about rational design. Both had experience in dealing with

Washington. They proposed the most sophisticated project." South Ump-qua was awarded a one-year planning grant intended to enable them to prepare a four-year grant proposal. Cox was notified at the very end of the school year and decided to delay the formal announcement until Fall Inser-vice Day, just before the opening of school.

The announcement was a bombshell, in several ways. ES promised a very large sum of federal money to a district that was unaccustomed to large-scale grants or contracts. Cox's success fulfilled the board's request that he bring in all the federal money he could manage. But many teachers, especially those who pre-dated Cox, were outraged. They felt that the superintendent had operated unilaterally, committing them to a course of comprehensive action without consulting them in advance. In a district with little tradition of coordinated effort of any kind, Cox's action seemed to some both threatening and autocratic.

Many teachers came around quickly, evidently recognizing that their only chance to influence the direction of the next five years was through ac-ceptance and cooperation. Others remained angry and bitter, telling friends in the communities about Cox's high-handed treatment of his teachers. Mc-Caslin, recalling the period, says, "All of us were into it before we knew what we were doing. Some of the teachers made negative noises in the com-munity during the first three months. By the end of three years, those teachers were happy, but the noise came back to haunt us."

Community members were concerned about more than the complaints of some of their teacher neighbors. Citizens had many questions about ES: Aren't our schools in good shape now? If so, why do we need to go to the federal government for more money? Why are teachers being pulled out of classes to plan for this new program? What are these Experimental Schools people experimenting on, anyway? Our kids? Such questions worried parents and taxpayers throughout the planning year. And there were few answers from the administrators who were planning the project. "I would have served the district better had I gotten staff to share information with the community instead of attending primarily to program," Cox says. "We saw political issues as an intrusion. I'm not proud of that, but that's the way it was."

Attending to program was enough to keep nearly everyone frantically busy. Teacher committees met constantly, generating more than seventy proposals for a variety of changes. The administration and school board ap-pointed an Experimental Schools Coordinating Council, whose members were chosen from among the business and professional leaders of the three communities. School staff visited another ES site, in Tacoma, Washington, to see what was being done there. Cox met with each faculty member to solicit ideas for the program. By mid-year, some of those involved with ES planning felt that more ideas were being generated than could be processed. According to John Hunter, who was an elementary teacher in Tri-City at that time, even the most enthusiastic staff members were frustrated by a sense that they didn't know how anything they suggested fit into a whole plan. "There wasn't enough time," he says. "Some teachers were angry because Dea asked them for feedback and then didn't use it. They couldn't see how their ideas were going to be used."

Nevertheless, a coherent proposal was generated, and Cox submitted it to Washington in August 1973. It is an impressive 127-page document proposing what the ES guidelines required: a comprehensive plan for the improvement of the entire school system. "It was the best kind of design," evaluator Herriott says. "It had multiple small components, which is far better than a few larger ones." The design focused on changes in the elementary school program but included new components (especially curriculum restructuring) at the junior high school and high school levels. South Umpqua asked for about two million dollars, spread over a four-year period, to implement these reforms.

At this point, the first of a series of serious negotiations with Washington began. Like other ES projects, South Umpqua suffered from changing dictates from the federal officials. Control over the program was shifted from the U.S. Office of Education to the newly formed National Institute of Education. Directors changed, emphases shifted, ground rules altered. Over the five years of the South Umpqua ES project, five different program officers monitored the effort. Each had a slightly different idea of what the district should be doing. The first round of negotiations gave only a hint of what was to come. The visiting committee insisted that the district reduce its funding request but would not say by how much or along what lines. The administration worked nonstop to cut the proposal, against an NIE deadline. Again, teachers and Coordinating Council members were not consulted. There was no time.

The final application requested $1.1 million, focusing mainly on the development of "Person-Centered Educational Processes" (essentially, individualized planning and instruction). The final proposal emphasized materials acquisition, at the insistence of the federal visiting committee, and staff development, reflecting Cox's sense that good teachers are the key to good education. Something both comprehensive and tailored, more or less, to Cox's curriculum reform plans had finally been created out of months of faculty and administrative work.

In the meantime, community concern about what was going on in the schools had coalesced into an organization, led by a young minister from one of the fundamentalist churches. This group, called Concerned Citizens for Education (CCE), did not form in immediate response to ES, but it chose the program as one of the first of its targets. The CCE questioned the impact of ES on the district, focusing on what its members considered a surplus of administrators. At this point, however, the group seemed content to ask questions and talk to the school board about their objections. Community and staff seemed willing to wait and see what would happen next.

The first year of implementation (1973-74) was eventful. Everything seemed to happen at once. New positions and programs were created; concepts and curricula already at work in one school were extended to the rest of the district, in accordance with Cox's plans and ES guidelines. The elementary schools felt the impact of ES most strongly. The administration was determined to get elementary instruction individualized, which they thought would be best accomplished by converting classrooms to a "learning-station" approach to teaching. Each elementary teacher was assigned a half-time aide to facilitate individualization; college professors were imported from the university at Eugene to provide training in the learning-station approach. Further, each elementary school got a new "instructional leader" (IL), chosen from the ranks of the regular teaching staff, whose job was to help teachers (in some fuzzily defined way) make the transition from conventional classroom to individualized centers of learning.

The elementary schools were also flooded with materials: art and music supplies, a new reading series, a new math curriculum, a wide assortment of games, individual learning packages, and the like. The fifth grade adopted MACOS (*Man: A Course of Study*), a nationally famous curriculum for social studies; another multimedia curriculum, *People and Technology*, was chosen to replace the outdated Latin America program for the sixth grade. A member of the Coordinating Council recalls that there were so many new materials in the Myrtle Creek school that teachers didn't even know what was there—which caused some comment about waste in the community —and one elementary school teacher noted that "a lot of problems came from people not knowing how to handle all that money at once."

There was also some grumbling among the teaching staff about budget control. According to the music teacher, ES money was used for musical instruments and other supplies for her program, but she had little to say about how it was spent. "What they bought was poor quality, and not what I needed," she says. She, among other teachers in the Myrtle Creek school, declared a preference for a smaller, teacher-controlled budget rather than larger expenditures controlled by the administration.

At the same time, effective small-scale programs from individual schools were implemented throughout the district. An annual trip to Terramar, an outdoor conservation education camp on the Oregon coast, had been a staple of the fifth-grade curriculum at Canyonville for several years. Classes raised money for the trip from bake sales, parents chipped in, and local merchants helped pay the costs of children whose parents could not afford to contribute. The cost of Terramar was now paid by ES, and all of the fifth grades in the district participated. A Friday electives program, a successful volunteer effort in Canyonville, was extended to the other elementary schools.

At the junior high school level, ES was a vehicle for curriculum restructuring. The junior high school was quite traditional; each student took a set number of full-semester courses. ES curriculum money funded the reorganization of the program into flexible, teacher-designed, nine-week mini-courses that allowed students substantial choice. In addition, classes in art, music, and drama were initiated.

The high school had the least ES investment and the fewest results. The vice-principal for curriculum, who was a high school teacher during the ES years, says, "It got us kind of organized. Teachers got used to writing down their courses because they had to under ES. Of course, they also got used to getting paid to do it, which gives us a bit of a problem now that we don't have the money to pay them anymore." Several innovations were tried, with varying success. First, a new freshman orientation program was developed, which involved parents and incoming freshmen in a guided planning process for the high school years. This was popular with the community, according to a member of the Coordinating Council who views it as one of the best and most permanent achievements of the ES program. A student-run storefront, intended to be stocked with student-made crafts, was a disaster. Merchants objected to tax-funded competition, and there weren't enough things to sell. A final innovation, a job placement service for high school students and graduates, never quite got off the ground.

Throughout the district, ES money went into a wide range of materials and experiences that were intended to enrich students' lives. ES money bought expensive equipment for the physical education program, countless bus trips to events and places of interest, artists in residence who helped students design and paint murals on school walls, and so on. Looking back on the ES experience, one former instructional leader says, "Some things that people now are calling 'frills' are experiences those kids will never forget." And school people, even those critical of the program, agree that it expanded the world of the classroom as it had never been expanded before.

By the beginning of 1974-75, Dea Cox had accomplished nearly all the tasks the school board had set for him when he was hired. The faculty had been radically upgraded. The curriculum had been transformed by ES-funded materials and courses. He had acquired more federal dollars than the school board would ever have envisioned a single program supplying. And, at last, even the new cafeteria was open (with an ES-funded Food Services Program to go with it). With the help of ES, the district was moving ahead like an express train.

## Trouble in Camelot

Unfortunately, the express train was going in the wrong direction for some people, and it was going too fast for others. There were those in the community who didn't like Dea Cox, who said he was distant, high-handed, and insufficiently responsive to community concerns, especially about sports issues. There were those, especially among the fundamentalists, who felt that the new books and multimedia curricula taught attitudes that were liable to lead young people astray. And there were those who were flatly unhappy with Experimental Schools. ES brought new administrators to a system already considered "top heavy" by local residents. Although Cox argued that there were only ten administrators in the entire system, including principals and vice-principals, some citizens tended to lump together regular administration with federal program personnel. They watched with some dismay as the new, beautifully landscaped administration building (called the "head-shed") filled its fourteen offices with Cox's staff.

Others were more concerned about what was going on at school. One principal, who titled the Friday electives program "Friday Fun," got a spate of angry letters and calls from parents. Townspeople complained when they saw school buses pulled up next to the local golf course in the middle of the day while the physical education classes practiced their strokes. By the 1974-75 school year, some of the original members of the Concerned Citizens group had become active critics of the program in the schools. ES became a ready focus for their discontent. According to one fifth-grade teacher, never a fan of the program, "It was a handy thing to blame things on. If your kid got into college, fine; if not, it was ES's fault."

The outside critics got some of their ammunition from within the schools. Some of the long-time elementary teachers felt bullied into the learning-station approach to teaching and found allies in a few of the community women who had been hired as aides. "They took away all the desks," one teacher recalls. "There was a kind of rootlessness about it. I felt, and I still do, that children need a place to sit down and get ready to listen. They need more structure." Another teacher complained that ES forced teachers to incorporate "time-wasting" activities into their classrooms. Others were not so negative; one young woman, who came to Myrtle Creek the second year of ES, remembers it as an experience akin to McCaslin's "Camelot." "Exciting things were happening here," she says. "The school was relaxed, exciting—there were learning stations, Friday electives, field trips, terrific media. Those were great times." But for those looking for negative feelings about ES, there were sufficient teachers to supply them.

If some teachers felt that they were forced to follow a program they did not like, others felt uncertain that they knew what the program was at all.

The instructional-leader strategy seems to have been a problem for the latter. According to Cox, the instructional leaders (ILs) were the great success of the project. He believes they made teachers more flexible, more responsive to individual student needs, more able to use materials and resources in creative ways. The teachers were not as clear about the value of the instructional leaders, perhaps because they had no part in creating the role. One teacher, whose attitude was echoed by others, called the whole concept a "disaster." "Ours ran around like a chicken with her head cut off. She was a glorified go-fer. You can't have an instructional leader leading people who know more than they do." This unflattering portrait is particulary interesting because it describes the leader Cox feels was the best in the program, a person he describes as "dynamic, intelligent, someone who insisted on systematic organization around the needs of kids." Cox agrees that the ILs often appeared to be "glorified go-fers" but says that this appearance was part of the strategy. "They were supposed to act as go-fers, to encourage change from two steps back. They were successful when the teachers changed without knowing it."

This kind of "invisible" strategy has built-in problems, both with surface credibility and assessment. In fact, the instructional leaders themselves were not always clear about their role. They held long meetings in which they tried to hammer out a common definition of their role, not altogether successfully. No one seemed quite sure whether the ILs were administrators, teachers without classrooms, or resource people for teachers and principals. "As ES went on," says John Hunter, recalling his days as the Tri-City Elementary School instructional leader, "it was less and less clear about our role. We knew we had a full-time job, but how we were to relate to teachers and to principals wasn't as clear. There was some tension between the teachers and the instructional leaders—you know, 'Who are you to tell me what to do?'" He thinks these feelings would have been less strong if the leaders had received more formal instruction in the individualized approaches they were supposed to foster in teachers. "I got some training later on," Hunter says, "but I really could have used it that first year."

The national ES program emphasis on "comprehensiveness" also caused problems with local implementation. Ideas that were fine at one school became targets for criticism when they were moved to other schools. Consider, for example, the fate of the Friday electives. The original Friday electives program was simple: parents would volunteer to teach a skill or topic to a small group of children every Friday afternoon. The volunteer would determine how many children would be in the group, and the classroom teachers would "float," resolving problems, handling discipline issues if necessary, and generally helping out. When this simple, informal program became part of the ES comprehensive reform, it began to look too casual.

Parent complaints about "frills" pushed the administration to demand evidence that the electives were really teaching something. According to Doyle McCaslin, "The volunteers only knew how to give the kids an experience. They didn't know how to make sure the kids got what they should out of it." The program became hedged with requirements: volunteers had to write out lesson plans; the electives had to take a fixed length of time; some means of evaluation had to be worked out. "When we were doing it on our own, it was fun," one teacher says. "We had beautiful mothers. They would volunteer to do what the kids wanted, or say what they would rather do, and then they'd do it. It was fun." But expansion of the program and formalization of the requirements apparently took the fun out of it, as did the rising complaint level from community people. In the end, according to another teacher, "When the Friday electives finally went, you could hear the sighs of relief."

Even without the problems of transplanted programs, the ES structure seemed to compel a level of formalization that took its toll. Concepts had to be too elaborate, scale had to be too large for small ideas to survive. Two teachers in Canyonville decided to build a nature trail. They started it themselves, digging up wildflowers and replanting them at the edge of a brook where the trail was to be. Then the project became part of the ES venture. According to one of the teachers, "They decided that the paths weren't level enough and brought in a bulldozer, which killed all our plants. So we replanted. Then they decided to make concrete paths, so nothing that got planted ever grew. It wound up not being a nature path anymore. It would have been better if they had left us alone."

While school people were learning to cope with new problems, strategies, materials, and roles within the system, a storm of public disapproval was rolling toward them from without. The mid-seventies were difficult years for school systems in Oregon; in 1975, ten districts could not get their budgets approved in time for the beginning of the school year, and South Umpqua was one of them. ES was not the only source of controversy, but those who survived those years see it as the factor that "stirred people up." In discussions of the period, the pendulum image recurs. School and lay people agree that ES represented a progressive swing so strong, and so public, that a powerful opposite reaction was virtually inevitable. According to Doyle McCaslin, "The nay-sayers were in the community to begin with. But ES really brought them out."

It brought them out in droves. A group of parents suddenly concerned with student misbehavior formed a volunteer "parent patrol" to police the corridors of the high school. Some members of this group expanded their areas of concern, protesting the inclusion of certain books on optional reading lists, complaining about the dismissal of a track coach, arguing against the "open campus" policy at the high school. School board meetings became long protest sessions, with parents complaining about a wide range of perceived problems.

When the 1976 school budget failed in April, and again in August, Cox felt compelled to make a public statement at a joint school board/budget committee meeting: "By all standard criteria, this is an outstanding school district. Tests show the reading levels to be up. Our athletic program is one of the most successful in the state. A winning athletic program is usually a sign of academic achievement. Outside the district, South Umpqua has a reputation as one of the better schools in the state. We are seen as a pace-setting district." But not at home. Cox says now that he made a conscious decision not to deal with the backlash against ES: "Towards the end, I spent less time dealing with problems. It would have meant my role would have been more political, less educational." As Mickey Moore, a long-time school board member and supporter of Cox, puts it, "Dea Cox is an educator. He didn't give a hoot about public relations. If there was money laying around out there which could benefit the kids, he wanted it. And I agreed."

Citizen criticism of the schools got stronger and more strident as the year moved on. Finally, in the fall of 1976, one protesting group fixed on the issue that provided a focus for a great deal of community anger. The issue was MACOS, the fifth-grade social studies curriculum that had been successfully pilot-tested in Tri-City, and which had been chosen for comprehensive implementation in the other fifth-grade classrooms, in part because of its noncontroversial nature.

A major part of the MACOS curriculum is a series of films on the Netsilik Eskimos showing the life of that culture in great and nonjudgmental detail. During the period following the adoption of this curriculum in South Umpqua, it had become the target of attack by a Texas couple who apparently had as their state mission the purging from American education elements that they considered anti-Christian or antipatriotic. Fundamentalist Christian groups in the South Umpqua district found this couple's newsletter persuasive in its attack on the "secular humanism" said to be presented in that curriculum. Led by a minister, this group lodged a formal complaint with the school board in September 1976, touching off a struggle that ripped the three communities apart for the rest of the school year. The MACOS battle was fought through the press, through the mails, and in the churches, stores, and homes of the three towns. The "anti-secular humanist" group sent around a circular describing the curriculum as an effort to "promote cannibalism, wife-swapping, infanticide, the killing of the elderly, and other revolting subjects." Parents who were unaligned with any of the fundamentalist churches became alarmed at this description of what ES had brought to their children.

Cox sees the MACOS fight as a local manifestation of a national right-wing movement, which caught fire in South Umpqua among those who saw the recent changes in southern Oregon as a direct threat to their values. "Some teachers allied with the fundamentalists," Cox says. "Mainly those we ran afoul of earlier on—teachers who were forced to get their certification, or who felt the heat when we were insisting on quality teaching." These teachers, Cox believes, fueled the conflict by feeding inflammatory information to the leaders of the protest movement.

A counter protest group called Citizens Advocating Responsible Education (CARE) formed around the MACOS issue, defending both the curriculum and the administration's point of view. Michael Hallinan, a local bookstore owner (and newcomer to the region) wrote a six-part article on the controversy for the Roseburg newspaper. These articles presented both sides of the issue but were easily read as pro-MACOS. The existence of CARE made formal and public the wrenching battle in the community. Anti-MACOS people accused the school of having made a deal with the government: fifth graders would be subjected to MACOS in return for a pay-off in federal funds, represented by ES money. Pro-MACOS people talked about separation of church and state, about curricular choice. They pointed out an alternative social studies course had always been available to fifth graders whose parents didn't like MACOS, but only seven children had ever had that alternative requested for them. Mickey Moore saw the fight as a reflection of an older quarrel. "We have a group around here," he says, "who are 'anti.' It's a group of church people who want to tell all of us what we can have in school. Church isn't being separated from state the way it should be in this district. And that's the way they want it."

In December, Cox resigned. The school board that had hired him and had supported the ES program from the beginning had changed almost completely. The professional and business leaders who had dominated school politics for more years than anyone in the schools could remember had been replaced by working-class people who tended to represent the more conservative, fundamentalist segment of the community. In his letter of resignation, Cox said that a major reason for leaving was his inability to work with the new board. Others felt that there were other reasons: that he was trying to stem the MACOS battle; that he was simply finished and ready to move on; that he was forced to resign as a result of the ES backlash. Looking back on that period, Cox himself says, "We weren't willing to work on politics. We said we'd work on education and to hell with the rest of it."

If Cox intended to reduce the MACOS tension by resigning, he failed. The battle continued, even more viciously. Protesters circulated an anti-MACOS petition, eventually gathering 900 signatures. Some of these, according to one long-term resident, were acquired in unscrupulous ways. "People were high-pressured in church," he says. "They were told that all

Christians would sign the petition. They went to the senior citizen residence and told them that MACOS was teaching fifth graders to kill old people. Of course they signed. I could have gotten 600 of those people on that petition to sign something supporting MACOS. It all depends on what you tell them." One teacher says that some local businesses came out against MACOS because of boycott threats; other citizens reported threatening phone calls and warnings about house bombings. In these normally peaceful, live-and-let-live communities, such tactics frightened and polarized people of every persuasion.

Finally, the school board held a series of public hearings on the MACOS issue. One teacher says of the final hearing, "It was like sitting on 'his' or 'her' sides at a wedding. There were some very supportive parents who sat with us, and a lot of people on the other side." The pro-MACOS teachers felt confident that the board would support them. It didn't. The board finally voted to continue MACOS to the end of the school year (with an available alternative curriculum), and then to eliminate it from the schools. The audience, which consisted primarily of anti-MACOS people, applauded.

## The Final Impact of ES

MACOS is gone now, and so is Experimental Schools. What remains of the $1.3-million spent over the five-year period? Certain tangible changes have been institutionalized and are likely to persist. Teacher aides, most of them mature women from the communities, are firmly entrenched in the primary grades. The teachers feel they are invaluable, and they are given credit (along with the Macmillan reading series) for the rise in primary reading scores between 1973 and 1978. The quantities of curriculum materials purchased with ES funds (with the exception of MACOS) will be around until they are worn out, used up, or outdated. And when they are replaced, teachers and principals feel that it will be with other articulated curricula. The days of each teacher selecting books for a particular class are probably gone. Some of the teaching staff, lured by the excitement of ES and Dea Cox's educational dream, are still in the schools. Some intend to stay for awhile; others are looking around. Certain programs, most noticeably Terramar, have been adopted by all district schools with funding from the board. Unless budget restrictions eliminate all such "frills," Terramar is likely to remain as a fifth-grade program.

Other innovations are gone: MACOS, obviously; the high school job placement program; the instructional leaders. The learning-station approach has been modified or eliminated in most primary classrooms as teachers turn back to more traditional practices. The Myrtle Creek school recently purchased a whole set of new desks. The junior high school principal says that the semester course system will probably be reinstated during the next few years, although the students will still be able to make some choices among courses. The change on which Cox most depended is gone, too. The "new educational leadership" recruited from all over the country did not outlast the administration that recruited it. All the young administrators Cox brought to South Umpqua have left. "You can structure an environment to attract young leaders," Cox says, "but you can't make them stay."

Cox believes that the rate at which his programs and policies have disappeared is sad but inevitable. "We spent money on a lot of things that didn't work, trying to find things that would," he says. "A phenomenal number of things happened for a 10 percent budget increase. It's no surprise that a lot of them are gone now." Herriott, looking at South Umpqua from a national perspective, agrees: "There seems to be as much continuing there as anywhere. No innovations last all that long—the deck is stacked against educational innovations."

Whether or not one is satisfied with the attrition rate, it is easy to count the tangible ES products that remain in the schools. It is harder to assess the psychological residue of the experiment. Some perceive positive results. "There is increased awareness in the community of what good education might be," Dea Cox says, and many agree. Mickey Moore says that ES was good for the teachers, and therefore good for the schools: "We acquired things that we would never have gotten otherwise. The teachers are enthused about them. And if the teachers think it's good for kids, it's fine with me." And several teachers agree with the one who said, "I can't believe the changes. The changes in the school are incredible. There is no way I could have believed two years ago that I would be standing up at a school board meeting and applauding the vice-superintendent."

Others feel that the psychological costs of ES were not worth the gains. Among them is Doyle McCaslin, who feels that ES, and especially the MACOS controversy, provided a forcing bed for community dissatisfaction with the schools, which has resulted in parent pressure groups attacking everything from sex education to Judy Blume books in the school library. "We wanted a critical mass of funding to accomplish certain things," McCaslin says. "What we got was a critical mass of opposition to go with it."

Many teachers agree with McCaslin that ES cost more than it gave. One teacher says that the program was "doomed from the start. We teachers just don't have the expertise to develop new programs. Now we have the new programs, but, oh Lordie, the misery in between." And another says, "I'm positive that education needs a lot of money. But I'm convinced that there are better ways to spend it. ES gave the schools a lot of money to do new things—that weren't the three R's—and parents worried about that." Many feel that ES cost the schools community support. One teacher says, "ES caused a split in this community. Before, people supported our school. Now there's lots of negative feeling, a sense that a lot of people are moving in on us, telling us what we can and can't do. The pendulum is swinging to ultra-conservatism."

It would certainly appear that public support for federal projects is a casualty of ES. A highly successful preschool program, funded by Title III, was voted in by several surrounding districts but defeated in South Umpqua. This program, which predated ES, began in the South Umpqua district and was very popular with local residents until after ES. Most school people attribute its defeat to "ES backlash." McCaslin, in fact, says that by 1978 there were rumblings in the community about voting against Title I funds and the small amount of money that the district received for Indian education. "A lot of people don't like all that government money," according to one teacher. "They want it all out."

There is a widespread belief in South Umpqua that the "ES backlash" would not have been so severe had implementation strategies been modified. The fast rate of change, the lack of teacher involvement at the earliest stages, and inattention to public relations in the community are all cited as factors in the strong negative response. "There might not have been a backlash if we hadn't accelerated change," Cox admits. And the principal of the Canyonville School, a long-time resident of the region, agrees: "Maybe if we had gone a little slower, gotten teachers involved earlier so that they would have sounded more positive to the community, it would have worked out better."

But there are clear reasons why the project was implemented as it was, some stemming from the personalities involved, some from the ES model itself. Cox takes some of the blame. He perceived himself as an educator, he says, not a politician. His articulated, sophisticated plan for improving the quality of education in South Umpqua appealed to the Washington profes-sionals; at home, his impatience with distraction and delay made him ap-pear autocratic and manipulative. As one teacher says, "Dea and Doyle made all the decisions. They kept saying we had a lot of *say* about what happened. But that didn't mean we had any *do*."

The ES model also had significant impact on what happened in South Umpqua and elsewhere. According to Herriott, the effort to "impose district-wide implementation of comprehensive change was an unwise strategy, especially in newly consolidated districts." Cox agrees, and adds, "We never were clear about what was meant by 'comprehensive.' And had we not been constrained by that concept, we would have designed more spot strategies for particular schools. That would have worked better." Her-riott agrees that the less comprehensive ES programs had more elements that stuck once the federal funding was gone, but pointed out that such programs were not what the federal government wanted. "Cox and McCaslin knew how to design and implement a program," he says. "They had the best sense of what the government had in mind."

Time was another ES-imposed pressure. The administration felt that it suffered from continuous deadlines—produce a proposal, develop a plan, get results that can be measured. "We had to nail ourselves down too early," McCaslin says. "That may have gone a good way towards doing us in." Time pressures also limited teacher and community contribution to the programs developed. Cox cites the market researchers of the 1950s, who found that housewives preferred cake mixes to which they had to add fresh ingredients, even if the final result tasted the same as the prepackaged mixes. Adding ingredients evidently gave housewives a sense of ownership toward the cake, Cox argues, and schools need the same opportunity. "Schools must put their own ingredients into strategies if they are going to work to keep them," Cox says. But the ES process, even with the planning year, did not seem to allow enough time for that.

Was the ES experience a success? It depends on what you wanted from it. Various teachers and community people see it as an unmitigated disaster, the source of tensions and conflicts that continue to haunt the district. Mc-Caslin, who believed in its potential to fulfill an educational vision, says that he would not have involved the district in the program if he had known what he knows today. But Cox disagrees: "I'm interested in education and the process of change, in the improvement of education. I believe the South Umpqua schools are better now, and that it couldn't have happened without the ESP." He does not believe that ES did anything to enhance the capacity of the South Umpqua communities to address their own educational problems. "That wasn't the point of the program. If you wanted to improve education in the district on a permanent basis, ES didn't work. But if you wanted to see how change affected a rural community, we learned a great deal. ES was an experiment—they wanted to find out how much change you could get in a rural school in a limited period of time. We found some answers to that. I was, in many ways, a carpetbagger. It might have been different if I'd known I had to stay. But ES was a professional thing for me."

### Notes

1. Michael B. Kane, *Educational Change in Rural America: An Interim Report to the Experimental Schools Program* (Cambridge, Mass.: Abt Associates, 1976).

# 7
# Taking Education to the Crossroads: Texas's Regional Education Service Centers

*Ralph G. Bohrson*

Drive down U.S. 277 in West Texas where the miles stretch unbroken to the horizon. You feel alone, isolated. You never reach the horizon, and you think you must be experiencing infinity. Both locals and visitors may on occasion share a common feeling of boredom in this setting, but only the outsider is lonely. In many ways the people of this rural outback—12 per square mile—are closer than people are in White Plains, New York, which is not congested even at 5,000 per square mile, or in New York City, where at a density of 26,000 there is little elbow room. Rural Texans share common primary concerns: hold the land, make it yield its riches, provide for future generations, protect from outsiders, live, love, learn, drink a little, go to Vegas or to Honolulu if it's a *real* anniversary, work, fight the mesquite, find time for family, see friends, laugh often, and take nothing for granted. Cities like Dallas, Houston, San Antonio, Fort Worth, and even Austin are rich, brassy, and economically segregated. It is because of these Texas cities with their magnet-like hold on millions of people that rural Texas seems so much more empty. It explains in part why the towns, churches, and schools are small, close to the land, and dear to the hearts of the few who stay or return from places like Corpus Christi, Waco, and San Angelo with complaints about rush-hour traffic.

Rural people worry about the quality of their schools. They expect the schools to educate their children for the future, wherever that may lead—city or ranch, nearby or far away. Ask the rural professionals and they'll say they are constantly improving their craft, but the critics will say that rural schools have never met the standards of the best city schools. Parents aren't certain who's right. Texas ranchers and planters may want their sons and daughters to have an education equivalent to that in Houston or its suburbs, but every hamlet has its traditions, possibly not understood by the standard bearers in Austin or Washington, D.C.

This raises the age-old question: How do you assure high quality throughout the school system without forcing uniformity? Raising the state's standards for education may create greater problems for the village schools without measurably improving them. Moreover, improvement usually means increased cost. Seemingly oblivious to the advance of labor-saving mechanization in agribusiness, mining, and even on the mom-and-pop farm, education continues to be proudly labor intensive with a clamor for more teachers, not fewer, and for human aides, not teaching machines. Traditional answers to the rural quality query have been to get bigger, get richer, or get help from the outside (and in turn give up a piece of local freedom).

For rural Texas—indeed for much of rural America—bigger and richer are fanciful solutions. Reaching the size of cost and program effectiveness is unlikely with even ten children per square mile. And even in Texas—the land of Neiman-Marcus and J. R. Ewing—rural districts cannot get rich enough to hire teaching staffs in numbers to offer programs comparable to those in Dallas or Houston. Until the mid-1960s, rural educational improvement in Texas seemed to require a form of outside service option without the inevitable external controls. The device selected in 1965 by the state legislature was a form of service cooperative designed to maintain and upgrade local schools, channel federal aid funds legally to those schools, and enforce state standards. Today twenty Regional Education Service Centers (RESCs) blanket the Lone Star State and, according to their advocates, bring rural education into parity with the best schools in Texas and elsewhere in the country.

The notion of both serving and regulating rural schools through an intermediary was not new to U.S. school systems in 1965. As early as 1829, the county was the unit of local school administration in Delaware. After 1865 the role of the county superintendent was defined in detail as a form of intermediate local school governance. Even so, the county superintendent became not so much the enforcer of rules as the master teacher. S/he generally considered teachers to be students, a group to be guarded, the junior members of an emerging profession. Enforcement resulted from demonstration, not coercion, and local control was maximal. As important as it was for the county superintendent to be the intermediary for the state, s/he was seen first by local folk as the lantern that brought the light to the country school.

Times changed. The cities grew, and with improved transportation, one-teacher schools were consolidated and tiny districts were re-formed into larger units with professionally educated superintendents, who as often as not communicated directly with the state, bypassing or otherwise making superfluous the elected county school official.[1]

In response to the growing expectations for schools and the proliferation of state laws that made supervision more demanding, national rural school reformers envisioned another form of intermediate unit that would go beyond demonstration teaching, supervision,· and guidance and would provide services directly to schools to help teachers stay abreast of new curriculum movements and teaching trends. The concept was later enlarged to include services for special student populations as well. A 1953 report of a national commission formed to define this intermediate unit called it

> an organization within the legally established structure of school administration which includes the territory of two or more basic administrative units and serves as the intermediary between the State Department of Education and quasi corporate units having immediate responsibility for maintaining the schools. It may have a Board or Officer or both responsible for performing stipulated services for the basic administrative units and for inserting leadership in their fiscal, administrative and educational functions. Leadership and services in the administrative unit promotes and strengthens local control and responsibility. It assists local districts and the state education department in finding and meeting more effectively the educational needs of children and communities by performing functions which can best be administered by an intermediate type of organization.[2]

One year later, Howard Dawson, executive secretary of the National Educational Association's Department of Rural Education, introduced the subject in his foreword to the Rural Education Association's *Yearbook:* "As people develop educational programs related to the real needs of each community, they discover that there is need for services which are beyond the reach of most local school districts, *even those which have been reorganized.* The problem which community schools face is how to get these educational services at a reasonable cost while at the same time preserving local community autonomy [emphasis added]."[3] By then the service role pioneered by the county superintendent was an accepted need for all rural schools. Today several geographically large states have organized multi-county units that can combine supervisory and regulatory functions for the state while offering services to teachers. In a few cases the units offer their clients other forms of schooling (e.g., vocational and arts education) as well.

The Texas version of the intermediate service agency, the Regional Education Service Center (RESC), came into bud in 1965 and into full bloom in 1967 with a change in guidelines for Title III of the federal Elementary and Secondary Education Act (ESEA). The change shifted the support of innovative efforts in local districts to regional centers for the dissemination and implementation of innovative programs. Building on the state-supported media centers legislated in 1965 and implemented in 1967, the state allocated approximately half of its annual $10 million Title III entitlement for the next five years to establish the twenty RESCs. Consistent with the service intent as stated by Dawson, but adding the federal notion of educational innovation, the Texas RESCs are area facilities (organizational and physical) established for the purpose of planning, coordinating, and/or providing basic educational programs and services to students in elementary and secondary schools and to children, youth, and adults, in a group of communities. Centers may facilitate creative and educational change by stimulating activity in all stages of the innovation process; and by serving as a communication link in a network to identify and solve educational problems and to disseminate information about innovative and exemplary programs. A center might offer services in the following areas: education manpower development, curriculum development and consultation, pupil personnel, special education, data processing, adult and vocational education, instruction, cultural enrichment, communication, and educational planning.[4]

The study team went to Texas to see what role a well-established intermediate unit structure had played in improving education for children in rural areas. We sought to determine to what extent the regional center is a fundamental institution working on behalf of rural schools. We asked whether the centers can help define services for a truly effective education that reflects the uniqueness of locality and the pride of ethnic diversity while maintaining high educational standards. We asked taxpayer-like questions of the professionals: Is it working? Do we get the same return on our educational dollar that San Antonians get? Will the kids hold up under scrutiny at college and on the job market? Finally, we asked: If the rural schools work, is it because of or in spite of the structure? In Texas, for instance, does the insertion of one thick ply of bureaucracy between the state and the localities strengthen rural education overall? Is the bureaucratic insert an insulating device preventing needless state interference in local decisions, or is it the professional educator's method of frontier management—a way to enforce, keep order, and maintain "one best system"?[5] The answers to the questions were not clear cut; perceptions vary depending on whether the view is from the state office, the centers' headquarters, a nearby district, or one far away.

We picked the West Texas region (Region XV) because in setting and lifestyles it is an archetypal rural microcosm and because its director, Charlie Bitters, a career education reformer (now retired), was for a dozen or more years in charge of the Texas Small Schools Project (later the Texas Small Schools Association and now the Community Schools Association) operating out of the state education agency. If anybody knew the needs of small schools, it was Charlie Bitters, and if any region had an abundance of small schools, it was Region XV.

## The Region XV Spread

From his office, Bitters presides over a domain almost the size of Maine, with forty-eight public school systems, eight nonpublic schools, eighteen counties, and several ranches of 40,000 and more acres. The center's total staff of about fifty includes twenty-seven professional, itinerant consultants who, according to the center's brochure, know the "school's individual situations and mold services to fit them."[6] Their operational creed displayed prominently in the office is, "Services available anywhere should be available everywhere."

Region XV, large even by Texas standards, is varied in its needs, although no more so than Texas or rural America overall. Driving from San Angelo southward through the region, the world seems an endless view of mesquite, cotton and peanut plants, wheat, maize, sheep, goats, cattle, and fences; people appear more as blips on the radar screen than as the landlords and serfs who in their separate and unequal ways dominate the setting. The seat of Tom Greene County, San Angelo, is the region's nerve center and its population center at nearly 100,000. The "second city," Del Rio (population 30,000), lies 157 miles south on the Rio Grande, the river "too thick to drink, too thin to plow," which is an international boundary too porous to stop the bands of workers who cross illegally to seek jobs, education, and (sometimes) official citizenship. For the adjacent school districts and for the region in general the legal and illegal migrants create a difficult institutional ambivalence. Migrants and bilinguals are worth money in state and federal aid, but not nearly enough for the problems created. Three-fourths of the center's income from Washington is for migrant education. On the other hand, bilingual education, requiring highly qualified, dedicated teachers, gets little or no federal money. Less than 1 percent of state revenue to the region is spent for that purpose.

Yet the combined Mexican and Mexican-American populations have been influential in other ways. Region XV's territory breaks culturally and agriculturally into a North XV and a South XV. The South XV, from Del Rio northward and westward, includes towns with significant Spanish-speaking student populations, viewed, as noted, most positively for the federal and state money they can be counted on to attract. The "more populous" upper tier districts are little concerned with bilingual or migrant programs. Their small enclaves of ethnics—second- and third-generation Americans, still called Germans, Czechs, and Poles—also include a few second- or third-generation Mexican-American land owners or business people as almost equals. However, if the center's ultimate purpose in equalizing services is to equalize educational opportunity—as those who fashion state aid formulas, court-ordered remedies, and educational service delivery systems claim—it has its work cut out for it.

Neither the socioeconomic structure of West Texas nor the governance structure of the center is simple, and, as so often happens, neither is one in programmatic alignment with the other. In the Region XV world, people are divided into four socioeconomic groups. The ranchers and planters, the latter with large holdings of cotton, maize, or peanuts, are usually the white upper class. The next group, the farmers, are landowning, often Mexican-American, families, not quite equal but "hard working, clean, and respectable." Then come the workers, more or less steady, hired help—cowboys and domestics on the big spreads—good folk, but almost poor. At the bottom, naturally, are the migrants, who by general acknowledgement are itinerant trouble: poor, illiterate, often illegal.

Region XV's constituents are both haves and have-nots, but its governing structure, written into state educational policies to assure programmatic congruence with regional interests and needs, include only the haves. The joint committee is composed of one person from (a) each twelve-grade school district, (b) each district with fewer than twelve grades, and (c) each four-year college or university with an approved teacher-education program. All joint committee members are appointed by their appropriate policymaking/governing boards.

Members of local boards of education elect the noneducators on the centers' boards of directors, who, with rare exception, represent the business-political interests of the area. The San Angelo center is governed by an all-male, all-Anglo board composed of two merchants, two ranchers, a real estate agent, an optometrist, and a retired county judge. (In comparison, the oil-rich midland area, Region XVIII, numbers as members two physicians, a petroleum engineer, a farm loan manager, the county auditor, a realtor, and an airport manager.) No board member may be engaged professionally in education, be a member of a local board of education, or do business in any way with the RESC.

The board of directors picks the executive director, who must hold a graduate degree, have administrative experience in education, and be approved by the state commissioner of education. In addition, each RESC is assisted by an advisory committee of at least twelve teachers, supervisors, and principals selected by the board from school districts served by the RESC. Other advisory committees are formed as needed within each region.

The entire scheme is held in statewide equilibrium by the statewide Advisory Commission on Regional Education Centers of twenty people (those who chair boards of directors of RESCs) and the Commissioner's Planning Council for Elementary and Secondary Education, made up of each RESC's executive director. These groups, together with the commissioner of education and the appropriate supervisors within the state education agency, are advised by statewide committees on programmatic elements of RESCs such as computer services, career education, crime and narcotics, and ESEA Title III-IV.

The governance and advisory structure assures a network of communication to the centers from the state and across regional lines, then back to the state from the district superintendents. The design at the regional level is expected to assure political awareness of local district preferences, most of which pay less attention to minority than to majority needs. According to textbook and legend, public education has always been the means to level the classes—provided that those at the bottom of the heap don't pretend too openly to equality. But equality has another dimension. As the nation's values become similar, if not more sane or urbane, and as television talk shows, the evening news, and popular magazines make young ruralites aware of Sunday brunch, backgammon, radical chic, and analysis, the school must somehow take notice of these outside life-styles and fads. Half of being educated is knowing what others are doing.

"Services available anywhere should be available everywhere." What's good in Dallas should be available somehow in Barnhardt, but if Barnhardt wants it and Menard doesn't, one should have it, the other not. By state guideline, each center's legally constituted board of directors "demonstrates its obligation to the clients it represents by soliciting 'participation as appropriate, from district personnel within the region, citizens, patrons, and students, in shaping operational strategies.'"[7] According to the State Plan revised in 1970, "The Center . . . is designed to provide *services* to school districts in a region in response to the needs and *wishes* of those districts [emphasis added]."[8] Apparently "one best system" was not the intent of the guidelines writers.

But what does one find by a closer look at a service region within the elaborate organizational structure, supported by an annual budget of slightly over $3 million? Region XV's information handbook lists nearly a dozen administrative, instructional, and direct student services:

*Administrative*
- *Data processing* through a neighboring computer 300 miles away with terminal and telephone access in the region's headquarters. Includes grade reporting, test scoring, class scheduling, payroll, and accounting.
- *Fiscal management and budgeting*, including recording and reporting of revenue and expenditure information for member schools and districts.
- *Public information* through newsletters reporting available and anticipated services, press releases, explanatory brochures, etc.
- *Special projects* and technical advisory services to help districts stay

current with contemporary educational trends and with rules, regulations, laws, and guidelines as they come from the state capital.

*Instructional*

- *Inservice sessions and workshops* on expanding library services, new curricular materials and teaching services, and assistance with guidance and counseling programs, including direct assistance to the 50 percent of the region's schools without guidance personnel.
- *Special training assistance* to schools under state mandate to develop "desirable teacher competencies" in a crime prevention and drug education program for all schools.
- *Direct delivery of materials and equipment* through a film, slide, and cassette distribution program and transporting of three air-conditioned driver education trailers with simulated driving stations.
- *Resource teachers and aides* to work directly with children of migrant farm workers. Records for migrant workers' children are maintained for the nation in a central computer bank in Little Rock, Arkansas, 800 miles away, and are available through a dial-up terminal at the regional center.

*Student*

- *Consultants in special education* for testing, evaluation, and special materials distribution from the regional library.
- *Coordination of programs* and distribution of special funds for hearing and visually impaired children.
- *Workshops and technical assistance* to help local schools reach "State Criteria of Excellence for Reading Programs," the Texas version of the national Right to Read program.[9]

Have the above services resulted from the needs and wishes of the member districts of the region, or are they programs the state and/or federal government decided should be introduced—or both? For the communities of Menard, Mason, Bronte, and Eldorado in the North XV, the best answer would seem to be both. They participate in the state-financed data processing programs for student accounting, finance, payroll, and tax accounting; the school bus-driver training program, driver education programs, and media center resources with biweekly deliveries (all state supported); and inservice programs, many of which relate to either federally developed programs (such as Right to Read and innovative programs of the National Diffusion Network) or programs mandated by the state and federal governments (e.g., migrant education and education for the handicapped). The district superintendents in the North XV spoke highly of Bitters's operation, suggesting only the addition of a teacher-recruitment service (rural schools still have difficulty locating specialists in art and music[10]).

Further to the south, Rock Springs and Del Rio are the only districts in the region with bilingual education, a program introduced in Del Rio by court order to respond to the needs of Spanish-speaking children. Because only two districts are involved, Region XV provides little if any help. Rock Springs fends for itself or gets help from Del Rio, which in turn seeks advice from Region XX in San Antonio, 153 miles to the east. The Del Rio director of instruction noted that his staff had gone to Region XX for assistance in migrant education programs as well.

Like other schools in the region, Rock Springs and Del Rio are served by the twice-weekly delivery of media supplies. They also participate in the in-service education programs and receive assistance from RESC personnel on the state education agency's new accreditation processes requiring local districts to write educational goals for student development, school organization, management, and accountability. The Rock Springs superintendent, a product of his own school system and community, was promoted to the superintendent's position from a position as "Vo-Ag" teacher. He would like to see Region XV hire more curriculum specialists to "come out and work directly with teachers." With the closest higher education institution 150 miles away, such a request is understandable.

## RESC: Serving the Local Interest?

The central offices from which the services originate in downtown San Angelo are in an "excessed" school building shared with the San Angelo public schools. The basement houses the media center and special education materials, which the schools order through a 182-page catalog by paying $1 per student. Air-conditioned temporary buildings house the computer complex for data processing of student records, scheduling, and fiscal management. A computer terminal on the second floor ties Region XV into the national migrant record system in Little Rock, Arkansas. The activities of the professionals housed in assorted offices are recorded in the computer with yearly printouts completed for each school providing it with a list of RESC staff development meetings attended by local personnel, a breakdown by professional assignment (administrative, aide, or instructional staff; elementary, junior high, or high school), and a listing of RESC consultants conducting local district visits, including how many people they met with, for how long, and for what purpose.

Region XV is firmly established as part of the basic educational matrix of Texas. The RESCs touch every school system—rural, suburban, and urban—and provide work for some 1,200 professional staff. They cover the state with data processes, films, mobile labs, drug and tobacco taboo kits, advisors, consultants, specialists, coordinators, and a full array of people carrying the unusual, sometimes artificial, vernacular of a proliferating profession.

To remain in power at the top of the regional centers requires that directors be a careful blend of state bureaucrat, district school superintendent, local politician, and country schoolmaster. They know the territory, they know each other, and they know who has the votes and the dollars. With one foot in the local soil and the other in the politics of Austin, they more than anyone make the RESCs work. (A recent statewide study of RESCs indicates that 200 Texas superintendents regard RESC leadership equally with RESC program quality as a leading influence on local education agencies' participation in RESC services.[11]) They survey vast rural expanses dappled with animals, vegetation, cropland, brushland, fence lines, roads, power lines, pipelines, towns, churches, banks, schools, and people. The regional directors can make the case that a special combination of those features makes each of their jobs different and each region different. The state may agree.

Back to the earlier question: What role does the intermediate unit play in rural Texas? Is it an instrument for local control or the state's vehicle to carry the one best system to the hinterlands? Clear answers are not in stock. Despite the guidelines' references to innovation, the superintendent who talks of innovation loses his or her job as rapidly as the one who claims his or her country school to be as good as the best in the state. City practices are suspect but sometimes coveted. Traditions can be seen as safeguards of a culture or impediments to progress. In theory, improvement through studied local innovation is possible. But to many professionals and parents, innovation is a four-syllable word.

In fact, it is difficult to introduce programs that come from outside the realm of traditional services funded from traditional sources. Rural people have always done it their way, whether in the Sauk Center of Sinclair Lewis, the Grover's Corners of Thornton Wilder, or the Eden and Rock Springs of Charlie Bitters. To be rural is to be conservative and to oppose tinkering with the basic structures of home, church, bank, school. *Loblolly*, the innovative magazine of the high school in Gary, Texas, lives because it seeks to define and affirm a town's history and culture. It keeps school and town close.

Charlie Bitters calls the regional centers a "two-way street." In the deliberate speech of a native West Texan he describes his role and that of his counterparts in the other nineteen RESCs that blanket the state, city, and countryside as "tellin' it like it is" to the old boys in Austin. The center staffs keep the Texas Education Agency informed of what local districts want and need; on the other hand, when new state mandates such as uniform accounting procedures and new accreditation requirements are issued, RESCs are there to help the school districts.

The official line all the way from the office of the assistant commissioner of education in Austin down through and including the thirty-eight teachers and superintendents in Rock Springs (enrollment: 525 K–12 students) is that RESCs are service centers oriented toward and responsive to the needs and desires of the districts served; they are not an arm of the Texas Education Agency. To put it another way, State Superintendent Marvin Brockette saw the service centers "as educational cooperatives and the local schools as stockholders in those cooperatives."[12]

RESCs, according to Austin, do not have official regulatory functions. Nor are the centers expected to provide direct teaching services under their cooperative arrangements with member districts. Principle number 4 of the TEA's 1978 criteria states that each RESC "gives primary emphasis to *assisting school districts* to improve their capacity to produce student learning." The guidebook follows with a note: "As a general rule the education service center is not directly responsible for producing student learning results, but is accountable for providing assistance to local districts to improve their programs aimed at producing student learning."[13] The guidebook further assures local districts that the centers will not compete with them. The assurance, however, does not extend to ESEA Title III (now Title IV-C), where RESCs would because of their regional nature appear to have preference over individual district proposals in securing funding.

Clearly, RESCs deliver services to rural schools that the schools alone could not provide—data processing, instructional media, special services for handicapped students, crime prevention and drug education, schooling for the deaf, driver training, certain kinds of vocational education, school bus safety education, education for children of migrant workers, and, in some rare cases, bilingual education. What is not clear is whether the need for those services originated with local rural school districts or with some state or federal agency. If one looks at the budget and source of funding it would appear that the RESCs are at least as much emissaries of the state and federal governments as they are agencies providing services for locally defined needs.

Fifteen of the twenty-eight special program areas of Region XV are federally funded (60 to 75 percent of the total budget) and therefore carry with them federal guidelines for operation. The remainder are state and locally funded and are similarly controlled largely by the state.[14] In program areas such as the media center or the curriculum library, where a service provided could be tailored to local circumstances, little evidence of local adaptation can be found. Tailoring of programs seems to occur more by opting to buy the goods or not than by changing the fabric or the pattern. Even the inservice programs—supposedly planned with local participation for local needs—appear to reflect the current educational fads, i.e., values clarification, teaching creativity, or assisting teachers to respond to guidelines of federal or state mandates.

The center's staff would not agree that it lacks the local view. For example, a number of districts needing help with health services resulted in Region XV's involvement in a coop effort that now provides nine itinerant registered nurses funded from federal migrant education sources. The RESC staff also asserts that because of their work, nineteen school districts participate in migrant education programs that because of excessive paper work would not otherwise exist. We discovered no examples of individual schools having adapted or adopted center-built programs for their special needs. Co-op efforts seemed more popular; certainly they are more cost effective.

Whether or not the RESCs are determined to be positive agents for rural educational improvement depends in part on philosophical and operational judgments—for example, whether the buyer buys into the one-best-system creed for education, or not. For operational considerations in nearly all overview evaluations of this kind, individual testimony weighs heavily in helping a writer sum up. One evaluator from an earlier study of the centers has doubts about the qualitative consistency from region to region and notes that even some Texas professionals

> saw the RSC's as self-serving fiefdoms that paid more attention to their own growth than to the needs/priorities of participating districts. Or, as one RSC director said, "We're in the business of laundering money." However, it is important to note that none of our respondents criticized the *concept* of an RSC; in theory, they though they were a good idea—especially if RSC guidelines could allow differential treatment for large and small LEA's [local education agencies]. This suggests the importance of RSC leadership.[15]

Applying another measure, the centers seem not to be serving as the force for equalization that reformers have sought. Insofar as an institution can serve as a conscience for its members, the centers fail. The professional educators do not collectively seem to view the poor or the children of the poor as targets of special concern—except when special funding arrives from Washington or Austin. Little inservice attention is demanded by local districts to help bring the poor and culturally different into economic, social, and political equality.

Several unpublished evaluations cite as a shortcoming the distance factor: the farther from the center's home base a school is, the fewer visits it receives. In an establishment of education that still equates the quality of service with the amount of time spent, the teacher and student at the end of the line appear to be hungrier than those close in. The extent of service is, of course, in large measure a reflection of managerial quality and money available. No one rides free from San Angelo to Del Rio. Yet the professionals in Del Rio seem not to mind that the RESC crew and their director don't get down there very often—and the RESC people seem not to care that they don't mind.

On the other hand, despite a shaky funding structure and organizational encumbrances matching in scope if not longevity the best creations of old-world educational bureaucracy, the centers seem to be working. Innovation is possible, sometimes evident. Professional growth, if not always upward, is there, and the intent to make rural equal to the best is an openly stated objective. On close (if not exhaustive) scrutiny Region XV meets the test.

The building slogan—"Services available anywhere should be available everywhere"—must be viewed temperately through spectacles that show clearly what a $25 average daily attendance budget will allow. The total budget of $3.1 million a year pays for the salaries, gas and oil, telephone toll charges, per diem, computer costs, and postage needed to carry the message across a 25,000-square-mile expanse—an area that has probably twice that amount invested in fence posts and barbed wire.

Another viewpoint would hold that centers are effective in making state regulations palatable to the region and local or regional needs palpable to the state. Bitters's contention that the RESCs are a "two-way street" seems to be held by the state commissioner of education, who was quoted as saying, "RESCs serve the Texas Education Agency, but the school district is the primary client of RESC services and so has major local control holding RESCs accountable for quality and type of service provided."[16] In some ways RESCs are on the cutting edge where they serve to advance a statewide data processing system, media distribution, or to make the work of state education officials easier.

A review of the services offered suggests that the Texas Education Agency and many of the small-school superintendents appear to subscribe to single-system philosophy. The RESCs, in spite of their independent governance, or perhaps because of it, provide the services and programs for which money is available, which for now reflect primarily a state or federal agenda.

Charlie Bitters maintains, without much refutation in Austin, that he ran "one of the best, probably *the* best, rural service center in Texas." His superintendents, except for a couple in the South XV, agree. They seem to think that the center serves a valuable purpose in providing for their isolated schools what in smaller states would come from the state education agency, if at all. The people who run the schools also seem to think that with battle-hardened Bitters keeping the state bureaucrats happy and at a distance, life was easier for them.

In summary, the centers seem to work within the limits of vision and dollar constraints imposed by law, a cautious profession, and careful constituents. One must note that what Charles Bitters did he did well, as do some of his RESC counterparts. One departs San Angelo with the impression that the Region XV personnel are devoted, able professionals whose convictions about the value of their guiding slogan are true, strong, and realistic, and that without their presence and work out of that old school building at the urban center of the region, most of the kids in West Texas would, without really knowing it, be "less equal."

We went to Texas to determine whether, after a dozen years in existence, the Regional Education Service Center is a fundamental institution working on behalf of rural schools or is an arm of state government designed to help align the small schools within the standards set for Dallas or San Antonio and their suburbs. We came away feeling that the centers are a little of both.

Education is expected to release people from the restrictions of superstition, ignorance, time, and place—to help the individual gain a knowledge of the dimension, scope, and degree to which personal freedom and social discipline can allow one to live. In essence the regional centers are expected to help the village schools in that mission, to help create windows on the larger society. The consultants, media specialists, and workers in migrant education are in their modern fashion serving as itinerant schoolmasters of the middle border, helping outback America stay in contact with progress.

The elaborate, cumbersome system of governance, policymaking, and professional oversight, together with the homage to local educational options, keep the centers free of snake-oil peddlers, revisionists, and arch educational fundamentalists. Local involvement means local contribution at $1.00 per average daily attendance for media, and that assures a certain local surveillance, if for no other reason than to reassure price-wary taxpayers that dollar value is received. Unlike other rural educational service devices, the RESC program as designed by Texans seems not so heavily dependent for effectiveness on an individual, social-political ethos, educational movement or source of funding. However, if after ten years the centers seem to function as much to make the profession comfortable as to speed new thought and practice out to the countryside, it may be only because the design and function are in equilibrium—which after all is one of the objectives of education.

### Notes

1. For an excellent, short history of the rise and fall of rural education during 130 years of industrial and urban development in the United States, see Jonathan P. Sher et al., *Education in Rural America: A Reassessment of Conventional Wisdom* (Boulder, Colo.: Westview Press, 1977); especially chap. 1, "The Urbanization of Rural Schools, 1840–1970," by Stuart A. Rosenfeld and Jonathan P. Sher, pp. 11–42.

2. Howard A. Dawson et al., "Tentative Statement of the Purpose of the National Commission on the Intermediate Unit," memorandum developed at the first meeting of the commission, Washington, D.C., 1953.

3. Robert M. Isenberg, ed., *The Community School and the Intermediate Unit, Yearbook* (Washington, D.C.: Department of Rural Education, National Education Association, 1954).

4. Governance and advisory structure was sifted from various state documents, but mostly from *State Plan, Procedures and Policies for the Operation of Regional Education Service Centers*, rev. ed. (Austin: Texas Education Agency, 1970), p. 17.

5. For a more detailed discussion of the "one best system," see David B. Tyack, *The One Best System: A History of American Urban Education* (Cambridge, Mass.: Harvard University Press, 1974).

6. *Education Center, Region XV, San Angelo*, descriptive monograph published by the regional office.

7. *Criteria for the Planning and Operation of the Regional Education Service Centers* (Austin: Texas Education Agency, 1978), p. 1.

8. *State Plan, Procedures and Policies*, p. 1.

9. *Education Center, Region XV.*

10. See *A National Problem, Recruitment and Retention of Specialized Personnel in Rural Areas*, National Rural Project Newsletter, Murray State University, Murray, Kentucky, December 1980.

11. *Criteria for Planning*, p. 5.

12. Personal interview with Ernest Chambers of the Texas Department of Education, January 24, 1979, Austin, Texas.

13. *Criteria for Planning*, p. 5.

14. Because of its large migrant education program, Region XV is atypical in funding percentages. Statewide, RESC funding is 30.4 percent federal, 37.6 percent state, and 32 percent local. State funds are used primarily as "incentives," never fully covering the cost of programs yet dictating how local funds are spent. (See "Factors Influencing Local Education Agency Participation in the Programs and Services of Education Service Agencies in the State of Texas," Report No. 6, ESA Study Series, 1979.)

15. Personal letter to Ralph G. Bohrson from the Rand Corporation, March 9, 1979.

16. Author's notes from interviews at the Texas Education Agency, Austin, Texas, January 24, 1979.

# 8
# Getting on the Bandwagon: Maine Schools Discover the National Diffusion Network

*Thomas Gjelten*
*Daniel Cromer*

On a wall in Bob Shafto's office above the National Bank of Gardiner hangs a map of the state of Maine stuck all over with red pins. The map is Shafto's scorecard: Each pin marks a school district where he has helped the staff put into practice a government-certified educational innovation. Shafto is the Maine agent, or state facilitator, for the National Diffusion Network (NDN), a U.S. Office of Education (OE) operation encouraging the spread of new education ideas among local school districts. The programs promoted through the NDN have been judged by a panel of outside reviewers to be exemplary and replicable; the NDN catalog is titled simply *Educational Programs that Work*. It is Shafto's job to publicize the NDN programs in Maine, to help school administrators choose programs that address their educational needs, and then to coordinate the logistics involved in the local adoption of a national program.

The basic NDN sales pitch is clearly stated by a sign next to Shafto's map:

*School districts no longer have to re-invent the wheel, wasting valuable time and money, in the process of improving their curriculum.*

Through the National Diffusion Network, in other words, districts may now gain the benefit of someone else's trial-and-error experience and adopt a kink-free innovation, one that has already been tested and approved by experts and made ready for instant implementation.

Behind each red pin there is a story. At Oak Hill High School in Sabattus, Shafto arranged for eight teachers to implement Project Adventure, an approach to the teaching of academic skills, physical education, and self-awareness through outdoor experiences. It was originally developed at a suburban high school in Massachusetts; Oak Hill now has its own ropes course, built with the assistance of teachers from the Massachusetts high school. In Madawaska, on the Canadian border, Shafto helped three teachers try Strategies in Early Childhood Education, a model for a continuous developmental program bridging preschool, kindergarten, and first grade. It was imported from Wisconsin. And at York, on the southern coast, he assisted in the installation of Individualized Language Arts, a New Jersey program that stresses basic writing skills. Like other programs in the NDN repertoire, each was originally developed with the support of federal funds.

Shafto is on the road at least two days a week visiting schools. He knows personally many of the teachers and most of the principals and superintendents in Maine. In his office, he spends much of his time on the telephone with them—responding to requests for information about specific programs, informing people of upcoming awareness sessions (when the original developers of NDN programs come to introduce them to Maine teachers), and scheduling training workshops in which school staff are trained in the procedures for implementing NDN programs.

The job requires diplomacy, efficient organization, and subtle persuasion; Shafto has them all. His boss in Washington, NDN Director Lee Wickline, cites Shafto as one of the best examples of how a state facilitator should go about his work, and for good reason. By May of 1979, Shafto's infiltration of the state's public school system was so complete that two out of every three Maine school districts had an NDN program in place and operating—a program Shafto had facilitated. In Lisbon, one of the first districts to adopt an NDN program, Superintendent Dick Ladner says, "The NDN operation did in a few months what I tried to do for fifteen years."

Across the state, some programs have failed, and some districts have soured on NDN. Shafto has had difficulties in the smallest, most remote rural schools and, like other facilitators, has had trouble breaking the bureaucracy of the largest city schools in the state. But between the extremes, he has met with remarkable success. "I would say that Maine schools have changed because of Bob Shafto," says Lee Wickline. Whether and how Maine schools have improved because of Bob Shafto and the NDN is a more complex story.

The state of Maine, with over 400 public elementary and secondary schools, is a tough assignment for a roving school reformer. There are the schools of Portland (the state's only "city"—population over 80,000), with over 10,000 students enrolled. There are the schools of the bilingual Franco-American towns along the St. John's River on the Canadian border, the mill towns and paper-company towns of the state's interior, the vast potato-growing region of Aroostook County, and the coastal fishing communities. There are also the two- and three-room schools for children isolated in the

Allagash wilderness and for those living on the outlying islands ten or twenty miles off the coast. The challenge of school improvement is further complicated by the fervent localism of Maine's rural communities, many of which have 200-year-old traditions of local control and grassroots democracy. Native Mainers prefer to muster their own energies to solve their own problems through their own devices, and are often suspicious of outside intervention.

Shafto, a former high school biology teacher in his early thirties, has been directing the Maine Facilitator Center single-handedly since it opened in 1975, one year after the National Diffusion Network was organized. No Maine school official had bothered to respond to Lee Wickline's original memorandum announcing the availability of OE grants to support state facilitator projects. But Ed DiCenso came to the state education department in the summer of 1975 "to get something creative going" as the new director of the ESEA Title III program in Maine, and one of his first acts was to apply for the NDN funding.

Under OE guidelines, an NDN grant for a state facilitator project had to go through a local school system; DiCenso chose School Administrative District (SAD) 11, located in Gardiner, a small town about six miles south of Augusta, the state capital. The superintendent there, Merle Peacock, was in DiCenso's judgment "the kind of a person who was forward looking and who encouraged innovation." DiCenso's proposal was approved by OE in the fall of 1975, and he began looking for a candidate for the position of facilitator. Bob Shafto was his first choice; he knew that Shafto had been given a grant the previous year to install a K–12 environmental education program in his school in Calais. He considered him to be a competent and hard-working teacher who knew firsthand what it was like to adopt a curricular program that had originally been developed by another teacher for another group of students. Shafto accepted DiCenso's offer, and in November the Maine Facilitator Center opened for business.

### The Shafto Strategy

Though he arrived on the NDN scene a year behind most other state facilitators, Shafto quickly became known in that circle as someone with "a good operation," in the recollection of a former facilitator from another state. He earned his reputation in the only way that would impress other facilitators: by getting adoptions. Within eighteen months of his center's opening, Shafto had twenty-one separate NDN programs operating in over 250 Maine schools—more than half of the state's 400.

How did he get such quick results, in a state known for its innate conservatism? Shafto personified the ideal NDN facilitator; he came into the position fresh from five years of teaching and a year of directing the environmental education project. He was sensitive to teachers' needs and knew the difference a well-designed instructional package could make for a classroom teacher. He brought to his work a belief in its importance and a missionary-like commitment to spread the NDN gospel. Shafto's success, in fact, cannot be easily explained by the adoption of an innovative approach in his work as facilitator; his accomplishments were notable, but the procedures Shafto followed in Maine were basically the same ones that others before him (particularly Glen Belden in New Hampshire, his mentor) had used. What did distinguish his approach was a strong sense of strategy from the beginning and an intuitive awareness of how to appeal to school administrators.

His first move was to write to every superintendent, principal, and private school director in the state, advising them of the existence and function of the center. He enclosed in the letters mail-back cards on which the recipients could indicate their area of greatest curricular need. To each superintendent, he sent a copy of his basic text, the OE catalog *Educational Programs that Work.* He was not besieged by responses, but those who did answer provided Shafto with his first core of contacts in the state's network of schools. He telephoned each respondent personally, introducing himself and explaining his services further. He confirmed their curricular interest and then sent them descriptions of programs in their need area that had received NDN developer-demonstrator grants and that could therefore offer free staff training and adoption assistance to interested school districts.

Based on his informal survey of perceived educational needs in Maine and on the recommendations of Glen Belden, Shafto immediately began to schedule a series of awareness sessions. These were a standard part of the facilitators' operating procedure. Typically, program developers would come and make a short audio-visual presentation of their program, demonstrate the use of program materials, and answer questions about its operation. Eleven such sessions were presented at a "Mini-Education Fair" in January; the night before, there had been a snowstorm, and schools were closed that morning, but fifty-five teachers and administrators showed up. Shafto had publicized it through more mailings and phone calls to his original contacts.

In February, Shafto mailed out the first issue of his newsletter, "The Maine Facilitator." In it, he reintroduced himself, announced upcoming awareness sessions, and reported on Maine districts that were having teachers trained to install NDN programs in their own schools. Although this was a facilitator's normal approach, Shafto was already demonstrating a keen strategic sense. He took pains to separate himself and his operation from conventional state-managed programs. "What's This All About, Anyway?!" was the title of his opening column, which began, "Maine Facilitator Center. Hmmmm. Sounds like another one of those Augusta inventions designed to give some down-and-out a job. No doubt a number of people in the Maine educational community have responded in the above manner when first hearing of the Facilitator Center. Perhaps a few words . . . are in order to help dispel that myth." It was the first step in what was to be an integral part of his strategy—the presentation of his center as an independent organization, untarnished by whatever reputation "Augusta inventions" held among local districts.

"The first thing I did here," Shafto now explains, "was to ask myself, what are people assuming? Federal programs . . . Augusta . . . money . . . paperwork . . . three weeks to answer a letter. Then I tried to do things that were diametrically opposed to those assumptions. When I got a letter, I responded to it the same day, usually by phone." In his dealings with local school personnel, Shafto sought to be responsive without being viewed as an interference—a delicate task. He met and introduced himself to as many school administrators as possible, in addition to teachers, education department personnel, and even state legislators. He was careful not to use his network of contacts as a base for lobbying on behalf of NDN program promoters; he wanted simply to establish personal relationships with as broad a range of individuals in the state's educational system as was possible. His low-key approach came to be appreciated. "He never pushed hard," says Frank Joy, a superintendent of two community school districts and a supervisory union in Hancock County, on the downeast coast. "He just let me know he was there if I needed him. And then, if I asked him, he'd go out of his way to help."

Even as Shafto was busy distinguishing the Maine Facilitator Center from the state education department, he was laying the groundwork for what he hoped would become an NDN *movement* in Maine, with subtle suggestions that the districts that were adopting NDN products were a select group. Like his initial mailing, the first issue of his newsletter went to every school official in the state. This time, however, an announcement was made that the future "Facilitator" mailing list would be limited "to those who have had previous written or telephone contact with the center or who have attended any of the awareness sessions that have been held." If an administrator were not in that group but wanted to receive future issues of the newsletter or other Shafto mailings, he or she would have to contact Shafto's office and ask to be included.

The move, Shafto explained, was due to "postage rates being what they are," but it also fit neatly into a larger effort of building a feeling of exclusivity among his clients. Shafto needed to know who wanted to be served and to reinforce their sense of being a part of a special group. He presented himself not as a program salesman or representative, but as a professional whose job it was to assist school staff sincerely seeking to strengthen their educational program. His choice was not to waste time on uninterested districts, but to concentrate on a cadre of committed teachers and administrators, hoping that others would join on their own volition, enticed, perhaps, by the example of their peers. Writing in the first newsletter, Shafto made just that appeal: "If you have delayed getting on the bandwagon, do so today!"

Meanwhile, he continued to schedule two or three awareness sessions a month. They were casual affairs, held in motel conference rooms or school cafeterias. When possible, he scheduled two or more presentations at a single session on a single theme, such as reading programs. There would be no charge to schools sending representatives, the majority of whom were principals and central office personnel. Shafto was always present, circulating among the attendees and playing the role of all-purpose facilitator. "Someone has to be there to find the missing video cords and ask the questions when the developer is begging for them," he says.

Only a few carefully selected programs in the NDN repertoire were introduced at the awareness sessions. Through his discussions with local school people. Shafto began to get a sense of the needs and biases typifying Maine schools, and he considered those factors in planning the sessions. He asked his neighboring facilitator Glen Belden which programs were doing well in New Hampshire. By filtering out at the earliest stages those programs that didn't fit rural Maine or hold a potential for widespread adoption, Shafto was hoping to ensure that the early impressions of NDN would be positive ones. This matched his strategy of movement building; he figured that an NDN trend would develop most quickly in Maine if a series of schools had a series of successful adoption experiences, and for that reason he was likely to recommend low-risk programs involving a minimum of institutional change or philosophical adjustment.

Shafto's "bandwagon" strategy can be seen in other ways as well. He worked hard to find an appropriate program to match a school's particular needs, but he was willing to sacrifice a bit in the way of totally customized service to each school district in order to gain the benefits of what he called "cluster adoptions"—adoptions of a single program by a whole group of schools in a region, simultaneously or in close succession.

If there were sufficient interest indicated in a program introduced at an awareness session, Shafto arranged a training workshop at a local school, or, if several districts were involved, at a central site. Either the original developer of the program or a trained staff person would provide a comprehensive orientation session lasting from one to five days. Again, there was no charge to participating schools, as long as they were able to release their staff for the workshop. The Facilitator Center, in fact, would often reimburse schools beyond commuting distance for the overnight expenses of their teachers in attendance.

The training procedures varied widely. In some cases, prospective teachers actually worked with classroom students during the course of their orientation. In others, they took turns practicing with each other. The well-financed developers provided program materials for teachers' classroom use free of charge. Others either sold them to teachers or showed them how to make their own. Often, teachers had to sign "agreements" with the program developers, promising they would implement the program exactly as it had been developed. "Program fidelity," it was argued, was essential if the teachers were to expect the same results that had been achieved in the original setting. Again, Shafto was on hand, managing the logistics, giving the trainers feedback on how the workshop was going, and interjecting questions when he thought a crucial point was being overlooked.

Shafto kept careful track of the teachers' experiences as they returned to the classroom to implement the NDN programs. "This is the Weight-Watcher School of Educational Change," he explains. "It is absolutely essential to monitor the progress in adopting programs." Typically, he would visit an adopting site personally three to four months after a training workshop. "I'll sit down with the staff and talk about the program, what level of use it has in the school, what problems are emerging. I'll decide what would be an appropriate intervention. I'm really the linker. I say, 'Tell me the problem. I'll see that you get some help.'" If local circumstances were demanding a modification in the program design and implementation, Shafto would arrange for the developer to personally assist the teachers in making the necessary changes, if possible. After another interval of three or four months, Shafto would visit the school again. Often, his support was as much moral as it was technical. "I try to pump them up," he says. "I say, 'Hey, there's 100 of you in Maine now—you're not quacks anymore. You may be the only two in this building, but you're part of something that's really exciting.'"

With a few modifications, his operation has remained a consistent one since the early days. He continues to maintain selectivity in his dealings with schools, periodically weeding out of his newsletter mailing list those districts not responding to his invitations and apparently uninterested in network activities. (He has, in fact, identified the "red-flag" districts where a lack of administrative support seems to doom his every attempt to make inroads.) In his planning of awareness sessions these days, he asks his fellow facilitators for their recommendations of not only the best programs but the best presenters. "I've never had an adoption occur through review of written materials alone," Shafto says. "So much depends on the presenter. I've seen a charismatic presenter sell a whole roomful of people on a program after a lackluster one had presented the same program in the same area a month before and not gotten a single adoption. It makes me wonder what they're buying—the program or the presenter?"

He has learned from Maine educators what types of programs are most eagerly received. Currently, they are the ones that have sprung up in response to the accountability movement. As the Joint Dissemination Review Panel (JDRP) demands objective evidence of a program's positive impact before giving it their approval, the NDN catalog is full of programs boasting of improved achievement test scores or leaps in students' reading levels, and they are all popular. Programs providing a means of implementing competency-based approaches are also in high demand.

There have been changes in Shafto's technical assistance to local districts, mostly due to the sharpening of his skills through experience. He now pays considerably more attention to what he calls the "front-end work"—the preparation of school staff for an adoption. He no longer arranges training sessions automatically for any district that asks for them; he wants to be sure all the ingredients are there that are necessary for a successful adoption. He has developed an "appraisal activity" to determine the readiness of school staff. The core of it is a detailed questionnaire for each of the programs he represents. It begins, "What evidence is there that there is a need for the program in the school?" followed by "What other possible approaches might meet this need? Have they also been explored?" It goes on to ask how many staff members had attended an awareness session on the program or visited an adoption site and to what extent principals and central office personnel had indicated their support for the program's adoption. It then requires the staff to provide a detailed plan for the program's adoption, identifying who would be involved in it and what steps would be taken to install it, and concludes by asking for a plan of evaluation and long-term program maintenance. Shafto visits the prospective adopting school personally and takes the staff through the questionnaire, item by item.

Shafto is more cautious in this phase of the adoption process than he used to be. He is reluctant to authorize school staff to go through training for a program if he has reason to believe the program is going to fail. He has strong feelings that all staff to be involved in a program should have attended awareness sessions for it, rather than just the training workshop. He has to be convinced that principals, in particular, support the program and accompany the teachers to sessions if possible; he has concluded that the principal is the key person in the determination of the fate of an adoption attempt. And he looks for a "critical mass" of staff commitment to the adoption.

Shafto has recognized that he is an education change agent, an intervenor, and he has learned how to play that role. "I'm a third party," he says. "I can say things to an administrator that teachers can't." When a teacher expresses interest in a program but doesn't have administrative support, Shafto may be able to help: "I'd call back and explain, 'Here's what we do, here's what we offer. Why don't you go to your principal and suggest that I come to the district to talk about the program.' Then if the administrator's mind is made up, I won't get involved. But if it's not, I'll talk to him about it."

Shafto is becoming increasingly involved with superintendents, though it is with principals that he still works most often. He has become familiar with the informal network that exists between the state's superintendents and has learned how to break into it. He plays a largely advisory role with them and has become for many of them a helpful, nonthreatening guide in their efforts to build a reputation for their system as one that is modern and progressive. "They say, 'I can't work with all these things,'" Shafto explains. "They can't see much difference between them. They want someone to help them sort through it and recommend programs that are known to produce good results. That's my role." His candid advice enables them to build a progressive reputation for their system without having to suffer the risks and potential embarrassments of trial-and-error experimentation.

When he is asked by a school staff member to "talk to" an administrator not yet convinced of the merits of a certain program, Shafto uses "the old bandwagon approach. . . . The most important thing is peer influence—what are they doing in the next town. If I feel one is a little unsure, I'll mention a superintendent who's just as conservative as he is, but who has an adoption. I tell them, 'You're not alone, you're not out on the limb. It's a low-risk operation.'" In the same vein, Shafto has introduced a special feature in his newsletter: the "adopter profile," in which he emphasizes the accomplishments of a particular school system (carefully chosen) and its enthusiasm for a new NDN program. He sees that each area of the state is represented on a regular basis. "I want to get across the idea," Shafto explains, "that, 'If So-and-So can make that program work, I know I can.'"

Shafto's accomplishments in Maine are undoubtedly of his own making, but the strategy he has followed there conforms closely to the "person-intensive" approach originally envisioned by NDN designers. Shafto personally credits the NDN operation as a whole for his own success in Maine. "It's a good network," he says. "The strength of it is its smallness, its responsiveness, its closeness to local agencies. It's very much a practitioners' program. The developers and trainers are people who are teaching. By and large, the facilitators come right out of the classroom, too; not from a management or administrative background." Shafto has used this advantage expertly. In a 1979 survey of Maine school districts' experiences with the NDN—part of an evaluation of the Maine Facilitator Center—the writers reported that respondents "contrasted their feelings about the Facilitator Center with their feelings about other governmental agencies. The Center is quick and concrete in its responses; the other agencies are apt to be slow and vague. The Center's services involve little or no paperwork; other bureaucratic services are often characterized by what is perceived as meaningless paperwork and red tape."[1]

Similarly, when asked to prepare testimony in April 1979 on considerations pertinent to Governor Joseph Brennan's choice of a new commissioner of education, Rockport principal Mark Higgins used the occasion to call for a "reexamination" of the role of the state department in curriculum development in Maine schools. He cited Bob Shafto's services as an example of what the state department should be doing: "The Maine Facilitator Center, with a staff of one director and one secretary, has in the last three years influenced more curriculum change in Maine schools than has the Department of Educational and Cultural Services, with the exceptions of vocational education and special education."

Shafto admits that he understands how local school people feel about state-paid education specialists and that he has deliberately sought to act in ways opposite to their expectations of him. And he admits that he is aware of the comparisons that are made between the state department and his own operation. But he does not encourage them, and he is careful to point out that local school people "seem to forget that I have many more resources to draw on than does the Curriculum Division." His own dealings with the state department have been for the most part harmonious. The Facilitator Center was opened by Ed DiCenso of the state's Title III (now Title IV-C) office, and close relations with that office have continued.

The Maine plan for expenditure of federal Title IV-C funds (earmarked for the "improvement of local education practices") provides for four types of grants to local districts: *innovative* grants, for the development of new educational programs (the type of grant that led to the development of most exemplary programs now in the NDN); *demonstration* grants, for the dissemination of an exemplary program to other schools; *adoptive* grants, to cover any local costs incurred in the adoption of state or nationally validated programs; and *mini* grants of up to $1500, for teachers to carry out innovative programs on their own. Because most adoptive grants went to schools wishing to adopt programs in the NDN (about one-third of NDN adoptions in Maine each year are underwritten by Title IV-C adoptive grants), Shafto has been called in to help administer them, first by Ed DiCenso and later by his successor, Lois Jones. The Title IV-C staff apparently considers Shafto an ex-officio staff member, referring to him in their literature as the "adoptive grant monitor," referring phone calls about adoptive grants to him, and taking him with them on their annual information tours of the state.

What Shafto has demanded and achieved is independence and freedom for his facilitator project. He sees his headquartering in a local district, outside of Augusta, as an important advantage in a state where government programs are viewed with suspicion. He appreciates the flexibility this has given him in such matters as the scheduling of meetings on short notice and the mailing of leaflets, simple things that might be complicated if he were located in Augusta. He has worked to preserve his independence. In both his newsletter and his awareness workshops he has maintained "purity," disseminating information only about the projects with which he is associated. He does not advertise other exemplary innovative programs, even those that impress him. "If I opened it up, I'd have book companies and A-V [audio-visual] companies in here every day," he explains. But it has also meant that state-department projects are excluded. About the only state-department news Shafto mentions in his newsletter concerns the availability of Title IV-C adoptive grant money and the procedures to go through in applying for it.

Relations between the facilitator and the state education department have been an issue in other states as well. Originally, all facilitator projects were required to be based in a local district because their funding came under ESEA Title III. When NDN received its own authorization and appropriation in 1976, that restriction was lifted, and now only about half of the state facilitator projects in the nation are based in state education agencies. Proposals for a facilitator project may be submitted by local administrators, administrators of intermediate service agencies (covering several districts and administratively independent of both local and state agencies), or by state personnel. The national staff takes no formal position on the matter, although Lee Wickline explains, "We feel, and we have said so, that the most effective facilitator projects are in the local agencies. We've said there are great advantages to the facilitators sitting outside the state agency because they're seen as nonregulatory and nonthreatening. We've cautioned state agencies that if they expect the state facilitators to be effective, they must be given a lot of autonomy." On the other hand, Wickline tells facilitators that there are advantages to having close relationships with state departments and that "they should be in a position where they can make recommendations about formula-driven grants."

One of the consequences of an independent operation like Shafto's is that it focuses attention on one individual. Shafto is an important man in the state, a self-admitted "gatekeeper" who screens the JDRP programs that are to be introduced to the state, an individual who through his work with the Title IV-C advisory council is able to direct thousands of dollars in grant money to districts of his own selection, and a confidant of many of the state's school administrators. The problem of dispensability was Shafto's first lesson of educational change, learned when he was at Calais adopting the environmental educational program: "It worked beautifully, but it was a lousy change strategy," he says. "It only worked as long as I was there. I didn't train any teachers to develop curriculum materials themselves." He wonders if he has made the same mistake—becoming indispensable—as state facilitator. "That bothers me," he says. "If I left this job, it'd be hard for someone else to take over, in spite of our records. You need the experience base." He is finding, however, that districts are becoming "less dependent on me." While he has increased his assistance at the front end, he is giving less at the back end, after the adoption has taken place. "They're learning that if they have a problem with the program, they can call the developer about it, not me. . . . I try to make myself less necessary. I try to get people to do as much for themselves as possible."

Conferences have grown out of the "subnetworks" Shafto has established among school districts sharing a particular program adoption experience. Through them, the school staff share their failures and their successes and cooperate in the arrangement of additional inservice sessions. In some cases, the subnetwork of adopters has become so formal that they distribute their own newsletter among themselves, keeping each other informed of the progress of their adoptions. "It's one way of insuring long-term maintenance of projects after they are adopted," Shafto explains. "It relieves me of some of the burden, and I don't have to guess what follow-up is needed." Shafto is a leader among state facilitators in the nation in his establishment of subnetworks, and he was featured in a March 1979 NDN report that called subnetworks "the wave of the future for the NDN."

He has been forced into such developments by the enormous growth of his operation in Maine and the increasing demand for program training and adoption assistance. In the summer of 1979, Shafto finally hired an associate director to help him, but he made the move with some ambivalence: "I'd never want to work in a larger organization. I'm a smaller-is-better person. I think when you get diversification, it's not good."

Shafto is now one of the most experienced of state facilitators, and his reputation as a remarkably successful promoter of NDN programs continues. Four years of following school districts' experiences under NDN programs have led him to some conclusions about the process of educational improvement. He is increasingly confident that the adoption of proven programs is the surest route. "I used to say to myself, 'I'm not a meddler. I don't have the answers,'" Shafto explains. "But maybe I've over-reacted." He is now ready to argue that perhaps there *are* answers. "I believe there are ways of teaching that are more effective than others. We begin by identifying the practices that work. Then we train other people in these practices. Why is it that educators don't do it more often? The medical profession does; when new techniques in heart-bypass surgery are found, they are disseminated, and doctors learn them. We haven't yet accepted teaching as a science. I'm convinced it is."

It is not that Shafto personally has the answers. The answers to an education problem can be found in the NDN catalog: "When I explain the work of the Facilitator Center, I say, 'Here's an overview of what there is. I am not an expert on any of these 200 programs. But I can *connect* you to the experts.' That's the part that's been missing."

So, are the schools of rural Maine being improved because of their increased access to the assistance of outside experts? To answer that question, one must first understand the conditions in rural Maine schools and the context in which adoption takes place.

## One example: ECRI at Sumner High School

The Flanders Bay Community School district, covering an area surrounding the village of Sullivan in northern Hancock County, serves some of the lowest-income families in Maine. There is high seasonal unemployment here, and underemployment persists all year. The region is sparsely populated and industrially underdeveloped, though the St. Regis Paper Company owns vast tracts of woodland in the area. The year-round residents make the most use they can of the land on which they live—heating their homes with wood, growing their own gardens, raising their own chickens and pigs, and fishing and hunting to stock their freezers. Many of the men work in the woods, cutting firewood and pulpwood to sell on the open market.

Four hundred sixty-six students attend Sumner High School, a decaying wooden building two miles east of Sullivan. The thirty teachers offer a comprehensive secondary program, including a vocational shop course. David Seerman is an English teacher at the school, a position he has found frustrating. "Kids are workers in this area," he says. "They make good money, some of them. School is secondary to them. Parents push them to work and make money, but they don't push school. There's a lack of rapport between the school and the community." One of the biggest problems, he says, is the "low morale among the teachers."

A high percentage of Sumner High School students are reading below their grade level, a condition that has concerned Frank Joy, superintendent of schools in the Flanders Bay district. He has in recent years been increasingly frustrated with reading teachers who seem unable to improve the situation. He blames it on inadequate training. "Reading teachers learn how to diagnose reading problems in college really well," he says. "But nobody teaches them how to solve those problems."

The task of treating reading problems at Sumner has fallen most recently on Elaine Baum, the high school remedial reading teacher. She had not yet found a program that helped her in that effort when she attended an awareness session on reading programs sponsored by Bob Shafto in 1977. One of the four approaches presented at the session was a program developed more than ten years earlier by the Exemplary Center for Reading Instruction (ECRI) in Salt Lake City, Utah. Ethna Reid, the director of ECRI, developed the program after carefully researching the work of teachers who were successful in teaching reading skills. She identified the "behaviors" critical to their success, then translated those behaviors into specific teaching directives and developed a program for drilling teachers on the particular techniques. The JDRP reviewed teachers using the ECRI program with 700 Utah students over a three-year period and found first graders reading at a 3.8 grade level, second graders averaging reading scores in the 95th to 99th percentiles, Title I pupils averaging 1.4 to 3.2 years' gain per year, and secondary students averaging more than 2.5 years' gain per year. Shafto has been impressed with the program and has publicized it widely in his newsletter. It was the first NDN program to be adopted in Maine. By the time Elaine Baum heard about it, the program had already been widely adopted in Maine schools and was the most popular of the NDN offerings. To date, more than 800 Maine teachers have been trained in the ECRI technique, and more than twenty-five Maine school districts are using the program in their classrooms.

A program that reduces the teaching of reading to a set of highly structured prescribed exercises (students drill on such routine tasks as where to write their name on the paper, how to number it, and where to record their score until, by design, those actions become habitual), and virtually guarantees dramatically improved student achievement in reading levels as a result, apparently has a strong appeal, particularly among the schools serving the working class youth of rural Maine, where reading attainment has never been high.

After he'd heard the figures on ECRI quoted to him, Joy promptly sent Baum to observe ECRI in action at Lisbon Elementary School in Lisbon, a mill town of 10,000 in the central part of the state. "Elaine came back really enthused," Superintendent Joy recalls. "She was wondering if there was any particular program that fit our needs. We'd been through everything here—gadgets, the scratch-and-sniff books, filmstrips, you name it. But nothing was working. It didn't show results where it counted—in the achievement scores. Then came ECRI. The test results indicated that it worked. That impressed us—the research."

In October 1977, a training workshop for ECRI teachers was held at Sumner High School. Twelve teachers attended. By December, the program had been implemented at the high school and at an elementary school in the district, under the leadership of Elaine Baum. And, just as they had hoped, students' reading achievement scores improved considerably in the first semester of the program. Joy was pleased. He strongly urged teachers to learn the ECRI technique. When he hired new elementary teachers, he told some of them that one of the responsibilities they had as a teacher was to go through the ECRI training. It didn't always pay off. "I made a mistake with some of them," he notes now. "I didn't give them a choice. I said they had to go through that first training. I didn't do it tactfully."

David Seerman was one of the teachers who took the original training. He is now using ECRI in his ninth-grade English class. He likes the program because "it gets right to the teaching of skills" and because he is better able to monitor students. "It's easy to teach," he says. "They tell you how to teach each skill, mechanically. It's a formula. What particular words to say, even when to stand and when to sit." But he qualifies his praise for the program. "There's a vicious cycle here. Kids just don't like to read. TVs are more popular than books. ECRI may cure a few symptoms, but it's the whole cycle that's the problem."

Sumner students have no strong feelings about the program. Joy suggests that the attitude of most students is, "We don't want anyone to know, but we kind of like it," though he notes that his own eleventh-grade daughter told him she felt "insulted" by it: "You see, the program assumes kids don't know anything beforehand. It starts at ground zero." Baum reports that many students enjoy the responsibility placed on them (they score their own work and chart their own progress). "I like it because we get a chance to read more," says a student in Seerman's ninth-grade class. Another student, however, doesn't like the "lack of variety" in reading class since ECRI took over.

Parents in the Sullivan area, Joy says, have been impressed by the large gains made by their children in achievement scores and are relieved to see heavy emphasis on basic skills again. The program's stress of rote learning and drill and its attention to such details as penmanship hark back to earlier days, and in a tradition-minded community, that has been a welcome sign. The school board was so impressed by ECRI that, for the first time in its history, it authorized a small line in the budget for "inservice education" to enable more Sumner teachers to be trained in the program. Some members suggested that perhaps the program should be implemented "across the board," with all teachers required to go through the training, although Joy has not encouraged that.

## NDN's Impact on Maine schools

Both Elaine Baum and Frank Joy credit Shafto for the adoption of ECRI in Sullivan. Since then Joy has followed Shafto's schedule of awareness sessions carefully. "We're absolutely dependent on the Facilitator Center," Joy says. "We don't have any grants-writers here. We'd have no idea what was available." He sees Shafto as an "arranger, not a salesman. He just asks, 'Are you interested in any of this?' There's no high-pressure tactics. He has no quotas to meet. He's just aware of what school systems need and are looking for, and he'll go out of his way to help them." Dick Card, assistant superintendent of SAD 58 near Phillips, attributes the success of the Maine

Facilitator Center to Shafto, personally: "It's Bob. He's got a nice approach. You get the feeling he has expertise. When you feel somebody knows what they're doing, you tend to listen to them."

John Emrick, in a Stanford Research Institute evaluation of the NDN, has noted that between the two change agents established by the network— the program developer-demonstrators and the facilitators—there has developed "ambiguity, and, in some cases, conflict" over what is the proper business of the NDN. "Facilitators saw their role as legitimizers and catalysts, as advocates of a change process rather than of a particular project," he explains. "This has been a major source of dissatisfaction among some developers, who preferred to view facilitators as spokesmen and brokers for their individual projects."[2] It is from the developers that has come the NDN emphasis on program fidelity, the insistence that adopters hold strictly to the prescribed procedure in implementing JDRP-approved programs. Shafto respects their concern: "There are critical elements in a program. Using four out of five parts of it doesn't guarantee 80 percent of the results. You can't pick and choose." He notes, however, that "exact replication is often impossible—there must be mutual adaptation."

Nevertheless, Shafto does not believe that the gains that come from a particular program adoption are all that NDN has to offer to schools. He believes (and in this matter, he is back in the facilitators' camp) that some of the most important benefits of an NDN adoption are the secondary ones, those that come from the adoption experience rather than the program itself. In a traditional community, the process of adopting an NDN program may bring about an increased acknowledgement of teachers as professionals, who deserve to be treated as such. "Many school boards, particularly rural ones, believe that a teacher should know everything there is to know when he or she starts teaching," Shafto explains. "With NDN, teachers are constantly improving their performance as professionals by being trained in better practices. School boards are beginning to recognize the need for that, in the form of inservice." The willingness of the school board in Sullivan to authorize local funds for teacher retraining is not an isolated incident, he says.

He has also found that districts that have made it through one successful adoption are more likely to consider another one. It is "stimulating professionally," Shafto says. "A school experiences organizational effort and togetherness. That doesn't happen very often, and when it does, it produces enthusiasm." It is his commitment to generating that feeling among school staff that most inspires him in his work, he says: "When I go into a workshop in a local school, the first thing I say is, 'I'm not in the program-selling business; I'm in the business of positive organizational change.'"

As with any organizational change, new roles have emerged. To the extent that Shafto has been successful in getting superintendents involved in the NDN movement, men like Dick Ladner in Lisbon and Frank Joy in Sullivan have emerged as curricular leaders in their school systems instead of just fiscal agents. "I've had a lot of people tell me," Shafto says, "that they've seen all three groups—teachers, principals, and superintendents —come out of their roles and all talk the same issue: curriculum."

For those reasons, Shafto sometimes goes after adoptions simply for adoptions' sake. Numbers are important to him, and there is considerably more to his operating strategy than the mere matching of schools with programs that meet their needs. His insistence on independence for his operation has made it possible for him to present himself as one person, working alone—untainted by the bureaucracy, unencumbered by red tape, and unbeholden to higher-up officials. He has intentionally sought to create a movement, through his use of the bandwagon appeal, his pursuit of cluster adoptions, and his support of the NDN subnetworks. He has worked hard to remove many of the elements of risk that are inherent in the adoption process, trying to make educational change as comfortable and nondisruptive as possible. Finally, he has maintained expert political neutrality between teachers, administrators, and state department personnel.

Some evidence of the soundness of Shafto's strategies may be found in the fact that of all the fifty-five facilitators working in the nation (including single facilitators serving the entire states of California, Illinois, and New York), Shafto is ranked thirteenth in the total number of NDN program adoptions arranged. Of a group of seventeen facilitator projects considered by Lee Wickline's NDN staff to cover areas and populations similar to Shafto's, he is ranked number one. In Maine, the researchers who surveyed both users and nonusers of NDN services concluded that "there is a pervasive feeling of good will about the Facilitator Center and its work." And it is not hard to find tributes from people such as Lisbon's Dick Ladner, who says, "The Facilitator Center is the best thing that's happened to me as a superintendent."

When the Facilitator Center opened in November 1975, there were two known JDRP-approved programs operating in two sites in Maine. By Shafto's latest count, there have been over 600 adoptions since then, spread among 102 of the state's 158 districts. What has this massive infusion of exemplary programs accomplished? Have Maine schools, as Lee Wickline suspects, changed as a result?

The NDN itself wants an answer to that question in the form of hard, objective data showing measurable changes. In a few cases, local districts have provided the center with test-score results showing impressive gains; in others, such nonacademic changes as improved attendance and reduced police contacts (on the part of students in a special program for "disaffected youth") have been claimed. But such data is difficult to obtain and expensive to gather and organize. Neither teachers nor administrators have been trained as researchers, and when they are faced with the tasks of isolating variables and establishing control groups, they become frustrated. The researchers looking at Maine NDN reported hearing questions "about what is making the apparent difference. Is teacher enthusiasm and directed energy the major factor in success? . . . Is the feeling that a whole school or system is working together on a new program a factor? How can we say that it is this program that makes the difference? Maybe it is the new principal or the smaller classes." In Sullivan, even Elaine Baum is suspicious of ECRI's claims. "I have to wonder if it's the 'Hawthorne Effect,'" she says. "You know: Any new thing that catches students' attention works well for a while." Furthermore, claims made for a particular program have varied across the state. Some districts have been ambivalent or even disappointed with a program while others have been enthusiastic. In the end, the researchers concluded, the "impact data" was not a major factor in a district's decision of whether to continue using a program: "In many districts, the program will probably continue if someone with power likes it, and it doesn't cost too much. . . . A program is used until something better comes along."

One much-discussed possibility is that there have been major philosophical shifts in Maine schools as a result of the NDN movement. There is only one Maine-developed program in the NDN—a bilingual unit for use only in Franco-American communities. There are two New Hampshire programs, though neither has received dissemination funding from NDN. There are no programs from Vermont. Thus, Maine districts are adopting programs almost exclusively from outside northern New England. Have the state's schools become more cosmopolitan as a result?

An inescapable point about the enthusiastic reception given NDN here is that it has happened in a predominately rural state. Moreover, Maine is not an isolated case in this regard. One of the most publicized findings of the Stanford evaluation of NDN was that the network dissemination activities have tended to concentrate on "nonminority rural school systems." The first explanation considered was that the programs disseminated through the NDN might be of more interest to rural schools than to urban schools. But, say the researchers, "we examined the diffusion patterns across several classes of innovations, [and] found no evidence to indicate this nonurban bias is innovation or developer-specific." To make matters more complicated, it turned out that although the typical adopter was rural, "the typical developer was suburban or urban." Why would rural school systems lead urban systems in the replication of programs that were originally developed in urban or suburban settings?

One explanation might be that the NDN, in its focus on the local educational unit, its reliance on a traveling extension agent of educational expertise, its highly personalized service, and in its offering of technical assistance to school systems too small to employ their own curriculum specialists or grants chasers, has all the features of a model custom designed for the realities of rural areas. The point has also been made, in a journal article on the NDN's impact on southern Appalachian school districts, that the NDN is ideal for rural districts because of its cost efficiency: "Rural and low-income school systems with minimal financial resources lacked the funds to try attacking their problems in new and different ways. *Yet in many cases the innovative programs that would eliminate their specific difficulties had already been tried elsewhere and had proven successful.* Making this information available to them would show them how to solve their problems and in the process serve to stretch their limited funds [emphasis added]."[3]

If attacking problems "in new and different ways" requires more resources than are available to low-income rural districts, then they will have to leave it up to the well-endowed suburban districts to do the trail-blazing for them. The fact that the Stanford evaluators found that the typical NDN program developer was a suburban district bears this out; what NDN may have turned out to be, therefore, is a brilliant strategy for supporting the roles of suburban districts as innovators and rural districts as imitators. Does this mean that where NDN has had an especially strong impact on a rural area, such as in Maine, the schools have become "suburbanized"?

In this regard, it is important to remember that there is an exception to the rule that NDN programs have been warmly received in the rural schools of Maine. The state has a large number of small elementary schools in remote communities, often serving fewer than 100 students and under the administration of a principal who is also a full-time teacher and a superintendent with an office in a distant town and perhaps a dozen schools under his jurisdiction. Very few of these have adopted NDN programs. "When I think about it," Shafto observes, "we have not been successful in the rural-rural schools. It seems like there has to be a minimum size." An explanation for this exception might be that although the NDN model, particularly as refined by Bob Shafto in Maine, is ideal for most rural school systems, the prerequisite is that they are large enough and similar enough to urban or suburban schools that they may accommodate a program originally developed for an urban/suburban setting. Wickline would deny this. "If there is any common thread running through all the NDN programs," he says, "it is individualization, and that is something that applies equally well in rural and urban areas. I believe that the NDN is a generalizable model, that it should work as well in either rural or urban areas."

There is another possible explanation for NDN's troubles in rural-rural schools, and it suggests as well a new perspective for the consideration of how NDN may be changing Maine schools. Shafto believes that the lack of adoptions in these schools is due to the fact that the teaching principals who administer them see themselves more as teachers than as principals, and the superintendents are too distant: "You need the element of an administration," he says. "Otherwise you have no leadership. Teacher turnover will kill you." Indeed, several signs indicate that NDN program adoption in this state is a phenomenon more closely identified with administrators than with teachers, in spite of the facts that most of the NDN programs are classroom instructional programs, that most of the developer-demonstrators are practicing teachers, and that Shafto himself has come from a classroom teaching background. NDN's special appeal in rural areas may more precisely be its special appeal among rural administrators.

Virtually all contacts between a local school system and the rest of the professional education world are channeled through the principal's or superintendent's office. It is to them that Shafto directs his mailings, and it is on them that he relies for local intraschool publicity. It is with them that he has worked most often and built the closest relationships. Not surprisingly, they are among his strongest supporters. When the state department was considering whether to continue Title IV-C funding in support of the Facilitator Center when it was experiencing hard times in the period between the changeover from its old authorization to its new appropriation, a group of superintendents volunteered to go to Augusta to communicate their enthusiasm for it. Shafto could count on their support again if he needed it. "I could get a roomful of superintendents who would go up there and say, 'The Maine Facilitator Center is worth having.'"

The 1979 survey showed superintendents to have the highest rate of questionnaire return (among teachers, principals, and superintendents) and the highest rate of positive comments about the usefulness of Shafto's services. More significantly, it showed that the *selection* of an NDN program for use in a district was a decision usually made by school administrators rather than by the teachers who would finally implement it in the classroom. The survey writers reported:

> A pattern common to the projects visited is the articulation of need and the identification of possible solutions in the form of programs by central office personnel, usually an assistant superintendent, curriculum coordinator, or project director. In most districts, both identification of need and access to resources depend on these individuals. . . . In many cases, there remains a question of how much the need articulated by central office personnel was accepted by all staff involved in program implementation.[4]

The preponderance of administrators in the NDN movement must also be explained as a result of Shafto's own strategy. His use of the "bandwagon" appeal, for example, is aimed at them. In fact, awareness sessions have become such a customary meeting place for superintendents that, according to the 1979 survey, "stimulation and socialization may have become . . . as important factors in attendance as searching for a specific program to meet a specific need." It is administrators, moreover, who have had to answer publicly to the demands of the accountability movement in education and who have had to explain low achievement-test scores and agree to do something about basic skills. Programs such as ECRI, which hold out the promise of dramatic gains in test scores, are particularly attractive to administrators. Maine teachers, however, are apparently not always convinced that a new program can make as significant a difference as the administrators envision. The survey writers, in asking whether NDN programs were so different from other programs operating in a district, found that "teachers tended to perceive more similarities between 'what we were already doing' and the NDN program than administrators did."

Shafto has insisted that teachers attend workshops and adopt NDN programs on a purely voluntary basis, but some administrators have not been so patient. In several cases, administrators have required their teachers at least to attend workshops where programs were being presented. The pressures may have produced some resentment on the part of teachers and a fear, unreasonable according to Shafto, that "if I can't make this program work, it'll mean I'm a failure."

Maureen Giunta, an English teacher at Ellsworth High School, traveled with some of her colleagues fifteen miles down Route 1 to an ECRI workshop at Sumner High in Sullivan. She didn't like it at all. "It didn't allow any flexibility for me the teacher," she says. "It was all rote. It didn't allow us time to sit and discuss the story. Everything was pre-programmed. I give the cue, they respond. I like to give the kids a chance to express themselves, rather than just respond to a cue." The basic tenets of the program, she says, "the ideas that you have to repeat when it's necessary and drill when it's necessary, are ones that any good teacher already knows." She has not been an eager follower of NDN programs in general, because she suspects "they take away any creativity from you. You don't have to think anymore. I'm going to pull back from anything where they say I have to do it in a certain way. I wouldn't want to be locked into anything. I like to be free to try some of my own techniques—things that have worked for me in the past." If Giunta's reaction is typical, it may help explain why more teachers haven't jumped on the NDN bandwagon.

If the NDN is primarily an administrator's network, has its impact on the schools been any less? It may be that it is Bob Shafto, not the dozens of developer-demonstrators with their "tested and proven" programs, who is changing Maine schools. The survey writers found in investigating the training workshops that "what is most remarkable about the training as described by the respondents is the general lack of enthusiasm for it." They found that their training needs were more in the area of "local or regional support systems" than in the area of further contact with the program developers. Most helpful of all, the survey said, were facilitator-led sharing sessions, where they "move beyond 'show-and-tell' to group problem solving, a form of technical assistance by peers."

This may be the type of change that is of greatest permanence and significance. The programs may eventually be discarded, and the teachers may lose interest in the developers' show-and-tell promotions, but change has occurred. Technical assistance itself is a new concept in many schools—the idea of someone from outside the system, a facilitator, sitting down with teachers and administrators to work out the problems of a new program. The "subnetworking" of rural schools around anything besides extracurricular athletics is itself a notable phenomenon. The involvement of superintendents and principals in issues beyond those of management and finance is a development that may have far-reaching implications for curriculum reform. Of the two NDN change agents, the facilitator and the developer-demonstrator, it's the facilitator—the "technical assistance broker" in director Wickline's words—who is probably accounting for the changes that are taking place. With two-thirds of Maine's districts now in the NDN column, the changes are substantial.

## Notes

1. *Study of the Maine Facilitator Center,* "Report: Phase I—Summary of Survey Responses," and "Report of User Site Interviews" (Portsmouth, N.H.: RMC Research, 1979).

2. John A. Emrick, *Evaluation of the National Diffusion Network,* vol. 1: *Findings and Recommendations* (Menlo Park, Calif.: Stanford Research Institute, 1977).

3. Judy Barry, "Stretching Education Dollars and Ideas," *Appalachia,* June-July 1977, pp. 27–32.

4. *Study of the Maine Facilitator Center.*

# 9

# The Urban/Rural Program: Can the Government Buy Change in Rural Schools?

*James Branscome*

There is a lot of talk these days about networks in education. There are formal networks, informal networks, social networks, and—pending the outcome of some sizable National Institute of Education studies—there may be other types yet to be discovered. We doubt, however, that any will equal the Cud network, which starts out in Fort Gay, West Virginia, runs up and down hollows all over Wayne County, links up with nearby Kentucky, and occasionally—when the weather is right—bounces over strip-mine-mangled mountains to excite folks 150 miles away in "Bloody" Harlan County, Kentucky.

Cud is not an acronym. It is a huge, fist-sized plug of Bull Durham chewing tobacco crammed into the left jaw of a disc jockey who spits and spins out "golden oldies" from the 1950s into the airwaves of Appalachia over WFGH public radio. For the Cud network, the fans are grateful to the Office of Education, which—after five years and $1 million—left the FM station behind at Fort Gay High School as its most visible accomplishment in Fort Gay, West Virginia.

This is not, however, a story about Cud. It is a story about the Urban/Rural Program, a federal experiment in teacher retraining that stretched from the slums of Puerto Rico to the Makah Indian Reservation at Neah Bay, Washington. To tell the story of Urban/Rural is to spin a yarn about the "good old days" of the 1960s when educators opted to sail off in new, experimental directions in renewing American education. The propeller was a now-extinct brand wistfully called "many dollars." Depending

James Branscome, a freelance writer, worked from 1970 to 1972 for the Stanford Leadership Training Institute, under OE contract, to help establish the School/Community Council at Fort Gay.

on who is remembering the program, the ship either sank on the shoals of disappointment or charted a new course that opened up a whole new world of educational practice. In any case, Urban/Rural lost its propeller.

The story begins, not surprisingly, in Washington, D.C. Prior to 1965, the Office of Education and its parent, The Department of Health, Education, and Welfare, were so ill funded and low ranked that few soldiers of educational change even bothered to salute. OE primarily gathered statistics and maintained a small staff that rendered technical assistance to state education offices and institutions of higher learning.

In 1962, when President Kennedy appointed Francis Keppel as commissioner, OE began to think of ways it could win a new role in educational policy. The result was the passage in 1965 of the landmark Elementary and Secondary Education Act, a package of reform-oriented amendments wrapped in a billion dollars' worth of enticement. The problem was poverty and the answer was compensatory education. America's poor classrooms would never be the same; bare rooms were filled with exciting new personnel, methods, and technology.

By 1967, ESEA was a fully molded program that left OE little more to do than write checks to the states and local educational agencies administering the program. In response to OE suggestions, Congress in 1968 passed the Education Professions Development Act, a far more flexible piece of legislation that directed OE to remedy educational personnel shortages and to reform training for professionals in the field. Section D of the act was open ended; OE had the discretion to develop "programs or projects to improve the qualification of persons who are serving or preparing to serve in educational programs in elementary or secondary schools."

The commissioner of the new Bureau of Education Professions Development (BEPD) was Don Davies, a former head of the National Education Association's Teacher Education and Professional Standards Commission. Davies was a strong advocate of changing the rule that teacher training had to be as closely tied to teacher training institutions as a pig is to its skin. He wanted a new emphasis from OE that would "free the creative energies of teachers and other staff members . . . by taking the training to where the people are."

After a 1968 BEPD task force recommended a school-based, locally planned program of teacher retraining in poor urban and rural areas, Davies appointed an Urban/Rural Task Force to work out the details of the program. John Lindia, a Davies assistant, was named to head the group of eight BEPD employees who worked on the job part-time. Two OE interns, John Rude and Michael Brannon, were assigned to the team and did most of the work. The OE history of Urban/Rural provides an important insight into how a small group of self-acknowledged lower-level employees influenced OE to move one significant step further in program design:

> Rude soon emerged as the day-to-day head of the Task Force. Following Lindia's advice, members of the group decided to observe some of the nation's more prominent community-run schools; in preparing for its first report to Davies and BEPD, the Task Force visited the I.S. 201 complex in Harlem, the Ocean Hill Brownsville district in Brooklyn, and the Adams-Morgan Community School in Washington, D.C. After these visits, the Task Force began to think about Urban/Rural as a federally sponsored experiment in promoting significant community participation. Rude commented "we were very much influenced by what we saw at those schools." The Task Force began to think about community control as a major element in Urban/Rural.[1]

It is important to remember the milieu in which the program designers were then working. Martin Luther King, Jr., had been killed only the year before. The riots that followed, the heavy war on poverty, emphasis on citizen involvement, and a general idealism about the ability of federal money to buy change all combined to produce a leap of faith about the role of federal involvement in education and the nature of teacher-training programs. Cooler heads at BEPD, like Bill Smith, recently head of the Teacher Corps, joined Davies in trimming out some of the program's designs that would not pass muster with state and local administrators (such as community control in project schools to the point of firing teachers), but the community input, school-based model of training remained.

The site selection process consisted of (1) willingness of the state to participate and to identify schools meeting poverty criteria, (2) willingness of the state and local education agencies to waive any regulation that might conflict with program design, (3) federal rules dictating national distribution formulas for federal funds, and (4) priorities on Model City sites in urban areas. The 1970 Program Information Document written by OE summed up the Urban/Rural mission as writing "a new script for educational performance within the school." In the same document, Davies noted:

> The Office of Education will not dictate to local projects. Local school superintendents will not design them. They will be the creation and responsibility of the entire school staff and local community. The result will be a school with a new environment which is stimulating and satisfying to the child and teacher alike, and in which the academic achievement and human development of children will be significantly increased. In a sense, this will produce an approach that is at the same time revolutionary and old-fashioned. Revolutionary in terms of involving an entire school staff as change agent; old-fashioned in terms of the total participation by school and community that was practiced when this nation was struggling to grow.[2]

## A New Script for Fort Gay

Not very much has ever happened in Wayne County, West Virginia. No major Civil War battle was fought here, and with one exception, no great general or statesman ever visited the county. That exceptional visit was paid in 1960 by presidential aspirant John F. Kennedy during the West Virginia primary. The young millionaire expressed shock at the poverty he saw in Wayne County's hollows and promised that the New Frontier would have the revitalization of West Virginia high on its agenda.

Kennedy's visit marked the beginning of a new discovery of Appalachia. David Brinkley stood on a rickety, one-lane bridge across the Tug River in Wayne County and told his NBC viewers of the stark poverty of the people and their fascination with Kennedy. In return for the attention, Wayne Countians named the bridge the "David Brinkley Bridge" and hung a sign with his name from its beams. In 1971, an overloaded truck dumped the bridge into the river. Only a few days later, the favorite joke in the county was about how "the sound of the bridge hitting the river bottom was the only damned thing we've heard from the War on Poverty."

The flood of social legislation in the sixties had little impact on Wayne County. The Community Action Program (CAP) never really got started in the county before it became buried in the battle for the spoils with the poor lining up as a majority to be whipped by the minority—the politicians. The county school board kept Head Start out by refusing use of school property. They used Title I (ESEA) federal money to purchase a TV broadcasting unit and a TV set for every classroom and administrative office.

The county school system developed its own special explanation of community action in Wayne County. In a brochure written for submission to the Office of Education (BEPD), the school officials explained: "The Office of Economic Opportunity and Community Action Groups have not been active in this area because of the lack of leadership and organization. Most of the indigent people are content to leave the welfare of their families to the Department of Public Assistance." In 1970, the county's average family income was just over $3,000. In some hollows the number of persons on welfare assistance was 60 percent of the population; in others, it was 90 percent. Of the 1,000 first graders who entered the county school system in 1960, only 600 remained to graduate in 1972. Many of the county's unemployed bet their eighth grade against the chance of a job "up North" and left for Ohio and Michigan industrial plants. For some of those left behind, there were jobs in the county's largest industry, education. In 1970, the system employed 600 people: 500 teachers and 100 others in custodial or supportive jobs. The qualifications for a job as a teacher, other than a college degree from nearby Marshall University, have always been kinship and unswerving devotion to the local superintendent. For other jobs, like driving a bus, kinship and votes will suffice. In both cases, outsiders need not apply.

Wayne County would seem an unlikely area for an experiment in "school-community parity in decision-making"—especially parity, defined by Urban/Rural (U/R) guidelines as "mutual, collaborative decision-making on the part of those rendering and those receiving services." Nevertheless, in October 1970, Wayne County School Superintendent Sam Hubbard was advised that his system had been selected by OE to participate in the program. Provided that both he and the community agreed to accept the program, OE promised $750,000 over a five-year period to conduct teacher retraining. The guidelines stipulated that the money be spent on a cluster of schools. After preliminary negotiation, Superintendent Hubbard and OE agreed on three schools in southern Wayne County: Fort Gay High, Fort Gay Elementary, and the Thompson Elementary School on Mill Creek.

The program called for the development of a School/Community Council (SCC) composed of both teachers and members of the community. The SCC was assigned a number of organizing and implementation tasks, including: (1) assessing the education needs of the school and community; (2) developing a long-range plan for improving education resources of the school and community; (3) implementing this plan through a program of school staff training and the employment of a school development team manager; and (4) developing procedures for evaluating the program and assuring that, to the extent possible, it was coordinated with the other federal programs in the school.

The Stanford Leadership Training Institute (LTI), under the direction of Dr. Robert Hess, was given the task of organizing the community input of the SCCs and providing the whole SCC with technical assistance in carrying out its job. The Stanford LTI in 1970 hired nine regional coordinators to work at the local level with the U/R sites in twenty-seven states and Puerto Rico.

My first job as a regional coordinator was to meet with the school system of Wayne County and to negotiate the formation of an SCC. In addition, I had to hire a local community person (a "local facilitator," as LTI called them) who would be responsible for the initial community meeting to decide whether local people would accept the program. Due to delays at OE, it was actually May 1971 when I arrived in Wayne County to begin my work. At the time, I was twenty-five, half the age of Superintendent Sam Hubbard. In my few years of traveling around my native region, I knew more than I needed to know about the power of school superintendents; and Sam Hubbard had spent fourteen years surviving as one. The idea of him "negotiating" with me over "parity" struck me as something more than absurd. But, with the OE promise "to hold the system at bay," as one OE staffer had told us at an LTI meeting, I headed for Fort Gay, a village that sells beer to dry Louisa, Kentucky, across the river in return for that town supplying groceries, motels, and other amenities.

Sam Hubbard is a mountain professional; and he wasted no time in telling me that he remembered "signing something" about parity but that it really did not interest him because OE had "already advised me that I have fiscal control." I carefully pointed out that the SCC was to have administrative control of the program and the funds, and that he was to sign the checks. He carefully reminded me that in West Virginia the county sheriff signs all the checks, and besides: "I have the power through the Board of Education to stop the program. We don't want any rabble-rousers around here like those community action groups in Crum [a nearby community]. . . . I guess I'm from the old school. I'm trained in education. We know more about education than Mrs. John Doe, housewife, though I know we've got to listen to them more. But the community shouldn't tell us what to have in schools, what teachers, etcetera. They're not going to start administering things."

Lesson Number One: Don't ever challenge a professional to a battle with a piece of paper; he'll let you win every time. Sam Hubbard had seen plenty of guidelines in his time from Washington and he knew from experience that they didn't bite. We both signed our names to an "interim agreement" saying that an SCC would be formed, have control over spending the funds, plan the program, and be able to hire its own personnel. I left Hubbard's office and headed to Fort Gay.

The principal at Fort Gay High School had heard that "his school was in some kind of new program" but he didn't have time to talk about it. It was raining hard and he had to round up the bus drivers before the roads flooded out. It was also class ring day for the seniors. Sam Hubbard had told me this principal was a dedicated man, but I was not surprised a year later when he went to work selling class rings full-time. By contrast, Leonard Thompson, at Fort Gay Elementary, couldn't have cared less about class rings or the weather. "As long as it's good for the kids, I'm for it," he said. "I'm glad to hear that the government has finally decided that some of the things we used to do in country schools are all right after all." Seven miles out on Mill Creek at Thompson Elementary School, Mavis Martin, principal, knew all about the new program and she hoped the money could be spent for teacher aides (it could not). The Thompson School had 159 students and six classrooms. Two of the six teachers had not been certified. Its kindergarten room, the janitor said, had been built as an apple bin.

Up the road and across one bridge from the Mill Creek School, Damron's Store is as country as they get. The lone gas pump is on the outside, right under the sign that says "We honor government food stamps." Inside is a pot-bellied stove and about everything you need to survive in Mill Creek. After a Pepsi and a bag of peanuts, I explained that I was looking for a "local facilitator" to get moving on this new government program. Hazel Damron was very sympathetic. She was more lively and knew more about the local schools than anybody I had seen all day. We agreed on a salary, and she was off and running.

With Hazel Damron's cooperation, we worked out an agreement with Sam Hubbard for a twenty-one–member School/Community Council. Nine would be teachers (three from each school) chosen by their peers, ten would be community people chosen at an open meeting of the community, and two would be high school students.

In May of 1971, I returned to the Thompson Elementary School to address a meeting of community people to discuss the U/R program. About seventy-five persons turned out, most of them having responded to local facilitator Hazel Damron's personal contact and extensive newspaper and radio announcements. I explained the U/R guidelines in detail and then opened up the meeting for questions and responses. The general response was one of skepticism. The audience seemed to believe that I had described just another federal program; many said if they could not buy equipment with the grant, they were not interested in it. Others said that trying to reform their schools was going about the problem backwards—economic development had to precede educational development. After more than two hours of discussion, the group voted to accept the program. After another two hours, they finally managed by secret ballot to select twelve men to serve on the council. (Dozens of women were present, but the Scot-Irish tradition of male domination prevailed.)

After the meeting I met with the council to discuss the program in even more detail. By midnight we were all exhausted, but the group was more enthusiastic than they had been at the start. I urged that they use the U/R program as a means of attacking other educational and economic problems in the community, that they view education in more than just school terms. Before the meeting ended, I also advised them to meet as a group several times without the teachers present to get to know each other and to think through carefully what they thought were the major needs in their schools and communities. As it turns out, telling them to have these private meetings was the best advice I ever gave the council. It allowed them to gain some confidence in their own group and to assess thoroughly what a school should be.

The SCC set to work immediately to complete a needs assessment and to make proposals for change in the schools. Though they had an option to pay themselves from the $25,000 planning grant for attending the weekly meetings—some lasting until 2:00 a.m.—the members, including teachers, voted to serve without pay. With U/R, OE had promised a different kind of program; the sky was the limit—except for equipment purchases. The $250,000 of first-year money would be there when the people were ready.

The LTI provided the SCC with consultants on request and designed a three-day training session for the community members. Our emphasis was on insisting that the community do as much as possible by itself. We warned them about snake-oil consultants bearing packaged programs and instant solutions; about local teachers' colleges that helped create the educational mess and got government "reform" money to mess things up some more; and about OE, which had never behaved this way before. It was good advice. The snake-oil salesmen came in droves; the SCC turned them away. The teachers' colleges came from four states, as far away as Michigan; they went home penniless. But then came the government, the one that was supposed to "hold the system at bay." Sorry about that $250,000 start-up money, they said, it has to be cut by a hundred thousand. Sorry about that promise of no deadline, it's the first of October. Sorry about saying any community input is better than a Pert-chart, we must have a line-item budget.

The SCC decided Washington could sit on its collective duff and make contradictory statements to all those people "out there" if it pleased. They were going to act as if nothing had changed. On September 2, they sent me their draft proposal, minus a line-item budget but full of good educational sense about Fort Gay schools. The proposal included statements such as:

> This council feels the principal way to solve the problems of our educational system is to involve the general public in school activities. We, therefore, will concentrate our efforts along these lines. Under a second priority, the secondary problems of reading and math, as well as vocational education, will be studied and possible solutions found and inserted into the school curriculum. Different types of classes, lectures, and demonstrations will be offered to teachers and parents to increase their knowledge of child behavior.

Components of the project included: (1) career education in grades K–12, (2) individualized instruction, (3) health and nutrition, (4) language arts, (5) community school development, and (6) adult education. Even though the council had been told repeatedly by both LTI and OE that equipment was *verboten*, they insisted on an FM radio station and a press to print a community newsletter.

Still active, even with a full-scale reorganization going on and no full-time staff for U/R, OE decided the proposal deadline would be November 1, not October 1. A sigh of relief at Fort Gay. Then on November 9, a staffer called to say he had seen their proposal and it "would never see the light of day in the grants-management division." What about those promises other staffers had made about loose proposals being the best proposals? This staffer said he did not know, he had just come "on board." Rather than complain about OE, he advised, the SCC should be complaining about the Stanford LTI because "it is obvious from your proposal that you have not taken advantage of consultative expertise." By the way, he said, the deadline had been moved up to December 15.

The SCC decided that all its effort could not go down the drain. Hazel Damron contacted the state office of education, which in turn contacted Marshall University, forty miles away in Huntington. Marshall put three consultants to work for three days. The result: a proposal with Pert-charts, organization schemes, a complex evaluation model ("which requires a clear description of the context into which input, process and product matrix is cast"), and a report schedule. The proposal became a sixty-seven–page jargon heap, rather than a twenty-page piece of educational brilliance. Simple statements such as the one above were changed to read: "Objectives: the objective of this project is to develop in a rural school service area a model school/community development program which results in the merging of school and community resources in a mutual reinforcing and supportive role to improve education and community life."

Meanwhile, Sam Hubbard had been demonstrating that the purse strings could be used to choke community control as effectively as anything else. Expenses submitted by the SCC never got paid. As Larry Pelfry, the SCC community chairman, said at one point in exasperation: "I guess we're all pretty tired. I'm not really sure what we have to talk about tonight. I'm pretty fed up with this situation. I'm owed $400 and would wash my hands of the whole thing if I didn't think that's exactly what they wanted me to do. . . . Everybody blames the money problem on somebody else. You go and hire consultants and get 'em to come in on these things and they don't ever get paid. Nobody gets paid."

As dismal as the situation looked in some respects, it was hopeful in others. To the community members' surprise, Leonard Thompson and Joe Wellman, the new principal at Fort Gay High, took the community's side in some of its battles with the teachers. The SCC was also learning it had political clout. It intervened with the school board and obtained an addition to the Thompson School for a kindergarten room (which the superintendent had planned to build in another area of the county). It also pushed for and got commitments from the school board for a new vocational school in the southern end of the county. Thanks to a controversy over an overspent school budget, Sam Hubbard had little time to concentrate on monitoring the SCC. The major impediment that remained was the Office of Education.

On January 13, 1972, Robert Fillion, the third OE project officer assigned to Fort Gay, arrived. The SCC minutes of two days later reflect the outcome of his visit:

> Many changes must be made in the proposed budget and material rewritten to justify the items proposed. Mr. Fillion did not look favorably on the Career Awareness, Vocational Education, and Community School programs. Since

these were of vital interest to the SCC, it is hoped their approval can be obtained in the future. Mr. Fillion indicated prior to leaving that he had enough information to release some money, but revisions must be made by the end of February to obtain the full grant.

The council went to work again. This time, however, they were fed up. At their next meeting, having met weekly since the inception of the project, they voted to pay themselves $10 per meeting.

In February 1972, the council was still at work, even though it had had no word from OE about the approval of its proposal. They hired Mike Sullivan, an Ohioan with federal projects experience at the secondary level, as school development team manager. They also hired Sue Crabtree, a local woman with no college training, to be its community services counselor, a person who would go to the homes of all parents to explain the U/R program and to provide whatever services the family needed to better prepare their children for school. Several members also attended a community education workshop at Flint, Michigan, and were asked by the Mott Foundation to submit a proposal for funding of a community education program. Optimism began to rise again.

In March the SCC received word that its proposal was "unfundable" and that the SCC should come to Washington with a representative of the school board to negotiate the proposal. The SCC prepared for a good fight. When Hazel Damron, Larry Pelfry, Joe Wellman, and Henry Ray (assistant superintendent) got to Washington, they learned that the OE project officer in charge of negotiating had never even read their proposal. A subordinate told them, "You must not be able to read," among other insults. This was more than Henry Ray, a man who is normally soft spoken, could take. He gave the project officer a tongue lashing. After a two-day ordeal, the Fort Gay people won. They would get an FM radio station ($8,500), a press for a community newsletter, a career awareness program, an adult learning center, and all the other items on which they had been insistent. Despite the jubilation at Fort Gay, Hazel Damron's response was, "We knew it would be approved someday if we just fought long enough, so we just went on about our business." In April 1972, the long-promised grant came through.

April was a watershed month for the council. Negotiations with a contracting university for teacher training were under way. Sue Crabtree was winning high praise from all quarters for her success in getting into the community homes and explaining the U/R program. By now she was helping people find welfare, food stamps, and hearing exams for slow learners. Her work balanced the bureaucratic-management attitude taken by SDTM Mike Sullivan.

The council's finest hour was their sponsorship of Mountain Heritage Day on April 22. It was organized by the community education staff leader,

Mike Ferguson, a former teacher at Fort Gay and an early member of the council. The flyer that went out in the community newsletter explained that the Heritage Day was to be an Appalachian celebration complete with an apple-butter stir, craft making, fiddling, and a salute to all things that make mountain life still an alternative culture. More than 750 persons turned out in the rain to attend the Heritage Day. It was the largest gathering in Fort Gay history. "For the first time," says Larry Pelfrey, "the politicians came to ask our help." This first Heritage Day was to be one of several throughout the year.

By summer, teachers at Fort Gay were taking resident courses in Fort Gay on subjects ranging from career awareness to "Appalachian culture and its impact in education." Things were changing in Fort Gay—slowly perhaps—but the old game of accusing activists of being "rabble-rousers" and "outsiders" was not working for the politicians this time. After the turn-out for Heritage Day, the SCC had a fighting chance to survive.

### Looking for the New Script

Prior to our visit to Fort Gay to interview the major participants of U/R about their experiences, we had reviewed the reports from Stanford LTI, summarizing their views of the program's accomplishments. We were intrigued with their positive statements about U/R's success (Fort Gay was recommended to NIE in 1978 as one of the best programs), which were summarized by Dr. Robert Bush of Stanford as follows:

1. School-Community Councils, with approximately equal representation of school officials—mainly teachers—and community people, can be established and can achieve parity in structure and operation in making decisions about inservice education.
2. The work of such councils, through shared decision making by the main parties affected, has a positive effect on morale in the district; improves the variety, quantity, and quality of inservice education; and, where the evidence is available, leads to better learning of students.
3. The communities, after six years and with the aid of federal support, are trying to carry on and to incorporate the experimental work into their regular school programs.[3]

The program produced four surprises, according to Bush: (1) rural areas did a better job of inservice training than urban areas that had more money; (2) "sharing power" with the disenfranchised "increases power"; (3) "the negative stereotype about Washington bureaucrats that is pervasive in this country was not true in the U/R program" except "in the early years"; and

(4) "universities are not useless appendages" deserving the criticism leveled against them by inservice education consumers. "When the schools and communities were free to seek training, they drew on the institutions of higher education more heavily than on any other single source, and learned how to ensure that these services were of high quality and related to their needs."[4]

These glowing testimonials scarcely squared with my experience with Fort Gay's SCC, the university, or OE staff. Moreover, in reading carefully through the entire report, it became clear that the Stanford experts themselves had considerable doubts about their conclusions. For example, the bold assertions about successful participation and sensitive OE support were qualified later in the document which saw a fundamental dilemma in the format that gave community people parity in educational decision making when in some instances they did not have the time to develop adequate experience and competence. The inflexibility of the program, said the report, forced the SCC to purchase expertise that, given time and training, it could have developed itself. The situation of "too much too soon" was compounded by a limited sense of what the Office of Education might regard as an acceptable proposal and implementation plan.

With these official conclusions as a backdrop for our interviews, it quickly became obvious that there were several U/R programs at Fort Gay: The program differed depending on the personality speaking. It also became clear that any fair summary of the project at that time would vary considerably from the conclusions reached by the LTI. Nearly a million dollars' worth of effort later, U/R at Fort Gay was still a story of personalities; most of the outcomes had to be recorded from the subjective views of those most involved.

Sam Hubbard, the once-feared county education master, was found outside Fort Gay High doing bus duty. He had been busted to the lowly rank of math teacher as a result of the election of a new school board. Befitting the diplomatic response officials give visiting evaluators, Hubbard made some complimentary but general remarks about U/R. He then described his role in the early days as trying to defend the SCC at a time when it was under attack for being "the steak crowd that went to a lot of meetings." It was a short interview because he had to depart to get another bus on its way.

At Fort Gay Elementary, new principal Mike Ferguson was holding forth in the more plush first-floor office that had been built by the SCC to house the team manager, the administrator hired to carry out the program on a day-to-day basis. A no-nonsense and opinionated young professional, Ferguson had wanted to be team manager. He had never risen above the role of being in charge of community participation. From an early program enthusiast, he had turned into a pessimist about the accomplishments.

Ferguson's first impression regarding the U/R program was that it was going to "pay for student teachers" who would come to Fort Gay to reduce teacher/student ratios. This was, of course, inaccurate. But it is a good example of the kind of distortion that occurs as information gets passed down from the federal to county to local level, with the effect that what's heard is more consistent with the pinch being felt by various local actors than with the federal program's actual purposes. "U/R was too much of a teacher-oriented college degree program," Ferguson said. "The people who are really sharp moved on," he observed, estimating that of 120–130 people (a high estimate) who were affected by the program, only 30–40 remain. The percentage of remaining teachers who have master's degrees is up sharply, even so. But Ferguson doesn't think the training had much effect on their actual classroom behavior.

Ferguson said that his own tenure as principal at Fort Gay Elementary had improved the school far more than U/R. "I expect more from the teachers," he said. "The atmosphere here used to be just completely lackadaisical. Now that's changed." There has been about a 50 percent turnover in staff since he became principal, he said.

At Fort Gay High School, Clarence Spencer, former assistant principal and active SCC member (including the chairmanship for three years), was on bus duty too. He had been busted to an old job—shop teacher in a dingy, unkept building that had precious little shop material. "I supported the wrong candidate in the last election," he said philosophically, trying to be heard above the soap opera that students were watching on the Title I–supplied television. In Spencer's view, the quality of the inservice education programs sponsored by the SCC was generally "below standards." It was "too easy," "too much of a gift. All teachers had to do was to attend class; and they did little else. I worked out every dime of a college education," he said.

The decision of members to pay themselves $10 per meeting was portrayed as absolutely pivotal by Spencer. "The council built in this business of paying members $10 a meeting. If you don't come to the meeting, you don't get your $10, so sometimes people would come for the first of a meeting, then say they had some kind of emergency or other at home and had to leave early. Now, you know no board of education is going to pick up that $10 a week," he said, referring to the OE and LTI hope that local systems would take over the program in a smooth transition when federal funding ended.

Throughout the conversation with Spencer, one got a picture of the SCC as a group undermined by trifling venalities. For example, no one would serve as secretary for less than $20 per week. This set off bickering in which people said, "Well then, the chairman should get $20 per meeting also." He smiled a foxy smile when he told us this was an attempt to get him to change his position and vote in favor of the $20 per meeting for the secretary.

Asked for his advice on how to improve U/R, Spencer said he could tell us what not to do: "not to put much money in, because the more money you put in, the less result you'll get. We used to approach things like we were asking 'Now how are we going to spend this much money?'" He said 58 percent of the U/R money went into what he called "administration"—office staff, stipends, and consultants. More important is this statement: "We were paying big salaries to all these people from outside, so we started thinking about paying ourselves."

Spencer's story of how U/R ended at Fort Gay is revealing: "We were going to have a really big to-do—you know, a covered dish supper and all. And we'd celebrate and start planning for the future. But only about two or three people showed up. When there's no more money, nobody cares any more." So a group that had met virtually every week for over five years never met again once the federal dollars ran out.

At the Mill Creek school Mavis Martin was in her twenty-second year as school principal. U/R had turned her teaching staff into a better certified group. Martin said she saw two main foci of the U/R program: certification and overcoming community apathy through community involvement. She appeared to conceive of community involvement mainly as a process of increasing parents' familiarity with and support for the school program rather than as one of increasing parents' participation in education decision making.

Some curricular changes resulted from U/R, Martin said (although both of the examples she cited have now lapsed). As a result of a visit paid by some parents and teachers to an open-classroom project in Georgia, the Thompson School instituted an open-classroom program in grades four, five, and six. But opposition from parents was not long in coming; even some of the parent SCC members, who had been very enthusiastic about the Georgia project, turned against the program, and the open classroom was subsequently abandoned. Martin and the two teachers agreed that initiating the program with fourth, fifth, and sixth graders accustomed to more traditional instruction was a mistake. Students had a difficult time charting their own learning paths and an even more difficult time explaining to their parents what they had done in school each day, the professionals agreed.

An attempt to initiate a core curriculum also failed to become institutionalized, though for reasons that were less clear. The two teachers indicated that they had tried out a whole range of ideas and techniques to which U/R-sponsored courses and workshops introduced them. They said that they still used quite a few but had dropped others as time went along. We got the impression that exposure to new possibilities was exciting to them, that they probably rushed back to their classrooms and tried innovations with considerable enthusiasm, but that after this wave of excitement passed, not a great deal was left behind.

When we visited the radio station, we had no trouble figuring out how BEPD money got spent for this project. Keith Spears, the teacher and former disc jockey who started the station, was interviewing his old friend, former Congressman Ken Hechler, who was trying to win his seat back. Before the mike that would broadcast the Cud network that evening was Hazel Damron's 15-year-old son, reporting the news for high-school credit.

Spears said the U/R program came along during his first year of teaching, a time when he was "gung ho, and very sure that the world was going to change in a very short time." When he heard that the goal of the program was to bring the school and community together, he went to the SCC with the idea of a ten-watt FM station. "They said that's a great idea. That's fine. All you have to do is get it okayed by the federal officials," he said. "Right away, I ran into a big problem. It was a kind of chicken or the egg thing. The FCC said where's the funding coming from, and the U/R people said you don't have the documentation," he remembered. Hechler's office intervened successfully, which may explain the OE hostility at the Washington negotiating session mentioned earlier.

At first, the station broadcast all of the SCC meetings, but there were complaints, Spears said, that SCC members were doing a lot of grandstanding because they knew their remarks were being broadcast. The practice of broadcasting meetings was abandoned, but the station continued to cover the activities of the SCC. It also began broadcasting city council meetings and some Wayne County school board meetings. A radio station might not represent a major innovation in many urban and suburban districts, but in a community the size of Fort Gay, the impact was undeniable.

Spears said that the council deteriorated over the years because it became divided along "clannish" family lines. Cliques were always forming, he said. These splits did not occur along social class lines, apparently because the membership was mostly middle class (the SCC didn't span class lines enough to divide that way). The biggest single issue dividing the group, according to Spears, was the question of whether members should be paid $10 per meeting to attend. He said that in addition to dividing the SCC, the decision to pay members undermined community support.

At the end, a number of SCC members resigned before their terms were up, partly because of nervousness about the possibility that the project might have overspent its budget. People said they were resigning "for the good of the community," Spears remembered, but it was more a matter of "rats leaving a sinking ship." The people who were around at the end had to cut everything back and "they're the ones who got the bloody noses," he said.

Newspaper editor Dan Watts covered the first meeting of the SCC and later became a SCC member. He said the lasting impacts—the community library and the radio station—"had nothing to do with the real objectives of the program." He too estimated that 30–40 percent of the teachers trained used the experience as a ticket to a better job in the cities. And as a regular reporter of the school board meetings, he assured us that the SCC had had little lasting impact on local school politics. "It still all comes down to who gets the janitors' jobs," he said.

As it turned out, the Fort Gay program ended up tied to Marshall University in Huntington, the teacher-training school that originally furnished the area with most of its teachers. It was not a direct contract relationship because Marshall refused to waive tuition fees. Central Michigan State University got the contract, but they subcontracted much of the teaching to Marshall professors. We were given no reason to think that the course offerings were unique in any way except that they were taught at the scene.

Dr. Charles I. Jones, the professor at Marshall who helped write the final SCC proposal, was clearly disappointed that the final outcome did not result in a Mott Foundation–style "community school" at Fort Gay. "When you have a program like this that's not run by specialists in the field, it usually goes down the drain. Laymen typically just rediscover the wheel," Jones told us. When we asked Jones why the university refused to agree to a contract to run the SCC retraining, we got this reply: "You realize that every question you're asking me is political dynamite because everything that went on down there is tied into the political structure in Wayne County, and that's tied into the administration here at Marshall."

Finally, and significantly, our lengthy interviews with the three most active community participants failed to confirm the overall LTI conclusions. Larry Pelfrey, the early SCC chairman, and Jarrett Peters, the Veterans Administration counselor who had pushed hard for vocational education training, both had moved from the area to Huntington, the largest city in the western part of the state, citing their frustration with the SCC as part of the reason. Neither is currently involved in school or civic matters in his new area. Both expressed doubt that they would ever again be interested in serving on the board of a new school program.

Hazel Damron, the former LTI facilitator who remained on the SCC to the end, is no longer involved in school matters and has no interest in becoming involved in more school battling. When we interviewed her she was working as a secretary at the county health department. Like Pelfrey and Peters, her reflections on the program resulted in stories of political intrigue. Her concluding comment on the program surprised us all: "Stanford was too far away," she said. "They offered to help, but by the time you got anything from them, it was too late."

## Conclusions

It could be said cynically that U/R at Fort Gay represented the most expensive teacher retraining project ever undertaken. Assuming that 100 people (teachers and community) benefited from the training, the cost was still over $9,000 per participant. Looked at only in terms of the number of teachers who got master's degrees (30), the cost was $30,000 per participant. But this was, after all, an experiment in a different kind of teacher training, controlled by community people who potentially could influence more than teacher credentials.

We have no problem conceding that some good things happened at Fort Gay as a result of the project, but as to "parity," the notion of a new script for educational performance, the hope of a restructuring of the professionalizing system, and the promise of better educated children, we are forced to conclude that the LTI's final report and the LTI staff's impressions of the Fort Gay experience are inaccurate.

A major objective of U/R was to achieve parity in decision making between the school and community. Conceptually this notion was designed to help close the gap between professionals and lay people, a desirable goal and perhaps even an accurate perception of what is needed in an Ocean Hill-Brownsville where the school administration is predominately white and the community is black. Although bringing the school and community closer together in Fort Gay was desirable, an equally important problem was dealing with the reality of the political and kin factions that plague the operation of the schools. The U/R program in Fort Gay may have made some progress in bringing the school and community together; however, the SCC served primarily to provide another arena for the political factions to play out their struggle.

The redistribution of power from politicians and central office administrators to a local council would have been useful had the locals—lay people and professionals together—reallocated dollars and attention away from political patronage and routine performance of bureaucratic functions and back to concerted efforts to improve the quality of the program for children. Unfortunately, however, this does not seem to have been the case.

U/R and the people involved in it were a product of the times, some of them clearly captives of a political and social philosophy that was untried and not welcomed by a large segment of educators and community people. Perhaps the most significant observation we can make about the program is that its creators tailor-made it for urban areas and its evaluators found it worked best in rural areas.

Throughout our study of U/R, we were constantly surprised at the extent to which education planners believe that money from Washington can buy change in rural (or, for that matter, urban) areas, especially over a short period of time. They seem unable to comprehend that conservative schools may be what some conservative communities want.

It is clear that the OE planners wanted a program that would break the symbiotic relationship between teacher-training universities and teacher retraining. To do that, they hired one university teacher-training school, which was unable—with few exceptions—to keep the sites from hiring the same teacher-training schools they had always dealt with. And that one chosen university sent in an evaluation of its efforts that defended all teacher-training schools.

We wish no quarrel with Stanford's assertion that good things happened as a result of U/R in communities across America. We do quarrel with the claim that U/R was one program testing one model nationwide. We doubt that there is either the will or the money to try to duplicate it.

### Notes

1. Alan Weisberg, *Urban/Rural School Development Program: An Account of the First Two Years of an Office of Education Experiment in School-Community Parity* (Stanford, Calif.: Stanford Center for Research and Development, Urban/Rural School Development Institute, 1973).

2. "Urban/Rural School Development Program," mimeographed (Washington, D.C.: U.S. Office of Education, 1970); introduction by Don Davies.

3. Bruce Joyce, ed., *Involvement: A Study of Shared Governance of Teacher Education* (Syracuse, N.Y.: National Dissemination Center, 1978).

4. Ibid.

# 10

# San Juan, Utah: Ending a White-Indian School Battle by the "Process Method"

*James Branscome*

The San Juan County School District is not a typical rural school system. Its size alone places it in a class by itself. Serving the Utah quarter of the Four Corners area (the only point in the United States common to four states' boundaries), it covers 8,000 square miles, about the size of the state of New Jersey. Its boundaries are clearly defined by the Colorado border on the east; Lake Powell, formed by the Glen Canyon Dam, on the west; and the state of Arizona on the south. The San Juan River cuts across the bottom third of the district, marking the northern boundary of the Navajo Reservation.

Stark contrasts characterize both the geography and the people of San Juan County. The magnificent desert vistas of Monument Valley seemingly stretch forever to the south, and the Abjato Mountains dominate the high desert plateau to the north. The Green and the San Juan rivers wind their way through the county, providing some of the best river rafting in the country. Cattle and sheep of both the Indian and white ranchers roam freely across the highways with only painted stripes on the road serving as cattleguards to mark the boundary lines between one spread and the next. Ranching and irrigated alfalfa and pinto beans, once the basis of the economy, are now rivaled by oil, gas, and uranium production. Thanks to the energy development, San Juan County's population has increased dramatically, showing a 6.3 percent growth rate (compared to a 7 percent loss for the rest of rural Utah).

The county's population of 10,000 averages 1.2 persons per square mile. The majority of the district's residents live in two population centers: Monticello (population 1,431) and Blanding (population 2,250). The school district offices, Bureau of Land Management, and National Park Service are in Monticello, and Blanding, twenty-two miles to the south, serves as the region's trade center. Both are predominately Anglo communities with a high percentage (97 percent in Blanding) of Latter Day Saints (Mormons). As one travels south of Blanding toward Bluff, or to the southeast toward Montezuma Creek, the well-kept homes of Blanding and Monticello are replaced by dilapidated homes and trailers of Native Americans, many of whom still hold to traditional beliefs and life-style, speaking only the native language.

In 1975, the district's 2,700 students were served by seven elementary schools, five of which were located in outlying areas. The one junior high and two high schools, however, were in the two population centers, which meant long bus rides for the Navajos, who in 1950 made up only 2 percent of the student body but now constitute half the student population in San Juan High.[1] For some students, an eighty-five-mile bus trip, plus a two- or three-mile walk to the bus, meant four or five hours each day getting to and from school.

The schools obviously were not geographically situated to serve the Navajo students. They were even less prepared programmatically to cope with students whose first language was Navajo and whose culture was far removed from that of the predominant Anglo/Mormon population. In spite of efforts by the district through a Title VII grant to establish a Curriculum Development Center for bilingual/bicultural instructional materials, and in spite of the "Oljato Study"—an initiative of the Utah Board of Education, the district board, the Utah Navajo Development Council, and the Navajo Tribal Government—to see what could be done to improve educational opportunities for Indians, time ran out. Riding on the wave of civil rights activism, the Native American Rights Organization in 1974 filed a class action suit against the school district, charging unequal access to educational opportunity.

### The Northwest Regional Educational Laboratory's Rural Futures Development Program

One of the major program thrusts of the Northwest Regional Educational Laboratory (NWREL) in Portland, Oregon, was rural education. Building on their earlier experience of developing curriculum materials designed to expand the rural school's limited course offering and accommodate the unique needs of American Native populations, the Northwest Lab officials were prepared to launch a more comprehensive approach to improving education in rural communities. Having looked at the work of Asahel Woodruff, Ron Havelock, John Williamson, Richard Schmuck, and Phillip Runkel on how people learn and how organizations can be changed, the Lab began evolving a program through which all segments of the rural community population could participate in a problem-solving process around

the issues of improving education. The Rural Futures Development Program (RFD) was "designed to aid rural people in creating their own solutions which would fulfill needs that are unique to their own environments."[2]
The underlying principles of the program included:

*Participatory decision making.* Support for school programs increases when those who feel that a decision affects them are given the opportunity to influence the decision and the way it is made.

*Choice.* Educational solutions are not the same for every community; communities improve the quality of their educational programs when they become skilled in selecting solutions that match their values and resources.

*Process.* When people follow a systematic procedure for making choices and changes, they can make the best use of existing resources.

*Comprehensiveness.* Because complex relationships exist between students and adults, between teaching and learning, and among schools, communities, and support agencies, a global change strategy, not a parade of separate innovations, is needed.

The RFD assumed that:

- All individuals have the right to participate in decisions that affect them.
- When decision making is shared, the decisions that are made accurately reflect the opinions and knowledge of the entire group.
- Change is inevitable, but if change is planned, educational opportunities are more likely to improve than if they are simply allowed to happen.
- When people from the community and school communicate, support for school programs increases.
- As people develop skill at solving problems and communicating with one another, they become more self-reliant and the chances that educational improvements will succeed increase.
- Every individual has worth and dignity.
- Conflict is natural and common and can be dealt with constructively.
- A process facilitator is helpful to persons seeking to bring about planned change.[3]

The RFD program required a team of process facilitators (PFs) to install a seven-phase school-community process that included: creating an awareness of the strategy, forming school-community groups (SCGs) made up of recognized opinion leaders, conducting needs assessments, searching for alternative solutions, planning for action, carrying out the plan, and assessing the results.

In the fall of 1974, this strategy was ready for field testing. Rowan Stutz, the director of the Lab's Rural Education Program (REP), was from Utah and had worked for the state department of education in rural school improvement. He was therefore familiar with the situation in the San Juan County schools. The need to find a resolution to the class action lawsuit seemed the perfect opportunity to test the RFD strategy. At a September meeting of the local school board, Bob Green of NWREL was in Monticello presenting a "plan to improve educational programs and facilities for students in the southern end of the district. Basically, this plan would provide the Indian people with an opportunity to help identify their school needs and to make recommendations to the Board of Education concerning any future programs or facilities within their communities."[4] When it was clear that implementing the program might lead to an out-of-court settlement of the charges brought by the Native American Rights Organization, the board directed the superintendent and the attorney to draft a memorandum of agreement with the interested parties.

Not long after, a legal notice appeared in the *San Juan Record* (the county newspaper) announcing job vacancies for four community process facilitators. The four PFs would take care of the first two school-community groups to be established in the southern end of the county at Montezuma Creek and Oljato. As the two communities were overwhelmingly Navajo, the need for hiring individuals who were neutral in terms of their community relationships was tempered a bit. Three of the PFs were Indian: Jim Dandy, Robert Angle, and Clyde Bennally. The fourth was an Anglo woman, Jan Christiansen, who had been teaching in Salt Lake City. The local socio-cultural characteristics of the area not only required some modifications of preconceived notions of who the PFs should be, they also dictated some unique considerations in the forming of school-community groups. The "opinion leaders" of the Navajo were those who were already in leadership positions within the tribal chapter structure. These representatives needed to be joined with representation from the minority but controlling population of the oil and gas companies, the trading posts, and various religious groups.

Although NWREL had tried parts of the RFD strategy in a variety of field settings (Healy and Juneau, Alaska, Neah Bay and Okanogan Valley in Washington, and the Montana State Education Agency in Helena, Montana), San Juan provided the first opportunity to put it all together: refining the process, testing facilitator training procedures, and trying out the RFD products (a series of how-to manuals that could be used independently of Northwest Lab assistance). Five manuals were to be produced: *RFD Guide for Training School-Community Process Facilitators, RFD Manual for School-Community Process Facilitators, RFD Guide for Schools, RFD Guide for School Boards,* and *RFD Notebook for School-Community Groups.*

The interrelationships between the Northwest Lab and San Juan were multifaceted. In addition to identifying and training the local process facilitators, the school-community process needed to be initiated and maintained. Materials were tried out and revised and the whole program evaluated with an eye to marketing the strategy in other communities. Keats Garman, an anthropologist newly hired by the Lab, moved on site to assist with training, provide support and guidance to the fledgling PFs, and relay firsthand information to the development team back in Portland, Oregon. Formal training sessions were conducted by Lab personnel who made the 1,100 mile trip to the district on a monthly basis.

The educational problems needing attention in Montezuma Creek and Oljato were obvious and had already been the attention of previous studies and the class action lawsuit. Much of the usual work of the early phases of the SCG process could be shortened. The need for high school facilities in the southern end of the county needed validation, with some assurance that if they were built, students now attending school elsewhere would enroll. Further, once the school board agreed that the schools should be built, sufficient support had to be generated so that a bond issue could be passed to finance the school construction. If the above steps could be accomplished, many of the issues leading to the lawsuit could be resolved and educational opportunities for the Navajos would be greatly enhanced.

Although the agenda for the SCG process was fairly clear from the start, achieving that agenda was no small task. Four newly hired PFs needed to understand the concepts behind the notion of a process facilitator and learn the skills necessary to carry out that role (establishing working groups, keeping the group process going, agenda building, staying on the task, searching for alternatives, and making recommendations). Perhaps most importantly, the PFs needed help in establishing and maintaining a position of neutrality in a school-community process that relied on the power of persuasion to get things done. Functioning school-community groups have been notably difficult to establish under the best conditions. Creating such groups in a less than favorable climate within a bicultural, bilingual situation was even more difficult. Only the on-site direction and leadership of Keats Garman and the less desirable option of legal action continually in the background made it happen: SCGs did get organized. "Needs assessments" were developed and conducted in two languages, options were considered on where new school facilities should be built, and recommendations for new schools were made to the board.

The recommendation for two new facilities, one at Montezuma Creek and one in the Oljato area, were accepted; architects were hired and plans were made for a bond election. In a little over a year, the real test of the effectiveness of the SCG process was at hand. Would the voters turn out and vote in sufficient numbers to approve the bond issues? The answer in this case was clear: Precincts in which the SCGs had been operating in the southern end of the county voted for the bonds; precincts in the northern end of the county where SCGs had not been formed voted against the bonds. The school-community process paid off: Those saying yes were 61 percent of the votes. With SCGs effectively in place in the Indian communities, others were formed in Blanding and Monticello, where the groups focused on teacher performance, extracurricular activities, and the honor system. In addition, an in-school task force trained by the PFs was formed at Blanding to work on teacher concerns.

The RFD was active in San Juan County for twenty-two months, from August 1974 to June 1976. REP reported that the "installation" of the strategy at San Juan for 1974-75 cost it $36,382 and the school district $109,000. The major cost of the period was $93,000 for the salaries of the four PFs. The second largest expense, $65,000, was for the Lab services to continue the program past 1976, picking up the estimated $50,000 annual tab with special federal impact funds.

## A Process Facilitator Looks at the RFD
### (September 1978)

Jan Christiansen, one of the PFs in San Juan County, literally bubbles with enthusiasm about the RFD. To her, a disenchanted former teacher, the program represented the most effective way to involve community people in educational decision making. As far as the school system is concerned (and many SCG members as well), Christiansen *is* RFD. She began with the program in September 1974 and only recently (since this interview) resigned and moved away because of the lack of opportunities in the rural county.

"The original concept was that we would phase out," Christiansen reflected, "but it hasn't worked out that way. Our role has changed significantly. There used to be a lot of skill training, but now we're consultants and linkers." To her, the major benefit of the program was that "there is nothing sacred that our people cannot get into. They are entirely independent. There is no censorship by the board." Every time the SCGs have gone to the board, she said, their well-thought-out plans have been approved. She, like most other observers, attributes the existence of the SCGs to the Navajo lawsuit. "There is no question that the lawsuit triggered the movement of getting the SCGs going."

Christiansen admitted that coming into the area fresh from a teaching position in Salt Lake City, and previously in Oregon, caused her some trouble starting out as a process facilitator. "It took me six months to figure out what I was doing down here," she said. She said the hardest task was determining how to transfer skills she learned from RFD trainers. Knowing how to get a group going is one thing, but figuring out how to keep the group focused on a task can be a formidable job, she said. Some of the most effective training she did for the community members of the SCG involved taking them to districts where model programs were being conducted.

Through lengthy analysis of a particular problem and how best to solve it, the SCGs develop the capacity to "weed out the impossible, the unrealistic. The operating principle is no surprise. The board has never said no to anything. If the people had not had good experience in getting the system to respond, they would not continue." It was the overwhelming passage of the bond issue for the new schools, with the heavy affirmative vote coming from the southern (Indian) part of the county, that first demonstrated that the SCG was learning the process of empowerment. (Several of the women trained in the Blanding SCG used their skills to successfully confront the city council over building sidewalks in the community.)

She saluted the program's flexibility as a major asset. As an example, she said the strategy called for "opinion leaders" to be the primary people sought for SCG membership, "but we modified it to suit our needs." In getting a group going, she said she "hit the businesses, the ranchers—anything I could think of. The same names kept coming up. I went to them and asked them to form a temporary group." On the reservation, the PFs went to chapter meetings and called community meetings to explain the program. Interpreters translated into Navajo. (Later that was reversed as SCG meetings were conducted in Navajo, with English translation provided.) The PFs suggested formation of twenty-member SCGs, with thirty initially to allow for dropouts. As soon as the groups met, a chairperson—always a community person—was elected. The group was immediately given a short course in agenda planning. In the following months, the PFs thought out the best methods to use in skill transfer. Each group decided the tenure of members and replaced members who dropped out.

Because of previous Bureau of Indian Affairs practices, Christiansen said, the Navajos tended to conduct very formal meetings concentrating on drawing up legalistic-sounding resolutions. Also because of BIA practice, the first-year members on the reservation were paid $25 per meeting, plus mileage. When the budget was cut, the $25 was cut, causing some of the people "to be really upset. We still pay mileage of 15¢ on the reservation because that precedent was firmly set." Christiansen was concerned that attendance would drop off at Oljata once the school construction was completed. "We'll have to work harder to keep them going."

Training for the groups concentrated on problem solving, conducting meetings, data interpretation, and evaluating alternatives, among other things. The PF is a resource linker, finding answers to questions and frequently running interference with the district office. The PFs also do much of the group's paperwork and telephone calling. Paid by the district, they must be responsive to the SCG and the school and at the same time remain neutral on policy questions. A PF is forbidden to take leadership positions.

In addition to the new schools on the reservation, Christiansen cited other early impacts of the program: It developed a needs assessment that focused community attention on specific school problem areas; once reading was identified as a problem, RFD was a resource linker in getting in-service training for teachers; and it changed teacher evaluation at Blanding High, with administrators being forced to spend more time in the classrooms.

## The SCG at Montezuma Creek

In Montezuma Creek, three things are inescapable: the Navajos have not lost their culture (the hogans and crafts and language prove that); there has been an SCG here; and the community is proud of the modern, impressive structure soon to become the home of the White Horse High School Raiders. Navajos demanded the school, their bond vote funded it, they helped design it, they helped set the curriculum, they participated in hiring the principal, and they aim to have it run to suit the community majority.

Billy Totochini, chairman of the SCG for two years, has no doubts about the new school. To him—a college-educated Navajo who does recruiting and counseling work in county schools—the new school will mean "the people will become more involved in their children's education. Too many of our people think of school as a place to learn to read and to speak English. That will change now." Totochini carries two large looseleaf binders stuffed with resolutions to prove that "almost everything we've recommended to the school board has been done." He says the issues successfully resolved range from attendance policy to curriculum.

Wes Jones, a Navajo teacher at the nearby Aneth BIA boarding school for elementary students, is the current SCG chairman. He is less sanguine than Totochini on future developments. "The SCG had input into the building of the school, but now that it's ready to open in the fall, the principal has not showed up to any of our meetings where we wanted to discuss bus routes and curriculum." Jones, one of the natives who has helped turn the Aneth school toward cultural teaching and continuing education for adults, is worried that vocational education and cultural programs will not get their proper place in the high school curriculum. The Aneth teachers are now 35 percent Indian; he doubts those percentages will prevail at White Horse.

Ed Tapahah, a young Navajo who works at the local health clinic, is concerned that his time on the council may not pay the dividends he wanted most: a staff that would communicate with parents and understand traditional culture. He believes the communication is still open with the school board, however, through the process facilitator.

Emergency medical technician Linda Wetzel, who keeps the clinic records and runs the ambulance, feels whipped by the school board. She thinks the board now feels it has satisfied the malcontents on the reservation. "It's pretty easy to get discouraged," she lamented. "We pass a lot of resolutions on how the school should be run, but the board doesn't listen and the principal claims he's too busy to meet with us. We always end up with the assistant principal. But every once in a while, somebody comes in and gives us a pep talk, and we get to thinking things will get better. But overall, I think they want to appease us as long as we keep quiet and don't get in the way."

According to Christiansen, not all the Navajos were convinced the new high school was a good idea because it will be about 97 percent Navajo. "There were mixed emotions," she said, "because of the history of poor schools on the reservation. The educated Indians were the most concerned that there will be no Anglos at Montezuma Creek. They've been to college and they know that all the opportunities are in the white world." The Utah Navajo Development Council, located in Blanding, hopes that situation is changing. It now sponsors a glove factory at Montezuma Creek and hopes its housing project will be able to build the homes for the twenty-three new teachers who will be moving into the community. A sit-in protesting how monies earned from the gas field were distributed may also bring more revenue back to Utah from the Window Rock reservation headquarters.

## The Process at San Juan High

When principal Paul Brooks leaves San Juan High this year for another school district, he would like to take the SCG and teacher task force with him. He credits the SCG for improving school-community relations, instituting a new honor system, improving the teaching of reading, encouraging extracurricular activities, and building the town's sidewalks. He credits the teacher task force with improving faculty reception to new ideas and with the building of a faculty room. But, he adds with a smile, "I really appreciate it that they are advisory only." Brooks indicated he had turned down some of the proposals presented him by both groups.

Five hundred six out of 873 of San Juan High's students are Indian. Brooks estimates the school will lose about 240 students to Montezuma Creek. About 70 percent of the school's graduates go on for advanced training of some kind, the principal said. "What we've got is a whole bunch of agencies ready to pick up our kids. The armed services are always poking around here." Student performance figures are not available for the school, but Brooks said it is average for the region. "Some of the new people moving in have come in and told us their kids might need to be moved ahead a little bit because they're pretty intelligent. We put them into the regular classes. They seem to fit there."

Janet Wilcox thinks the Blanding schools could use some improvement.

She ought to know—she has six boys in the system or aimed for it. A former local newspaper reporter who once covered SCG news for the weekly *San Juan Record*, she now edits the monthly newsletter of the Blanding SCG (the only SCG newsletter). To Wilcox, the SCG's best efforts in the three years she has been involved went into changing the teacher evaluation program at Blanding. She chaired a task force that met weekly for four months to make the evaluation available to teachers and to make the reports more objective. The task force discovered that teachers had not been evaluated the two years previous to its formation. Teachers are now evaluated three times a year.

Wilcox said that training for her sixteen-member SCG meant that "complainers have been turned into people who help schools solve problems." Asked to contrast the SCG with a PTA, her reply was that "the SCG is more problem-solving oriented. The PTA provides services—back to school nights and band uniforms. We're looking for problems to solve." She said the group avoided working on problems it could not solve by carefully planning its agendas. "Jan [Christiansen] meets with the chairman before each meeting to plan the agenda," she said. "That keeps issues from coming up that we can't handle." She is convinced the SCG would flounder without the PF. "The PF has to be here for the SCG to survive. We'd be very dependent on the school leaders if she wasn't here."

## The View From Bluff

All you would have to change to make Bluff a movie set for a nineteenth-century western are the Coca Cola signs. This small community on the edge of the reservation and the San Juan River has the most Indian school in the district—5 whites out of 104 elementary students. It serves a very traditional Navajo population that until ten years ago had no bridge to San Juan. One enterprising parent ferries students across the river to school in a basket.

Bluff has no SCG, but it reportedly has plenty of problems with Anglo-Indian relations. (An SCG is planned for next year.) It was here that we met district superintendent Dr. Donald Jack and assistant Mel Walker, who were visiting Bluff Elementary School. Jack quickly answered the question of why San Juan County was interested in the RFD. "We are looking for something to pull our county together. You've seen the distances and the cultural differences. We knew we couldn't make it without new ways of doing business. We had reached the point . . . where we saw that we had to have programs that had credibility from one end of the county to another."

As the central office sees it, the only times the process does not work well "is when the group is not being led properly. Once in a while a facilitator gets out of his role—rather than helping people understand the problems, the facilitator becomes a leader. If the facilitator is out front, the people become less involved." Walker says that communication with the community is much better as a result of the RFD. "It used to be after a board meeting all we had done was to air the complaint. Now there is a process."

## The View From the Lab

In a final evaluation report submitted to the National Institute of Education in December 1976, the Northwest Lab reported on a survey of the program's impact. It found that 80 percent of the Navajos surveyed thought the SCG had increased community participation in education. Sixty-five percent of the Anglo community people surveyed knew little or nothing of the program. Twenty-six percent of the school staff responding knew little or nothing of the program. On the whole, however, two-thirds of the respondents interviewed thought the program had improved educational decision making in their community. Originally, the Lab had hoped to evaluate the San Juan experience in light of "unanticipated consequences of strategy implementation." It abandoned that plan after "it became more and more difficult to determine which were and which were not anticipated outcomes. This was due, in part, to such factors as the incomplete installation of the strategy and the political and cultural idiosyncrasies of this site."[5]

The Lab also recommended that the various relationships between the education agencies be more clearly defined, that PFs be better trained on their role, that all PFs receive the same salary and training, that the school board be better informed as to what was planned, and that the NWREL staff members make certain they refrained "from becoming involved in promoting their own solutions to onsite problems."[6]

## Some Observations and Conclusions:

It is clear that the San Juan County School District provided an atypical site for the NWREL's pilot effort of RFD. One could argue that if the process could work in a situation as difficult as San Juan, it would work anywhere. On the other hand, one might conclude that unless a district is faced with a crisis as severe as the one in San Juan, there is little likelihood that a school system will spend the extra dollars needed for process facilitators and their training or voluntarily give up some of the decision-making process to the broader school community. The study team's site visit approximately five years after the strategy was initiated and three years after NWREL ended its active involvement provides some clues to this issue.

First, it is clear that RFD was useful in San Juan. Through the SCGs and the broad participation of the Navajo people, the school board responded to the demand for schools in the southern end of the district. The SCGs were also a mobilizing force to get the bond issue approved; the schools are now a reality. The SCGs in other parts of the district, Blanding and Monticello, were responsible for involving more of the community in the discussion and the making of recommendations on important educational issues. Whether or not the Navajos would have achieved as desirable a solution through legal action or a neutral conflict management referee at less cost to the district will never be known. Those involved in the project say no, although they readily admit that if the multimillion-dollar development costs of RFD were considered the cost of the San Juan settlement would be high indeed.

It is also clear from our visit that with the resolution of the legal issues and the ending of the Lab's involvement, the level of RFD activity declined. Part of this was due to the fact that with no outside resources one full-time PF and one half-time PF were trying to maintain all of the SCGs in the county, where previously there had been four PFs for only two SCGs. There was also evidence that with no outside Lab force to maintain their neutrality, and with the PFs now being paid by the district, the SCGs had tilted toward being an arm of the school district.

Further clues to the viability of RFD as a rural education strategy can be found by looking at its use and impact beyond the San Juan setting. The involvement of the state department of education was a part of the San Juan pilot and indeed the concept of broader community participation in educational decision making has emerged as an important priority for Utah. The education code now flatly states: "Funds expended for community education shall be used to support the concept that the schools belong to the people and to find ways to engage the community in determining the role the schools shall play in solving individual and community problems." The RFD process is held up as one way to get this community involvement. Yet, when NWREL initiated the RFD process in a number of communities in Washington, none was successful in making the formal process an ongoing part of the district program. Some aspects of RFD have also been used by districts in southwest Minnesota to meet state-mandated planning requirements, but, again, the activities were temporary in nature.

RFD, although attractive in theory and even useful in unique conflict situations such as San Juan's, appears to have a number of basic design flaws. To be effective, it needs skilled, *neutral* process facilitators. Unfortunately, neutral funding agencies are not readily available, so the PF tends to be either a public relations person for the district or a community organizer. Without a neutral PF, conditions for maintaining a broad-based, rational problem-solving process are simply not present in most communities. A second major flaw relates to RFD's tendency to "package" process. There are some general guidlines critical to group process, but each setting is sufficiently different to require some reinventing of the wheel.

Finally, institutionalizing broad-based participation in educational decision making seems unlikely. Such participation takes time, on the part of
both the institution and the community. Neither side is inclined to invest
that kind of time unless there is a hot issue. Conflict around rural school
systems is not unusual, and because of the personal nature of small communities, these conflicts can become both unpleasant and damaging.
Although total RFD design, as conceived by NWREL, is not likely to find
wide acceptance, access to some kind of RFD process could be useful in
resolving these problems.

## Notes

1. Keats Garman and Donald Jack, "Local Control and Self-Determination: The
San Juan Case," paper presented at the Rural Conversations Conference, College
Park, Maryland, May 29–31, 1979.

2. *RFD Journal for School-Community Process Facilitators* (Portland, Ore.:
Northwest Regional Educational Laboratory, 1975).

3. *RFD Manual for School-Community Process Facilitators* (Portland, Ore.:
Northwest Regional Educational Laboratory, 1975).

4. *San Juan Record*, September 19, 1974.

5. Joan L. Goforth, *Final Evaluation Report Site A* (Portland, Ore.: Northwest
Regional Educational Laboratory, 1976).

6. Ibid., p. 19.

# 11

# The Leadership Development Program: Facilitating New Leadership for Rural Education

*Paul Nachtigal*

The story of the Leadership Development Program (LDP) is a story about people: 700 individuals from rural America who were singled out as having the potential to provide a new cadre of leadership for rural education. It is also the story of a small number of Ford Foundation personnel who evolved a program of fellowships that would serve as an alternative to the academic schooling approach to leadership development.

Dean Bennett, a 32-year-old native of Yarmouth, Maine, was one of the first of the 700 to be selected for an LDP fellowship, which provided a salary equivalent and expenses to pursue a year's program that had been specifically designed for him. Bennett was an industrial arts teacher in Yarmouth Junior-Senior High School. Before entering the field of teaching he had been a journeyman cabinet maker. In his teaching, he wanted to bring the two worlds of industry and conservation together. Bennett's fellowship would allow him to develop a curriculum that would "make conservation and its problems a real and powerful concern for each student to the extent that he will be stirred to take positive action in the wise use and management of our natural resources, including the human resource."

Bennett's year of study and travel included time at a conservation school at Bryant Pond under the auspices of the University of Maine. He studied at the University of Michigan with noted conservation authority William B. Stapp and in Aspen, Colorado, where he shared ideas with Robert Lewis, a former teacher and consultant on outdoor education. Bennett returned to Yarmouth to establish a regional environmental education program serving the schools of Yarmouth, Falmouth, North Yarmouth, Cumberland, and Freeport. Later, Bennett was to become director of the Natural Resources Council of Maine, where he helped establish six additional pilot programs in other high schools around the state.

171

## In The Beginning

The genesis of LDP lies largely with Edward Meade, Jr., a program officer with the Ford Foundation who had been responsible for the Comprehensive School Improvement Program, a series of grants to institutions for the purpose of implementing the curriculum reforms of the 1950s and 1960s, which tested new organizational patterns for schools and the instructional use of the latest technology. One lesson that emerged from this program was that projects with good leadership went well; where the leadership was lacking, results were disappointing. A second lesson was that although the grants to institutions did not always result in the desired institutional changes, the processes inherent in these school improvement programs—e.g., the chance to travel, to observe innovative programs, to work with experts in the field, to escape day-to-day routine, to think about new educational practices —were useful in the development of educational leadership.

As the foundation turned its attention to the problems of rural education in the 1960s, there were good reasons to focus on the leadership issue. An abundance of federal dollars was available from the Great Society programs to support school improvement efforts. What was lacking was the creative leadership to put those dollars to good use. The urban migration of the fifties and sixties had siphoned off much of the younger rural population from which future leadership could emerge. If the foundation could create a program for identifying individuals with leadership potential, and then through a program of fellowships provide the experiences that develop leadership qualities, a real contribution could be made to rural education.

In conceptualizing such a program, Meade likened it to "the baseball scout who goes around to these little towns looking for the left-handed pitcher, the fast baller, the kid with that little spark of something extra. We are looking for the left-handed pitcher, the potential leader who still lack[s] the tools of leadership. We could help him get the tools." With little more than this concept to give the program a focus, the LDP began operations in the Northeast, serving Maine, New Hampshire, Vermont, and New Brunswick, and the Deep South, including Alabama, Georgia, Mississippi, and South Carolina. Regional representatives—LDP "scouts"—were hired to search out potential leaders with "something extra" and to help develop a program of activities that would give them the "tools of leadership." After a year's operation, the program's aims and activities had been refined sufficiently to appear in a Ford Foundation brochure as follows:

> Men and women selected have already demonstrated to some extent leadership qualities in their local school or community. The program is not for those already in positions of recognized authority. The program is expected to

enhance this leadership potential with the hope that Fellows will contribute more effectively to the improvement of the rural areas and small towns where they work. The fellowship helps to broaden personal and professional outlook through exposure to different people and programs in many settings. Consequently, usually Fellows undertake little if any formal academic study.

Once selected, Fellows receive support for periods up to 12 months. Programs are planned to open new insights and to foster personal growth by combining activities such as apprenticeships, travel, visits to model projects, and writing. Generally the program will not support extensive work toward the advanced degree or extended travel. Other public and private grants are available for those purposes.[1]

The Southeast was tailor-made for the program. The rural South, with a high percentage of low-income blacks, had for years seen its young people migrate to northern urban centers for employment. The civil rights movement was now at its peak, and the region was finally beginning to shake off the constraints of segregation. New leadership was needed at the local level to keep pressure on education agencies to comply with desegregation guidelines and to test the nation's commitment to racial equality. The rationale for establishing the Northeast region was not quite as obvious. It was a definable region, rural, and, according to members of the foundation's board of trustees who summered there, had its share of poor.

Rufus Huffman, an early Southeast fellow, was a teacher in Union Springs, Bullock County, Alabama. Huffman, 40 years old, had a broad agenda for his LDP year. As a sixth-grade teacher, he wanted to find ways to liven up the curriculum to keep kids interested in learning. Knowing how to present his ideas visually would help. He also wanted to know more about the desegregation process in the public schools: where the forces were to make it happen and what to do in school when it did. Huffman was not only a teacher, he was also becoming a political force in the black community of Bullock County. He had stood for tax assessor the year before, an unheard-of move in Alabama and one that angered the white minority. He was, of course, not successful; the Voting Rights Act of 1965 had little impact by the spring of 1966.

Huffman's year of training included a visit to an innovative education institute where he learned to build his own teaching aids. It also included time with the Bedford-Stuyvesant Legal Defense Fund, where blacks faced problems similar to those in the South, but in a very different setting. At the heart of his program were the five months spent with Dan Dodson, then chairman of New York University's Human Relations Department and a leading national consultant on school desegregation. As an intern, Huffman accompanied Dodson to conferences across the country wherever desegregation issues had reached the boiling point.

At the end of his LDP year Huffman's school did not want him back. The confrontation techniques learned in the North were not welcome in Alabama, but Huffman faced down the superintendent and forced his way back into his sixth-grade classroom. In the end, the battle was primarily symbolic: six weeks later the Office of Economic Opportunity overrode Governor Lurleen Wallace's veto of a twelve-county social agency that Huffman had been instrumental in proposing. He left teaching to work for the agency. Fourteen months later, the NAACP asked Huffman to become education director for the Southeast region. Ten years later he ran for county judge of Bullock County and won easily. Ironically, he was now in a position to control much of what happened in a school system that earlier did not want him back.

The LDP was designed to reflect local regional needs. As there was little formal structure to the program, particularly at the beginning, it reflected the strength and interests of the regional representative. It was the rep who conceptualized, however vaguely, the problems of rural education in the region and how leadership might be developed to address those problems. The rep was responsible for establishing a selection committee and a selection process. And although committee members spoke their own minds, they were appointed by the rep and therefore tended to see the world of rural education in a similar way. The rep was primarily responsible for recruiting applicants. In consultation with the fellow and others, the rep was also responsible for developing the individual programs and determining to a large extent where the fellows traveled, who they worked with, and what ideas they were exposed to.

To initiate the program in the Northeast, the foundation, using established contacts, hired Peter Briggs, then director of freshman admissions for Harvard University. Thirty-three-year-old Briggs had grown up around Boston and his great grandfather had been governor of Maine; he was an establishment New Englander. Bringing the aura of Harvard with him, Briggs was welcomed by the education establishment. He interpreted his role with LDP as "finding people with a good idea and with a good reason for taking a year off [from school], and a feeling that that reason would benefit the school."[2]

Briggs spread the word about LDP through the schools of education, state departments, district superintendents' offices. More than 250 applicants vied for the twenty available fellowships; only 18 were selected that first year. (Many were overqualified: they held advanced degrees or their interests were too limited to be of potential benefit to the school community.) Selecting the fellows was one thing; developing a program for each one was quite another. Being familiar primarily with the world of academia was not much help in developing "nonacademic" programs, so Briggs turned to the foundation for assistance. Using the cumulative experience of foundation officers, each fellow's year was pieced together and the LDP was under way.

Lois Jones, an English teacher in Winthrop, Maine, was typical of the Northeast fellows. She was interested in finding ways to individualize and humanize instruction. Her LDP year included a National Training Laboratory (NTL) workshop at Bethel, Maine; a Gestalt workshop at Esalen Institute; work with Carl Rogers and William Glaser in California. Although the LDP was not designed to support graduate work, Lois took graduate courses at the University of Massachusetts, starting a master's program in humanistic education. She returned to Maine after her fellowship, finished her doctorate, and is now the ESEA Title IV-C consultant for the state department of education.

Briggs didn't stay with the program for much longer than a year. He left to pursue a longtime dream of being headmaster of a private school and was replaced by Paul Judkins, a native of Maine, who had also done time at Harvard and was currently business manager of the University of Maine in Farmington. The change of leadership brought few real changes to the program. The rural education problems of the Northeast were perceived to be well within the purview of the schools to address. Schools needed to become relevant to a wider range of students. With better leadership, this could happen.

Although the Southeast region began at the same time with the same general guidelines, it very quickly took a different turn. In the Northeast the schools were seen to hold the solution to better education, but in the South the segregated school system was a large part of the problem. If education was to be improved, longstanding traditions had to be broken. To initiate LDP in the Southeast, the foundation selected Dorothy Hassfeld as regional rep. She was 30 years old, Anglo, originally from Toledo, Ohio, and was recently back from a Peace Corps assignment in Nigeria. At the time of selection, she was working on an internship at Alabama A&M, a black college at Huntsville. Hassfeld, highly committed to the cause of social and racial equality, had been recommended by Ben Gibson, vice-president of the College Entrance Examination Board. When first contacted about the program, she thought she was being offered a fellowship and was surprised when they asked her to run the program.

Although she was in general agreement with the purpose of LDP, Hassfeld left after a year, largely out of frustration with the loose guidelines and operating procedures that required continual negotiations with New York on what could and could not be included in the fellowship. She felt the psychological distance between the problems facing local black educators and the demands of the eastern establishment was too great. As a replacement, the foundation hired K. Z. Chavis, a charismatic black educator who had been a teacher, a principal, and a staff member of a foundation-funded innovative education program in North Carolina.

Chavis was considered for the job in the beginning, but there were questions about a black activist being accepted by the white superintendents. The fact that a little over a year later he was appointed to the position was due both to the rapid changes resulting from the civil rights movement and to a better understanding on the part of the foundation that the rural education problems of the Southeast were of a different order than those of the Northeast. Establishment educators were not the important actors in a suitable strategy for the South. Chavis, with his background, his intuitive political sense, and the fact that he was black, gave a needed legitimacy to the program. Through the next eight-plus years, he orchestrated the individual grants program into a regional leadership effort, bringing fellows together in semi-annual workshops and creative program planning that placed new fellows with old. As in the Northeast, the personnel change appeared to strengthen the capability of the program to pursue the directions established by the original regional reps.

Soon after the Southeast and Northeast programs were in operation, an organizational change in the foundation resulted in Ed Meade's assuming additional responsibilities as head of the newly formed Office of Public Education. It was clear that an additional staff person was needed in New York to manage and give further guidance to the fledgling LDP. Ralph Bohrson, who had formerly directed the Western States Small Schools Project (Ford Foundation funded) and later monitored the foundation's Comprehensive School Improvement Program, moved to New York to take the assignment with the provision that he could add another region in the Southwest to serve rural Mexican American and Indian populations. This was agreeable to the foundation; they had from the start wanted to add regions across the country.

A careful search by Bohrson resulted in his naming David Grant, a Chicano, to head up the third component of LDP. Grant had been a teacher and junior high principal in Santa Fe, attended Columbia University to work on a doctorate, and was working in the newly created Regional Educational Laboratory in Albuquerque when the LDP offer came along.

Geography and cultural differences found in the Southwest contributed to a greater diversity of rural education problems than was found in the other two regions. Ideological differences existed in some areas between the old-line Hispanos and the young activist Chicanos. Along the lower Rio Grande Valley, Chicanos were challenging the Anglo power structure. The Indians had their own unique problems with the Bureau of Indian Affairs (BIA). With new LDP leadership, however, the institutions could be made to operate more effectively, particularly if one could tap the abundance of federal dollars being made available for migrant education, bilingual programs, and Indian education.

In opening the Southwest region, Grant also turned to the established education networks to seek applicants, advertising the program in local school systems, colleges, and universities and through the BIA. His initial round of fellows tended to be teachers and principals and, much to the foundation's dismay, largely Anglos.

One exception was 26-year-old Jesse Santana of Douglas, Arizona. Douglas is a border town; it is also a company town. The Phelps Dodge Copper Mine provides the majority of the jobs for the town's residents (75 percent of whom are Mexican American). The mine also provides all of the town's pollution: The tall stacks of the smelting operation lay a grimy pall over the shabby housing twenty-four hours a day. Santana, a Douglas native, returned after a two-year hitch in Vietnam to teach fourth grade and then fifth grade in the Douglas public schools. He was the bilingual educa tion coordinator for the elementary school when selected for an LDP fellowship. His goals for the year were "to find out how minority groups throughout the Southwest and elsewhere are being helped through educational means [and] to get as many federal programs in the school system as possible to help the Mexican American and Anglo children of Douglas."

Santana's program included a stay in Washington, D.C., to learn where the federal dollars were and how to get them to the local community; a trip to San Francisco to work with the Mexican American Legal Defense and Education Fund; and time with two regional community-action–oriented agencies, the Southwest Council of La Raza and the Home Education and Livelihood Program. His program, with minor modifications, was the same one that most Southwest fellows experienced. Dubbed the "chile circuit" by New York, this itinerary was the source of an ongoing disagreement between the foundation and the regional office New York maintained that LDP, because it was an individual grants program, should tailor the fellowship year to each individual's needs. Grant argued that the series of activities, with a few modifications from time to time, was useful for all fellows and therefore the region. And, by cycling fellows through the same agencies, a full-time slot could be created by the various agencies and filled by fellows, providing them with a real working/learning experience. This battle over programming continued until the end; Grant persevered on the basis that he, better than New York, knew what was best for the Southwest.

With the program operating in three regions, program planners began to think of other regions that should be added; Appalachia and Puerto Rico were two under consideration. Discussions for geographical expansion were accompanied by a desire to expand the clientele served by the program. There was a growing concern among those running the Leadership Development Program that the practice of selecting only educators (primarily teachers, as principals and superintendents were already considered leaders) might not be the most effective way to improve rural education. The experience of past fellows suggested that teachers, no matter how well prepared or how innovative, could have only limited impact on the school beyond their classroom and virtually no impact on the community.

The original proposal for the Leadership Development Program had called for "a program to identify and develop individuals—*teachers and public servants*—who will accept leadership tasks during the next quarter century [emphasis added]." Because schools were a reflection of local communities, the development of new community/policy-level leadership might be a more effective way to bring about improvement in rural education.

Plans for expanding the operation of LDP to additional regions were tempered by the deteriorating economy, which severely reduced the foundation's funding capacity. As a compromise, one more region was established, a region-at-large, which was to serve sections of the country not included in the three established programs. In many ways, this was a token program with only half of the quota of twenty fellowships allotted each of the other regions, even though the territory, thirty-two contiguous states plus Alaska, was many times larger than any one of the other three. The region-at-large did, however, serve two important functions in the larger scheme of things: (1) the foundation could not now be accused of discriminating against some sections of the country; and (2) the region-at-large project was to be more experimental, testing the LDP concept with individuals not part of the formal education structure.

To run the region-at-large, Bohrson turned to Paul Nachtigal, with whom he had worked in early rural education improvement programs in Colorado. Nachtigal was currently working half-time as a consultant to the foundation. He was already somewhat familiar with foundation procedures, and his travel in connection with his school improvement consultant capacity could dovetail with LDP activities. The region-at-large could be in business with relatively little difficulty with Nachtigal working out of an already established office in Denver.

In order to make the most effective use of the limited number of fellowships, Nachtigal targeted areas of the country that seemed most in need of a leadership program. The Appalachian region was clearly one target area, the southern border states not covered by the Southeast region was another, and states containing Indian reservations or large Native American populations was a third. Most of the fellows in the region-at-large eventually came from Appalachia, Indian communities of the Midwest and Northwest, and the native villages of Alaska.

The Appalachian region was made to order for testing whether or not LDP would be useful for developing community leadership, which in turn might be a constructive force for improving rural education. School systems in the coal fields tended to be so politically controlled that an LDP fellow selected from within the system for the purpose of changing that system was sure to lose his or her job. This realization led to identifying individuals outside the education field, such as Edith Easterling of Poor Bottom, Kentucky, as the target group. Easterling, a natural community leader, had started Marrowbone Folk School, a small cinderblock building in Poor Bottom Hollow in eastern Kentucky. Here, community people would gather around the potbellied coal stove to talk about their problems and socialize. Applying for Social Security benefits and securing welfare assistance or disability payments were topics of discussion, along with the problem of getting and keeping the children in school, which was located at the mouth of the hollow. Because of their dress and hillbilly speech, the back-hollow children felt uncomfortable at school and dropped out. In some cases, poor children eligible for free lunches were made to sit on the stage to eat while the rest were seated on the gym floor. ("It's easier to account for free and paid lunches," parents were told.) Easterling would discuss such problems with the parents, who would then gain the courage to go to the school and demand that their children be treated like the others.

Easterling's fellowship year allowed her to observe the work of organizers such as Cesar Chavez of the United Farm Workers in California and Connie Harper, a former LDP fellow from Alabama who had established a Headstart and job-training program for the rural communities around Montgomery. Easterling also spent time with a community college that was supposed to have a strong community outreach, but she found she knew more about relating to communities than they did and ended up helping them with their program.

## A Decade of Refinement

The ten-year life of the Leadership Development Program, with the exception of the region-at-large, took on a cyclical nature. Selections were made around the first of the year so applicants who were teachers could arrange for leave or inform their superintendents that they would not be returning for the following school term. Program development took place through the spring; fellows started their program year in the summer so they would finish in time to cycle back into the academic year. The region-at-large was never bound by these constraints because only a few of its fellows came from the ranks of the education profession.

The fellowship programs that were meant to be individually tailored to the particular needs of the fellow and his or her local community were not always unique. Once a program had been designed for the year, however, each fellow was remarkably free to pursue it in his or her own fashion, with modifications being easy to make. One of the more powerful learning experiences of the program may have been this freedom. In effect, the fellows could make as much or as little of the programs as they wished; they made their own mistakes and had to live with them. And although some misused this freedom, wasting time and money, most took the responsibility seriously; in fact, many fellows perhaps took it too seriously, feeling guilty if they did not put in a "full day's work," often missing the opportunity to see the sights and experience a culture in a part of the country to which they might never return.

Each new crop of fellows initiated discussions of whether or not LDP was tapping the right strata of potential leadership. This discussion invariably took two directions. First, were people being selected who were overqualified, that is, already leaders due to position or academic training and therefore not in need of the fellowship? Second, had we reached far enough down into the high-risk category, identifying individuals who had that certain spark but who without the program would definitely not have the opportunity to develop their potential? The questions were never fully resolved partly because there was never clear agreement on how to define leadership. What was clear was that as more fellows were selected from the fringe of the socioeconomic mainstream, the problems of operating the program increased. Certain program activities—extensive travel, budgeting program expense money over a three-month period, making one's way into establishment organizations to learn and observe, filling out the proper quarterly reports—were foreign to some of these people. Without more personal assistance than LDP was prepared to offer, the project was of little use to some fellows and perhaps even detrimental to others.

Nachtigal argued that if the program was to improve education in poor minority communities, it was necessary to develop a new cadre of leadership within that population. To do so, however, would have required a major restructuring of the program. There was little support from other regional reps for such a move. Those changes would have to wait until the LDP itself had runs its course (at which time many of the changes were incorporated in one of its spinoffs, the Southern Appalachian Leadership Training Program).

In the later years, more fellows were selected from the ranks of community leaders, although they remained a minority. The Northeast did recognize the existence of an Indian population, a number of whom were selected for the program. The Southeast, although remaining a majority black program, included a good percentage of whites. The Southwest did indeed select more and more Hispanos, Indians, and blacks. The region-at-large selected fewer of the very high-risk individuals toward the end.

Ralph Bohrson urged that LDP become an ongoing commitment of the foundation. But the foundation saw its role as experimenting with a new approach to leadership development, which it had done for ten years; it was now time to move on to other priorities. The Northeast region was the first to go. The regional representative was kept on for a time to tie up the loose ends with past fellows and explore other funding sources, but the existing model that called for $15,000 per fellowship was too expensive for local funding sources and the program ceased to exist.

The foundation's strategy with the other two regions was a bit different. The first step was to find a regional agency to administer the program while the foundation continued to provide funding on the assumption that once the program was regionally established, financial support might be easier to come by. The Southeast region was spun off to the Southern Regional Council in Atlanta; the Southwest region went to a regional office of the Washington-based Center for Community Change. But here too, the cost of the programs was such that when Ford Foundation dollars were gone, the programs closed.

Still another strategy was tried with the region-at-large. Two continuing efforts were funded: an Indian Training Program operated by the National Indian Training and Research Center in Tempe, Arizona, and the Southern Appalachian Leadership Training Program in Appalachia. Both modified the model to better fit the population to be served, and in the process reduced the costs, enabling the program to attract other funding.

## Impact of the Leadership Development Program

What did the Ford Foundation get for its $10 million investment? Did the program develop leaders who then improved rural education? No systematic follow-up study has been conducted that can fully answer these questions. There is, however, some evidence to suggest that it was a good investment. Dr. Douglas Derrer, hired by the foundation to take a critical look at the program after four years of operation, concluded:

> The program generally has two main effects on Fellows: awareness and self-confidence. Both increase. Fellows learn more about the world outside their small, rural communities, which some of them have never left throughout their lives save for a tour with the military. They see the national government, they talk to and work with famous statesmen, educators, scientists and the like. They travel over this country, Canada and abroad. They see schools, projects, programs, poverty, and degradation, wealth and opulence that they never knew existed. For many of them it is a fairytale, dreamlike experience. And they begin to blossom, to open up, to change.
>
> The Fellows seem to awaken to two things about the same time; the complexity of the problems with which they are concerned (poverty, education, discrimination, community organization, etc.) and that they have some of what it takes (confidence, esteem, people skills, intelligence) to cope with these difficulties. Some become discouraged by what they see or by the seeming im-

possibility to achieve change at home. However, most become more committed and more confident that they can make a dent in these difficulties; these
also have usually learned some patience.[3]

Finally, his report states that the LDP provides the opportunity for fellows
to take a measure of themselves and compare this measure with the people
they meet. To find they are not wanting, that they do all right with the big
names of the city is "a powerfully reassuring realization."

A more recent documentation of the program by David Nevin, who spent
the better part of two years tracking down past fellows, relates both successes and failures but concludes on balance that LDP made a difference,
both to those who were fellows and the communities and regions from
which they came. "In the end [LDP's] success is in the quality of the individual experience and the use which individual fellows make of it," Nevin
stated. "I think the LDP succeeded in that it has left behind some seven hundred men and women who are better equipped to deal intelligently and
generously with their society, whose ideas and information range are expanded, whose personal perceptions are broadened and enriched."[4]

In spite of this assessment, the foundation is an institution and concerned
ultimately with institutional change. The question of whether or not LDP
had any institutional impact, particularly on rural schools, was always implied, if not openly asked. Nevin addressed this question by saying, "And
no matter how high the program impact on the individual, the force he
brings to the institution still is largely his own fiber and intellect and
courage. But within these limitations, it seems to me that there was considerable effect on schools and other institutions. . . . Many fellows became
principals, assistant superintendent and superintendent of schools. Some no
doubt were helped by the program's conferring effect, some were motivated
to struggle for positions to which they might not otherwise have aspired,
some received training through the LDP that made them natural candidates;
certainly all the fellows who achieved such positions applied concepts they
had encountered in the program and ran their offices with the broadened
consciousness that followed the program experiences."[5]

In addition to becoming school administrators, a surprising number of
fellows found their way into elected offices, as mayors, county judges,
county commissioners, and school board members. Others became tribal
leaders, noted authors, state education agency officials, a leading spokesman for rural education, and an investigative reporter who has influenced
the operating policies of the Tennessee Valley Authority. One could never
establish a cause-and-effect relationship between LDP and these leadership
positions, but the number of fellows achieving leadership positions in a
short time is impressive.

Although on balance the LDP as a foundation effort was considered a good investment (the Ford Foundation generally considers its programs to be high risk), the results were not all positive, and the program was not without its problems. There were fellows who remained relatively unchanged, going back to their old jobs and settling in with little indication that the program had made any difference. And there were those for whom the program appeared to cause problems, or at least exacerbate problems that were already there. The LDP year was a powerful experience and, as Derrer indicated, was responsible for some dramatic personal change. In cases where one member of the family experienced such change and the other did not, marriages were strained and in some cases dissolved. Even in cases in which the family accompanied the fellow, the disruption of moving, taking care of small children by either spouse in strange cities while the fellow was elsewhere, engaged in exciting new experiences, did little for furthering family relationships.

The target for LDP was to be the depressed and submerged groups of society, specifically "Negroes, poor whites, Mexican Americans and Indians." The program did tap a new population for a fellowship program, reaching both those who did not have the advanced formal education usually required by such programs and those from a lower socioeconomic level than is generally represented. Most of those who met with success in LDP, however, had been socialized into the American mainstream, had the ability to prepare a credible application, had some notions of how to budget time and money, and knew how to find their way to other parts of the country and the people with whom they were to work. Filing quarterly financial and narrative reports was within their capability. The fellows who made the most of LDP were employed before the fellowship and were therefore receiving a regular salary that could be matched by LDP, and they had personal agendas that fit the larger social structure; i.e., there were job slots and leadership positions to which they could aspire after the program.

When LDP selected individuals outside the mainstream, problems with the program increased. Assistance was needed to prepare an application that would adequately represent their case. If they were on welfare or employed seasonally or less than full-time, a salary equivalent was difficult to determine (at least one fellow could take no reimbursement without jeopardizing his disability status). These individuals could not survive on their usual income if they were to live elsewhere. The general guideline of establishing a fellow's salary equivalent was defensible as long as all of the fellows came from basically the same socioeconomic group. When efforts were made to include a more depressed segment the result was to keep the "poor" poor and the "rich" rich. And if the program had given a person $8,000 a year during the fellowship when he had made $4,000 the year before, there was the problem of what this would do to his expectations and his ability to go back and live in his home community after the LDP.

In the final analysis, LDP was designed to equip people to work better within the system on the assumption that by doing so, the operation of the system would improve. For those who had learned to cope with the American mainstream and for whom the system was open, these assumptions held true. Such was the case in the Northeast and, as a result of the civil rights movement, in the Southeast and the Southwest as well. However, for those who had not gained access to the system or for those to whom the system was not responsive, as was the case in Appalachia and on certain Indian reservations, LDP was severely limited.

### Notes

1. David Nevin, "Left-Handed Fastballers: Scouting and Training America's Grass-Roots Leaders" (August 1981), report to the Ford Foundation.

2. David Nevin, "In Search of the Left-Handed Fastballer" (Washington, D.C.: 1978), report to the Ford Foundation.

3. Douglas S. Derrer, "Educational Leadership In Rural America: A Review and Analysis of the First Year of Research and Study of the Leadership Development Program" (San Francisco, Calif.: 1972), report to the Ford Foundation.

4. Nevin, "In Search of the Left-Handed Fastballer."

5. Ibid.

# 12
# "Have You Considered Reorganization?" Iowa's People United for Rural Education

*Faith Dunne*

Alden, Iowa (population 879), seems an unlikely spot for the head-quarters of a protest movement. The three-street farm town is dominated by the towering bulk of the Alden Co-op Elevator and anchored by its pleasant, rather nondescript school. The corn fields begin at the edge of town and stretch as far as the eye can see, stopping only reluctantly at the clusters of hand-planted trees that mark the farm dwellings. In north-central Iowa, life is focused on the land. The houses, mostly in simple frame structures, are dwarfed by the shining metal grain storage sheds and the tall brick silos flanking the barns. And this is as it should be: North Central is one of the richest food-producing regions in the United States, and Alden's land is bountifully productive, even for North Central.

The Alden community is affluent, close knit, conservative, and stable. A core group of long-time residents, mostly farmers and local business owners, run school and community affairs, generally with the support of a more transient group of Ralston-Purina employees and others who work in nearby Iowa Falls, a town of 6,500 people. Alden is a typical North Central town: prosperous, somnolent, and emblematic of the virtues and limitations of Middle America. It is also the political center of a growing conflict involving farmers and school superintendents, statisticians and small-town merchants, the Iowa Department of Public Instruction and legislators from places as diverse as suburban West Des Moines and North Central's Steamboat Rock.

The conflict is about schools. Iowa has 443 school districts, the fourteenth highest number in the nation. The 181 smallest districts, which run K–12 programs with fewer than 600 pupils, are all rural, all closely identified with the small communities they serve, and all embattled. The Department of Public Instruction (DPI) questions whether these schools should continue to exist, particularly in a period of sharply declining enrollments and tightening money. Small schools cost more, DPI officials say, and deliver less in the way of program diversity, teacher quality, and adequate facilities. Further, they argue, there is no rational impediment to consolidation in Iowa: The state is culturally homogeneous; the terrain, especially in North Central, is virtually flat; and the towns are relatively close together. Pupils could readily be bused to a central location or to an already existing facility in a nearby larger town. Iowa Falls, for example, has suffered from declining enrollments, too; they could easily absorb the 470 children in the Alden school district.

Unfortunately, this does not appeal to the citizens and parents of Alden's school children, nor to the residents of more than 200 other Iowa school districts. Alden wants its children in Alden, not in Iowa Falls "where nobody knows them." Many rural community leaders argue that the small rural school offers more, not less, of the things they feel are important: community interaction, adequate supervision, basic skills training. The "big guns," however, are all on the side of the DPI. They have the statistics, the professional expertise, and the power of legislators who sit on the Senate Education Committee and the School Budget Review Committee. But the local community people feel that they have their children at stake and are willing to fight, like any guerrilla force, with whatever weapons they can muster. The battle lines are clearly drawn.

Alden is at the center of this war largely because Janet Kinney lives there. Kinney is a tall, open-faced, ebullient woman whose giant spectacles and tousled head of blonde curls belie her extraordinary organizational powers. She is the secretary of People United for Rural Education (PURE), a grassroots political organization that claims to represent the interests of the rural school districts against the power of the DPI. The central offices of PURE are in Kinney's house where, armed with an IBM typewriter and a Xerox machine (paid for out of PURE dues) and a desk overflowing with papers, DPI documents, House Files from the current legislative session, and newsletter page proofs, Kinney manages this remarkably complex four-year-old organization.

PURE now has thirty-two local chapters and 2,755 members. At the heart of the organization are Kinney; Joyce Losure, the organization's president and chief spokeswoman; and James Jess, superintendent of the small, rich CAL Community School District serving the towns of Coulter, Alexander, and Latimer. These three have been the prime movers of PURE since its inception, and it is difficult to imagine the group achieving what it has without their combined talents and efforts.

## PURE History

How did two farm women and a school superintendent launch a nationally known small-schools organization? Former State Senator Earl Willits, a long-time opponent of small schools, claims—only half in jest—that it is because of him. In January 1977, Willits introduced a bill in the Iowa legislature to mandate the reorganization of districts with fewer than 300 pupils, K–12. This was the first step in a DPI plan to consolidate Iowa's schools into districts with 1,000 or more students, in keeping with the recommendations of the Iowa-based Great Plains School Organization Study, which concluded that the 1,000-pupil district was the smallest efficient and adequate educational unit. Public hearings were scheduled for February 1977, and the bill, if all went well, would be brought out of committee during the spring legislative session.

The hearing on the Willits bill drew a range of opponents to consolidation. Losure, vice-chair of her county chapter of Farm Bureau Women, felt that she had both an official role and a clear obligation to express her disapproval of school closings. In addition, she felt a personal commitment to carrying on anticonsolidation work of her good friend, Judy Greiner, who had died suddenly just before the initial hearing on the Willits bill. Kinney, who was secretary of her local Parent-Teacher Organization, had been interested for some time in the potential of rural schooling. She was a product of Iowa's rural schools and had spent a considerable amount of time informally investigating the use of essentially rural classroom techniques (such as peer tutoring and cross-age grouping) in the most "advanced" suburban classrooms. "I wanted to find out how you get better quality education without busing the kids all around," she recalls. The prospect of reorganizing Iowa's small schools into 1,000-pupil districts violated her most basic educational values. She decided that she had to take action on the Willits bill, on behalf of her own children and in support of what she saw as an endangered way of life.

Jess had a professional as well as personal stake in the Willits bill. The three communities that make up the CAL district were passionately committed to remaining a rural school system; a 1975 poll had found 96 percent of the voters rejecting the concept of consolidation with a larger town. Further, the district was quite ready to raise the tax money to support its school. In 1975, 350 residents of the district had traveled in busloads to Des Moines to back Jess's request of the legislature that CAL be allowed to raise more money in local taxes than the state law allowed. "We won," Jess remembers. "The legislature was overwhelmed by 350 people from one community filling the galleries, demanding to be allowed to spend more of their own money."

That victory encouraged Jess to pack up 150 local citizens to go to the Willits hearing, where more than 1,000 small-schools supporters gathered to oppose legislated consolidation. Jess testified at the hearing, offering data from his doctoral thesis suggesting that small schools got better support from their communities than large ones. Kinney and Losure were impressed by his talk and decided that the time had come for action—although they weren't sure what form that action should take. They set a date for an initial meeting, not entirely certain what that meeting would produce. "We just wanted to get our heads together," Kinney says, "and see what we could come up with."

On her way to that meeting, at the Losures' Kamrar hog farm, Kinney turned on her car radio and heard that the Willits bill was out of committee and about to be placed before the legislature. By the time she got to the Losures', Joyce had heard the news, too, and the two held their initial meeting on Interstate 35, en route to the State House in Des Moines. "I was in my jeans and my fringed jacket," Kinney recalls. "We really looked like hicks. But we went right in there just as if we knew what we were doing."

At the State House, they were advised to register as lobbyists and poll the legislators on the Willits bill. By afternoon, the two were official "rural schools lobbyists," and by the end of the day, state senators were under the gun from Iowa's newest lobby. Some of the senators responded with anger. Kinney says, "Some of them accused us of playing God. They said we had no right being down there at the State House. They said we were setting rural education back fifty years." But Kinney and Losure were not about to be stopped. They polled all fifty state senators, and were ignored by only two. Many legislators took time to talk to them, as did Gary Olney, legislative liaison for the DPI. "I remember the first time I met them," Olney says. "They were just private citizens then. They seemed like sincere people, though, willing to work hour after hour to get some comprehension of what is going on in education in Iowa."

The North Central–Des Moines shuttle continued into April, through the heated (and well-attended) debate on the reorganization bill. Then, Losure recalls, "One day somebody said to me," 'The administrators are organized; the teachers are organized; the DPI is organized. Who's speaking for the children?' Janet looked at me and I looked at Janet, and we decided." The next day they began sending out letters. They sent out twenty-one invitations to an organizational meeting at the Kinney farm on April 27. "We invited people we had met at the hearings or the debate, or people we had read about in the paper," Kinney says. "We hardly knew any of them." But the issue was enough to draw sixteen people to the initial meeting: twelve homemakers ranging from young married women to grandmothers, and four professional educators, including James Jess.

By the end of the meeting, PURE had been formed. The group had brainstormed names, drafted bylaws, and adopted a statement of purpose: "To promote the qualities that have been inherent in rural education and to pursue educational excellence that will enhance rural community life." Late in the afternoon, five housewives drove to the office of a local insurance man who was a notary public to file nonprofit incorporation papers. "We were legally 'United' by the time the day was over," Kinney says. "If we had known what we were getting into, we might not ever have done it."

During the four-hour trip home from Alden, Marilyn Burdic was astonished at the amount that had been done in a single meeting. As she wrote later in the PURE newsletter, "What I didn't realize then was that this was the pace that would be maintained and sometimes escalated!" The pace of the next few months was truly dizzying. PURE passed a set of bylaws and elected a hesitant, hard-working board of directors—all rural women, none with any professional background or educational expertise. Kinney and Losure sent news releases to every newspaper in Iowa, describing the fledgling group and soliciting interest in its mission. The sixteen originators sold memberships to everyone who would stand still long enough. Ten dollars bought a big red-and-white button and a subscription to the monthly newsletter, a twenty- to thirty-page offering describing PURE's activities and those of its member school districts. With Jess's help, the board designed a brochure describing PURE's mission and its educational goals; copies of this flier were sent to all school superintendents with fewer than 750 pupils and to the school board chairs in the same districts. By October, the organization had 312 members scattered across the state, in virtually every section of rural Iowa. Most of the membership was concentrated in North Central, the richest rural area in the state and the region where resistance to reorganization is strongest.

At this point, the board felt that there were enough members to establish a traveling committee, headed by Losure and Jess, who could go to community meetings across the state, extending the information network and recruiting members. "I remember one of our first community meetings," Losure says. "It was a nice harvest night and we were afraid that nobody would have time to come. But they did come, and listened to us, joined PURE, and then went back out into the fields." The community meetings were successful. District and individual membership continued to rise, and a number of small-town businesses, farmers, and other friends of PURE began to make cash donations to the organization. The list of donors reads like a guide to rural Iowa: $25 from the Terril Co-op Elevator; $100 from the Latimer State Bank; $20 from the Dows' Parents and Teachers Who Care organization; $100 from Mrs. Lois Hanke of Fonda; and $51.05 from Chris Kinney, Janet's 11-year-old son, who sold greeting cards and contributed the proceeds to PURE. The ranks of the faithful may not have been large, but they were willing to contribute money, time, and organizational experience to a cause they perceived as their own.

### The PURE Communities: North Central Under Siege

Stratford, Iowa, about twenty miles north of Ames, is a farmer's town. Shakespeare Street, the main east-west road, is dominated by the Farmer's Savings Bank, the feed store, and the two huge farm implement dealerships that face each other at the edge of the village. The 331-pupil school is the center of Stratford. Its superintendent, Louis Doty, was one of the four professional educators who came to the April 1977 meeting that formed PURE, and Stratford citizens have been staunch and open supporters ever since. "Don't ask me about the school," says the man who owns one of the Stratford gas stations. "I'm prejudiced. I graduated from that school in 1925, and my boys graduated from there. I think it's fine and so do they. They did all right, too. One's a dentist, and the other's teaching school over at Jewell. Got his master's degree. You can't tell me that's a bad school."

The elementary teachers agree. "We have plenty of materials—more than we need, really," says one teacher. "And we're small enough so every child's problem can be taken to heart personally. How can that be anything but an advantage?" The well-stocked, cheerful classrooms seem to bear out this confidence. There is certainly no lack of attractive, packaged materials at Stratford, and no lack of the kind of individual attention that enables children to use them. Elementary test scores are high, partly, perhaps, because most children come from affluent backgrounds, but also, the teachers say, because "teachers feel more responsible to get work accomplished in a school this size. If the fourth grade isn't up to the mark, everyone knows who is to blame." The elementary teachers here are strong PURE supporters and hope that PURE can help the community keep its cherished school. "The community here really wants to keep this school going," one teacher says. "If the school goes, they'll lose their sense of identity. The whole town will just fold up."

The high school faculty is not as certain that the effort is worth it. There are two distinct groups of high school teachers: some are middle-aged, long-time residents of the area, who are clearly in the school to stay; the others are young, with one or two years of experience. According to high school principal Al Delay, most of the younger ones will "graduate to bigger schools where there are better offerings." The younger teachers see reorganization as inevitable. "It's just the last phase of consolidation," one says.

By and large, the high school teachers do not feel that there are distinctive advantages to smallness. "Three is too small for a speech class," says the speech teacher. "Five is too small a group for PE," the gym instructor agrees. "And thirty is too large for general science," the science teacher says. "But it's a required course and so I have to teach them all." Small, they feel, is inflexible; small means too many preparations and too much teaching in their minor subjects; small means reduced course offerings. Looking down the grades at the seventeen-child kindergarten class, the high school teachers do not see how the Stratford Community School can survive. "At some point you have to start eliminating teachers," the principal says. "And that means cutting programs below the minimum necessary for good education." No one knows what happens then.

At the moment, with 115 in the high school, Stratford is managing to maintain its program, although some teachers have as many as seven preparations and teach a remarkable range of courses. The home economics teacher, for example, manages eighth-grade home economics, courses in clothing, foods, marriage and the family, and interior decorating, in addition to classes in practical reading, writing, and ninth-grade English. Some of these are one-semester courses, but she teaches all of them in a single calendar year. It is, she feels, quite a load.

The Stratford high school students seem confident, competent, entirely at home with one another. This is hardly surprising as most of them have been together in the community and in the school their entire lives. They have a casual but clear expectation that they will excel, especially in group activities: the band marches annually in the nearby Dayton Parade, the Chamber Choir competes throughout the state, the basketball games draw literally hundreds of spectators. They seem less devoted to class-work—which is presented, generally, to very small groups in highly traditional ways—but they are cooperative and reasonably diligent. It would appear that the school's expectations of them and their expectations of the school are mutually fulfilled.

The high school teachers may debate the educational merits of the Stratford school, but the town is willing to organize, to fight, to levy extra tax dollars to maintain the school. The arguments made here in favor of small, community-based education are repeated over and over, in virtually the same words, all over north-central Iowa. "We have the philosophy that kids don't need 200 courses to choose from to have a good education," says the principal of the Alden school. "They need to be taught the basics, and a sense of responsibility. That's best taught with fewer people involved. We can do that best right here." "We maintain a good, sound educational program here," agrees a businessman from Goldfield, which has a 215-pupil school. "They've got a lot more courses over in Eagle Grove, but I interviewed one girl from over there who couldn't even spell. They say we sacrifice education for team sports. It's just not true."

The central arguments, however, are not educational but social. The most ardent advocates of small rural schools feel that their way of life is be-ing threatened, that the state equalization effort will destroy the com-munities that are the center of their lives. "A lot more than the school is at stake," says a Goldfield resident. "Rural areas need service centers—banks, stores, elevators, churches. When the service centers lose their schools, the whole town dries up. If we go to 1,000-pupil districts, Goldfield will not survive as a prosperous, thriving community."

Why is the school so critical to small-town survival? "If the kids go off to school someplace else, that sends families in one direction or another. Families go to church where the kids' friends are—the mothers run errands where they go to pick up the kids or to do work for the church. First thing you know, younger people won't move in, and the older people won't vote for services. Windows start getting broken in the stores. I've seen it happen. The school goes, the town just dries up."

Economic survival isn't the only issue of concern. The survival of com-munity spirit is another. The small rural communities support their schools with almost fanatical devotion. When the now-defunct New Providence School needed a new baseball diamond several years ago, the men of the community brought their heavy equipment down to the field one weekend and built a playing area worthy of a state championship game. In Goldfield, it took "about a week to collect the $10,000 we needed to buy land to put the new school on." In several small communities, large sums of money for band uniforms or sports equipment materialize virtually overnight. As Kay Banwart, a PURE organizer in West Bend (school enrollment: 394) puts it: "Kids can get anything in West Bend that they need. If we don't have it, we'll get it for them." This rare brand of unequivocal school support ap-pears to stem from a combination of affluence and the high level of school/ community interaction typical of these small towns. "The school and the church are the center of most of the town activities around here," a Gold-field resident says. "That's important to everybody. When we have a good girls' basketball season—a championship team—it pulls the whole town to-gether." This is true not only of athletics, although a good team is still the biggest drawing card a school can have in Iowa. There were only 174 school-age children in New Providence immediately before it closed, but the school could count on an audience of more than 200 at their annual play. And the West Bend FFA (Future Farmers of America) Chili-Oyster Supper can depend on a crowd far larger than the students' parents could provide.

This kind of interaction is important to the students as well as to the com-munity. Several seniors at the Meservey-Thornton School (enrollment: 261) said that high school students work hardest on projects that involve the community, such as the homecoming floats and the ice cream socials and chili suppers with which seniors raise money for their graduation trip to Chicago. "It makes a lot of difference living in a small community," one girl says. "You know everybody and you get used to everybody working together."

Parents see the close-knit relationship between the community and the school as a way of keeping their children from growing up too fast, from coming too soon into contact with alien, urban values. "Parents want their kids in a school where they can participate in a lot of activities in the afternoon," one PURE member says. "That way they can't get into trouble. They want to have the younger kids walk to school, and know that the neighbors are watching out for them. They don't want their kids on some bus."

The small-schools proponents agree strongly about the virtues of their educational mode. And they also agree strongly about the nature of the enemy without. Advocates of the embattled small-school districts can identify nearby towns that are "just sitting there, licking their chops, waiting for us to give up," as one PURE member puts it. Reorganization has serious financial implications in Iowa, where state aid is delivered on a fixed, per-pupil basis, and virtually every district suffers from declining enrollments. Few towns in the 5,000–10,000 range would object to a sudden influx of 200–400 students, each accompanied by a state allocation of funds. And in Iowa, where schools are allowed to raise money in excess of the state allocation only by special vote, the pressure to pull in extra pupils is strong. "It got to the point where I'd follow moving vans to see if maybe the family had kids," one small-town school board member says. More than one school superintendent spends some of his time convincing parents of large families that his district is an attractive place to live.

But the characterization of these larger communities as "vultures, out to get us" is more emotionally than intellectually reflective of the actual attitudes. In the rural communities, the larger towns are seen as greedy, educationally sloppy, and ill controlled—and their schools are viewed as places where lunchroom vandalism and rude student behavior are the norm. The presence of an external enemy seems to fuel the resistance of the small-schools proponents by giving them a concrete, nearby model of precisely what they do not want for their children.

For the community-based–schools advocates, the problems are not all external, however. Not everyone, even in PURE's highest membership communities, entirely agrees that the virtues of small schools outweigh the varied programs and better facilities available in larger districts. Several rural schools have had difficulty holding on to the small enrollments they have because several families have pulled their children out of the community school. In the last years before the New Providence high school closed, several parents decided to transfer children's guardianship to relatives in nearby communities so they could attend larger schools, "mostly for their athletics," according to Stephen Swanson, the former New Providence superintendent. Other students are taken out of local schools after

elementary school, for fear that the community-based institution will provide inadequate college preparation. This fear is not unfounded. In small
schools, says Swanson, teachers are required to teach courses in fields about
which they know very little. "One of our smartest students had to drop
chemistry at Iowa State. She had done very well here, but her teacher only
had maybe six hours of chemistry in college. The teacher just couldn't do it
all." In several rural communities, especially those with the very smallest
schools, the parents agree with Earl Willits, who says, reflecting on his own
rural schooling, "I see opportunities in Des Moines that I never had. I want
my kids to have access to lifetime sports, to cultural resources. Half my high
school class had to get married a year after they graduated. It's not all
sweetness and light out there."

### The Role of PURE: Is the Cavalry Coming?

Iowa's rural schools face a range of educational, political, and demo-
graphic problems. What, exactly, do they expect of a nonprofessional,
volunteer, politically amateur organization like PURE? Practically
everything, it seems. First, PURE is expected to be an effective lobby. In
1977-78, this function was left almost exclusively to Losure and Kinney,
who felt that organizational support focused and intensified their determination. In the winter of 1978, "we drove back and forth to Des Moines
through rain, sleet, and snow, every day of the session," Kinney says. "If
there was a meeting outside the State House, one of us would stay there and
the other would go to the meeting. Otherwise, we'd both stay." Between the
two lobbyists, PURE monitored virtually every open meeting held by the
DPI, the legislative committees on education, and the School Budget
Review Committee. "If you need to find me," Kinney told a friend at one
point in that long, snowy winter, "just call the State House. They'll know
where I am."

As the organization grew, however, Kinney and Losure gained increased
political backing from the membership. In West Bend, PURE activist Kay
Banwart found that "they could call me and say, 'Kay, your legislator is not
listening to us on House File such-and-such.' I could get a hundred people to
call that legislator right away. Then they'd listen." Banwart now says that
this kind of legislative pressure has a bonus attached; it is a way to build
PURE loyalty and membership. Every time a new issue arises in the
legislature, she tries to get "five new people to write. That gets them
hooked—and then they build a group. We make people aware that they
have rights. That's how we build."

In addition to its lobbying function, the organization is expected to serve
as a rallying point for small-schools improvement concepts. Early in the life
of the organization, Jess, who was sensitive to the DPI's growing criticism

of PURE as a one-issue anticonsolidation organization, took this on as his special charge. "We had to get beyond consolidation as an issue," he says. "Consolidation was enough to get people on the bandwagon—but then we had to go somewhere with them."

Jess felt that the next step was to hold a convention—a major event that would combine educational idea gathering with political solidarity. "We kind of groaned at the thought of it," Kinney recalls. "All that work. But we went ahead and did it." PURE was ready for a celebration at the end of its first year of life. The organization had grown from 16 to 1,500 members. They had $14,482.83 in the bank. The Willits bill had gone down to defeat and the DPI was sufficiently conscious of PURE to be openly critical of them. They had done more than survive.

The First Annual State Convention was the crowning event of that successful year. Held in Des Moines in February 1978, the conference drew more than 300 Iowans and visitors to a two-day series of workshops, banquets, and speeches. Entertainment was provided by drill teams, swing choirs, and bands from Iowa's smallest schools; their precision and self-confidence provided unspoken testimony to the success of small-scale education in the state. The major banquet, attended by Governor and Mrs. Ray, was addressed by Jonathan Sher, education director of the National Rural Center and an early PURE supporter. Other out-of-state guests spoke warmly of the positive qualities to be found in small rural schools to passionately approving audiences. For many of the hard-working PURE originators, the success of the conference was a culmination and a reward.

National recognition followed. In late November 1977, PURE had been nominated for a National Volunteer Activist Award. Losure and Kinney had taken time out of their hectic December schedule to respond to the questions required of nominees. "It was one of the best things that ever happened to us," Losure says. "It made us sit down and think about what we were doing" at a time when the activities of the group were expanding so fast that it was difficult for the board to keep up with what was happening to its own organization. Late in March, the awards were announced and PURE was one of nine national winners. The award gave the group a morale boost and some state and national publicity. Kinney and Jess went to Washington to accept the award on PURE's behalf; stories and pictures of the event filled the summer newsletter.

The Volunteer Activist Award catapulted PURE into a new and demanding position. As Jess remembers, "Calls started coming in from all over the country," asking for organizational advice, innovative practices, and monitoring techniques. "We began to realize that there were a lot of rural communities with a lot in common." With Jess's encouragement, the PURE board began to think about expanding outside Iowa. In May 1978, a small group of PURE representatives were invited (at Jess's recommendation) to speak to a class at Minnesota's Southwest State University. In June, Jess and Losure returned to Southwest State to participate in their Rural Life Institute, Losure as a panelist, Jess as a featured speaker. In July, Jess and Losure represented PURE at a Center for Rural Affairs meeting in Ponca, Nebraska. It became clear that the organization's leadership could easily spend most of its time on the road.

### The Costs of Victory

Even in mid-1978, when PURE was flush with a sense of triumph and reward, these multiple demands taxed the resources of the leadership. The board decided to expand by four members that summer, to take some of the workload off the shoulders of the original five. This move was clearly necessary for survival, but it also removed some of the intimacy, some of the pioneering sense that had held the core group together over the first year and a half. PURE was clearly evolving into a new kind of organization, at once less amateurish and more diffuse. "We're quite a group," Kinney said proudly that summer. "I'm proud of the kind of people we attract." But she also confessed that she knew less about where things were going and why.

Spring 1978 had brought some small triumphs at substantial cost. Losure and Kinney (with help from everyone they could muster) pushed two House Files through the legislature, one permitting small districts to share employees and resources, the other allocating funds to help cushion the blow of declining enrollments. "We got those in over the DPI's body," Losure says. In addition, PURE lobbied hard for changes in legislative language. Months of effort resulted in the change (in one bill) from "It is . . . the policy of the state to *encourage the reorganization* of school districts" to "It is . . . the policy of the state to *encourage economical and efficient* school districts which will insure an *equal educational opportunity* to all children in the state." Equivalent effort wrought a change from "promoting reorganization of school districts" to "providing for reorganization." Even after all the battles, the significance of these victories was not clear. Robert A. Benton, state superintendent of public instruction, dismisses their importance: "Frankly, I do not give credence to changing the word from promoting to providing for. I can't blindly ignore what is happening with the school enrollments figures." And the DPI *Dispatch*'s September 1978 issue announced that the much-argued phrase was to be interpreted as "encouraging reorganization," infuriating PURE board members who had spent most of the winter and spring making sure that it was not to be read this way.

Pressure at home continued to build, even as PURE's reputation outside the state brought increasing numbers of invitations and requests for organizational assistance. Late in 1978, reports began to filter in from PURE's member districts that the DPI was stepping up the reorganization pressure. The state's intermediate service agencies, operating under the supervision of the DPI, were pushing their smaller districts to consolidate. In addition, the School Budget Review Committee, charged with distributing the $2.5 million earmarked for schools with sharp enrollment declines, gave the smallest districts less help than the PURE membership thought fair. "Have you considered reorganization?" small districts were routinely asked. Few stock questions could have irritated the PURE board more.

In response to this sense of frustration, the PURE board sent a strongly worded letter to the State Board of Public Instruction that read, in part:

> The People United for Rural Education feel that it is time for you as a State Board to recognize that the officials in our State Department of Public Instruction have an obligation to interpret laws and policies as they are passed by our legislators and signed by our Governor. That they are not free to interpret them as they see fit into their way of thinking. Also, we feel that you as a board should apply the necessary pressure on the Department of Public Instruction to be a state agency that is interested and responsive to the needs of Iowa's smaller rural schools. The people of Iowa's small rural communities are tired of being treated as if they are second-rate citizens by the Department of Public Instruction. Our needs, desires, and opportunities to preserve our rural life style are just as important to us as are the life styles of those citizens living in the more populated areas of our state. Our small rural schools which are located in many of our small communities are an important part of our life style, the educational opportunities we want for our children, and the future development of our rural communities. We are interested in seeing that our schools continue to offer our children quality programs and equal educational opportunities.

The state board scheduled a meeting with representatives from PURE in mid-October. The PURE board turned out in force. Joyce Losure and Marilyn Burdic, flanked by James Jess and Roger Baskerville, another small-school superintendent, were the official representation; the rest of the group sat with absorbed attention around the edges of the panelled board room. Losure, in fact, said virtually nothing, and the discussion became a low-toned, verbal battle between the two superintendents and State Superintendent Benton. Jess declared that Kinney and Losure "spent a year getting 'reorganization' out of that House File, and they don't like the Department's acting as if it was still there." Benton responded directly to Jess: "I don't want to personalize this, Jim," he said. "You and I are professionals—we can work out our professional differences. But the PURE Board never came to us. In all candor, . . . I resent the idea that we interpret the law as we please. All I can say is there is no way I deliberately misinterpret the law."

The Board of Public Instruction (BPI), essentially an observer in this discussion, expressed concern that PURE felt the DPI was pushing consolidation. "You have to recognize that some small schools *are* deteriorating," one BPI member said. "We have to deal with some small districts who are doing nothing to help themselves." The BPI members went around the table expressing, for the most part, their rural sympathies and their appreciation for their own rural backgrounds. One board member seemed to express the feelings of the group: "There are problems of rural education that have to be faced. First of all, there is a need to preserve rural life styles. But you have to define what it is. The small family farm is an endangered species. We don't know what it's changing to. Our obligation as a State Board is to prepare children to handle change without fear and with success. We are concerned that there isn't a full range of program choices in a small school. Smallness isn't necessarily goodness any more than bigness is. It can become insular, self-perpetuating—and it can fail to prepare children for the future."

After that statement, board chair Jolly Ann Davidson brought the session to a close, asking the PURE representatives to say what it was they want the board to do next. Jess said that PURE wanted more communication, and Davidson assured the group that the board wanted increased communication as well. The meeting ended on a conciliatory, if somewhat uncertain, note. State Superintendent Benton asked to be invited to the next PURE conference, already announced for February 1979.

After the meeting, the PURE members were not certain what had been accomplished. They felt some sense of victory—Benton had been put on the defensive about the sensitivity of his department, and had actually asked to be invited to the February conference—but they weren't clear about what the next step would be. Kinney wanted a DPI column in the PURE newsletter, describing the services available for small rural schools. Losure wanted some clear evidence of increased responsiveness from the department toward the smaller districts. Jess wanted to see the establishment of a rural-schools office within the DPI. So much effort had been invested in gathering the internal resources to confront the Board of Public Instruction, apparently, that too little had been used to generate a universally agreed upon and practical program for reform.

As fall wore into winter things did not get easier. PURE had become a sufficiently influential organization that Iowa policymakers had begun to expect expertise from them. State Senator Ray Taylor, a North Central legislator and long-time PURE supporter, reports, "I've heard legislators on both sides of the argument say, 'What does PURE think about different issues?'" But with this rise in influence comes a rise in responsibility. "We can't pretend that we're the dumb clucks who don't know anything and have to have things explained to us anymore," Losure said that winter.

"Now we have to do the explaining." Kinney adds, "We're making enough noise now so they have to keep the discussion going on small schools." They had learned the hard way that the pressure has to be incessant if the countervailing forces that push toward consolidation are not to be renewed.

By the 1979 PURE conference, the group's leadership was both more professionally adept and more cynical. Losure said at that time, "On the one hand, the government is working for community betterment, but on the other hand, they're closing the schools. How many young people are going to move into a community without a school? How do they expect to 'better' a community that way?" But she and Kinney had learned a good deal about the uses of language and language interpretation over the two years of PURE's battles with the DPI. They had come to feel that constant, nit-picking vigilance was the price of small-school survival.

They had also realized that the PURE board and a handful of superintendents could not continue to carry the organization unaided. Kinney and Losure were already working full time, without pay, and were pouring thousands of their own dollars into expenses for their lobbying and community organization trips. The superintendents all had full-time jobs of their own, in small districts that demand a great deal from their administrators. Help came in mid-1979, in the form of a VISTA volunteer couple assigned to the organization after months of complex negotiations between the regional office and Washington. This couple, and the volunteers who succeeded them, spent most of their time attacking the problem of centralized membership. Although PURE expanded its local chapter roster in the first two years of its life, its center of power remained North Central, where Iowa's farm wealth is concentrated and where towns can afford to badger the legislature to permit them to raise additional taxes. In the southern counties, where the land is hilly and poorer than North Central, the PURE message had been less persuasive. It was Kinney's ambition to have the VISTA workers change this trend through community organization. "I want to look at districts where we don't have members and find out why not," Kinney said in 1979. "I want to find out how we need to change to get members in all the rural school districts in Iowa."

The first pair of volunteers, Margaret and Harold Benson, spent most of their time on this effort. They traveled from town to town, visiting at the schools, talking to community leaders and administrators, conducting "Have Coffee with PURE" meetings, setting up booths at local events. Their efforts paid off: the PURE membership expanded from 1,800 to more than 2,500 between 1979 and 1980. But it was a slow, laborious process.

Even VISTA could not adequately reduce the overload carried by the PURE board. By early 1980, PURE was engaged in a major membership campaign, in an ever-expanding national network of small-schools districts and colleges interested in rural schooling, and in efforts to influence national as well as state legislation. In Washington, PURE was a leader in the (unsuccessful) battle to get an Office for Rural Education into the new Department of Education. In Iowa, PURE was doggedly pressuring the legislature to adopt a new funding formula that would provide a stable financial base for small districts. In the western half of the country, Jess, Kinney, and Losure were operating a speaking circuit that would have done credit to best-selling novelists, shuttling from conference to meeting in thirteen states and Washington, D.C.

It was clear to the board that it was time to reorganize. Jess was appointed "national advisor" to PURE, and Roger Baskerville assumed the duties of "state advisor." The organization's commitment to a national role was formalized and expanded. Losure was elected to the board of directors of the National Rural Center in Washington, D.C. Jess was asked to join the advisory board of the ERIC/CRESS (Educational Resources Information Center/Clearing House on Rural Education and Small Schools). Thomas Minter, deputy commissioner of the Bureau of Elementary and Secondary Education, agreed to deliver the banquet address at the third annual PURE conference in January 1980. The PURE newsletter's calendar of events began to sound less like a grassroots organizational roster and more like the schedule of a national rural education center. Jess's long-time dream of Iowa as the locus of expertise on small rural schools seemed within reach.

But there is only so much a volunteer organization can do. PURE vice-president Kay Banwart remembers the 1980 conference as a time of mixed elation and panic. "We had a reception and people from other states came and said, 'Please help us!' Now, I'd love to reach out and help others—but we can barely manage ourselves." While the membership drive continued and the lobbying efforts gained strength as the membership grew, PURE began to look for ways to reduce the workload on the board. Baskerville, as state advisor, organized an advisory council, a group of eight small district superintendents who took on a number of tasks formerly handled by board members. "They take the local chapter organizational meetings that are 300 miles from my house," Baskerville says with relief. "It takes some of the pressure off the core group."

Jess, as national advisor, has also looked outside the core group for help and thinks he has found it in the Rural Education Assocation, a fledgling group that recently split off from the Rural/Regional Education Association. According to Jess, the new REA wants to be "a national voice for rural education" and has the organizational capacity to bring it off. "I came back from their 1980 conference and told Janet that I think we should focus on this region as long as we are going to remain volunteer," Jess says. Kay Banwart agrees with this assessment of PURE's resources. "I'd love it if Jim Jess would stand up and say 'PURE is going national—we're setting up a

Center—bring us your problems and we'll handle them!" But we can't—and do you know why? Money. We can't possibly take on more responsibility."

### The Future: What Can PURE Do?

The expectations of PURE are complex and varied, depending on who is doing the expecting and what their biases are. The small-schools communities of Iowa hope that PURE can push the legislature into changing the state aid formula—at the very least to convince the legislature to take the lid off local spending and at best to get some kind of weighting system that would channel more program-support money to schools with fewer pupils. In North Central at least there is a lot of anger about the difference between the tax rate and the amount of money that comes back from the state in the form of school aid. "It's not a matter of someone having to send us tax dollars to keep our school open," one Goldfield resident complains. "We don't get our own money back." Legislators like Willits and State Education Committee Chair Joan Orr say that such claims ignore the state's tax breaks for agricultural land, but such arguments are not taken seriously by the residents of rural communities. It seems clear to them that they pay out a lot in taxes and don't seem to get much back for their schools.

In addition, the PURE communities want the organization to push the DPI and the legislature toward educational deregulation. Iowa has a high level of state curriculum regulation, and some of the mandates seem to the PURE membership to be directed at their lifeblood. Until 1980, every Iowa high school had to offer and teach two sections of a foreign language each year. That meant, according to one PURE member, that "even if no one wanted to take Spanish 2, you had to teach it anyway. You had to go up to some bright girl and say, 'Gee, Sue, we're in kind of a jam—you've got to take Spanish 2, even if you don't want to, or we're in trouble with the state.'" That particular regulation is now off the books—thanks, PURE claims, to its pressure. But other, similarly restrictive mandates continue to be enforced, and PURE is expected to do something about it. "We want help in getting some of the requirements modified," the Alden high school principal says. "People are fed up with not having rights they used to have by law—such as the right to offer the curriculum we want our children to have."

The people in these small communities believe in the commitment and efficacy of PURE. They see the PURE leadership, in fact, as their chief means of leverage on the legislature. Representative Del Stromer says that communities like the ones he represents see "Janet and Joyce as real people who will speak up for small schools in Des Moines. They believe the State School Boards Association will go for big schools in the long run. Janet and Joyce won't."

Finally, the member communities in Iowa expect the organization to keep them informed about what is going on in small rural schools all over the state. PURE tries to respond to this need, as a basic contention of the organization has been that it is not for small schools for their own sake, but for quality education delivered on a small-scale basis. Information is disseminated largely through the newsletters, which combine old-fashioned Iowa boosterism with descriptions of small-schools–oriented educational innovations. The annual conference, which draws about 300 participants yearly, is another forum for sharing ideas among small-schools proponents. Its offerings range from survival strategy planning sessions to nuts and bolts curriculum workshops.

The Department of Public Instruction and the consolidation-oriented legislators have a different view of PURE—and different expectations. Although Baskerville feels that PURE has now achieved respectability (and clout) with the legislature as a formal lobby, there are Des Moines officials who see the organization as a first-class nuisance, a one-issue organization with no positive orientation. "PURE is working on fear," one DPI official says. "They have a strictly negative thrust. They know what they don't want, but not what they want. They don't even look at the virtues of the other side of the fence. When you don't know or understand what's on the other side of the fence, you're suspicious of it. They don't understand that they can't protect things the way they were." According to another official, "They can't produce what they promise. Reorganization is inevitable. The best they can do is to stall it off."

Willits feels that PURE can, at best, produce a kind of standoff. "The legislature won't vote for mandatory reorganization, but it won't vote any money to keep the small schools alive, either. At that point, the little schools will just get squeezed to death. When you get a high school of seventy kids, you have to spend all your money on the required courses. That's just not good pedagogy." Both DPI people and some legislators have doubts about PURE's potential efficacy. "Legislators will be polite to them, but they don't take them seriously," according to a DPI representative. And Willits adds, "There are some legislators who have really played games with those women."

Expectations from the world outside Iowa add to the tensions at home. Baskerville feels that the publicity PURE has received has "vaulted us to a level nationally that we can't achieve here at home." Outside Iowa, he feels, PURE is considered the voice of grassroots rural education; within the state, the organization is often perceived as representative of a fanatical faction. "I can take my dog and pony show to Washington," Baskerville says, "and everybody listens. Around here, they've seen my dog and ridden my pony and they just don't pay much attention." Kay Banwart echoes this. "People at the conference come from all over the country and they all say PURE's terrific. But sometimes I have the hardest time with the person next door."

Ready access to influential and admiring national audiences tempts some of the PURE leaders to push for an emphasis on a broad role for the organization. "Professional people are needed to develop good rural education policy," Jess says. "But grassroots people are needed to get the Congressmen to pass it. It amazed me what happened when we got in touch with D.C. [Senator] Grassley set up meetings with Tom Minter and we got a chance to talk about our problems with inappropriate regulation, and research needs, and discrimination against rural areas. They were really accessible."

But much work remains to be done in Iowa, a fact that holds PURE back from full-scale pursuit of a federal-level role. "I think that enrollments will stabilize in a few years. If we can get through that time, there will be lots of alternatives for us," Baskerville says. But getting through the next few years, he believes, will require the kind of constant attention to local events that has characterized PURE's first four years. "We have won a lot of battles over the last few years," he says. "But we have made a lot of bitter enemies by not listening to the powers that be." It is his feeling—as it is Losure's and Kinney's—that the Iowa war is far from over.

## Why PURE?

Most rural school reform comes either from the outside (in the form of state or federal government intervention) or develops locally (a Foxfire project here, an exchange program there). PURE is an exception. It began as a statewide organization, with no state support. It became a national voice, without federal assistance. It has remained throughout its struggles stubbornly amateur, in a field of hungry professionals. How has this been possible?

First, it seems clear that an organization like PURE depends on affluence. The PURE leadership is not rich, but they have the luxury of disposable cash and expendable time. PURE can be run on a shoestring budget because Kinney and Losure pay the bulk of their own expenses. Jess can devote hours each week to the needs of the organization because his district can afford to hire administrative assistance to run his tiny school when he is on the road.

Affluence has indirect effects as well. The schools North Central is fighting for are, by and large, good schools by any standard. They have been richly supported over the years, drawing good faculties and building fine facilities to educate young people who are highly motivated and well supported at home. The test scores in the small districts are as high as they are anywhere in the state; their rates of vandalism, drug and alcohol abuse, and violence are lower than they are elsewhere. The West Bend parent who will pay money, write letters, and attend meetings to support PURE does so in defense of an entirely defensible institution. The extent to which that quality is the result of local wealth and the extent to which it is the product of smallness may be arguable. The results are incontrovertibly there.

Further, the comfortable, independent farmers of Iowa have a sense of entitlement, a habit of power, that makes an organization like PURE possible. Iowa farmers are accustomed to having (and using) political clout in the legislature, through the Farm Bureau, and with their congressional delegation. The notion of government as a distant creature, inaccessible and arbitrary, is not their notion; most of them know their state legislators well and are acquainted with their federal representatives. Janet Kinney and Joyce Losure might have felt like "hicks" when they wandered into the State House dressed in clothes appropriate for the soybean fields, but they felt like *entitled* hicks, whose right to form a lobby was fundamental to their perception of the political process. A history of affluence and access may not be required to develop this sense of political efficacy, but it certainly does not hinder its growth.

This sense of the legitimacy of political action is fed by a feeling, prevalent among rural Iowa taxpayers, that they have been ill used. It is strongly believed in North Central that the Iowa farmers produce most of the state's wealth, that they pay most of the state's taxes, and that the response from an ungrateful government is first to deprive them of their fair share of the school finance funds and then to deprive them of their community schools. Questions about equalization do not sit well with the PURE membership; they believe that the present funding formula deprives their children of educational opportunities readily available in the pleasant suburbs of Des Moines.

The recent resurgence of interest in rural issues has certainly helped PURE's development. "Rural is in vogue now," Jess says. "And who's done anything? We have. So people have begun to come to us." Indeed, PURE has had substantial outside help, on an informal basis, from its inception. PURE has never had any problem getting nationally known rural educators and federal policymakers to speak at its conferences; it has been written up frequently in publications with national distribution. To scholars and policymakers (especially outside Iowa), PURE is the emblematic grassroots organization. And, as rural education draws the attention of more and more people who have never seen a cow, it is convenient to set up a single organization as the voice of rural America.

Finally, PURE's success is a reflection of the quality of its leadership. Jess, Kinney, and Losure are all canny politicians who know how to distinguish a viable issue from a silly fight. The board is still dominated by strong, committed rural Iowans, mostly women, who are willing to devote endless hours of time, energy, and personal funds to research, lobbying, editing, traveling, selling, and organizing. "I'm just a West Bend Bulldog," Kay Banwart says of her board role. "When I say I'm going to dig in, I dig in." PURE may not be able to win its battle with the legislature and the DPI, but it won't be for lack of persistent and determined leadership.

As an amateur organization, PURE has accomplished a great deal—more, perhaps, than a similar group of small district superintendents could have done. "It's *People* United," Baskerville says. "Not Administrators United or Board Members United. I'm really glad it's lay controlled. That makes us more effective." But it also runs some risks. First, there is the risk that the organization cannot outlast its original leadership. The leadership itself says that this is not the case. "Any of us could be replaced tomorrow," Baskerville claims. In spite of their disclaimers, the core group has the experience, the recognition, and the particular chemistry that made PURE cohere. It is not clear to what degree a new board could take its place. Kinney claims that the trick is to arrange an orderly transition—to train new people to take over the roles of the present people in the core group before the original cadre resigns. But orderly transition is more easily proposed than accomplished when heavy investments have been made.

Another risk is that PURE might win its four-year-old battle. It is not clear that the organization could withstand an end to the crisis that brought it into being. The original leadership envisions a long life for the organization; they see it as a permanent group of small-schools advocates, devoted to the protection and improvement of small-scale rural education. But they are not at all certain that their adherents will stick with them if the emergency goes away. Losure says, "So many people are crisis oriented. If we can show we can do something for them, for their school, they'll join. But if there is no crisis, we just don't know." The PURE leadership has come to believe that only continual militant monitoring of what Baskerville calls "the powers that be" will bring any measure of safety to small rural schools. They are afraid that modifications in the state funding formula could bring an end to the sense of urgency that has provided them with essential backing, leaving the field open for future consolidation efforts by the DPI.

Finally, and perhaps most importantly, PURE runs the risk of debilitating overextension. The expenditure of the last four years has left the original core group thoroughly exhausted. At the end of four years, serious questions remain. What is PURE's national role? What are the issues that will unify North Central and the poorer counties of the southern tier? Can PURE organize small-schools movements in other states? Can PURE continue to build membership in Iowa? What are the priorities? Where is the central focus? There is no consensus on the answers to these questions, even among the PURE leadership.

In mid-1981, PURE is continuing to perform its juggling act. All the oranges are in the air, held aloft by skill and Iowa stubbornness. How long that can continue—or how the central dilemmas can be resolved—is still an open question. A growing number of rural communities across the country are waiting to see how PURE works it out.

# 13
# Elk River, Idaho:
# The Pursuit of Quality Schooling
# in a Threatened Community

*Thomas Gjelten*

Clues to the meaning of "educational improvement" in Elk River, Idaho, can be found in a visit to Dale Yates's high school physics class. Students work at small lab tables under bare fluorescent bulbs in a cramped basement classroom. Juniors and seniors take the class together: Physics is offered just once every two years, alternating with chemistry. The curriculum consists of a series of prepackaged, individualized units, patterned closely after the state science curriculum guide. Yates, who also teaches earth science, biology, and four separate math courses, wrote the physics units himself, in a series of late-afternoon work sessions.

Similar units have been prepared by history teacher Rick Campbell and junior high math/science teacher Wes Snow. They are all the products of a school-wide K–12 curriculum plan developed by a faculty committee at the Elk River School. The committee was formed by the teachers themselves. Much of the work, in fact, was accomplished during the last half of the 1977-78 school year, when Elk River was without a superintendent and there was no administrative pressure on the teachers to do curriculum planning. The curriculum development began instead as one phase of a long-running, cooperative effort at Elk River to improve the local educational program—one that has won the school a widespread reputation in the state.

There is a story behind this improvement effort, and it has many implications for isolated rural communities across the nation. It does not feature frivolous experimentation or even spontaneous bursts of pedagogic inspiration, but rather earnestness and sobriety. The stakes in this case have been high: the survival of the Elk River School, which is considered to be absolutely essential to the survival of the town itself. Elk River is a tiny logging town set deep in the north Idaho woods, twenty miles from its nearest neighbor town. Totally vulnerable to the company policies and practices of two or three major timber corporations, Elk River has never been free to face its future with confidence. For over fifty years, life in this community has been characterized by economic and political insecurity. "Will there be jobs here for the next generation?" "What can be done to give the town some autonomy?" "In whose hands does the fate of the community rest?" These are questions that have been asked in Elk River over and over again.

The town was built in a hurry—and looks like it. It was put together in 1910 by construction crews working for the Potlatch Lumber Company after the company had selected a remote spot along Elk Creek as the site of a new milling operation. With the opening of the mill and the completion of a railroad to serve it, there would be work for several hundred men, and the company needed to accommodate them and their families. Lumberjacks and carpenters were brought in and within a few months, out of the mud and stumps and tents, there emerged a little city, complete with stores, a post office, a church, a bank, a hotel (which doubled as a school), and a company-operated electrical-generating plant.

It is today a compact and unassuming town, neatly laid out. The houses sit in straight rows, each the same distance from the street. Most are small, wood-frame bungalows perched on concrete pilings, with shiny tin roofs steeply slanted so the snow will slide off. Potlatch built almost all of them, using just two or three basic plans, then rented or sold them to the mill-workers. Wooden-plank sidewalks—replacements for the original ones laid down by the lumber company—still border the town's gravelled streets, retaining the old-time flavor of the community.

There had been several logging camps in this section of Clearwater County before 1910, but no permanent community until the mill was built. By 1915, 1,000 men were employed in Elk River, and the town, with a population of over 2,000, was prospering. A new school and a hospital had been built, and there was a local newspaper, the *Elk River News*. The superintendent of the lumber mill, Bloom Corbin, was also the town mayor. "He just ran the whole place," remembers "Ma" Vine, who arrived with her lumberjack husband in 1919. "He'd walk up and down the streets—if he saw a man sitting on a bench, he'd offer him work at the mill. If he took it, fine. If he didn't, he wasn't welcome around town much longer."

Then, as suddenly as it had boomed, the town busted. In 1930, Potlatch decided to close its Elk River mill and move the equipment to Lewiston. The town's electricity was shut off. The residents were shocked and furious; after having created the town, Potlatch was now abandoning it. Hundreds of men were put out of work overnight. Those who had bought company houses on the security of their employment at the mill could no longer afford to keep them—but neither could they find buyers. Many homes were simply given up. The population of the town plummeted as people left to find work elsewhere. Those who stayed behind were forced to compete for the few remaining jobs, all in lumberjacking. The depression was on, and everyone shared in the hardships.

The town never recovered from that blow. John Morris, whose father had a drug store in town during the mill days, was one of those who stayed. He operates the store today in a much quieter and less prosperous Elk River of 380 residents. He expects the town to stay that way. "Since the mill closed," he says, "the only work available has been in the woods, and it's not going to change much. As long as the trees keep growing, they'll keep cutting them, and there'll be a town here. But it's never going to be a boom town again."

The old Potlatch Lumber Company—now the Potlatch Corporation—is still the major employer, followed by another larger timber corporation, Diamond International. These days, Elk River is a mustering point for logging crews working in the nearby area. Each morning, six-passenger pickups swing through town to pick up men for the commute to the current cutting area. Loggers earn decent wages; many make more than $20,000 per year. But the work is as hard as ever, and the future outlook for employment in the industry is, at best, uncertain. Most of the areas being logged now have been logged once before, twenty or thirty years ago. Some men are concerned that the time may come, alarmingly soon, when the hills around Elk River will be timbered almost clear, and there will not be enough trees left to sustain a major logging operation.

A diversification of the town's economic base has never been accomplished. It would seem that the already-cleared hills surrounding the town could provide an ideal site for a ski resort. The prospect was seriously considered for a while, according to Morris, one of the unofficial town fathers, but "when the chips were down, the money wasn't there." Similarly, the Elk Creek Reservoir, a tranquil and picturesque fishing spot, and the spectacular Elk Creek Falls might be potential attractions to campers and fishing enthusiasts, but tourism hasn't caught on, either. "Oh, there's been some talk of it," says Morris, who would benefit from the business it might bring to his hardware/liquor/drug store, "but, hell, we're awful deep in the woods, a long ways from the highway. About all we get is a few RV campers, and they bring everything with them." Thus Elk River remains at the mercy of the logging industry.

The instability of the economic situation has had repercussions. There is no new housing available in the town. Neither the banks nor FHA will guarantee mortgages in a one-industry town when that industry is on feeble footing. For the same reason, the houses that are already owned in Elk River have low resale values—as little as one-fourth of what they might bring in Moscow or Lewiston, two cities of about 20,000, southwest of Elk River. The town's tax base, consequently, is sinking.

A further aggravation in Elk River are the hard winters. "There are a lot of people who don't stay in Elk River too long," John Morris says. "When they get older, they have a tendency to move out, to get out of the snow belt." But for those who were born and raised here it is home, and most stay. In fact, the domination of the town's very existence by timber corporations may have actually kept the town united. Each family's struggle is understood and shared by the others; all are equalized in their dependence on logging.

If the common experience of hardship has nurtured a strong sense of community among Elk River residents, it is probably their isolation from the rest of the world that has preserved it. Elk River is among the most remote of the tiny towns dotting the rugged wilderness of Idaho's panhandle. It is surrounded on all sides by mountains, including Elk Butte, whose 5,790-foot peak effectively blocks TV reception in Elk River homes. The town lies at the terminus of State Route 8, a narrow logging road that winds its way into the hills from the Palouse agricultural region north of Moscow. It is twenty miles past Bovill, a ranching and logging town of about 500. Until 1973, the road was unpaved and on many winter and spring days barely passable. As a consequence, life in Elk River has always revolved around local community events. Not surprisingly, there are those who view the paving of the road to Bovill as a mixed blessing and lament the diminished sense of local self-sufficiency since then. "It's taken the business out of town more," says Morris. "Now people go to Moscow or Lewiston to do their shopping."

Nowhere can a strong community will be seen more clearly than in the town's attitude toward its school. Eighty-four Elk River children from kindergarten through grade twelve attend the two-story wooden building that sits authoritatively on a hill at the entrance to town, its belltower overlooking the main street, the creek, and the green hills beyond. It is the symbol of the community's independence. "This town is built around that school and all that goes on there," says Ted Malm, the current chairman of the Elk River school board and himself a native of the community. "It's our entertainment for the winter, it's . . . everything." The townspeople are united in their defense and support of it. "You know, this little town doesn't have that much," says Virginia Hill, an Elk River graduate. "If we lost that school up there, we wouldn't have anything. There's nobody in town that wants to see that school go."

Because there is no family in the Elk River district that lives beyond a walk from the school, there is no busing. Nor is there hot lunch; students and staff alike walk home at noon each day. A few children start drifting back about ten minutes later, and to supervise them, one teacher stays at school to stand playground duty. On the Elk River playground, duty may consist of playing a short game of soccer with some sixth- and seventh-grade boys, twirling the jumprope for a group of girls, or talking with individual students about their latest crises. Older students mix freely with younger ones on the playground. "That's something really good about a school this size," says Superintendent-Principal Jack Deits. "It forces the age groups together. You're liable to see a high school kid sitting down on the ground with a second-grader." By ten minutes to one, on a warm and sunny day, almost everyone has returned. Teachers and students stack up on the front steps, looking over their town and talking about the latest school and community news, before going in for afternoon classes.

There is in the Elk River school a feeling of camaraderie among students and teachers that is not found in larger schools. "I think we have good rapport here with the students," says industrial arts teacher and assistant high school principal Ray Ireland. "I notice a kid a little out of it, and I know something's gone wrong with his family—best leave him alone." Similarly, Mary Simeone, who teaches English, home economics, speech, and German, says, "I'm personally involved in the life of every one of my students. Almost everything I teach is one-to-one. It's like being a tutor in a private school."

The individualized math program recently introduced by junior high teacher Wes Snow in his classes is not entirely new. "We were already doing some of it," he says. "You can't help but individualize in this school—but now it's more systematic." Other parts of his teaching have been influenced by the unique conditions at the Elk River school. In social studies, "I put a heavy emphasis on current events," he says. "Not local news—which is mostly scuttlebutt—but national news. We look at it from our perspective, the effect of the recession or the gas shortage on the lumber market, for example. You can bring it out so much more clearly in a one-industry town like Elk River. And we talk about using the forest resources, choosing between the timber industry, which wants to cut down everything, and the environmentalists at the other extreme. I try to get them to see that balance. They're the ones who'll have to make the decisions in the future."

The school staff has tried to be attentive to community needs. In a town without a doctor or hospital within an hour's drive, widespread knowledge of first aid measures is crucial, and local emergency medical technicians have been brought into the school. And "civic-mindedness" is stressed, says Ray Ireland. "For example, we still have Earth Day. With their teachers' help, kids devise a project to clean up the community in some way. Then we send them out. They've cleaned up the park, painted the fire plugs, made street signs, things like that."

Discipline problems are minor at the school. One of the most persistent problems is unauthorized absences, and Deits and Ireland are firm on it. Students must bring written excuses from their parents each time they miss school, and even then the excuse must be a good one. Some older students are tempted to work in the woods instead of coming to school, and they may have parental support. The administrators remind them that their state aid depends on their average daily attendance and that each day a student is absent is a cost to the district in revenue. It is apparently a traditional problem at Elk River. Ray Hill, who has been hauling logs since he was 14, recalls that when he was a student at Elk River High School, "I always tried to talk that superintendent out of going to school when I needed to work. He'd let me have a week, maybe two, in the fall, but that was all."

Like his wife, Ray Hill is a native of the community and a staunch supporter of the school. "I think Elk River has always had a good school system," he says. "As far as I can tell, their standards have always been pretty high. We have a lot of real bright kids here, and we've always had good teachers. The kids have to really get in there and earn their grades." The townspeople have demonstrated their support for the school, the Hills say, by taxing themselves beyond their legal obligation to pay for it, and they have shown their belief in the virtue of education by the way they treat the teachers who come to Elk River to live and work. "A teacher is still a pretty respected person in this community. We haven't had all those changes like some of the larger towns have. I've got a lot of admiration for the teachers. They ought to get all the support that we can give them—financially, too, as much as we're able."

Although the paving of the road has made trips to the movies in Moscow more feasible nowadays, it is on school-sponsored events that Elk River people still depend for their diversion: music programs, films, holiday celebrations, and, especially, sports. Students take their responsibility for entertaining their community seriously, and virtually every one of them goes out for at least one extracurricular activity. An active core of students participates in all of them; for that reason, work on the school yearbook often has to wait until the spring track and tennis seasons are finished.

Teachers depend on the community as well for their own social life and traditionally have joined in community activities. "They've always been taken in as part of the community," says Lillian Yangel, a native of the town and for many years a teacher herself in the Elk River school. "I remember when we were kids—teachers would take us out on wienie roasts and sleigh rides." Virginia Hill agrees: "The teachers here mix right in. They're active in church affairs, they're involved in everything." It's what's expected of Elk River teachers, according to board chairman Malm.

The strong local support for the school was one of the first things to impress Jack Deits, who came from California to assume the leadership of the Elk River school system in the summer of 1978. "This is the biggest little school I've ever seen," Deits says, "and I'll tell you one reason—the school board and community support education 100 percent. Whatever they can do for the teachers, they do."

If Elk River teachers are a satisfied lot, it may be partly due to the fact that their salary scale (1979-80 base: $9,770) is one of the highest in the state, for any size school. When fifth- and sixth-grade teacher Van Thompson came ten years ago, it was the highest-paying school district in Idaho and it furnished four houses to teachers at low rent. He has stayed, and he is happy. "The people in town know us," he says, "and they're going to do what they can for us."

But Elk River teachers are not complacent when it comes to their work at the school. They realize that the futures of the school and the town are intertwined, and their efforts at curriculum development have occurred in an atmosphere of urgency. Just as the future of the town's economy is dependent on a distant corporation, the future of the town's school is dependent on a distant bureaucracy: the Idaho Department of Education in Boise.

### The Pressure to Improve the School

It is the thought of consolidation that alarms people here. Though the nearest high school is thirty-eight miles away, townspeople continue to fear that the state department might one day make a push to close Elk River High and bus the students out of town. "I think there's more danger now than there ever was," says John Morris. "Before, the roads were crooked and rough; you couldn't get over them. Now they're straightened out and paved."

It was not until the late 1960s that the Elk River school began to face the threat of consolidation. The state education department sponsored a University of Idaho study of various school district reorganization options and then encouraged the state legislature to consider one of them for action. In 1969, a bill was introduced that would have initiated a consolidation movement in Idaho. It had the backing of the state department. With its less-than-fully-accredited high school, Elk River would have been a vulnerable district.

The superintendent in Elk River that year was R. Dee Merrill. The community could not have had a man more suited to their needs of the moment: Merrill also happened to be a member of the Idaho House of Representatives, the first active school superintendent in Idaho to be elected to the legislature. Though he was a professional educator, it was his understanding of tax issues for which he was known in Boise. He soon learned to put his expertise to practical—and political—effect. "I was a tax bug," Merrill recalls, from his office in Harrison, Idaho, where he is currently superintendent. "I headed a coalition—we fought the utilities. I was known as 'the shotgun' because I shot from the hip. I talked a lot. We could get anything passed we wanted to—tax-wise."

Merrill used his position of influence to kill the consolidation bill. It was only an initial victory, however, in a struggle that was just beginning. Elk River's problems ran much deeper. The town had already begun to suffer the effects of economic decline. Its assessed valuation was falling steadily and hence its ability to add local dollars to state school funds also declined. The immediate danger may have passed, but if the district continued to lose ground in its capacity to finance its school, it would be facing a more serious threat in the long term.

The state department, meanwhile, was beginning to pay considerably more attention to a school's accreditation status. There are three levels in Idaho: full accreditation, accreditation on an "advised" status, meaning that deficiencies in the instructional program have been identified and recommendations to correct them have been made; and accreditation on a "warned" status, where the recommendations are in fact stern orders. For a high school of about thirty students, the state accreditation standards represented a major challenge, and Elk River had never made it past the "advised" level. It had too few courses and too many teachers teaching outside their field of training.

By 1973, the financial and academic situation was approaching the crisis stage. Something had to be done if the community school was to survive. Merrill had by then retired from the legislature, though his counsel on tax matters was still highly regarded, and he continued to travel frequently to Boise to advise his former colleagues on pending legislation and lobby for particular bills. His support of a bill continued to be a major factor in the determination of its fate. In the process of his lobbying, he earned many favors, which he cashed in on behalf of his community. He was instrumental in getting the state highway department to approve the paving of the Bovill–Elk River road. He also managed to get Elk River designated as a recreation district, which entitled it to state funds for facilities and programs. But his crowning accomplishment was the solution he worked out to his district's school finance problem.

Merrill devised a plan by which a local school board could petition the state board of education to recognize a school as "remote and necessary." Once designated, the school would receive supplementary state aid adequate for its needs. The idea was that there are schools such as Elk River's that are necessary by virtue of their distance from other schools in the state, yet without the necessary revenue to support them. Merrill convinced the state superintendent of public instruction, Larry Engelking, of the merits of his proposal, and Engelking offered Merrill one of his aides to help in the drafting of a bill. Under the bill's provisions, schools would be guaranteed enough money to operate an acceptable educational program. "Acceptable" was defined as meeting all accreditation requirements (in the case of a high school) and passing a special instructional review by the state education department (in the case of an elementary school).

From the beginning, it was clear to everyone that it was Merrill's own bill, written exclusively for his own school. "It was known all over the state as the 'Elk River bill,'" he admits. He had friends introduce it and monitor its progress and when it was placed near the bottom of the House legislative calendar (and thus certain of being tabled), one of them called and alerted him. He immediately flew to Boise. He convinced the majority leader to get the bill moved up on the calendar for quicker attention. Another meeting with his old friend, Idaho governor Cecil Andrus, brought a promise from Andrus that when the bill was passed, he would sign it immediately. Shortly thereafter, the bill became law. "That was my greatest accomplishment," says Merrill. "I've never lobbied another bill. I just gave it to them [Elk River residents] as a going away present, because they'd been good to me." (Merrill left Elk River that year.)

As a result of Merrill's lobbying, the Elk River school was kept alive, but there was a price. It would now be the object of much more attention from the state department than it ever had been before. "There's no other system in the state that's scrutinized like Elk River," Superintendent Deits says As Dick Nelson, a state department official who has worked closely with the Elk River district, explains, "When you ask the state board to make up the difference in your budget above what is brought in by local revenue, you really have to have your house in order."

Elk River used its supplementary state aid to hire two additional teachers, enabling the preparation load of the other teachers to be reduced and allowing the seventh and eighth graders to be switched from a self-contained classroom arrangement to a rotating schedule, as used in the high school. The level of expenditures was also raised for new textbooks, teaching supplies, and equipment.

But the money didn't mean that Elk River's problems were solved overnight. The state department continued to control the school's fate through its accreditation process. Each year, the Elk River school board had to make its petition to the state board and, under the terms of the statute, had to prove that with its extra funding it was able to offer a quality program. As one state education department official explains, "The premise of the 'remote and necessary' law is that all children, regardless of where they live, deserve a good education. As it stands now, the only way we have of determining whether a program is of minimal quality is the accreditation process. It's not perfect, but it's all we've got."

There had always been pressure on Elk River to get its program accredited, but with the new dependence on state aid, the pressure was sharply increased. The teachers noticed it, and not without some ambivalent feelings. "In recent years, the state department has gotten stronger and more demanding," Ray Ireland says now, "and I think rightly so. We used to do some things in a shoddy manner." But then Ireland qualifies his words: "Not that the kids ever suffered, though. Above all, the welfare of the students has been uppermost, at least in the minds of the teachers." Ireland respects the state department's concern for maintaining its standards but would never back down in his defense of small rural schools: "I think small schools bring out the best in a teacher. In fact, I've thought that when you have a teacher who isn't certified to teach a class, he puts more effort into the class. He has to work to get the background for it, and the effort shows in his teaching."

In the years following Elk River's qualification for extra aid, the state department's division of instruction continued to deny the high school complete accreditation (as it did for about 25 other high schools of the 130 in the state). The reports cited curricular weakness in the areas of foreign language, fine arts, and home economics, and said that Ray Ireland's informal guidance counseling wasn't certifiable. The school board began to get nervous. "Pretty soon when you're running on this remote and isolated money, they [state officials] get discouraged on you," says board chairman Ted Malm. "There's always the threat they'll take it away; without it, you can't survive."

In the spring of 1978, Superintendent Rudy Armitage, who had replaced R. Dee Merrill in 1973, suffered a stroke and was forced to retire. Ray Ireland had to fill in as acting superintendent for the remainder of the year. Once again, the year passed without the school getting off the "advised" list on the accreditation report. The school board's search for a new superintendent that summer concentrated on one requirement: that he or she be able to get the school completely certified. "That's the main thing we needed—accreditation," Malm recalls. "You have to leave all that stuff to your superintendent. You depend on him for everything."

The man they chose for the job, Jack Deits, was a tough-minded former principal and teacher whose most recent experience had been with high school students at the California Youth Authority. His first priority as superintendent was to study past accreditation reports and initiate changes in the school program in response to their recommendations, if possible. With $2,000 in the salary account—saved in the hiring of new teachers—Deits hired a counselor to work at the school one day a week: Dan Miller, a retired University of Idaho ROTC Commandant with a Ph.D. in psychology and a certificate as a psychological examiner. Deits also convinced Mary Simeone, the high school English teacher, to add German I and II to her teaching schedule. Finally, he juggled teaching assignments around, dropping some courses and adding others. Within six months, the division of instruction at the state education department granted full accreditation to Elk River's high school program.

Actually, it was not just the superficial changes that impressed the accreditors. The school had in the past few years begun to move forward in other ways, primarily through the leadership of the teachers. The faculty curriculum committee had been working to organize the entire K–12 curriculum around a series of specific goals and objectives. The district had also just completed an eighteen-month "needs assessment" involving students, staff, and community representatives. The self-directed process is voluntary in Idaho districts, but the division of instruction had convinced the Elk River superintendent that it was in the district's best interests to volunteer. Dick Nelson of the state department engineered the entire process, beginning in December 1976. He visited Elk River and, in an open community meeting, explained the seventeen-step flow chart outlining the model the state department had prescribed for the needs assessment.

A steering committee was appointed by the school board (two teachers, the superintendent, and six community "patrons") to coordinate the project. They held a "speak-up" session to identify community concerns. They constructed a questionnaire using the information gathered at the meeting and mailed it to all members of the Elk River district. The responses—residents' ideas of the needs of the school—were then compiled, along with information from student achievement tests. Next, a needs-assessment committee was appointed, the needs were ranked and analyzed, and a priority list was drawn up. Nelson was impressed by the interest shown by Elk River community members in the project. "In a small community like that," he says, "you can get everybody. Communications are clear; it's easier to identify what the community wants."

Twenty "learner needs" of the Elk River district were identified through assessment and reported to the state department. They were grouped in three categories: "extremely critical," "critical," and "important." The top need of the school district was said to be "a systematic curriculum and extracurricular process for all grades, K-12." More advanced courses, special education classes, and the reinforcement of basic math skills were among the critical needs, while a variety of vocational skills, leadership skill development, an effective counseling system, and "more exposure to actual situations in preparing for lifetime employment" were listed as important.

The needs for systematic reading and testing programs were selected as the priorities for implementation in the 1978-79 school year. (Better testing in the "content areas" was what the group was seeking—Elk River was already using Science Research Associates—SRA—achievement testing in basic skills areas.) The committee's final report, written by Jack Deits shortly after he took over the superintendency, suggested ways the needs could be resolved and concluded with a timetable for implementation of the recommendations.

The recommendations of the committee closely matched the curriculum development that was already taking place at Elk River, and it spurred the work along. As a result, says Wes Snow, "We know where we want to go on a K-12 basis. We'd talked about curriculum development for years, but didn't have support for it. Now we have the cooperation of the administration and the community, and the time and resources to get it done."

Deits was impressed with the initiatives taken by his teachers and gave them rein to go further. "If you don't have teacher commitment to a curriculum, you won't implement it," he says. "That's the key—the teachers have to decide they want to use something." In the fall of 1978, elementary teachers Van Thompson and Mona Martin, while attending a regional in-service workshop, heard about a National Diffusion Network (NDN) program to individualize reading, math, and language arts instruction in grades 1–8 from the Idaho state NDN facilitator. (See Chapter 8 in this volume on the National Diffusion Network.) The program, called Model Classrooms, is a procedure for instructional management, not a curriculum itself. Teachers trained in the procedure learn to take their own texts and workbooks, or their own curriculum materials, and catalog and cross-reference them so that students can work through them individually with their own progress charts. The teacher's role becomes one of checking workbooks and talking over work with each student. The program was originally developed at Moses Lake, Washington, and Deits and the elementary teachers traveled there to learn more about it. As a result of the trip, an application was made for an Elementary and Secondary Education Act Title IV-C grant to pay the costs of the program at Elk River for the year 1979-80. The grant was approved, and plans were made to install the system in Elk River classrooms.

## A Better School for Whom?

In April 1979 Jack Deits submitted Elk River's annual petition to be recognized as a "remote and necessary" school. He was able to list several accomplishments for the Elk River district in the year since the last application was made: full accreditation of the high school program, the completion of the needs assessment, the curriculum work in math and physics, and the outline for further curriculum development in line with district goals. He noted the schools' adoption of the Model Classrooms program as well as another facilitator-promoted program in elementary physical education. He reported that the district had instituted a Right to Read project and a new special education program. It was a strong application, written with pride. Moreover, Deits was confident enough in his petition to be able to offer a mild criticism of the format he was supposed to follow in preparing the petition. He suggested that it implied a negative rather than a positive view of schools such as Elk River's by its emphasis on "needs rather than accomplishments, necessity rather than desirability, [and] remoteness rather than uniqueness." He said the special funding was needed not only because the school was necessary, but because as a tiny country school it was valuable—an "endangered species" worthy of preservation—and without the funding, one of the "last outposts of American education" would be forsaken.

Deits could have opened a little controversy with that argument. The state education department would automatically presume schools such as Elk River's to be handicapped in their educational potential, as it is committed to the definition of a single standard of quality education across all districts in the state. That definition inevitably puts high consideration on the number of curricular offerings in the school, the degree of specialization of a teacher's professional training, and the extensiveness of a school's facilities. As long as that view holds, the burden to prove excellence will fall on those schools least able to marshal an impressive array of resources. Deits said that he was rearranging the categories for the report in order to project the school as an "active, viable, and desirable" part of education in the state, but he stopped short of questioning the fairness of the state department's assumptions in the first place.

His caution is understandable. It is the school's constant vulnerability to a critical evaluation by the state department of education that has been the primary concern here for several years. Even now, the school's survival hinges on whether the state's curriculum inspectors are satisfied by what they see taking place at Elk River. As recent educational improvement efforts here have taken shape amid concern over losing accreditation status and hence the loss of the special funding, the improvements have been largely consistent with the state department's notions of what they ought to be. Deits noted in his petition that all the curriculum development at Elk River has been based on guides provided by the state department for that purpose. As a result, the program at the Elk River School could be as easily found in Moscow, Pocatello, or Boise.

"Eighty percent of what we do is pretty comparable to what kids would get anywhere else," says Van Thompson. "But as we do something, it comes out differently." Indeed, educational improvement efforts at Elk River seem to focus on adapting conventional techniques and materials to local exigencies. In order to offer a standard secondary curriculum, including advanced science and math courses, business courses, foreign languages, and industrial arts, Elk River has used state aid to hire additional teachers, bringing its student-teacher ratio in grades 9–12 down to 5.3:1. Similarly, the Model Classrooms project in the elementary grades represents a way for teachers to adapt standardized curriculum materials for use in a classroom that includes students of a wide age and ability span.

The adaptations of conventional approaches that have been implemented at Elk River have been wisely chosen and they have served their purpose. The Elk River staff *is* able to measure its instructional accomplishments in the same way used by suburban schools outside Boise—by student achievement on standardized tests. Many schools in the nation would love to have Elk River's composites: On the SRA basic skills section, students schoolwide scored at the 52nd percentile; for grades 7–11, the 66th percentile. Not surprisingly, the local educational improvement effort has won the praise of state department officials. State Superintendent Jerry Evans has watched the school for several years, and he's been impressed by it. "When you talk about the problems of rural education in isolated settings, and what a school district can do to maintain a quality program in spite of them, that's Elk River." For now, Elk River seems safely in the state department's good graces.

But does educational improvement aimed at getting your house in order in the opinion of state officials mean the same as improvement that would benefit your local community? The state education standards reflect a bias in favor of a comprehensive secondary curriculum oriented primarily to giving students a background for further education or training for specialized positions in a centralized, urbanized society. By adhering as closely as they can to those standards, the Elk River School staff is committing itself to an academic program that some might argue is not altogether relevant to unique local needs. How important is German I and II to life in Elk River? What about physics, in fact, when some high school students are unable to distinguish between white pine and birch in the woods in which they might be working? What assumptions about the worth of Elk River in comparison to the outside world of professions, industry, and bureaucracy lie behind the Elk River curriculum?

The Elk River teachers are not in the least confused by such questions. "We try to give them things so they can leave," explains Van Thompson. "Kids could go from Elk River to somewhere else and fit right in. And that's what we encourage them to do. Whenever we get into a situation where we're talking about job opportunities, I try to point out that there are a lot of things more enjoyable than getting up at 4 a.m. and logging. It doesn't take much to convince them. It's a fact that the only job here is working in the woods. There's nothing at all for a woman in this town." Apparently it is the school staff's intent to channel students away from Elk River, and it is an intent that has the support of school board member Margaret Pflanagan: "There's only one real world," she says. "We want them to be prepared for it."

Ray Ireland, whose father was a logging boss in a lumber camp near Elk River, has noticed that "kids aren't staying around after they graduate like they were six or seven years ago. We've taught them that. We've taught them to go. Maybe it's been our undoing—we've lost some potentially excellent community members; but I have to look at it from the students' point of view." Sophomore Kelly Kreisher's point of view is, "I don't want to marry a logger. I'm not going to stay here."

In fact, Elk River teachers are clear enough about their intent that they have carried the process one step farther, beyond merely giving their students the academic skills they need to compete with students from urban and suburban areas. They are at the same time building into the educational program experiences to increase the students' exposure to the world outside Elk River and to develop their ability to survive in it. Out-of-town field trips, for example, are a high priority at the Elk River school. In 1978 the school board and administration convinced the state board of education to buy them a new sixty-six–passenger school bus under the "remote and necessary" funding, to be used exclusively for field trips. The district also owns a van and a station wagon, and they are frequently all in use at the same time. "Their motors hardly ever cool off," notes Deits. In the fall of 1979, all the teachers at the Elk River school will be trained as school bus drivers. When that is done, according to Deits, "with very few exceptions, when a teacher wants to take a trip, he or she can just fire up that rig and go."

A large number of the school's field trips are to allow students to participate in activities at other schools. "Between athletics, Boys' State, Girls' State, the youth legislature, and music camp, just about every student participates in some activity that gets him or her out of town," says Mary Simeone. On a recent spring school day, third- and fourth-grade teacher Janet Thonney had her class attending a gymnastic meet at a college in Pullman, Washington, and the tennis team was at Sun Valley. One senior boy had qualified for the state track meet in Boise, and his coach had driven him there. "Parents here are determined that their kids get every chance that other kids would get," says Deits. "We'll always come up with the money somehow. As long as we operate this school, they'll be going places."

In 1974, says Van Thompson, the whole school went to the World's Fair in Spokane. "In 1976, we went to see the Freedom Train come through. We always try to pick something of interest to the kids." Thonney has taken her class to visit a lumber mill similar to the one that once operated in Elk River, to the post office and telephone company in Moscow, and to a bank in Troy, among other places. "Most of the parents like to have their kids go places," she says. "I've never had a parent say 'No' to a field trip." "I want them to see what's available out there," explains Ray Ireland. When he took his woodworking class to see a toy factory, "the kids were amazed to see people making seven or eight dollars an hour, doing the same thing they've been doing here in this class."

The school staff also tries to invite guests to the school from outside Elk River as often as possible. English teacher Mary Simeone scheduled successive visits by an environmentalist ardently opposed to the use of the powerful pesticide D-425 in the woods and then a representative of the U.S. Forest Service to argue in favor of the chemical. She has also written a proposal for a grant to get a poet to come to the school for two weeks and work with students on poetry writing. "I'm constantly looking for real live people for the kids to get close to," she says. "Anyone who can come here and have anything at all to offer, I'm all for. So that the kids know there is something else in the world besides school and TV and drinking on Friday nights." Elk River kids face a dilemma in deciding whether they want to stay, she says; they know, however, that "logging makes an old man out of you in a hurry."

No one would know that better than Ted Malm, the 49-year-old chairman of the Elk River school board. Malm has worked in the woods all his adult life. He's ready to verify that logging is a hard life, and he's convinced the school should encourage Elk River kids to leave town if they are able. "I don't think any man should have to bust his back for a living," he says. "That's what a lot of us do. What's it get him? It's just like—a miner doesn't want his boy to be a miner. A lumberjack doesn't want his boy to be a lumberjack. These people have worked hard all their lives. They don't think it's a way to go." Promoting options outside of Elk River doesn't do local youth a disservice, Malm believes, because ultimately "there's more who stay than who leave," and the work is there "for those that want it, you bet." Regardless of how hard the school pushes, there are still strong forces tying kids to their hometown, says Susan Swearingen, a high school junior. "It kind of gets scary when you think about going somewhere else," she says. "You can always stay here. A lot of kids see their parents here, they've been here all their life, and they're happy—so, why leave?"

Ray Hill, now a logging foreman for Diamond International, says that the future of the town is perhaps not as bleak as some might make it out to be, noting that there are jobs available in areas related peripherally to logging, such as fire protection, forestry management, or wildlife conservation. In fact, the school recognizes that option. The exposure to the outside world, in that case, serves as a sort of leadership development exercise. "As a teacher," explains Mary Simeone (who moved to the Elk River area eight years ago with her artist husband), "I want them to get out and see the world so they can make a responsible decision. I told my class the other day about a conversation I overheard in the post office. Someone was asking about the availability of land in this area—they were considering moving in. Kids need to know that some people are *choosing* to live here. We made that choice. The kids could, too, but it's got to be an independent decision."

## The Price of a State-Approved Program

The Elk River story has been widely told. As Hope Kading, Idaho's former representative to the Education Commission of the States, told me, "Whenever there's a group discussing remote schools and their inadequacies, someone always says, 'But look at Elk River.'" There is undeniably a tale of success here; but on a closer look, a variety of complicating questions arise.

It is first of all a story of a community *reacting* to outside pressures rather than *acting* on its own initiatives. And it appears that it will remain that way for some time: As long as the land around Elk River is controlled by the Potlatch Corporation, Diamond International, and the U.S. Forest Service, there will be little opportunity for diversified economic growth. And as long as the school staff must devote its energies and resources to the operation of a program deemed acceptable by the state's division of instruction, there will be little opportunity for locally inspired innovation in curriculum and programming.

"Educational improvement" at Elk River School has been seen as the various steps necessary to satisfy the inspectors from the state education department. Those steps have included: (1) making the educational program "systematic" by establishing specific goals and objectives for each course, based on uniform curricular standards set forth by the Idaho Department of Education; (2) adding German I and II to Mary Simeone's teaching schedule; and (3) replacing the informal counseling of Ray Ireland with that of a certified psychological examiner.

One of the consequences of this approach to educational improvement is that students here are being prepared for futures that are available only outside of Elk River. The state curriculum standards are designed with the understanding that secondary schools can all be measured by uniform criteria; these criteria are based on a view that the primary purpose of secondary education is to provide the background necessary for higher education and/or work in an urban/industrial society.

The question to be considered is whether there is "only one real world," as Margaret Pflanagan (a recent immigrant from California) believes, or several worlds—with Elk River being seen as a place unto itself, with its own schooling needs. It is, after all, an isolated community, and the problems it faces are clearly quite different from those facing urban and suburban communities in other parts of the state. Does that mean that the Elk River school program should at least take unique local realities into consideration? Ted Malm points out that there are more youth who stay in Elk River than there are those who leave, in spite of the school's constant orientation to the outside world. Are these youths being adequately served by the Elk River school?

It appears that the Elk River community is not particularly troubled by that question. Perhaps the forces that bind young people to their hometown are so strong that they don't need additional support, whereas the ideas of individual initiative, enterprise, and ambition must be constantly reinforced. Many people in Elk River are convinced that the grass may not be quite as green, but the opportunities for a prosperous and exciting life are greater on the other side of the mountains, an attitude implied in John Morris's explanation that industries would never locate in  Elk River "because their managers wouldn't want to live in a town like this." There are many hardships in Elk River, and in spite of the fact that the natural setting of the town is as lovely as people could ever hope for, the truth is that the outlook for the town's future is not an encouraging one. Given the situation, the community's approach to school improvement may be entirely reasonable.

The truth is, the question is largely academic. For the Elk River school to serve the local community, it must first survive, and right now it appears that the only way that it will survive is by meeting the standards imposed on it by the state department of education. Ultimately, therefore, questions about the appropriateness of this model of school improvement in a community of fewer than 400 residents must be addressed to state officials themselves. The real issue is whether the Idaho accreditation standards are either fair or practical when it comes to evaluating a thirty-student high school in a geographically isolated community. The Elk River staff have shown that, given adequate resources, they *can* satisfy the requirements for secondary accreditation—but the cost is heavy. Meeting those standards demands a determined effort; all the resources, both human and material, must be brought to bear on that single objective, to the exclusion of more creative (and perhaps more relevant) uses of those resources.

Meeting state standards also demands money. In his 1979 "remote and necessary" petition, Deits said that he needed $368,000 to operate his school (a per-pupil cost of over $4,300), of which over $100,000 would have to come from special state funding. He recalls the response he received: "They said, 'Well, Jack, your budget may be a little high compared to the rest of the state,' but I said, 'Well, I don't know how you can ask me to run an accredited program without it.'" Elk River's special funding is taken off the top of the state aid to education package, meaning that it in effect reduces the state aid available to other districts in the state, few of which are spending anywhere near $4,300 per pupil. Because of statutory restrictions, Elk River is still the only district to have applied for the special funding, however, so the loss to other districts is negligible. If other districts were included, "a controversy might develop," says Dick Nelson.

Elk River's ultimate vulnerability is also made clear by the fact that although it has enjoyed the luxury of generous state funding (the district has each year been given the full amount requested to operate its program under the "remote and necessary" guidelines), there are still those who doubt whether a school the size of Elk River's can ever have a high-quality educational program. Before Jerry Evans was elected to the state superintendency—when he was still an official in the division of instruction—he remarked to a colleague, "I'm going to take a real hard look at Elk River." He has since been pleased by what he has seen but still says, "No way would I consider it an optimum program." An optimum program presumably could be put together only in a much larger school—a consolidated school. The consolidation bill was "dropped as a legislative priority" by state department lobbyists in 1969, but it could reemerge. When economic pressures once again make consolidation a politically allowable action, it could spell trouble for Elk River.

But is it really necessary to choose between the consolidation of the Elk River school on one hand and, on the other, the maintenance of a program that is both expensive and of questionable relevance to local needs? If the school were instead given the freedom to experiment with interdisciplinary approaches, with a teaching staff of generalists rather than specialists, with experiential rather than laboratory- or classroom-based instruction, and with the use of local resources, substantial savings would undoubtedly be realized. And if the school were freed from strict adherence to the goals and objectives of a state-mandated curriculum, the educational program might be tailored more closely to the local socioeconomic realities, and there might emerge a truly exemplary model of education for tiny schools in isolated communities.

# 14

# Gary, Texas:
# The Rise of *Loblolly*

*Thomas Gjelten*

Teachers in Gary, Texas, learn quickly that high school basketball is taken seriously in their part of the state. The high school parking lot on a Monday morning following a showdown with nearby Latexo High School provides ample evidence: Virtually every vehicle has its windows covered with spray-painted slogans like "Bobcats are #1!" and "Go, Bobcats, Go!" With only eighty-nine students in grades nine through twelve, Gary High School is too small to have a football team—which has only heightened its feverish passion for basketball. The "school spirit" is shared by the community at large. On the nights of home games, the gym overflows with families and friends of the ballplayers. A group of mothers sells refreshments in the lobby; fathers cluster around the doorways. The fans are loud and enthusiastic. Cheering for the Bobcats, it seems, is cheering for Gary.

Gary is a town of barely 200 people in the lush pastureland of east Texas. The economy of the area has gone through a series of transformations since the region was settled in the late 1800s. In the beginning, it was based on lumbering; later, cotton and tomato farming were important. Oil and gas development and cattle raising have been the dominant activities since then. The newest hope for revitalization of the region is the mining of lignite, a form of soft coal that lies in long, shallow seams under Panola County grasslands and forests.

Gary has lost most of its commercial functions since the early 1900s, when it served as the shipping center to which local farmers brought their crates of tomatoes and bales of cotton to be loaded onto railroad boxcars. The town square is now surrounded by a gas station, a grocery, a general store, a post office, and a volunteer fire department garage. Around the outskirts of town sit five Baptist churches. Most of the families with children in the school live outside of town. Some men work in local cattle-raising, timbering, or petroleum enterprises, but most commute to work in neighboring towns and cities. A few travel as far as Shreveport, Louisiana, each day, forty miles northeast of Gary.

Social studies teacher Lincoln King tells his students that the area around Gary is in many ways more similar to parts of Georgia, Alabama, and Mississippi than to rural areas of Texas only 150 miles to the west. It shares with those states east of it a Deep South identity. Blacks and whites have lived separately throughout most of the history of the area. The schools in Panola County, where Gary is located, have been integrated only for the last seven years. Some local establishments maintained informal segregation even later. Gary itself is an all-white community. The Gary Independent School District is one of only a handful in the state with no black students; there simply are no black families living in the fifty-nine square miles between its boundaries.

Like many Class B schools in Texas, Gary's community school is organized as an independent district under the administration of a five-member local school board. There is one building for all 202 students K–12, a one-story structure built in the early 1950s. Elementary students have their classrooms in one wing of the school and take their recess in a playground behind the building; junior high and high school students attend classes in the other wing and congregate during breaks around their cars in the parking lot or under the trees in front of the school.

Superintendent T. M. Hooper teaches two high school classes, including advanced biology, "because I'm the only one certified to teach it." Until the school board hired a full-time maintenance man in the fall of 1978, Hooper was also responsible for much of the school's general repairs, working on everything from school buses to the building's plumbing. "Believe me," he says, "I know this baby from the ground up." He works closely with the high school principal, Stanley Yarborough, on most matters, including student discipline. "If I came in here at 8 a.m. each morning and locked the door and fought records all day, I'd go nuts," Hooper says. "I'm still in touch with the kids. I think too many administrators lose contact with them. In some systems, they're even regarded as the enemy. I like to keep feeling their pulse, knowing what's important to them." He has received the inside word on high school life in Gary through his two teenage sons and his wife Barbara, the high school English teacher. He is likewise familiar with the community, having grown up ten miles south of Gary in the town of Timpson.

Principal Yarborough also teaches—four math classes a day. His office adjoins a classroom, and he manages to monitor both scenes of activity simultaneously. On the wall of his office hangs a thirty-inch wooden paddle, but it is rarely used, he says: "These kids are honest. You ask them a straight question, you'll almost always get a straight answer." Both he and Hooper are part-time farmers, raising cattle and growing hay.

Most Gary youth seem to feel comfortable with their community. Although the employment future is bleak, many would like to stay, echoing the sentiments of eleventh grader Dwain Lake: "I won't probably ever leave Gary, myself. I'll probably have my house here. I'll probably end up getting a job somewhere else, like Longview or Shreveport, but I'll live in Gary. I like the way it's open, not just crowded in with everybody. You can have your own space."

The school remains the center of community life and identity. Though a ten-mile paved road connects Gary to Carthage, a town of about 5,000, school consolidation has never been a serious threat. "I'd fight to the death to save the school," says Bobby Strain, Gary school board member, and he undoubtedly would not be alone. "We're tough ones," says Mrs. Sistrunk, co-owner with her husband of G & S grocery, gas station, and general store—Gary's entire business district. "We haven't ever passed out. But if the school went, it'd be all over. You see it all around in these little towns. First the school goes, then the store moves out, then it's dead. People don't build there anymore. It just grows up empty land."

It is around the extracurricular athletic program that the community support of and involvement in the school has traditionally focused. Each year, there is an annual alumni homecoming, or "Roundup," as it is known in Gary. The central event of the weekend is a basketball game. The same spirit is evident in the Gary PTA. There are over 150 members, and the monthly meetings are often standing-room-only affairs. Many of the most active members no longer have children in school but continue to stay involved because of their support of the school. The group is highly successful in its fund raising; annual Halloween carnivals often net several thousand dollars. Most of their funds go to support school sports.

The central role of the athletic program is also evident in the school itself. A large glass case crammed tight with trophies stands in the front hallway, which is otherwise bare. The school gym is large and modern. It was completed in the fall of 1972, less than eighteen months after the wing of the school containing the previous gym had burned to the ground. High school classrooms, however, are sparsely equipped. The library is small and almost empty of students. The Gary PTA has helped the home economics department and the business program by buying them sewing machines and typewriters, but the science classroom still does not have full laboratory facilities. "Athletics is the center point in a lot of these rural schools," says Superintendent Hooper. "In many towns, the most important faculty member is the coach. I've known school boards to attract a good coach by offering him the superintendent job."

Yet the academic track record of Gary High School students is not unimpressive. About 50 percent of Gary graduates in recent years have gone on to college. Of those who have enrolled at Panola Junior College in Carthage in the last three years, more than half were honor students. "Our kids do just as well on test scores and in college as students from larger schools," says Yarborough. "I think the small size of our classes has a lot to do with it." Barbara Hooper agrees. "There's a relaxed atmosphere here," she says. "If they'll be still and listen to me for fifteen minutes, five days a week, I can teach them something that in a larger school, with hard discipline class-rooms, would take me two or three weeks."

Classes may be smaller and less formal than larger schools, but the instruction itself is thoroughly conventional. Social studies teacher King, whose classes range from geography to a mandated course, Fundamentals of the American Free Enterprise System, says that he uses classic teaching methods. "We use the book, and the questions in the book, and I lecture quite a bit. I don't think the traditional approaches are all bad."

## The Birth of *Loblolly*

In December 1972 Mary Nell King received as a Christmas gift from her uncle a copy of *The Foxfire Book*. It was a collection of articles on the crafts and folklore of Appalachian mountain people living in remote northeastern Georgia, written by students at Rabun Gap-Nacoochee High School in Rabun Gap, Georgia. The articles had been published previously in a quarterly magazine the students themselves produced, *Foxfire*. They con-sisted of interviews students had conducted with neighbors and relatives on subjects ranging from planting by the signs and mountain superstitions to violin making. The book was edited and introduced by their teacher, Eliot Wigginton.

King's husband Lincoln was fascinated by the book and over his Christmas vacation read it from cover to cover. He was especially im-pressed by the fact that a group of rural high school students had written it and by Wigginton's introduction to the book. In the introduction, Wig-ginton told the story of how the magazine had started, how it was put to-gether, how it was financed, and why it was so important:

> Looking beyond Rabun Gap and *Foxfire*, I can't get over the feeling that many similar projects could be duplicated successfully in many other areas of the country, and to the genuine benefit of almost everyone involved.
>
> Daily our grandparents are moving out of our lives, taking with them, ir-reparably, the kind of information contained in this book. They are taking it, not because they want to, but because they think we don't care.
>
> The big problem, of course, is that since these grandparents were primarily an oral civilization, information being passed through the generations by word of mouth and demonstration, little of it is written down. When they're gone, the magnificent hunting tales, the ghost stories that kept a thousand children sleepless, the intricate tricks of self-sufficiency acquired through years

of trial and error, the eloquent and haunting stories of suffering and sharing and building and healing and planting and harvesting—all these go with them, and what a loss.

If this information is to be saved at all, for whatever reason, it must be saved now; and the logical researchers are the grandchildren, not university researchers from the outside. In the process, these grandchildren (and we) gain an invaluable unique knowledge about their own roots, heritage, and culture.[1]

"I put that book down and said, 'We could do that here,'" Lincoln King recalls. He returned to school after Christmas vacation and told the administrators about his idea of starting a local history magazine with the freshman geography class. Principal Yarborough thought it was a great idea. From Superintendent Hooper, he received a tentative okay.

King went to the ninth graders, told them about the book, and asked them if they'd be interested in trying it in Gary. The area, after all, did have its own rich country heritage: Singer Jim Reeves came from Panola County, and movie star Tex Ritter was born, raised, and schooled in Gary itself. King explained to the students that they would, with his help, be responsible for choosing the subjects to investigate, for identifying the people who would be sources of information, for doing the interviews, for transcribing the tapes, and for editing. It was an ambitious idea. "I had no background whatsoever in journalism," King says. "I knew nothing at all about the technical aspects of preparing a magazine and was totally dumbfounded by the mechanics of photography. On top of that, we didn't have any money in the school budget for a project of this nature. But I told the kids that if they were interested in looking into it, I was willing to learn along with them and help in whatever way I could."

The students recognized an opportunity to escape from a textbook-and-lecture geography class and agreed to try to put together the magazine. King suggested that their first problem was to raise the money they would need to undertake the task. They decided to sell "stock" in the proposed magazine at two dollars per share. For one share, buyers were promised a free copy of the first issue. For the truly faithful—those who would buy five shares—they offered a one-year subscription to the magazine. "They really didn't know what they were buying, and we didn't know what we were selling," says King.

Between student-solicited advertising from area merchants and the sale of stock, the class raised enough money to buy a tape recorder, make a down payment on an IBM typewriter, and pay their $360 printing bill. Each day during "geography" class, King and the students discussed the significance of what they were setting out to do, as Wigginton had explained. The thought of leaving school during the day to go out and interview old people, however, did not quite fit in with the school experience students had come to expect and even to depend on in Gary. What King was asking them to do was unfamiliar and, inevitably, frightening. "At first I almost had to shake the kids," King recalls. "They are conditioned like the rest of us. They sit in school waiting for someone to tell them what to do. All of a sudden someone comes along and says, 'What do you think about this?' They had to learn how to make decisions."

King guided the students in their consideration of interview possibilities. One of their first choices was Tressie Cozart, mother of the local postmistress and an expert soapmaker. J. R. Brannon, a teacher at the Panola County Junior College and a Gary native, heard about the students' project from Mary Nell King and suggested that they talk to his uncle, Monroe Brannon, an 86-year-old Gary resident who had moved to Panola County with his parents in 1895 and had a near-perfect memory of the community's early history.

Small groups of students began going out daily, tape recorders and cameras under their arms, to work on the interviews. Because they did not have drivers' licenses, King usually accompanied them. Emma Blair, one of the students in the class, describes her first interview: "We were scared to death. Mr. King had to push us through the door. We had made out a list of questions to ask her. She had told us a few things about herself. We were scared and worried that she would hush and then we wouldn't know what to say, but it didn't work out that way. She just talked for hours. Every once in a while we would try to get her back on the subject. She took us out and told us all the names of her chickens and things like that."

During class time, when students were not out selling ads or subscriptions or interviewing, they would work on the tedious task of transcribing the tapes. Working from handwritten copies, the students would select the best portions to be included in their articles. In the *Foxfire* style, they wrote short introductions to the articles, which were primarily verbatim texts of the interviewees' comments on selected subjects. The edited portions of the interviews were typed on the staff's new typewriter and laid out in a six-by-nine-inch magazine format. At one class meeting, King and the students chose a name for the magazine—*Loblolly*, after the scrubby pine tree indigenous to the area.

In April 1973 the first issue was published. It was thirty-six pages long and contained interviews with Mrs. Cozart, on soapmaking; Monroe Brannon, on recollections of his boyhood in Gary seventy-five years earlier; and Carol Malone, a resilient and feisty widow who had raised four children on her earnings from a newspaper delivery route in Carthage for twenty-six years.

The magazine was an instant success. The first printing of 500 copies were sold out almost immediately; King ordered a second printing. "We were ecstatic," he remembers. "The kids were bouncing off the walls. It was the first time they had ever done anything in school that really mattered to

someone besides them and their teacher. Now something they had produced had been published and distributed for everyone to see."

Flushed with success, the students continued to gather more material
throughout the spring, preparing for another issue of their magazine.
*Loblolly* was the talk of the entire community. The little high school where
it was produced, meanwhile, was feeling the reverberations of the accomplishment and the publicity. In a school tightly bound by tradition and
custom, the sudden emergence of a new student activity prompted many
questions. What, in fact, had been created? Superintendent Hooper had his
own concerns. "We've got a good school system here," he says. "Our
greatest fault as a district is that we're sometimes a little too ambitious. We
sometimes get so wrapped up and involved in something that we try to do
things that we're just not big enough to do." Had he seen the production of
*Loblolly* in that light? "Yes, I questioned it at first. I didn't know if we could
do it. If something's going out over the Gary school name, I want it right. I
cannot tolerate mistakes in anything."

A major question centered on the scheduling of the *Loblolly* activity in
the following school year. King wanted to continue working with the same
group of students, the class of 1976, as they were planning the production of
the magazine as their bicentennial project. To devote another social studies
class to *Loblolly*, however, would mean skipping required academic content. But how else could the group be kept together? Additionally, work on
the magazine involved a high demand on student and teacher time and
energy. It exposed the school and the students' writing—mistakes and
all—to the community. It involved groups of students leaving school on a
daily basis, often unsupervised and occasionally missing classes in their
regular academic subjects. At one point, Superintendent Hooper was convinced that such a disruptive activity could not be continued at Gary High
School.

But the enthusiastic reception the magazine had received in the community, the undeniable excitement that had sprung up in the lives of the students who had put it together, and King's determination to work as hard as
necessary to keep the project going were all persuasive factors. When the
fall schedule of classes appeared, Superintendent Hooper had arranged a
journalism elective for the tenth-grade class. The object of the class would
be to produce the school yearbook and *Loblolly*. King would continue to
carry his regular load of social studies classes; the tenth graders who had
passed in their geography texts the year before in order to work on *Loblolly*
could not avoid the history class this year. But *Loblolly* would continue.

In October 1973, the second issue of *Loblolly* was published. King mailed
a copy of it to Eliot Wigginton in Georgia and a copy to Max Haddick,
director of journalism for the University Interscholastic League, which
coordinates high school extracurricular activities in Texas. After receiving

the magazine, Wigginton wrote King a personal note, complimenting him on *Loblolly*. He told King that he had reported the news of *Loblolly*'s emergence to the Institutional Development and Economic Affairs Service (IDEAS), a Washington-based group that had lately taken an interest in "the Foxfire Concept."

It was the response from Haddick, however, that proved to be the turning point in *Loblolly*'s growth, according to King. Haddick was extremely impressed, writing back to King the same day he received the magazine, "*Loblolly* is the finest magazine published by a school that I have ever seen. I don't know how you inspired this fine staff to do this outstanding work, but I wish I did. If I could isolate whatever technique you used to motivate them to do this, I would immediately write it up and send it to every journalism, English, and history teacher in the state." With the tribute, Haddick included certificates of citation made out to each student whose name appeared on the magazine's masthead. "That was the first real outside recognition of what we were doing," King recalls, "and it gave us a real boost." Student Lauri Gauntt remembers, "When we got that letter from Dr. Haddick, it made me realize that what we were doing was valuable, and I was proud of it, and it made we want to work harder. It made me more serious about the project."

Later, the IDEAS organization wrote to the *Loblolly* staff, asking for a copy of the magazine and information on how it had started. They were impressed by the Texans' independent initiative. Brian Beun, the director of the group, had seen a copy of *Foxfire* in 1970 and was convinced that it was an idea of enormous import that could be duplicated in other school systems. During the following four years, Beun later wrote, Wigginton and the IDEAS staff collaborated in the development of "a framework for extending Foxfire to cultures beyond its origins. . . . More than a dozen locally-interpreted Foxfire-type projects were initiated with IDEAS' help. Each was established in a diverse geographic and cultural setting of the country."[2]

But *Loblolly* had not been one of them. Until that point, King had had no contact with anyone in what was already a burgeoning Foxfire movement. He had been inspired by *The Foxfire Book* and by Wigginton's introduction to it, but the first two issues of the magazine had been put together on a trial-and-error basis. No one associated with the production of *Foxfire*-type magazines had visited Gary or had even heard of *Loblolly*. Not one cent of outside financing had supported the magazine (in contrast to *Foxfire* itself, which had received several thousand dollars in grant support).

King discovered that IDEAS had received grants from the Ford Foundation and the National Endowment for the Humanities to subsidize the production of *Foxfire*-type magazines, and he wrote back to the organization and asked for their assistance. Like other magazines, *Loblolly* received some small grants for the purchase of additional tape recorders and darkroom equipment, as well as a larger grant that enabled King and the students to continue operations during the summer months. Funds were made available to hire students to handle the mail, circulation and advertising business, and clerical work. But, having begun with IDEAS's help, *Loblolly* remained essentially independent of the national organization. For King, the major benefit deriving from his contact with IDEAS was the opportunity to meet other teachers involved in similar projects. "What he got from us," says Murray Durst, one of the original IDEAS staff who worked on the dissemination of the Foxfire concept, "was less technical assistance than it was the reinforcement of other people who were doing the same thing. He needed to talk to teachers who shared his situation."

As part of its support for the concept, IDEAS prepared to publish two handbooks for schools that were instituting Foxfire programs. *You and Aunt Arie*, written by Pamela Wood, advisor to *Salt* (a successful *Foxfire* type magazine published by Maine high school students), was to be a how-to student text for magazine staffers. *Moments*, written by Wigginton, was a pedagogical analysis of what he called the Foxfire Learning Process, written for teachers.[3] King was among five magazine advisors summoned to Washington to assist in the drafting of the outline for the latter book.

Largely due to IDEAS's efforts, there was developing a tight, mutually supportive network of Foxfire projects around the country. *Loblolly*, however, continued to be on the periphery. It was alone among the *Foxfire* offshoots in its independent origin. It was also the only *Foxfire*-type magazine to include advertising, a major diversion from what was a fairly rigid *Foxfire* formula. The *Loblolly* staff cared most about self-sufficiency, reliance on neither out-of-state readers nor frequent grants, and keeping the support and involvement of their own community, including local merchants. "We had no choice," says King. "We couldn't exist without advertising. Two-thirds of our printing costs are paid by ad revenue. Besides, it's one more learning experience for the kids, and it's one more way for us to be connected to the community."

Through 1974 and 1975 the *Loblolly* staff continued to put out an issue every three months, including summer issues. The class of 1976 remained solely responsible for it, working either during the journalism elective period or after school. In the process of putting out the magazine, the students were making friends with people sixty and seventy years their senior. They developed a particularly close relationship with Monroe Brannon, one of their original subjects. Because he had lived in Gary almost all his life, and because his memory was so complete and detailed, students used him as a source on almost every major story. "It was fantastic the way he could remember dates," says Lauri Gauntt, "the exact day and year that something happened. And it seems like he's done everything. He's been a pharmacist, he's been a detective, a farmer. And also you can tell by talking to him that he had a lot of fun when he was our age. He's still got a mischievous air about him." (In one story recorded in *Loblolly*, Brannon told the students about the days when clothes were made from flour sacks: "We went to a church meeting one night, and people got all happy and was shouting and carrying on. We had a favorite flour called Bellwood's Best. And this ol' lady fell over a bench, and her clothes flew up and on her petticoats, it said, '48 pounds of Bellwood's best.' That liked to have killed us all.")

*Loblolly* interviewers soon learned that Panola County was full of such enchanting characters. One of them was Corbett Akins, county sheriff for many years and, according to his own account, the only man around who has ever been shot between the eyes and lived to tell about it. Some girls visited the Women's Missionary Auxiliary of Good Hope Baptist Church in Timpson, whose members have raised over $5,000 for their church by quilting, to observe their craft. The staffers not only recorded their story, but also sat down with them, helped thread needles, and learned the art.

Max Haddick followed the magazine closely, offering advice and assistance ("Don't get slick!" was his constant admonition). In 1975, Haddick told King to bring his magazine staff to Austin for an Interscholastic League Press Convention, where they were surprised with an award from the chairman of the state bicentennial commission. *Loblolly* was the first officially designated high school bicentennial project in Texas, and it deserved special commemoration.

The following year, the staff prepared a 200-page bicentennial issue focusing on the economic history of Panola County. It was paid for by matching grants from the Texas High School Bicentennial Commission and the Panola County Commissioners Court. It was the closing effort of the class of 1976. The group of indifferent ninth graders who produced the first issue only under the threat of having to return to geography class had in their next three high school years followed with twelve more issues, each a higher quality product than the last. It had in that time become an accepted fact of Gary High School life. Children along the elementary wing of the school regarded the high school student journalists with the same reverence they felt for the local basketball heroes. They looked forward to the years when they, too, could go out on interviews and see their own names appear in print in those magazines stacked on the counters of groceries and drug stores in downtown Carthage.

The twenty-member class of 1976, all of whom had been active in work on *Loblolly* throughout their high school career, chose as their commencement speaker Max Haddick, their loyal patron. In their final year as *Loblolly* staffers, the class had trained fourteen juniors to continue the magazine after they graduated. Within a month after the seniors had left the school a summer issue, prepared completely by the juniors, was published. The following fall, the *Loblolly*/yearbook journalism class was formalized as an elective activity open to juniors and seniors, an arrangement that exists at the present time.

In the fall of 1978, the twenty-second issue of *Loblolly* hit the newsstands. It was a special issue on the escapades of Bonnie and Clyde in east Texas, as recollected by relatives, acquaintances, and people whose paths the famous outlaws had momentarily crossed. It sold out within two weeks.

## *Loblolly* as a Curricular Innovation

One doesn't need to read *Moments* to recognize the educational benefits of working on a magazine such as *Loblolly*. The obvious knowledge of local history that students gain often reinforces an understanding of regional or national historical events. By talking to old-timers about the variety of ways people have made a living in the southern portion of Panola County, students gain an understanding of the relationship between natural resources and economic activity and the ways in which local people are dependent on large networks of commercial transactions for their own livelihood.

The interviewing, transcribing, editing, and writing that go into a *Loblolly* article are opportunities for learning basic communication skills. In preparing for a *Loblolly* interview, King often had his students read the portion of *You and Aunt Arie* that described in detail how to conduct a proper interview. Students practiced with each other, working on how to keep a person on the subject as much as possible, what kinds of questions to ask to keep the conversation lively, when to listen, and when to interject. Back in class, students must transcribe oral conversation into written phrases and sentences, properly punctuated and spelled. They need to summarize lengthy portions, edit out others, and write their own introductions.

Heavily cognitive skills of organization and synthesis are also involved. King said that as students progress in the *Loblolly* class, they graduate to increasingly complex stories. He cited one student who worked on a story for an entire year—an article on the development of businesses around Carthage's central square. Such stories often involve dozens of interviews with different people and the research of written records.

The knowledge students gain of local history and culture contributes to a deepened sense of citizenship and an understanding of their personal identity as a share of a larger community identity. Annette Gray, for example, who prepared an article on Margie Neal, the first woman state senator in Texas and a Panola County native, reports that she "was proud to do a story on her. It's about time she was recognized. She's done a lot for Panola County!"

The subject matter of *Loblolly* is derived from the students' own experience. An interest in trapping led Dwain Lake to begin asking people about it: "That was one of the main things people around here did to make a living," he now knows. "I like to hear older people talk about how Gary was back at the turn of the century," says Charles Wyatt. "It used to be called Zuber. It was a real swinging town. All the farmers would come in with their crops and sell them. There were quite a few bars back then."

What the students are gaining through their work on *Loblolly*, says King, is a greater sense of pride in their own community and their heritage: "The success of *Loblolly* is in effect a stamp of outside approval of them and their culture. That's important, because this is a pretty culturally isolated area. Kids don't ordinarily get that many experiences dealing with the outside world, and it's easy to feel self-conscious about where you come from."

The production of a magazine is a complicated enterprise, and students engaged in it also learn practical vocational skills. Robert Pike, the Carthage printer who handles the *Loblolly* job, works to make the mechanical production of the magazine a real-life learning experience: "I let them do as much of the work themselves as possible. I want them to learn what it takes to get what you say into print. If they're not doing it right, I'll make them do it over. I feel like I'm giving them some basic knowledge." Handling the bookkeeping for *Loblolly*, which is a legal corporation, is another aspect of the business that students manage themselves. Advertising rates must be set to cover projected printing costs, and billing for ads and subscriptions must be done.

The publicity *Loblolly* has received has afforded many opportunities for its staff to meet the public. The project has been featured in prominent articles in Houston and Dallas newspapers and staff members have been interviewed on several radio and television programs in Texas and Louisiana. Principal Yarborough sees such experiences as some of the most important benefits of the magazine. "Their being able to communicate with adults, this is something that has fascinated me. When I was at that age, I didn't like to talk to teachers or older people particularly, and these kids have been on television, they've been on radio, and they have been at meetings. They've had to stand up and talk to groups of people. Being a small school, we don't have a public speech course, but this has helped a lot of them."

Because what they produce is seen by many other people, students learn a greater sense of responsibility for their work. The need to accomplish specific tasks is an opportunity for learning self-discipline and organization. Annette Gray, who worked on *Loblolly* in addition to the yearbook and still practiced two to four hours daily on basketball, says, "I had a set time for everything. I learned I could do a lot in five minutes."

Students working on *Loblolly* also learn *how to learn*. "I still don't know my way around the darkroom," King notes. "When kids needed to learn something, they learned from each other." When Larry Anderson, a reporter and photographer for a Carthage newspaper was in the school one day, students nabbed him. "They were having some problems in the darkroom," Anderson explains. "I answered some questions and gave them some advice." From that time on, students knew where to take their photographic problems. Lauri Gauntt advises that teachers considering the sponsorship of a magazine like *Loblolly* needn't hesitate for lack of special skills: "If a teacher has the desire to make it work, that's all that's needed. Because you can get help. . . . There's always someone who will come in and help if you ask."

Perhaps the most important benefit of working on the magazine is found in the affective domain of learning. "It puts students in the limelight for a while when they really need to be put there," says King. "It's still with me," said Annette Gray when she was a freshman at Panola Junior College. "It's right here. I'm able to meet people better. I've got a lot more poise. People know about *Loblolly*. I can go up to some of these kids [at the college] and say, 'I played a small part in that.' They can't beat it."

The view that *Loblolly* is a valuable learning opportunity and therefore deserves to be a key part of the school program in Gary has its supporters in the community. Ronnie Griffin, a Gary farmer and former school board member, sees ventures such as *Loblolly* as essential for rural schools: "You have to have more than just the Three R's in a school; you have to teach the kids about community involvement and about getting along with your fellow man."

The view that this kind of cultural journalism is a legitimate role for the community high school to play is underscored by the logic of having students do the research. "Older people are kind of shy," says Charles Wyatt. "It's easier for them to talk to kids that they know than it is to somebody else." Carthage banker Bill Applegate, a Gary native and an early *Loblolly* supporter, notes that students not only have greater access to the sources; they may also ask better questions. "These kids . . . get down to the nitty-gritty, what happened every day. If we were doing it, we'd talk about the political situation at the time, or something like that. But when the youngsters go to talk to Monroe, they ask him what kind of parties they had on Saturday nights."

Given the indisputable educational benefits of the experience of working on *Loblolly*, and the logical arguments for making cultural journalism a legitimate activity of a rural school like Gary's, has the *Loblolly* class become a standard part of the academic curriculum at Gary? Six years after the first issue was published, the answer is still no. As a journalism elective, the class remains outside of, and in many ways subordinate to, the required academic curriculum. Students working on the magazine are graded and receive credit for it as they might in another class, but the credits do not count toward graduation. Although Superintendent Hooper says *Loblolly* has "enhanced the reading and writing" program at Gary, he still insists that students get four years of basic English. As an extracurricular elective, *Loblolly* remains in the same category as the school yearbook and basketball.

Principal Yarborough sees extracurricular activities as "important because they keep the students interested in the school and the community interested in the school"—but they must be limited. "I guess I'm from the old school myself, where school has to be the most important thing," he says. "I have to impress on my kids that if they can't pass their subject, then they can't play basketball. So I do the same with *Loblolly*. If they come in and want to go on interviews, and they're not passing math, or they're having troubles, I say, 'Get your grades up first.' "

Barbara Hooper sees her job as English teacher as conveying to the students correct grammatical skills and an appreciation of classic literature. *Loblolly*, therefore, cannot be expected to be a substitute for a high school English curriculum: "They're interviewing old people whose communicating grammar is a mess. The kiddos are in a kind of dilemma. To retain the flavor, they've got to put it down like it's told to them. If they change it, they're not retaining it. You don't want to point out, 'Now this is a mistake, and this is a mistake,' because that's not the aim. The aim is to record history."

*Loblolly* has the endorsement and support of the Gary school administration but is independent of it financially. Aside from a $100 donation from the PTA, no local funds have gone to subsidize its production. Travel expenses are paid from *Loblolly*'s own account. Even substitute teachers, when required to cover King's classes while he is away on *Loblolly* business, are paid by *Loblolly* funds. The magazine, in fact, helps defray the yearbook's expenses through its provision of darkroom and photographic supplies.

King says that he's satisfied with *Loblolly*'s status. He has found that as an extracurricular activity *Loblolly* enjoys a special security. It is less vulnerable to a critical judgment of its academic legitimacy than it would be if it were offered through the English or history curriculum, and it does not need to conform to the structure of a conventional academic class. Furthermore, there is no evidence to suggest that students involved in *Loblolly* learn any less from it than they might if it were a formal class.

It is important to understand that at Gary High School, the fact that an activity is "extracurricular" does not necessarily mean that either students or faculty sponsors put less energy or time into it. There is, of course, the possibility that some students who are not performing to the satisfaction of their teachers in other classes may be discouraged from participating in *Loblolly* activities, but that does not seem to happen very often. "Most of the students who work hard on *Loblolly* are the same ones who work hard on other things," observes Superintendent Hooper. King believes, however, that working on *Loblolly* is one experience that does not seem to attract only the most achievement-oriented students. "There's room for many levels of achievement" in *Loblolly* work, he says. "Some of our best interviewers are very average students academically; their skill is being able to talk to these people well." Furthermore, the opportunity to work on *Loblolly* is still attractive enough to Gary students that the requirement that they maintain passing averages in other classes before being allowed to work on the magazine may be an incentive. "It's kept some kids in school who wouldn't have stayed otherwise," Hooper believes.

Extracurricular activities in schools like Gary's carry a special status. They are not the exclusive province of the highly motivated as they sometimes are in larger, urban schools where drama clubs, student newspapers, and the athletic programs each involve only a small percentage of the students. In Gary, according to Principal Yarborough's calculations, as much as 95 percent of the student body is involved in some kind of school program outside of the regular classes. To be sure, such programs are subordinated to the academic curriculum, but in some ways the distinction seems to be more like a formal separation, with the two domains each having its own set of educational objectives. Through the regular classes, students learn a strictly no-frills basic curriculum: traditional math, English grammar, standard science, and conventional textbook history. Parents want such subject matter taught, according to the superintendent.

But parents also care deeply about the extracurricular program and insist that activities in that domain are supported. It is, after all, in those extracurricular activities that "character" is built, and in many rural areas the virtues of character rival or surpass the virtues of book learning in the importance attached to them by the community. Notions such as self-discipline, teamwork, self-confidence, and pride in oneself and one's community are stressed in this domain of school activity. King and his students know they could count on the support of their community if a crunch came. Few school activities anywhere in the nation could hope to exceed the popularity of the magazine in Panola County. "People love them," reports Mrs. Sistrunk. "They like to keep the old timey ways alive. Every one of their issues was sold out. People get one, read it, talk about it, and start looking forward to the next one." When Sheriff Corbett Akins was asked what he thought students got out of their interview with him, he responded, "I don't know what they got out of writing it, but I sure as hell got a kick out of reading it."

The most dramatic accomplishment of *Loblolly* in school-community relations is its bridging of the communication gap between the youth and the older people in the community. As in many rural communities, those two age groups dominate life in Gary. The generation between is less evident, either because they have left, or because their work focuses their attention and energy elsewhere. Until *Loblolly* began, however, the younger and the older people passed each other without notice. Their increased respect and appreciation for the older people in the community is the first point that Gary students mention when asked what they have gained from the project. Says Kevin Hulsey: "Most of the old people you think are all grannies or something, or that they don't tell jokes or stuff like that. But they do." Until *Loblolly* came along, Lauri Gauntt knew Monroe Brannon, "but I never thought of talking to him. He was just an old man I saw at church who always gave me gum." Now actual friendships between old people and young people have grown up.

The growth of *Loblolly* has opened a whole new dimension for school studies: the local community. It is a new phenomenon at Gary High School, as it would be at most American high schools. Perhaps there is a preference for the carefully controlled medium of textbooks and laboratories, where there is no raw conflict, no disagreement, no ambiguities. As *Loblolly* has opened the school to the life of the community, there have inevitably been exposures to facets of experience a good deal less innocuous than soapmaking and sacred harp singing. A 1974 issue featured an interview with a local man who raised roosters for cock-fighting contests (which are illegal in Texas, with the owners of fighting cocks subject to heavy fines). The interviewers justified the activity this way: "On most Sunday afternoons, gatherings take place. These are called 'brush fights,' and owners fight their cocks more for the love of the contest than for the money involved." Nevertheless, one of the roosters the man showed the students was one who had earned him over fifty thousand dollars.

Students are never quite sure what their researching might uncover. In one case, a group of them prepared a story on a local lynching that took place in the early part of the century. When they went to talk to one of the descendants of a figure involved in the event, they discovered it was a family tragedy that no one wanted revealed. The story was filed away. In preparing their stories on Bonnie and Clyde's adventures in Panola County, students found people who were eager to share tantalizing recollections of the pair, but they also encountered others who were genuinely angry that more attention was being given to a sorry episode in Texas history.

Students stumbled into another controversy after they followed up a suggestion from the minister of a local Baptist church that they interview his mother, a faith healer. In their introduction to the article, students acknowledged their appreciation to the minister for his suggestion. A local resident obtained the article, underlined the reference to the minister, and sent it to the president of a local Bible college where the man taught, charging that he was endorsing his mother's views on faith healing—a violation of the college's teaching—and therefore that he should be fired. In the next issue of *Loblolly*, students had to insert a disclaimer, explaining that they had not meant to imply that the minister himself believed in faith healing.

John Dewey called such moments "first-hand contact of actualities" and said that they were the real times of learning. Eliot Wigginton saw the exposure of his students to the realities of life in their own community as essential steps in the shaping of their civic responsibility. But this is approaching a delicate area. *Loblolly* has for the most part stayed clear of problematic current issues. "I've suggested some more contemporary stories," King says, "but I don't think the kids really want to do that yet."

The remarkable thing about *Loblolly* is that it has emerged as a popular and well-integrated activity in a school that is otherwise almost untouched by innovative educational trends. It is all the more surprising because the Foxfire concept of learning is in several respects a controversial approach. Wigginton himself has noted the considerable potential for conflict that is latent in the process of adopting Foxfire-type programs in tradition-bound schools: "At the very heart of *Foxfire* is the conviction that students can learn about the community and about humanity only outside the classroom."[4] He has also stressed the need to abandon customary student/teacher role relationships in Foxfire programs, as such relationships are incompatible with the democratic nature of the decision-making process behind the production of the magazine. When besieged by questions from teachers anxious to duplicate his success but unaware of what it involved, Wigginton wrote: "How can I answer questions like that, knowing that the only way it can work is for the teacher to push back the desks and sit down on the floor with the kids and really listen to them for the first time?"[5] He has also told stories that illustrate the problems inherent in the existence of a *Foxfire* magazine class, with its basic "task-orientation" in a school that is characterized by a "schedule-orientation."

Gary High School, to be sure, has had to strain to accommodate the phenomenon of a student-produced magazine. But Superintendent Hooper seems to have accepted the idea. "*Loblolly* has been good for us," he says. "I won't say there haven't been times when the tail was trying to wag the dog, but that would happen with anything." The fact that *Loblolly* is living in the supposedly barren environs of a backwater high school suggests that the notion that rural schools resist innovations may not be all true; perhaps it is just that they wait for really good ones. It may on the other hand be proof that "*Foxfire* could fly anywhere," as one IDEAS staff member argues.

Has *Loblolly*, in fact, been assured of a permanent home in Gary High School? And could other such ventures be sustained in other schools? *Loblolly* certainly had its moments of uncertain fate. Superintendent Hooper, disturbed by the number of embarrassing mistakes in early issues, considered putting a stop to the magazine. The mistakes actually stemmed from a problem that was potentially more serious than the lack of administrative support: student carelessness and apathy. *Loblolly* survived, but what of its prospects for the future? Is it still vulnerable to apathetic slumps? Can high school students in other places hope to duplicate its success?

To answer these questions, the clearly nonrepeatable factors in the *Loblolly* success story must be identified and weighed. First is the role of outside recognition. The Gary magazine has had less of it perhaps than any of the other long-running *Foxfire* offshoots, but it has had its share: the nurturing support of Max Haddick, the connections to Wigginton and the Foxfire network, the front-page story in the *Dallas Morning News*'s Sunday magazine, the appearances on television interview programs. Such recognition cannot be guaranteed in the future for *Loblolly* and almost certainly won't be forthcoming to other rural schools who institute their own Foxfire programs. (On the other hand, the future *Loblolly* and its successors might have something potentially even more powerful: the existence of a precedent. Once an activity becomes a tradition in a rural school, it is securely situated.)

Second, one must understand the uniqueness of the individual who is able to initiate such a project and then to generate the energy in his or her students to make it work. King himself is a Yankee, Maine-born and raised. He acknowledges that it may have been his outsider's perspective on Panola County culture that explains his fascination with the idea of starting a *Foxfire*-type magazine. Even more problematic is the issue of the teaching ability necessary to sustain a Foxfire project. As Bill Applegate says, "It's a great idea for other schools. Of course, they haven't all got Lincoln Kings. This sort of program doesn't just generate itself. It has to have a lot of motivation and somebody that's dedicated and has ability." Wigginton makes much of the "special relationship" that must exist between a faculty advisor and the students in a Foxfire project. Lauri Gauntt, however, thinks that this kind of relationship might come after, or through, the process: "Our relationship with Mr. King grew after the project began. It wasn't special to begin with. He was just a teacher, he just taught geography, and he was just like any other teacher. But he got us started, and we looked to him for help, and we were kind of all learning together. Mr. King is our friend now; he was our teacher before. We've been through a lot together."

There are in the case of *Loblolly* lessons that apply to the feasibility of such a project for other rural schools. Most important, perhaps, is its strong localistic character. Of all the Foxfire projects that have proved durable, it is perhaps the most independent, the most oriented to its own community. Although they have received grants, "we'd like to think we could have done it without any," King says, and they probably could have. It's been three years since they received a grant, and they are not looking for one. "They're so damn complicated," King says. "The last grant application we did had to have twenty copies submitted."

King and his students truly do not solicit outside attention, relying instead on the strength and support that comes from their relationship with their own community and surrounding area. Ninety-five percent of their circulation is within Texas, 50 percent of it in local newsstand sales. Likewise, King has not sought to exploit his Foxfire connection. It is Max Haddick, not Eliot Wigginton, whom King and his students see as the patron whose support was most vital to the survival of the magazine. The local orientation of the *Loblolly* enterprise, in fact, may be one of the most important lessons of this story; if magazines such as *Foxfire* and *Loblolly* are to be feasible on a wider scale, it is logical that they would have to be much less dependent on heavy marketing, out-of-county sales, glossy packaging, and grant support. In each respect, *Loblolly* suggests an example.

King's emphasis on self-reliance has at times left him somewhat out of touch with other projects. In the beginning, *Loblolly* was one of the least-publicized members of the family of *Foxfire*-offshoot magazines that sprang from the IDEAS operation, and King is mildly defensive about it: "When we first came out," he says, "some people associated with the Foxfire movement looked down their noses at us, because we used advertising. They thought it cheapened the Foxfire image. . . . We may not look as slick as a *Salt* or a *Bittersweet* [a Missouri *Foxfire*-type magazine], but our story content is as good as anyone's." Actually, his independence from the network has impressed the Foxfire folks, including Eliot Wigginton: "Watching Lincoln's project evolve," Wigginton says, "has been one of the most humbling experiences of my career precisely because he did exactly what I hoped hundreds of teachers would do: take an idea, adapt it to their own particular student clientele, and run with it, without lots of hand-holding." And, as the network of Foxfire projects has grown to include over 100 sites across the nation, *Loblolly* is increasingly cited in *Hands On*, the Foxfire-based newsletter, as one of the best examples available.

Financially, King imagines that his magazine will continue to rely on local advertising and subscription support for its survival. "I don't have the time or the interest," he says, "to go out and really drum up support to make it big, to go to Austin to get state support, or to go out and get some grants, or to triple the circulation or whatever. I just don't ever see us going big." As a student-operated enterprise, however, *Loblolly*'s growth locally is also limited. Jim Stevens, editor of the local *Panola Watchman*—and a friend of King's and *Loblolly*'s—warns, "If it ever got to the point where *Loblolly* was competing with the local media—they've already gotten some ads that used to go to us—if it ever got big enough, then there'd be some resentment, for their using public dollars and facilities to compete with private media."

But if *Loblolly* were to grow, it is more likely that it would be in the direction of its potential as a community service project than in its potential as a student-operated business enterprise. Thad Sitton, in a report on *Foxfire*-type publications, has outlined a possible path of development for a project such as *Loblolly*, citing three ways it could serve the community through offshoots of a cultural journalism magazine: creating the tapes, transcripts, and photographs for a public community history center; creating the materials for a local history curriculum for use at all grade levels, K–12; and making its "personnel and resources available to field-research and produce reports on a variety of community social problems."[6] The delight with which Gary residents greet each new issue of *Loblolly* suggests that such expansion would almost surely be met with enthusiasm.

### Notes

1. Eliot Wigginton, Introduction to *The Foxfire Book* (Garden City, N.Y.: Anchor Press, 1972).

2. Brian Beun, Introduction to *Moments* (Washington, D.C.: IDEAS, 1975), p. vi.

3. Pamela Wood, *You and Aunt Arie;* and Eliot Wigginton, *Moments* (Washington, D.C.: IDEAS, 1975).

4. Wigginton, *Moments*, p. 5.

5. Wigginton, Introduction to *Foxfire 2* (Garden City, N.Y.: Anchor Press, 1975).

6. Thad Edward Sitton, Jr., "The Foxfire-Concept Publications: A First Appraisal," Ph.D. dissertation, University of Texas at Austin.

# 15
# Staples, Minnesota: Improving the Schools to Save the Town

*Thomas Gjelten*

When Albert Quie decided to run for governor of Minnesota in the fall of 1978, he chose as the coordinator of his campaign in the seventh congressional district a superintendent of schools, Duane Lund, from Staples. Quie subsequently won the election, defeating an incumbent Democrat in a state long dominated by the Democratic-Farmer-Labor Party. At a time when many school administrators were defending their programs and their budgets before suspicious taxpayers, the selection of a superintendent to fill an important political campaign position seems a surprising move. The fact that Quie carried the seventh district by a margin of 6 percent might alone justify the unusual strategy, but, hindsight aside, this particular district and Duane Lund himself present a unique situation.

The seventh—the largest and most sparsely populated of Minnesota's eight districts—includes all of the northwestern quarter of the state. It is primarily an agricultural region, and the constituency is a conservative one, made up of people living on farms and in small towns, close to their own family roots and holding tightly to their prairie values and Scandinavian-American traditions.

Lund is a native son, born and raised in Brainerd, a town of 12,000 on the eastern side of the district. Now in his early fifties, he has been superintendent in Staples since 1959. When he says that he intends for his school "to serve the community," he is speaking as a leader of the community. His work on behalf of candidate Quie is consistent with his long history of involvement in projects outside the immediate sphere of public education in Staples. As a prominent civic figure, Lund has been an unabashed lobbyist for business development in the town. He has held several state and regional leadership positions in education organizations and is among the best-known superintendents in Minnesota. He plunges into politics without hesitation, making friends with national figures and actively promoting his rural-people-are-the-backbone-of-this-country philosophy. Lund's career distinguishes him among small-town superintendents. There can be few others who are able to claim a background that includes four years as chief administrative aide to a U.S. senator in Washington, a doctorate, four books on Minnesota history, several national education advisory commissions, and speaking engagements across the country. Yet Lund has spent every day of his professional education career working in one school system, thirty miles away from his hometown.

"Don't worry about saving the whole world," Lund preaches to other educators, in a thundering voice arising from the depths of his massive frame. "Worry about saving one town—your town!" This has been his guiding principle throughout his tenure in Staples. He has in that time been the principal figure in a remarkable story of a town-school partnership for community development. It is a story that has been unfolding for over twenty-five years and has a cast of characters like a Russian novel. Before Lund tells it, he customarily prefaces his speech with a warning: "I don't have the answers. What works in Staples won't necessarily work in another town." But the idea that something actually works somewhere is usually sufficient to guarantee an audience, and the story has been widely told.

## A Town in Trouble

Staples sits in the very center of Minnesota, about 140 miles from each of the three closest metropolitan areas—Minneapolis/St. Paul, Duluth, and Fargo/Moorhead. With a population of 2,700, it is the largest town in Todd County and serves the surrounding area as a center of commerce and services. The Staples school district covers an area of 425 square miles and has a K–12 enrollment of just over 1,600. The last boost in enrollment numbers came in the mid-1960s with the consolidation of the remaining one- and two-room country schools in the area.

The town is neither glamorous nor affluent. Todd County was ranked last among Minnesota counties in median family income in 1960, although it managed to climb two notches higher by 1970. As a "division point" along the Burlington Northern Railroad's Great Northern route, Staples was where trains changed crews, providing jobs to over 300 Staples workers. Next to railroading, the area's only industry has been agriculture, and it was the farming families in northern Todd County who brought the income level down. The sandy soil of the area has never produced dramatic crop yields, and small-scale dairy farming is a risky and rarely profitable enterprise. Most of the graduates of Staples High School have traditionally been forced to leave the area in order to find work that suited their interests or training.

But, as the sign on the edge of town still proclaims, "It's fun to live in

Staples!" It is within a short drive of Minnesota's famous lake region, where the lakes coil in long chains around thick groves of pine and birch, and where thousands of visitors come to catch walleyes and hunt ducks. Staples is a clean, proud town, a place where people like to point out that they know the difference between a high standard of living and a good life and have chosen the latter.

The modern phase of educational improvements in Staples began under the direction of C. F. "Doc" Reichelderfer, chairman of the board of education for over 30 years until his death in 1973. It was Reichelderfer's belief that the key to a healthy community was a healthy school system, and he expressed this through his unwavering support for the town schools and the people who worked in them.

"Doc" was a familiar figure around the halls of Staples High School. Nearly every day he could be found somewhere in the building talking to cooks, custodians, students, teachers, or whoever happened by. Reichelderfer was a physician, but he rarely worked a full day at his practice. "Medicine, in fact, was his avocation," recalls Dr. Robert Mayhew, a Staples dentist, the current board chairman and for many years vice-chairman under Reichelderfer. "The school was his vocation. I think he spent about 50 percent of his time there."

Reichelderfer was as devoted to his town as he was to its schools, and he was determined that the community should support the schooling enterprise just as the educational system served vital community needs. When Superintendent of Schools P. M. Atwood retired in 1959 (having held that position since 1920), Reichelderfer led the board of education in the search for a successor. He knew what he wanted: a superintendent who would care as much about the town of Staples as about the school system itself. His first choice was Duane Lund, then a graduate student at the University of Minnesota.

After graduating from college, Lund had come to Staples as a teacher and guidance counselor. He was familiar with the community, having been there many times to visit his uncle who—like Reichelderfer—was a town doctor. During college, however, he had developed an interest in politics, and when an opportunity came a few years later to join Minnesota Senator Edward Thye's staff as administrative assistant, he left teaching and moved to Washington.

When Thye lost his bid for reelection in 1958, Lund decided to return to the field of education and entered a doctoral program at the University of Minnesota. All through his Washington years, Lund had remained close to Staples, and when Reichelderfer approached him in 1959 with an offer to return to the system as its superintendent, he quickly accepted.

Dr. Reichelderfer, the town physician and school board chairman, and Dr. Lund, the superintendent of schools, had a close relationship from the beginning. Each morning the 8:30-9:00 slot in Lund's appointment book was reserved for Reichelderfer. They would visit about school business, community problems, or perhaps hunting and fishing. From the school, Reichelderfer headed for Shorty Blessing's barbershop, where he was sure to hear the latest news as shared by Staples's main street merchants, professionals, business leaders, workers, and area farmers.

In 1959, the talk at the barbershop centered on the topic of Staples's future. The railroad was beginning to lay off workers, thus threatening the town's already precarious economy. As the year wore on, the outlook for the town's survival became increasingly gloomy, and conversations took on an edge of deep concern. By fall, the situation was downright frightening. The roundhouse, where locomotives were taken for mechanical repairs, was closed, and more than 100 Staples men found themselves out of work. The layoffs sparked rumors that Staples was about to lose its designation as a division point, and without the railroad jobs, the town would wither and die.

Panic swept the community. The market value of houses plummeted as people fearfully tried to trade down to something smaller and more affordable. Many refused even to paint their houses, thinking that any investments in them at this stage would be a waste of money. It was, said school board chairman Robert Mayhew, "an example of how rumors can almost kill a town."

In desperation, the mayor of Staples, banker Stan Eddy, summoned a gathering of community leaders. Superintendent Lund recalls: "The situation was that Staples was either going to die a natural death, or we were going to fight to see that it survived. . . . From the very beginning, we decided to fight and survive, but we had to set about establishing priorities, the things that we needed to do if we were going to build a community." The Staples leaders drafted an agenda for community survival, which they called their "bootstrap" plan. It included an agreement on the urgency of getting new industries to locate in Staples—to create jobs, to keep the retail business thriving, and to maintain a sound tax base. But the highest priority was education. Lund remembers, "Of all the things, it really thrilled me, the number one thing that came up was that we had to have a strong school system. If we wanted to bring in new industry or new business or attract new people, we had to be able to say, 'We've got a number one school system.'"

The young superintendent left the meeting that afternoon having taken that charge as his personal mandate for improvement in the Staples school system. Lund emphasizes that it was not a recognition of glaring weaknesses in the schools that inspired the ambitious drive to vitalize the system; rather, it was the idea of linking school improvement to broader notions of community development. "We had a good system at the time," Lund now explains, "a fine system; the community was proud of it; *but it wasn't well known.*" Because he was now concerned with making the community attractive to outsiders, it was important that it be *known* for its good education. Thus, Lund's assignment was to build a reputation.

## To the Rescue: A Strong, Innovative School System

Meanwhile, there were immediate and direct ways the school system could be of assistance to the community, particularly in its quest for industrial development. Most important among these was the expansion of its vocational training program. Dr. Reichelderfer himself had already taken the initiative in this regard. He had foreseen the need to diversify the industrial base in Staples for several years, and had made the establishment of a vocational-technical institute in town his highest priority as school board chairman. For two years, he and Mike Matanich, the vocational instructor, had been lobbying the state board of vocational education for the designation of Staples as a site for an area vocational-technical institute.

There was already a highly regarded high school vocational program in machine trades at Staples, but this designation would mean that the program could be expanded to include post-secondary students, that it could enroll students from outside the district boundaries, and that it could offer a wider vocational training curriculum. Most importantly, it would mean that Staples now qualified for the federal and state money appropriated to support vocational-technical institutes. It would boost Staples's attractiveness as a site for industrial relocation because there would be the assurance of a skilled, nonunionized labor force available for work in the Staples area.

Until that time, no rural town in Minnesota had been authorized to operate an area vocational school. Reichelderfer, Matanich, and Superintendent Atwood (along with Lund, who was still a graduate student at the time) had been to St. Paul to make their pitch before the state board. Jim Staloch, of the vocational division of the Minnesota Department of Education, was one of the team members sent out by the board to review the merits of the Staples request. What they found, he recalls, was that "everyone was 100 percent behind it—the school administration, the school board, the community—everyone." They were also impressed by the fact that Matanich had already secured a building for the program. A native of the area in Minnesota known as the Iron Range due to its widespread open-pit iron ore mining, Matanich had many friends among miners and company officials. In an ingenious arrangement, Matanich had convinced a mining company to donate a steel building to house the expanded machine trades program at Staples. It had been dismantled and moved to Staples on flatbed trucks. The positive thinking and enthusiastic preparations undertaken in Staples for the vocational school were persuasive considerations, and the request was approved, around the time that Staples leaders were outlining their "bootstrap plan."

The community rewarded the work of the school leaders by passing a $300,000 bond issue to construct an additional building for the vocational school. It opened in the fall of 1960 with sixty students and four teachers authorized to provide training in machine shop and related trades. Matanich was named director of the school. He had spent several years as a machinist in Chicago and in a mining company near his native town of Virginia, Minnesota. In Staples, he had already earned a reputation in the community as a dedicated and compassionate teacher (and football coach). His high school course in machine trades was nationally known.

With the new vocational school, the community had a stronger point on which to sell itself to outside developers. The Staples Development Corporation was organized with Shorty Blessing, the barber, as its president. By selling shares of development stock to community supporters, the group hoped to raise sufficient capital to help finance the moves of outside businesses to Staples. Their first target was the Ringer Company, a sportswear manufacturing firm then located in Duluth. In order to get the company to move to Staples, the Development Corporation had to finance their building. To do it, the group sold $60,000 worth of development stock in a truly community-wide effort. People sensed that this was an urgent priority. Lund recalls the campaign organized by the Development Corporation: "We had to raise some money, and in a dying community that wasn't easy. But we did it, we sold shares in the development corporation. It was an investment in the community. We never promised any money back, nobody ever got any money back. Even the kids helped out. They held dances and bake sales to raise money. There were adult dances, too. People of all walks of life bought shares and gave money." With the money, the Development Corporation bought land and constructed a building for the company, then agreed to finance it for them. The company moved operations to Staples and hired forty local residents, mostly women, to sew sportswear and outdoor garments at minimum wage. It was the first time a major employer had moved to Staples in as long a time as anyone could remember, and the community leaders regarded it as a great success.

At the new vocational school, there was space for more machine tools than Matanich had so far been able to purchase. The district was now qualified to receive outside money, but guidelines were not yet clearly established and the level of funding was much lower than it would become in later years. Lund and Matanich had an idea, however, that they were anxious to try. While Lund was working in Washington, Senator Thye had coauthored a bill authorizing the Department of Defense to loan machine-tooling equipment, which was being stored in caves and warehouses for a national emergency, to local school districts for use in vocational education programs. The bill had been passed, but the procedures for implementation had not yet been worked out, and there had as yet been no school district with the patience or the persistence to pursue the offer through the proper channels of the Defense Department.

Lund probably knew more about the "tools for schools" program than any other superintendent in the country, and he was ready to be the first to go after the opportunity. He led a delegation to Washington including Matanich, Reichelderfer, and Mayhew. "They were all flabbergasted that we were serious about it," remembers Mayhew. "We knew more about it than they did. We had to go right through their files ourselves." They were successful in their mission and returned to Staples with the news that the school would be receiving $650,000 worth of machine-shop equipment from the National Industrial Equipment Reserve. The only conditions on the loan were that the school district pay transportation costs and promise to keep the equipment in perfect operating condition. With the new building and the government equipment, Matanich was soon directing the largest and best-equipped machine-shop vocational program in the country.

The curriculum at the vocational school, originally limited to machine trades and related areas, rapidly expanded, first to include farm equipment repair and later heavy equipment operation and maintenance. Both programs stemmed directly from community needs: farmers needed help during those years to keep their farms alive. Matanich's farm equipment repair course was taught completely through the repair and rebuilding of local farmers' equipment, with the farmers being asked to pay only for parts used. In 1963 and 1964, grants received by the school under the Manpower Development Training Act funds enabled the expansion of the heavy equipment course. Like farm equipment repair, the course's curriculum was also set up around "real work," as Matanich describes it.

He chose to use community service projects as training exercises for students in the program. Their first task involved a weedy lake that had been given to the city by the railroad when it no longer needed a water supply for its steam engines. Nothing had been done to reclaim the lake for recreational purposes because of the expense. Matanich volunteered his students to do the work. They dredged the lake and hauled in 1,500 loads of gravel, creating a public swimming beach and a track for snowmobile racing, the first of its kind in the country. Matanich billed the city only for his fuel costs.

With the new vocational school well under way, Superintendent Lund turned his attention to the K–12 program and to the building of a school system that would put Staples on the map in Minnesota. His basic strategy was to fill the system with "good people." "You can't have a one-person operation," he advises. "You have to develop other leadership within the system." He worked slowly and quietly, hiring staff members with the talents and interests appropriate for the task. He wanted a staff who would be ready to make long-term commitments to working and living in the town and involving themselves in community affairs. In that regard, Lund continued to set an example for his staff. He remained an active supporter of the Staples Development Corporation and cochaired the planning committee for Staples's seventy-fifth anniversary celebration. Two people who met the superintendent's criteria were Dick Donat, a native of the little town of Upsala in Morrison County who was hired in 1960 as the agriculture teacher, and Dick Hegre, hired away from a school in the southern part of the state as the new elementary principal in 1964.

Yet, more was needed. How could Lund give his staff enough incentive to stay, enough freedom and challenge to develop their potential? How long would it take for the Staples system to become well known?

With the passage of the Elementary and Secondary Education Act by Congress in 1965, Lund recognized the opportunity he had been looking for. In expanded federal aid, there was a valuable resource for revitalizing his school system. He immediately designated Donat as the district's federal programs officer, with the responsibility of becoming an expert on the variety of funding programs instituted by the aid to education act. From his Washington experience, Lund knew the value of grantsmanship expertise. As a school district in a low-income county, Staples was qualified to receive substantial Title I funds (2.1 million dollars through the end of the 1978-79 school year). It would be essential to have one person with sole responsibility of seeing that the paper work was in proper order. Some of the aid programs, such as Title I, were allocated according to a set formula and were virtually automatic, but others were competitive, with funds being distributed according to demonstrated need and proposed activity. It would become Donat's job to match available federal funds with the ideas generated by Staples's school staff. An occasion arose soon after he took the position, at the suggestion of Dick Hegre.

Dick Hegre came to Staples with "fairly traditional ideas" about education. What changed them, he explains, was his exposure to vocational director Mike Matanich and his philosophy of teaching through "real-life" activity. "Mike gave me a much more positive attitude towards "change,'" explains Hegre today. "If he figured out a better way to approach vocational education, I thought, maybe there's a better way to approach elementary education too." No sooner had he settled into his new office in the North Elementary School than Hegre began to think about the old Lincoln School, now abandoned on the other end of town.

Superintendent Lund was at the time looking "for a vehicle to shake up our methods," as he later told a reporter. Between the two administrators, an idea about the use of the old elementary school began to take form. They saw in the building an opportunity to institute an alternative elementary program designed especially for students entering the system from one-room rural schools that were being consolidated. It would be an attempt to preserve some of the traditional features of the one-room schools in its incorporation of nongraded informal, individualized instruction, while at the same time offering the advantages of a larger school in its instructional resources and specialized staff. It would be, Hegre said, "a school for kids, with true individualization and personalization." The rural tradition would be further upheld by frequent parent-teacher meetings and the use of community resource persons in teaching.

With Donat's help, Hegre drafted a proposal—"A Model Non-graded Rural School"—and solicited $100,000 in Title III funds for the project. In the spring of 1967, Hegre and Lund met several times with rural school boards and parents in their country schools to explain the plan and answer questions. Their proposal was in the meantime approved by the federal government, and in the summer parents of all four districts voted to join the Staples system and send their children to the refurbished Lincoln School.

While the remodeling went on around them, the newly formed staff at the school met for six weeks of inservice training during the summer to learn nongraded, individualized instructional techniques. After only nine months in the new elementary school, Hegre returned to the Lincoln School as project director of the model school.

The doors opened that fall to sixty students, all coming from rural schools. Learning at the new school was to be fun. Letter grades were abolished, and students were taught according to their needs and interests. Children were free to choose between a variety of options in academic activities, though the amount of structure provided in a child's program depended on his or her "maturity level." Shortly after classes began, an informal open house was held for the parents on a Friday afternoon, the day rural people in the Staples area traditionally visited the town. Close parent-teacher contacts continued to be stressed, with school staff visiting each student's home at least once that fall. Conferences with the parents were held at the end of each reporting period.

Open classroom, individualized instruction, and nongraded organization were exciting new concepts in 1967, and the model school quickly became known throughout the state. In March of the first year of its operation, the school hosted a symposium, "The Nongraded Elementary School," featuring national speakers. Hegre identifies his exposure to the idea of nongraded instruction as an important factor in the reversal of his negative attitude toward educational innovations. With the experience he gained designing the model school and the insights he had from meetings with educational innovators across the country, Hegre was stimulated to continue looking for better ways of approaching elementary education for the district. Soon

Lund promoted him to the position of director of elementary education for the entire system.

Don Droubie, a former colleague of Hegre's from another school in southern Minnesota, was brought to Staples to become principal of the Lincoln model school. Under Droubie's direction, the model school continued to thrive, with federal funding renewed for two more years. The school staff was organized into two teams, one responsible for primary age children (roughly K–3), the other for intermediate (4–6). Students were grouped according to "levels" rather than grades. Optional activities continued to be offered to all students and most instruction was activity centered.

A successful open school, where all the students were enrolled by the choice of their parents, in a small town in rural Minnesota was a good story, and in the fall of 1969 a reporter from the *Minneapolis Tribune* visited the school. She was dazzled by how well it worked and returned to write a front-page article for the Sunday paper, "The Fun Path to Learning at Staples." She reported school administrators as saying that the Three R's are taught, but in Staples they are "relevance, readiness, and responsibility." An article followed in a national education publication about the school, and in 1970 it had more than 4,000 visitors from across the nation. Special observation windows had to be built to accommodate the crowds, and visitors' information packets on the school were prepared. Staples was rapidly gaining the reputation that Dr. Lund had set out to build ten years earlier.

Staples' economic fortunes had also improved. In 1967—the year the model school opened—there was a burst of industrial development after a long slack. The nationally recognized vocational school had been turning out some of the best-trained young machinists in the country—but they were all leaving Staples. That year, however, the Development Corporation scored its two biggest successes. Duane Lund, through his network of acquaintances, was familiar with individuals in the executive leadership of 3M (Minnesota Mining and Manufacturing), Minnesota's largest and most renowned native industry. They were operating a plant in a nearby city and had been planning to set up a machine-tooling facility to support it. Lund became personally involved in the negotiations to convince the industry to choose Staples. Two things were attractive to the 3M leadership about Staples: the ready availability of a skilled, nonunion work force and a building ready for them to turn into their shop.

The story behind the Staples Development Corporation's ability to arrange space for the 3M machine shop in town on short notice is illustrative of the school-community cooperation that has been the town's tradition. One of the vocational school's several machine shops in 1967 was housed in one of the original steel buildings donated to the school by an Iron Range mining company early in the school's history. The school board voted to move the machine shop out of the building and into the bus garage next door, kicking the buses out. They then sold the building to the Development Corporation, and the Development Corporation turned around and sold it to 3M—all in one day. The score was the best news of the decade, according to a Development Corporation slide show; Staples had not attracted just any industry, it had attracted "those magic letters, 3M."

Also that year, an executive of Benson's Optical Company from Minneapolis stopped to have his hair cut in Shorty Blessing's barbershop while on a fishing trip. He casually mentioned that his company was considering moving part of its operation out of the urban area. A short time later the Development Corporation sponsored a breakfast in the school cafeteria and announced that Benson's would move to Staples if a building were made ready for them. Within thirty minutes, several thousand dollars had been raised to finance a building.

The role of the school system in the development efforts continued to be major. The board of education under Reichelderfer's leadership was cooperating with the City Council and the Development Corporation in every way possible. Lund was contributing his personal influence to the cause of Staples's betterment. Vocational director Matanich dispatched his heavy equipment students to assist city and county crews in road and ditch work, landscaping for public works projects, and other special projects for the community welfare. When Staples's only homegrown industry, Northern Manufacturing and Engineering, a steel fabricating firm, began to expand its business, Lund recalls, "We helped them. We had the students prepare the site for their building through our heavy equipment program. We just helped them any way we could." The students were also at the controls of their bulldozers a short time later preparing runways for the city's new airport, another part of Staples's development strategy. The community service learning projects all followed from the Dower Lake reclamation. "That was just a start," says Matanich. "With that project, we realized our potential. It gave our students something to be proud of. It let them know their work mattered and that, while they learned, they were making a real contribution." Significantly, none of the vocational school's contributed work has brought them into conflict with local construction unions; there are no heavy equipment contractors in the Staples area, and Matanich has promised the union to stay within a five mile radius of the vocational school. Furthermore, the vocational school comes in only as a last resort. "It has to be work for which no monies have been appropriated," Matanich says. "We are not depriving men of jobs. The situation is simply this: If we don't take the project, it would never get done. The city can't afford it."

But while the vocational students were contributing their efforts to public works projects for the community, Matanich, Lund, and Reichelderfer were still concerned that the vocational school was not doing enough for people's needs in the area. As Lund explained, "The problem here for many years went beyond the threat of losing railroad jobs. Our small farms just weren't making it, and many farmers were giving up and leaving their farms. Since they had no marketable skills and weren't accustomed to city living, they were having all sorts of problems. Our school board was concerned and wondered if there were some way we could help keep the farmers on the farms."

Thinking that modern irrigation techniques may help to restore productivity to the dry, sandy soil on the farms around Staples, they tried to convince the state department of education to support an irrigation research and demonstration center there. Unsuccessful in that attempt, the Staples school board decided to do it themselves. The district borrowed money to purchase a 320-acre farm, hired irrigation specialists to manage it through the vocational school, and began teaching farmers irrigation practices. Crops were planted in 1968, and the farm has been self-sustaining ever since, with crops sold outside the immediate area to avoid competition with local farmers. "We are here mainly to show farmers in the area what they can accomplish through good management and irrigation," says Wil Meierhofer, farm director. "Farmers will drive by and notice our corn is head high, while theirs is only knee high. Our soil is the same as theirs, so they'll stop and ask what we're doing." From the beginning, the agriculture production and irrigation course of the area vocational school had been oriented primarily to local farmers. The first instruction in sprinkler irrigation techniques offered was made possible through grants from the Department of Labor and Manpower Development Training Acts, subsidizing low-income farmers to attend a twelve-month course. Six farmers in the Staples area were irrigating when the course began. In 1978 there were more than 300 farmers irrigating, with average corn crop yields rising from 40 bushels per acre to over 100, and with dry beans and other specialty crops assuming a new importance in the local market.

Inspired by the energetic and imaginative approaches being taken at the vocational school, administrators Hegre and Droubie were meanwhile eagerly searching for new, progressive programs for the elementary grades in Staples. The hefty federal grants already subsidizing their work enabled them to travel across the country occasionally. One idea that caught their attention was Dwight Allen's concept of "differentiated staffing." A series of proposals to implement it in the Staples school system followed, of which three were funded. The grants brought in over $180,000 in three years. Most of the funds went for inservice training for teachers and teacher aides and staff time to design a program. The result of the projects was a handbook for implementation of a model differentiated staffing system for an entire district. The idea was to reorganize instructional duties around a team approach, with everyone—from administrators to teacher aides—sharing in decision making and teaching responsibilities. Lund says that one of the most important consequences of the experiment was that "it got me into the classroom a few times a week," but he admits that it never really worked all that well. The concept has since been largely abandoned in Staples.

The projects did, however, help to create more publicity for the Staples district and add to its image in the state as a progressive rural school system. In 1972, the district received a Title V grant to do a statewide "needs assessment" of rural schools in Minnesota. That same year, Minnesota Education Commissioner Howard Casmey nominated the Staples Public School System as Minnesota's "expansion" site for the national Right to Read program. As such, it was meant to serve as a demonstration project for the national program and was supervised directly by the U.S. Office of Education. Under the three-year program, the Staples Public Schools received $109,000 to develop and implement an exemplary reading program for kindergarten through twelfth grade.

By 1973, the Staples school system was so well known in Minnesota that the Bush Foundation of St. Paul gave it $110,000 "to transfer successful projects from Staples to other rural schools around the state." During the 1970s, Staples teachers were kept busy getting or giving inservice training under at least a half-dozen major funded projects. Beneath the fascination with current fashions, however, there remained a commitment to traditional educational approaches. Lund continually advised his staff that they were free to innovate, but the ground rule was that they had to honor community concerns and expectations above all. At home, the parents were more likely to ask what grade level their children were working at than they were to inquire about the innovations taking place in their classrooms; even while the Staples staff were developing the system's progressive reputation around the state, they were keeping a watchful eye on achievement test scores and responding quickly to gaps in student performance measurements. "Through it all," explains Lund, "we always talked to our staff in terms of, 'Let's not forget the basics.' So when the current trend came along —back to basics—we were already there."

A state assessment and planning grant in 1975 made possible the testing of 9-, 13-, and 17-year-old students in the Staples system. Based on the results, another grant proposal was written and funded, this one for the implementation of "an elementary math program with emphasis on computation skills and their applications." The Three R's of "relevance, readiness, and responsibility" had reverted back to "reading, 'riting, and 'rithmetic." The Staples staff now proudly points out that although barely 51 percent of adults in Todd County 25 years or older had gone past the eighth grade in 1970, Staples students today have consistently been scoring at or above the Minnesota norm (which itself is above the national norm) on achievement tests.

Community tolerance for the innovative projects at the school was further explained by the fact that every one of the projects brought in thousands of extra dollars. In the first five years of the 1970s, when Dick Donat's notebook of successfully funded grant proposals was bulging, the Staples school system ranked at or above the 95th percentile of all Minnesota districts for the amount of federal dollars in their school budget. Dick Hegre jokingly recalls that during those years, "Whenever I stopped into the state department [of education] in St. Paul, someone would remark, 'Watch out, here comes Hegre with his briefcase. Hold on to your money.'" Donat was meanwhile becoming an expert grantsman and was beginning to put his knowledge to another use. "I was picking up some terminologies and some expertise, federal government jargon, all that, and building up a variety of contacts. And once I was doing that for the school, then it became logical that I spend evenings and weekends doing it for the city, as a community service."

The first major grant for the city acquired funds from the Economic Development Administration for sewer and water main extensions to a site the city was planning for an industrial park. In planning the location of the park, the Development Corporation (of which Donat was now the president) arranged it far enough out of town so that the utility extension—paid for by federal grants—conveniently went past the site of a proposed new hospital and a housing development. Because of the federal grants and the vocational students doing site preparation for the industrial park, the Development Corporation was able to sell sites in the park for much less than they would normally have cost, and clients soon began to move in.

In the next few years, Donat wrote grant proposals for a senior-citizens' high-rise building, a new fire hall, and a community center that includes an indoor swimming pool leased by the school. In addition, he helped local retailers prepare SBA (Small Business Administration) loan applications for expansion of their businesses. The proliferation of grants writing for the city inevitably spread over into Donat's school time, but no one objected. "Sure, there are times when I might be down in the Cities on Title I business, and I'll stop in at SBA or something like that, but the school board has taken the attitude that a healthy school system needs a healthy community to support it, so it makes sense."

Some of the grants work would be hard to separate. The school was anxious to have the city build a community center, which it could then lease for physical education classes. The arrangements between the school and the city leading to the financing of the center were complex, and, according to school board chairman Robert Mayhew, "Dick Donat practically put it all together himself. He's the only one who could have done it." As Donat said, "Why have the school over here and the city way over there? It's just a great waste of talent and resources."

## Strategies Behind the Success

The "City on the Move" is still moving in 1979, albeit at a slower pace. The latest development in Staples's industrial growth has again grown out of its school system. Three entrepreneurs who began as vocational instructors have since opened businesses in Staples resulting directly from their vocational program. The railroad is employing more workers than ever, due to a freight boom since northern Minnesota electrical generators have switched to coal for fuel. The roundhouse has reopened as the home of North American Transco, Inc., a freight-car repairing and rebuilding business. Deposits in the Staples bank have grown from $4 million in 1960 to more than $22 million.

The twenty-year effort to save Staples has been grounded in a determination to preserve and even exploit its small-town traditions. The fundamental strategy of community leaders has been to build on long-standing rural customs with contemporary resources and ideas. They love to point out the old-time values and classic American themes in the Staples story. Since the town rallied to its own preservation in the early 1960s, its citizens have referred to Staples as "The City with the Bootstraps." It is, they point out, an example of a town that turned itself around by hard work, persistence, and local ingenuity.

The central premise of the strategy is that the traditional closeness between school and community in a small rural town is the element that is essential to the town's survival and the one that most needs to be preserved. The precedent set by Reichelderfer is carried on by the current school board, as reported by a school-community advisory group in their introduction to a report they prepared for the state department of education in the fall of 1978:

> A number of years ago, the Staples Board of Education accepted the philosophy that a healthy school system needs a healthy community in which to educate children. The school system has been deeply involved in community activities, both on an individual and a system basis. . . . [The Board] should continue to encourage the school's role in community affairs. Industrial vitality, economic stability, social and recreational concerns overlap and intertwine to make a true educational institution. If wedges are driven between school and community, by fact or rumor, each in itself can survive, but maximum efficiency or quality of life will not be achieved.

Maintaining close school-community relations in a town experiencing crisis, however, is not easy. Civic and school interests are often perceived to conflict; in poorly financed towns competition for a share of the tax dollar is intense. What Lund and others did was to look at the *traditional* school-community closeness in Staples, identify the conditions that made it possible, and work to preserve those conditions in a contemporary context. The single most important condition, they determined, was that the people who had been working in the Staples school system were members of the community themselves, not passing itinerants or upwardly mobile professionals jumping from district to district.

That tradition has been successfully retained. There have been in the last fifty years only two superintendents and two high school principals in Staples. Each of the other important figures in this story—Matanich, Hegre, Donat, Droubie—has likewise committed his career to the Staples community and remains there in 1979. There are other examples of school professionals who have become influential Staples citizens and are buying houses and raising families there. They are officers of the Rotary Club, the Chamber of Commerce, and the Development Corporation. Along with the other professionals in town—the banker, the newspaper editor, the lawyers, the business owners—the educators are community leaders.

The phenomenon is partly explained by the value attached to formal education in the area. In Staples, more than 98 percent of students entering ninth grade have graduated from high school over the past five years; during that period, 77 percent of the high school graduates went on for further vocational or academic education.

The continuity of staff leadership has also been deliberately nurtured. Lund has sought to establish an atmosphere in which working in a small-town system is a unique professional challenge in its own right. Here, an educational leader has the opportunity of professional advancement as well as the responsibility of managing the partnership of school and community development efforts. Just as the vocational students care more about what they are learning when they do work that is really needed, the school administrators are more motivated when their work in the school system fits into the larger task of community building.

Under Lund's leadership, the Staples school staff has learned to make contributions to the overall "bootstrap" plan, and local business leaders appreciate it deeply. Ed Perry, manager of the local Ben Franklin Variety Store, credits the school system as being "the real catalyst for change in this community." When an article appeared in a national publication about Staples's school system, under the title "The School that Saved a Town," some people "didn't like the sound of it," according to Perry, "but it was exactly the truth." To win such accolades from local businessmen is surely an important reason school leaders choose to stay in Staples.

There is more, however, behind the support of long-term staff tenure and the development of local educational leadership in Staples. A close examination of the Staples experience with federally funded innovative projects reveals that the projects have less significance separately than they have together as a whole. "We're massively committed to innovation, and consequently government grants," Lund told a reporter in 1972. "I would say most of our programs from the elementary grades on up are in some way innovative." It's the *idea* of being innovative that is important and that brings in dollars. In the last thirteen years, the district has received more than $8 million in federal, state, and private grants to support its educational program. In that period, it has received more federal funding for innovative projects "than any other school district in the state of comparable size," according to the program specialist for the state department of education's federal programs office.

It is the flexibility and the opportunities for professional development made possible by grant money that makes it so worthwhile, Lund says, not the funded programs themselves. "I remember one of the first grants, for ungraded elementary education. . . . We got a lot of money, over $500,000, and I tell you, it made a lot of difference. You know why? Because we were able to pay teachers to spend some time together . . . sitting back and looking objectively at what they were doing and how they could do it better. Now, in the process, we did develop some serious commitment to ungraded philosophy. . . . But the important thing is, get the dollars—so you can do something."

Lund has used outside-funded innovative projects as opportunities for the development of local leadership. Recently, he and other administrators determined that there was a need for a K–12 energy conservation curriculum in the school system. They wrote—and had funded—a proposal to implement one. In selecting someone to direct the project, they considered how the position might be one in which a potential system leader might be developed. "If someone has talent, you want to give them an opportunity," explains Dick Hegre.

The system's accommodation of innovative ideas is partly explained by the benefits gained in the heightening of staff morale and loyalty. Don Droubie, for example, says, "If any teacher wants to do something different, this district will bust its back to make it possible." The projects have also made a wider variety of roles possible in the local system. "One reason teachers and administrators stay in Staples," explains Droubie, "is because here it's possible to advance within the system." The prominence of the Staples school system contributed to the designation of the town as a site for one of Minnesota's educational cooperative service units, of which Dick Hegre became executive director. The naming of the town as a site for a Teachers' Center project in the fall of 1979 similarly offered another professional position for a Staples educational leader.

Community support for the school system has been maintained by conventional indicators of quality: the above-average achievement scores, the high percentage of high school graduates continuing their education, and the absence of major discipline problems in the schools. Tolerance of the special projects is won because the community has been let in on some of the hidden reasons for the innovations.

It is the linkage of apparently unrelated elements in this story that makes it one of success: innovation with leadership development and image building, school business with industrial development, urban-type approaches with rural resources. The Staples school enrollment is as large as some suburban districts, and the pursuit of federal funds here reveals a sense of savvy that would rival the most sophisticated city school system; yet the local administrators still consider Staples to be a rural system and declare their intentions to retain those aspects of ruralness that they see as advantageous. It is an integration of disparate themes around one common idea: "the good of Staples."

The essential question is whether a strategy born in the late fifties in a small Minnesota town is still a feasible one for community revitalization and school reform in the eighties, in other rural towns. In Staples, everyone seems to have been on the same side, united in a common effort to save the town. Are the fragile alliances of people and ideas underlying this story still achievable? "Now is the real test," says Dick Donat. "We've had our heyday. Our heyday was in the sixties, when there was a real incentive of wage savings in rural areas, and when there was rioting in the streets in the cities. Now those factors are largely gone."

Two elements of the Staples success story in particular need to be highlighted. First, it is clear that there was a united community effort in Staples that is not often possible. Everyone was on the same side: the high school students with their bake sales to raise money for the Development Corporation, the school board moving its buses outdoors in order to make a building available to 3M, and the local labor force choosing to cooperate with developers and not to organize itself into labor unions. Within the school system, the key to success has been the continuous leadership by a few individuals.

Both of these elements will be hard to sustain in Staples and even harder to duplicate in other locales. Social change is now a fact even in rural Minnesota; as Staples has grown, its community cohesiveness has begun to erode. Union elections, for example, are increasingly hard-fought. Family farms are rapidly being replaced by large corporation farms. The school board is no longer able to speak with one voice for an unquestioning community, as it did under the leadership of Dr. Reichelderfer. Controversies regularly sweep through town these days, the most recent one involving the visit of a Planned Parenthood representative to a high school class to discuss birth control methods.

The toughest question to consider in the Staples story is: Should a local school system be so deeply involved in community development? And further: Is it the business of the school to have its resources and influence engaged in the effort to persuade industries to open plants in Staples, particularly when the profits from the operations are going to be leaving town? (That may be unfortunate, says Donat, but "it's jobs we're after—because it means more kids in school, more customers in stores, and more people in church.") Perhaps the school staff should stick to education and to the interests of the kids they enroll—interests that may or may not coincide with the community's interests.

For all the federally funded projects and innovative educational ideas that have been implemented here, this is more a story about community change than educational change. In the process of directing the school system's attention to the task of community revival, Lund himself has wondered if there have not been some groups who may have lost out: the nonvocational students, or the "gifted and talented" students, for example. There are, Lund candidly admits, "mistakes which have been made."

But, then, Lund never said he had the answers. He only explains what was done in Staples. There was a determination that a healthy school system needed a healthy community, and there followed a period when the school system was devoted to that end. Whether it was appropriate and proper in Staples is a question that can be answered only by the people of Staples, and whether it could and should happen somewhere else are questions that can be answered only by each community that hears the Staples story.

# Part 3

## Interpreting the Montage

# 16

# Rural America: Multiple Realities

*Paul Nachtigal*

As we began our study of rural education improvement efforts, we were faced with the central question: What is rural education? Everyone agrees that urban education includes schools serving big cities and the suburbs; defining rural as everything outside urban/suburban centers, however, is not very helpful. The rural population is too broad and too diverse for this definition to serve as the basis for creating public policy or designing school improvement strategies. In designing the study, we agreed that the definition of rural used by the federal government—"areas lying outside the standard metropolitan service area of 50,000 population"—is too inclusive. One of the obvious characteristics of rural education is small size. Although we agreed that communities just under 50,000 population were too big for this study, the answer to how large a community could be and still be rural was always "it depends." By some standards the largest population centers in North Dakota might be considered rural: The economy is based largely on agriculture, a large percentage of the residents have either worked the land or have family on the land, and the values and life-style would tend to be more rural than urban. On the other hand, relatively small population centers close to major metropolitan areas would likely be quite urban in nature, with residents commuting to urban jobs and adopting urban ways.

Isolation is also an important characteristic of rural education. Rural education certainly includes small schools that need to exist because of sparse population and/or difficult terrain. But again, the answer to how isolated a school needs to be is "it depends." Are schools serving small Iowa towns ten miles apart on paved highways not rural? The lack of a precise definition of rural is at least one reason that rural education has been largely ignored in recent years. Lacking clear criteria for differentiating between rural and urban, public policy has opted for the easy way out, supporting the notion of education being a generic enterprise. Thus the one-best-system concept has continued to prevail.

An important use of the case studies in this book is to learn what we can

FIGURE 16.1    Rural/Urban Differences

RURAL _____ URBAN

Personal/tightly linked .......................... Impersonal/loosely coupled
Generalists ................................................. Specialists
Homogeneous ........................................... Heterogeneous
Nonbureaucratic ........................................ Bureaucratic
Verbal communication .................................. Written memos
Who said it ............................................. What's said
Time measured by seasons of the year .............. Time measured by time clock
Traditional values ...................................... Liberal values
Entrepreneur ....................................... Corporate labor force
Make do/respond to environment ....... Rational planning to control environment
Self-sufficiency ............................... Leave problem solving to experts
Poorer (spendable income) ......................... Richer (spendable income)
Less formal education .............................. More formal education
Smaller/less density ................................ Larger/greater density

about the uniqueness of rural education. In Chapter 1 we discussed both some generalizable characteristics of rural communities as well as some of the differences that exist among rural communities. An examination of the generalizable characteristics suggests that these attributes result from small size and isolation, which dictate the general form of the social structure. Social interactions are more tightly linked in rural communities than in urban communities; personal interactions are more frequent. One meets the same people in a variety of social settings—at school, church, the local stores, the doctor. People tend to be generalists rather than specialists. It is necessary to be a "jack-of-all-trades" regardless of whether one is a doctor, a farmer, a construction worker, or an educator.

Figure 16.1 identifies and compares some rural and urban characteristics. As there is no clear-cut dividing line between rural and urban, it is useful to think of the characteristics as being on a continuum: Depending on factors of size and isolation (geographical and/or cultural), communities will display certain characteristics in varying degrees.

Although "rural" characteristics tend to be shared among rural communities, there are, as we tried to illustrate in Chapter 1, real differences that exist between rural communities. Devils Lake, North Dakota, is different in many important ways from Fort Gay, West Virginia; Wilmington, Vermont, is not at all like Goodman, Mississippi. The important factors that differentiate a rural community in one part of the country from a community of similar size and isolation in another part of the country appear to be related to (1) the availability of economic resources, (2) cultural priorities of the local community, (3) commonality of purpose, and (4) political efficacy.

Clearly some rural communities have a stronger economic base than others, and the presence of financial resources is evident in the way a community looks, the services and programs it provides, and the general lifestyle of its residents. Midwest rural communities, often settled by fairly homogeneous religious groups, still tend to hold to the puritan ethic of hard work and a level of competition that is reflected in neatly painted farmsteads, high academic achievement, and winning athletic teams. A similar community in another part of the country with approximately the same economic status may give less attention to the cosmetics of its buildings and perhaps be less concerned with high academics.

Compared to urban centers, rural communities traditionally have been fairly homogeneous economically and culturally. This, however, is changing rapidly in rural communities where, because of energy development, recreation, or proximity to urban areas, an influx of population has brought in new residents with different values and expectations. When this happens, as it has in Wilmington, Vermont, the consensus about what is best for the community begins to dissolve; goals and power structures need to be realigned. These transition periods in the life of rural communities can be particularly difficult simply because of the tightly knit personal nature of the social structure. Without the buffer of anonymity, strongly held views can create a substantial amount of heat.

The final factor accounting for some rural differences is the degree of political efficacy possessed by a community. In Staples, Minnesota, the political potency was sufficient to mobilize the resources from within the community as well as to tap resources from outside the community to achieve its goals. In Holmes County, Mississippi, the black majority does not have the kind of influence with the white minority that controls economic resources. Relatively speaking, the political process is much more open in the traditional midwest communities than it is in the rural communities of Appalachia (Fort Gay) or the Deep South (Holmes County). If a group of citizens gets excited in Goldfield, Iowa, the town council and the school board will listen and likely respond. This is less likely to be the case in situations where the power structure extends beyond the community or where political control is concentrated with large land holders or an energy corporation.

Our observations of rural America suggest that there are significant differences between rural and urban communities and among rural communities. What difference does this make to education and the way schools operate? Beginning in the mid-sixties, federal policy recognized that the one best system was not serving all student populations equally well. Poor minority children were not meeting with success in school at the same rate as the more affluent majority students. Our analysis of the case studies suggests a number of difficulties in implementing the one best system in rural communities as well.

The public school system as presently conceived is more in tune with urban characteristics. Quality and quantity tend to be equated: More courses offered, more volumes in the library, more lab equipment, and more teachers with specialized degrees mean a better school. If schools are of necessity small, they are then by definition second best. The specialization, bureaucratic structure, and professionalism that characterize the one best system tend to remove control from the local community and are therefore in direct conflict with the operating style and inherent characteristics of rural communities. The tight linkages of small rural communities make the school an integral part of the local social structure and demand that it operate in tune with that structure. On the other hand, education professionals, the majority of whom are "outsiders," attempt to run the school as the profession (urban oriented) tells them it should be run. Our conclusion is that a better fit is needed between local communities and the school system serving that community. Public policy, rules and regulations, and curriculum need to be carefully tailored to local needs; and one size/one style does not do the job.

To be effective, improvement efforts must be concerned not only with the education problems that exist within the four walls of the school but also with the larger community social issues—the sociopolitical milieu within which that school operates. This is obviously good sense in any community, large or small, but in urban areas true communities are more vaguely defined, if at all. School governing structures and communities tend not to coincide. Tight social linkages are missing and thus the latitude for schools to function apart from the community is much greater. In rural America these critical elements are still very much in place. Assessing the community's social dynamics is as critical as assessing children's educational needs in deciding how best to improve rural education.

Given this reality, what are the implications for educational change, for designing and creating school improvement interventions? Without question, the issue of securing a match between local needs and intervention becomes much more complex. Not only must the interventions relate to educational needs of children, they must also be sufficiently consistent with local mores to survive. From another perspective, intervening agencies must be as concerned with the rejection mechanisms present in the community setting as they are with the rejection mechanisms found within the school system. The tight linkages require that these issues be dealt with simultaneously in rural communities; one does not have the luxury of handling community acceptance of innovations as a separate issue.

It is clear from the thirteen case studies that the interventions that met with the highest degree of success (Staples, Elk River, North Dakota, PURE) had a high level of congruence with the social history of their areas and met educational needs that were clearly recognized and articulated by the local communities. Those that were less useful (Experimental Schools, Urban/Rural, Teacher Corps) failed to acknowledge the reality of the local setting. For instance, imposing a high-impact intervention of comprehensive change (as in Experimental Schools) on communities that had not fully adjusted to an unpopular school consolidation effort is asking for social turmoil that a rural social structure cannot easily accommodate.

Viewing rural schools and rural communities as integrated social structures, then, is the basic premise of an enlightened rural education improvement strategy. The additional complexity this contributes to establishing a match between local need and intervention requires an understanding and acceptance of the diversity of rural America. At the same time, one must impose sufficient structure and organization on this diversity to create a responsive policy of rural education improvement.

### Toward a Taxonomy of Rural America

As desirable as it might be to have policy and strategies tailored for each unique rural situation, in this imperfect world that is not likely to happen, even in an age of advanced information storage and retrieval systems. Analyzing the characteristics of the communities represented in the case studies suggests that they rather naturally fall into three categories, which if acknowledged in public policy would provide a giant leap forward in addressing the issues of rural education. One could at least speculate that successful differentiation at this level might lead to a finer tuning of policy. For now, we propose categories based primarily on the social, economic, and political realities found in these communities (see Table 16.1).

The first category of rural America, the Rural Poor, is still best described in the report of the President's National Advisory Commission on Rural Poverty, *The People Left Behind*.[1] This segment of rural America, by almost any measure of the good life, is well below the national average: lower median income, lower level of educational development, higher mortality rate, and lower level of political power and therefore self-determination. Economic and political power tends to be concentrated and often lies outside the local community. Appalachian coal towns and delta communities of the lower Mississippi are examples of these social/economic/political conditions. Under such conditions, implementing the

TABLE 16.1  Categories of Rural Communities

|  | Values | Socioeconomic factors | Political Structure/ locus of control | Priorities for schools |
|---|---|---|---|---|
| I. Rural poor | Traditional/ commonly held | Fairly homogeneous/ low income | Closed, concentrated, often lie outside local community | Mixed and low |
| II. Traditional Middle America | Traditional/ commonly held | Fairly homogeneous/ middle income | More open/ widely dispersed | High |
| III. Communities in transition | Wide range represented | Wide range/ low to high income | Shifting from "old timers" to "newcomers" | Wide range, resulting in school being battleground |

"in school" educational improvement strategies is likely to meet with little success. The more basic socioeconomic problems will need to be resolved first. For instance, in the Holmes County Teacher Corps program, in which the major intervention was concerned with inservice training of teachers and the locus of control was clearly with the university, little long-term impact is likely to result. Strategies that focus on community empowerment would perhaps have been more appropriate; a community leadership training effort along the lines of the Leadership Development Program or a community participation strategy like the Rural Futures Development of San Juan County, Utah, would appear to make more sense. Until local schools are more effective in securing funds from the economic and political structures of the community and/or the state little else is likely to happen.

The second category of rural communities, Traditional Middle America, includes the Midwest farm communities of Iowa, Nebraska, Kansas, and the Dakotas. Though not wealthy in terms of millionaire status, in comparison to the rural poor these communities are well off.[2] Solid family life, well-kept homes, and a puritan work ethic assure a high level of achievement at both school and the work place. Power structures are relatively open and political participation broad-based. Resources for educational improvement in terms of both money and people are available. School improvement strategies most useful to these communities would be those designed to serve as a catalyst, to stir school personnel and community leaders to reexamine present practices and dream of better things. The "idea broker" inherent in the National Diffusion Network or the challenge of a new approach to teacher training as presented by the North Dakota New School Program are examples of programs that can keep small school programs fresh and alive.

In both of the above categories, communities tend to have fairly homogeneous characteristics; the economic spread for the majority tends not to be large. Values and expectations are commonly held and preserved by population trends that are steady or on the decline.

Communities in Transition represent a third identifiable category of rural America. Recreation, energy developments, or proximity to urban areas that allows commuters to enjoy the rural life have resulted in an influx of outsiders who bring with them different ideas, different value systems, and new demands for services. Here the social structure is in a state of flux, and conflict between the old and the new is almost always focused on the school, as it still serves as the hub of the small-town social structure. The tight linkages that characterize social interactions in small communities serve to increase the intensity of those interactions when new ideas and new expectations generate conflict.

In this category, the case studies provide little guidance on how to intervene. There are clear examples of what not to do: one should not add to the turmoil, as was the ultimate result of the Experimental Schools Program in South Umpqua. The less-than-positive results of ES may, however, have been due as much to the way it was implemented as the design itself. There were in the design strategy provisions for broad-based community involvement, which, if carried out, might have resolved some of the growing differences within the community. Consensus building requires time, however, and the press of federally imposed deadlines prevented those provisions from being implemented. There are also elements within the Rural Futures Development Program that might be useful for working with school improvement in transition communities. Properly constituted school-community groups representing all factions of the community under the guidance of a skillful "process facilitator" could provide an arena for airing and perhaps resolving differences in expectations for the community's schools. ES and the Mountain Towns Teachers' Center both clearly point out the difficulty of successfully implementing school change without community involvement.

The rich diversity that characterizes rural communities is not so clearly reflected in the rural schools. One hundred years of implementing a common school system policy has resulted in more similarities than differences. The differences, however, are critical, as they have persevered in spite of efforts to provide equal—which has generally been interpreted to mean identical—educational opportunities. The differences have persevered because the linkages between rural schools and communities are still strong enough to offset the pressures of standardization that come from the one best system. Here again the differences are related to economic resources, cultural priorities, commonality of purpose, and political efficacy. Holmes County, because of inadequate state and local support, is forced to depend on an array of federal programs (40 percent of the total budget) to meet basic operating expenses. The low socioeconomic level of the local community plus the lack of commitment by local and state governments to the education of black children keeps the schools operating at a subsistence level at best. Rural schools of north-central Iowa, or west Texas, exist in a different climate. Many Iowa communities would increase the local support of schools if finance equalization laws would permit. Because they do not, ways are found to support the educational enterprise in other ways: Ten thousand dollars can be raised in a week to buy land for a new school, or ten lighted tennis courts are constructed by the community on school land for school use.

State legislatures of Traditional Middle America tend to be more aggressive and forward looking, establishing a more supportive climate for rural education in that section of the country. Studies are undertaken and programs initiated to fully credential all teachers, and educational service agencies are established to deliver programs to rural schools that would not otherwise be available. Teachers from a culture of the puritan work ethic set high standards for their own work as well as for that of their students. It is not unusual for rural communities to recruit teachers from local colleges and universities. The endemic socioeconomic problems facing rural schools in depressed areas also plague higher education, and the vicious circle continues. Through the same process, in more affluent Middle American communities the high standards are reinforced.

The traditional mix between locals and outsiders that characterizes a small school staff takes on different variations in each of the three categories of communities. Outsiders are likely to come and go much more quickly in the low-income communities, as those communities are not generally the top choice of job seekers. The proportion of outsiders to locals tends to be much higher in transition communities; a good example is Wilmington, Vermont, where the Mountain Towns Teachers' Center serves almost exclusively teachers who are new to the area. Here the turnover is also likely to be quite high. Again, most of the bright young teachers recruited during the Experimental Schools Project in South Umpqua did not last beyond the project. Adjusting to the isolation and the "fish bowl" existence is difficult for those who have grown up in urban and suburban areas.

Differentiating between the types of rural communities is basic to a more enlightened public policy for rural education, but there is also much to be gained by taking a closer look at size and density. As indicated in Chapter 1, the breakdowns used by the National Center for Education Statistics, grouping schools in enrollment categories of fewer than 300 students, 300 to 999, and 1,000 to 2,499, are important in thinking about school improvement interventions. In the larger context of American public education, even school districts that exceed 1,000 students would be considered small, and without question many are rural. San Juan County, Utah, and the South Umpqua District serving Canyonville, Myrtle Creek, and Tri-City in western Oregon are examples. The problems experienced and the appropriate solutions for districts in the largest of the three categories will be quite different from those in the smallest. Part-time administration and multiple teaching assignments require a different approach in schools of fewer than 300 pupils than in larger systems with full-time administrative support and more specialized teaching assignments. Support personnel, not present in smaller districts, are likely to be available in districts of over 1,000 to take care of federal accountability responsibilities. Direct services for both students and teachers may be needed in the smallest rural schools while in larger rural districts assistance may take on more of a consultative or technical assistance role.

Density of population has important implications for achieving a match between educational need and intervention. The problems faced in providing quality education in a 250-student school serving a 1,000-square-mile district in Colorado are very different from those of a similarly sized school in a district of 100 square miles in northern Iowa. The possibilities for sharing staff and services and for consolidation are much greater in the more densely populated districts. The percentage of each education dollar that actually goes into educating children rather than transporting them will vary a good deal.

There is still much work to be done in understanding what is rural and how rural education should be different from urban and suburban education. This study, we feel, has shed some light on the issue. Rural sociologists and others interested in rural education should take steps to further this understanding.

### Notes

1. The President's National Advisory Commission on Rural Poverty, *The People Left Behind* (Washington, D.C.: 1967).

2. Although communities in this category are often remarkably homogeneous, there are likely to be socioeconomic and/or racial minorities present, but in such small numbers as to receive little or no attention by the schools. Special classes cannot economically be provided. And because teachers are of necessity accountable to the majority whose parents represent the influential forces of the community, the special needs of these minorities are likely to go unanswered in the regular classroom.

# 17

# What Worked and Why

*Milbrey McLaughlin*

Determining which school improvement efforts worked and which did not is an inexact science at best. Evaluation schemes were not built into the programs studied, so there were no objective measures of teacher growth, organizational change, or student achievement that could be used to determine program success. Lacking such measures, our definition of what worked was limited to two more global indicators: the durability of the project over time and its continuing contributions to the original objectives of the program.

A number of the programs clearly had difficulty meeting even these criteria. For instance, participants of Urban/Rural and Teacher Corps acknowledge that courses offered in local communities and paid for by the project made inservice more attractive, but they also agreed that the courses were not much different from regular university offerings. In Urban/Rural, the School Community Council, the vehicle by which parity was to be achieved between the school and community for educational decision making, ceased to operate when the last federal dollar was spent. The only portion of the program that did continue was the FM radio station. And, as the case study points out, this was the one component of the program that local people refused to give up, forcing exemptions of program guidelines designed to prevent the use of funds for the purchase of equipment. The community outreach program, the most valued activity of Teacher Corps, may survive for a while in Holmes County, but both the formal inservice education effort and the internship program will cease to operate at that site now that the funding cycle is over. The activities of the Experimental Schools Program, many of which represented rather substantial change in the school program, began to meet with resistance even before the end of funding, and the growing backlash in the community dictated that the new administration "get things back to normal."

Other programs came much closer to meeting the criteria of durability and usefulness. The New School, now the Center for Teaching and Learning, continues to pursue the upgrading of North Dakota teachers twelve years later. The specific strategy of recycling less-than-degree teachers is no longer needed and has largely been replaced by a combined strategy of teachers' centers and off-campus courses to supplement the on-campus programs. *Loblolly* and PURE, both locally funded, did not have to pass the test of surviving the cessation of outside funding. Both have continued, with PURE expanding its purpose to look more broadly at improving rural schools in Iowa in addition to protecting their continued existence. The Leadership Development Program has continued with a modified format as the Southern Appalachian Leadership Training Program. The ultimate test for NDN has not yet been faced since it still receives federal funding. (Data are not available at this time to determine the success and continuation rates of the individual program adoptions.)

The varying degrees of success exhibited in the case studies led us to try out different frameworks for identifying critical factors in rural school reform. This can be illustrated by examining the strategies under the four themes of rural school reform, as outlined in Chapter 2. The programs we studied led us to seriously question the validity of Themes I (the rural school is the problem) and IV (the problems of education are generic). In answer to Theme I, we must note that we saw many excellent schools in our travels, with dedicated, experienced teachers and administrators apparently doing a good job of basic education. It is also clear that the solutions derived from Theme I, such as consolidation and professionalization, have reached their limits in several ways. The story of resistance to consolidation in Iowa suggests the existence of a different set of assumptions about what constitutes quality education. Local control and tight linkages to the community are perceived to be more important than the claimed efficiency and effectiveness of larger size. Rising transportation costs underscore the necessity of maintaining small schools in places like San Juan County and Elk River with their sparsity of population and difficult terrain. In fact, declining enrollments across large sections of the country will result in a growing number of small schools, many of which have already consolidated. Similarly, upgrading rural schools by standard strategies such as staff development encountered significant implementation problems in Vermont, Mississippi, and West Virginia. We suspect that the deficit model inherent in Theme I reduces the attractiveness of these strategies in most rural communities.

In terms of Theme IV (the problems of education are generic), we found a more mixed picture of success. The National Diffusion Network stands out as an example of a federal strategy that works well in a rural state, although it was not designed particularly for rural areas. However, in general, we found that federal strategies such as ES, Teacher Corps, and Urban/Rural led to either inappropriate designs or problems with federal administrative procedures in relation to the needs and dynamics of rural schools.

An inherent problem of the large federally funded programs was the unrealistic expectations of those programs for reforming education. Teacher Corps was "a means for creating a comprehensive approach to installing improvement, change and reform." For Holmes County, this translated into ten major objectives that ranged from "developing a model training program for T.C., professional teachers, teacher aides, student teachers and community leaders" to "initiating collaboration among university administrators, school district administrators, college professors, district teachers, teacher corps members, teacher aides, student teachers, school board members, local and state educational personnel." To accomplish either of these objectives could take ten years; Teacher Corps had only two.

The Experimental Schools Program was designed to bring about "comprehensive change" at all grade levels with "broad community involvement" in five years. Urban/Rural was to result in "a school with a new environment which is stimulating and satisfying to the child and teacher alike, and in which the academic achievement and human development of children will be significantly increased." The program would be "revolutionary in terms of involving an entire school staff as change agent."

As indicated earlier, clear examples of Themes II (necessarily existent) and III (strengths of smallness) were not available for study. Reforms that were locally initiated, such as *Loblolly* and the programs in Staples and Elk River, did appear to have higher success rates although not all were productive. The Mountain Towns project in Vermont revealed that local reformers can miscalculate in their assessment of needs or lack the resources necessary to carry through with their plans. In addition, the locally initiated success stories usually involved some form of inspiration or support from outside sources. Staples was liberally supplied with federal program funds, Elk River utilized consultants from the state education agency, and *Loblolly* received moral and political support through outside awards.

In the end, none of the themes turned out to be a universal prescription for planning future efforts or for explaining the variance in success among the different strategies. One of our efforts in the final chapter is to suggest the outlines of a new theme that could prove more useful and durable as a guide to future policy.

We also arrayed the case studies according to other criteria, in the hope of finding some critical dimensions that explained success or failure. For example, one can group strategies based on their problem definition: staff development (NDN, New School, Urban/Rural, Teacher Corps, Mountain Towns), community involvement (Staples, RFD, PURE, Urban/Rural), or curriculum (NDN, Experimental Schools, *Loblolly*). Each group, however, contained both winners and losers and we did not sense one of these problems as existing across the board in all the sites observed. There were also varying degrees of success shown in strategies concentrating on within-school variables as opposed to efforts from outside. Finally, heavily funded efforts were not necessarily more successful than those operating on small local budgets. In fact, there seemed to be considerable danger in "overfunding" a small school project in terms of its durability.

In sum, our analysis suggests that the critical elements for rural school improvement are very much community dependent and relate both to *what* is to be done and *how* the design is carried out.

### Centrality of Problem Definition

The success of rural school improvement appears to relate directly to the centrality of the problem definition to both the school and the community. In cases where a high degree of consensus was achieved concerning the relevance and significance of the objectives, projects continued and were useful; where the broad-based consensus was not achieved, projects ceased to operate when funding ran out. In other words, unless the locals are convinced it's worth doing, it won't work. And, as general research on the process of change shows, we found that levels of local commitment and motivation are not immutable givens; they can be generated (or depressed) in a local community.

Rural communities, particularly those populated by poor minorities, have a multitude of difficult and often interrelated problems: low economic base, isolation, and low level of local leadership and expertise. Typically, the educational problem addressed by a change effort is simply symptomatic of a sub-set of more pervasive difficulties. Further, rural residents, particularly those living in poverty, have fewer personal resources—time, energy, or money—to devote to anything beyond providing food and shelter for their families. Individuals in such communities will invest these precious resources only when the problem addressed by a change effort is accorded high priority. The community outreach programs of Teacher Corps came much closer to reaching this high priority status for the Goodman-Pickens community than did the inservice education aspects of the program.

Even in more affluent rural communities, projects failed in part because there was little local consensus about the importance of the problem as defined at the national level; consequently, commitment to project goals was not forthcoming. Although all concerned may support efforts to achieve "better education," if they do not perceive anything seriously deficient in their present practices they are not likely to endorse a school reform program.

This does not mean that federal policymakers or other outside planners must abandon their own goals and objectives and simply "put money on the stump" to effect change in rural school practices. What it does mean is that programs must offer a variety of methods and techniques within a broad conceptual framework that allows local decision makers to determine which educational needs have greatest priority in their communities and how these needs can best be addressed. For example, the North Dakota project was useful and has continued because parents as well as school people agreed with the legislature that schooling would be improved if teachers were all fully certified with four-year degrees. The Rural Futures Development Program of San Juan County, Utah, met with success because both educators and residents of the county saw it as a useful strategy in resolving the problems of equal access to education, which had been the focus of threatened legal action. The Staples school-community development effort addressed problems that were perceived to be critical to the survival of both the school and community; both eventually benefited. The proposed legislation to close the small schools of Iowa threatened a way of life for a large segment of the state; though it began as a parents' movement, many small-school administrators and teachers have since joined.

A careful examination of the case studies suggests that the success of rural school improvement programs depends on how well they fit local community needs as well as local educational needs. This finding is not surprising in light of the fact that rural communities tend to be tightly knit, personal, integrated social structures. Schooling in rural America is still very much the community's business. The professionalization and specialization of the nation's schools has severed most of the natural linkages connecting schools and communities in urban areas, but the integrated nature of the rural school and community are such that what goes on in the school immediately affects the community, and vice versa. Some of the programs examined, then, gained their legitimacy by virtue of the appropriateness of the problems being addressed.

## Process of Change

Compatible policy design and relevant objectives are necessary but not sufficient conditions for rural school improvement. Implementation strategies must also be chosen that are consistent with the facts of life in rural schools. Three key factors are important to consider in the rural school improvement process: (1) broad-based planning, (2) providing implementation assistance, and (3) building an institutional base.

### Broad-Based Planning

One way to insure the relevance of problems to be addressed by a rural school improvement effort and to mobilize incentives for change is broad-based planning. This means the involvement of all important actors in defining and planning a school improvement effort (a notion central to the Rural Futures Development strategy). Such a planning strategy serves a number of important functions in the change process. First and most obviously, involvement of all relevant parties, especially those who will be responsible for implementation, enhances participant commitment to an idea by bestowing a sense of ownership. Project goals and methods become theirs—something they helped to articulate rather than something imposed by a central administrator, project director, or outside agency. There is a second very functional value of broad-based planning. Participants in different roles have varying perceptions, not only of the problem, but also of effective solutions. In a rural community where the school's business is also the community's business, planners and advocates of change must enlarge their notion of the relevant actors in the planning process. In addition to school administrators, teachers, parents, and school board members, local business people and other local leadership must be included as well. The Rural Futures Development program required the involvement of all community opinion leaders as part of the design. And although the Experimental Schools project and Urban/Rural also called for extensive community participation in the design of local programs, in the final analysis federally imposed time lines and expectations of how proposals and budgets should be constructed negated local community involvement.

*Providing Implementation Assistance*

Implementation assistance comprises the technical advice, consultation, and moral support provided to project participants during the course of implementation. In rural areas, as in urban sites, it is essential for such assistance to be readily available as well as timely, relevant, and responsive to local concerns. Assistance that is scheduled in advance of particular project needs is likely to be out of phase with project activities and problems; problems rarely present themselves on a neat six-month or bimonthly schedule. In the absence of timely and appropriate assistance, project efforts are likely to go awry and project morale may be irretrievably lost.

Rural participants are likely to have greater and more frequent need for technical assistance than their urban counterparts. As a one-of-a-kind staff member, as is often the case, a rural educator has no one with whom to share ideas. Perhaps more importantly, rural educators have lived too long with the idea that only urban and suburban teachers are capable of implementing new educational ideas. Consequently, rural participants not only need a greater amount of technical assistance to keep project implementation on course, but they also require more in the way of hand holding—support for their efforts and assurance that they are making adequate progress.

It is equally important to provide assistance in appropriate ways. Urban residents have grown comfortable with outside experts and have become sophisticated in using their skills on a short-term basis. Outside experts—or outsiders of any stripe—mean something very different to rural residents. Outsiders typically are seen as subscribing to alien political and personal codes. They are considered insensitive to the facts of rural life and unaware of how things happen in small communities. They are viewed as passers-through, with no stake in community futures and no vested interest in the consequences of their proposals and activities. In short, outsiders are seen as wanting to do something *to* rural communities, not *with* them, and often meet with suspicion and distrust in rural school improvement efforts. The Leadership Development Program avoided this problem by providing the opportunity for local individuals to become the experts. Robert Shafto of the Maine National Diffusion Network worked hard at letting the small school educators know that he was one of them, delivering promptly the assistance requested by local districts.

## Building an Institutional Base

Building an institutional base means ensuring that sufficient expertise and support remain in the community to sustain a change effort when outside funding ends or when key project participants move on. Often rural change efforts are initiated and controlled by individuals with only short tenure in the community. An important aspect of building an institutional base, then, involves providing sufficient training to enable remaining personnel to continue project activities. Though problems of staff turnover plague urban and rural schools alike, they are more severe in rural communities. Rural school positions, for many educators, are either a first step in a professional career or an opportunity to demonstrate leadership and expertise. Planners and policymakers probably cannot do much to alter the high attrition of rural school staffs. What they can do is cast a wider net for project participants, with special attention to and including individuals who are committed to the community in addition to the "movers and shakers" who are upwardly mobile.

Another aspect of building an institutional base that is important to project continuation is the integration of project activities into ongoing routines. Change efforts that are "add-ons," that do not require the displacement of budget items, personnel assignments, or normal operational procedures are not likely to continue. The high level of outside funding for Experimental Schools, Urban/Rural, the Rural Futures Development, and the Leadership Development Program, in its original design, almost guaranteed that the programs would not continue. Small schools and small communities just do not have such resources. Even though the Mountain Towns Teachers' Center was funded at a relatively low level, the services provided were never integrated into the ongoing routines of the districts served and therefore the program was unable to continue.

## Leadership

Perhaps the most important factor of what worked and why was the quality of program leadership. Here again, our findings are consistent with other change studies. Where enlightened leadership was present, programs were much more likely to meet with success. (This, in fact, was the underlying reason for the Ford Foundation's initiating the Leadership Development Program.) In rural school improvement, understanding and trust of the local social structure appears to be as important as professional expertise in filling such leadership positions. In our visits, we found superintendents and program leaders who knew what needed to be done from the perspective of the professional educator, but because they attempted to move too fast, did not know the tolerance of local mores, or failed to get the trust and approval of the power structure, found themselves moving on.

Understanding and gaining the trust of the rural community power structure takes time. The short tenure of two, three, or four years, which too often typifies rural school administration, is not sufficient to establish oneself in a community. The Leadership Development Program recognized this problem and resolved it for the most part by selecting fellows who were established in local communities. The programs that met our success criteria tended to have this trusted leadership, for example, Duane Lund in Staples, Minnesota; Lincoln King in Gary, Texas; Robert Shafto in Maine. Good leadership in improving rural schools needs to keep its feet firmly planted in the local community while at the same time looking beyond that community for good ideas and the technical assistance to implement those ideas.

In summary, improving rural education will require policy that recognizes both the differences that exist between rural and urban areas and the diversity that characterizes rural America. In addition, the implementation process must be consistent with the characteristics of rural communities, recognizing their strengths as well as their limitations.

# 18

# One Practitioner's Notes

*Gordon A. Donaldson, Jr.*

Teachers, principals, and superintendents of rural schools and citizens concerned about rural schools seldom have the opportunity to see their own experiences from a distance. Most often, articles on rural schools, if they appear at all in professional journals, cover one aspect of school life or one particular case. We are left thinking, "O.K., that's the way it was at Otter Bend, but we're unique here." The case material in this volume is different. Its diversity permits us to see ourselves within a spectrum of educational practices and to consider its varied lessons for our own work.

I confront many, varied concerns in my work; the size of my school does not permit the specialization that could limit my problems to tidy dimensions. Instead, on a daily basis I must face the student with no lunch money, the teacher with an unorthodox curriculum idea, the parent with a bus complaint, and the citizen with a concern for wasteful practices. The wide-ranging pressures of rural school leadership belie neatly packaged solutions. The variety and the richness of detail in these case studies provide an unusual chance to improve our practices without forcing us to "buy into" a system that may not match the conditions or interests of our schools or communities.

### Obstacles to Improvement: Real or Imagined?

I occasionally am prey to a modest form of professional despair. Presented with a problem, my initial thoughts are of the reasons I or my school cannot overcome it. Meetings of my district's administrators, my faculty, my county's administrators, my local board, and our state professional groups frequently are tainted with a similar air of resignation. These case histories of rural school change have removed some of this despair for me by demonstrating how some commonly perceived obstacles to educational progress need not stand in our way.

First examine, for example, the matter of funding. Along with many colleagues, I view the inaccessibility or absence of money as a prime obstacle to change. The availability of funds in the cases described here, however, does not appear to be directly proportional to the success of improvement efforts. When money was thrown at districts, as in Fort Gay and South Umpqua, the desired results did not occur. In several instances, heavy expenditures of outside funds raised suspicions, threatened community control, and undercut local support for change. By contrast, when funds were generated by local people with outside help, as in Elk River and Staples, the programs were more successful. But as significant as money was in these cases, the community's and school leaders' roles in obtaining and spending the money appear to have been more critical to success.

Perhaps most encouraging, the Maine Facilitator Center and *Loblolly* experiences demonstrate how funds in ordinary school budgets can buy specific products that have significant effects on schools and on how their communities view the schools. Political organization of the sort accomplished by PURE and Superintendents Lund (Staples) and Merrill (Elk River) cost little to local taxpayers yet yielded important results. Texas's Education Service Centers are an example of a third avenue for greatly increased educational delivery for small local funding increases. Clearly, money need not be viewed as the insurmountable hurdle we often consider it. In fact, low funding levels can frequently lead to increased personal effort and an increased chance that a change will endure.

A second common obstacle to school change is the resistance of rural citizens (often including school staff) to outside ideas. We frequently are overly critical of the experts; we view new practices as "good for the cities but not for us"; we put up our defenses against people and ideas coming into our communities from out of state. Suspicions and opposition of this nature stalled or defeated attempts to institute changes in North Dakota, South Umpqua, and Vermont. Similarly, the Fort Gay school administration, part of a closed political system, resisted outside influences that threatened to disrupt local power and jobs. Indeed, most of the case studies identify some resistance to change, which originates from knee-jerk skepticism toward the outside and from a content with the status quo.

Yet we cannot afford to ignore the possibilities for improvement found beyond our communities. This volume documents numerous instances in which the barrier to outside practices was overcome. Most revealing are those in which the outside threat was a lawsuit or bill threatening to shut down local schools, causing the community to rally around its school to effect quick and potent improvements. In the examples of Elk River, Staples, San Juan, and PURE, we see local people seizing the initiative under pressure, refusing to accept a deficit view of themselves, and fashioning visible new procedures that use multiple outside practices for the sustenance of their schools and communities. I was most impressed by Jack Deits's advice to change the way we think about our schools as a first step: We must stress our accomplishments over our needs, the desirability of change over the necessity for change, and our school's and community's uniqueness over their remoteness if we are to see any progress occur.

A third obstacle is closely related to this defensive resistance to outside influences: an ignorance of alternative practices and an absence of updated training, born of professional isolation. I sometimes think, "If we were closer to resources to encourage, train, and stimulate us, we'd be doing a lot better." Again, the case studies reveal this obstacle to be a prime concern in many rural areas. Professional isolation (equated with professional stagnation) was a main target of the Vermont, Fort Gay, Mississippi, Maine, and North Dakota efforts. Strategies for change included on-site inservice training, exchanges, university-school teamwork, financial and academic degree incentives, and support networks of helpful and like-minded people. To overcome isolation, we must use to advantage such efforts to link us together and to give us access to resources.

And further, we must not sit idly waiting for others to contact us. In Gary, Staples, South Umpqua, and Elk River, local attempts at school improvement show that ideas and models for change must be sought by increasing professional contacts. Thus, locally initiated specific goals for school improvement led to professional exploration. That exploration was rewarded, and new visions of school practice and function emerged. I have witnessed this sort of upward spiral when colleagues sought out and used ideas, advice, and workable models to develop a local history magazine, a computer course, and community-based vocational training.

A fourth obstacle, the absence of a literature of shared experience that can both inform and support our local decisions, is addressed by this book. Perhaps more debilitating than our separation, our subjugation to central bureaucracies, and our poverty is the fact that we cannot find serious or creative treatment of ourselves, our pedagogical experiences, or our school problems in the literature of education. Most of these case studies are testaments to this void. Throughout the book, references to other models or systems of rural change are lacking—because they do not exist—and in the case of the federally funded efforts, one primary aim was in fact to develop ideas and programs of use in many rural areas.

We need look no further than the example of Lincoln King, whose Christmas gift of the *Foxfire* book prompted a change in curriculum with districtwide impact, to be reminded of the power of practical ideas shared through books, articles, and other professional means. This volume's cases, ranging as they do from a black Delta school to statewide diffusion programs, not only bolster our sense of importance and that of our efforts but also provide practical ideas none of us can afford to ignore. More current and systematic firsthand experience must reach us and more frequently, in periodicals, professional meetings, and books of this kind.

The most significant lesson of these experiences is that we should not allow ourselves to be defeated in our ambitions to improve our schools before we even start. Each of us has a particular constellation of obstacles; yet many ideas exist for mobilizing local support, for obtaining needed professional help, for ferreting out seed money, and for developing our own capacities as school leaders. The rising tide of interest in rural and small schools and the renewed commitment to proving and improving the quality of life in small communities will make our success more possible.

## Identifying Needs: Who Says We Should Change?

The experiences reported here make clear the fact that the itinerary of the idea for change from conception to fruition is extremely important. Critical to the success of a change effort are the community's and school staff's perceptions of where the idea originates, what perceived deficit the change is deemed to remedy, whether they can themselves alter and shape the directions of change, and what personal and community gain the change will bring. The case studies bring to light several generalizations I find useful in planning and establishing procedures for school change.

First, these cases confirm my belief that local changes, to succeed, must be authored by local people. Sites where changes moved most smoothly and became most integrated into the routines of school and community were those in which a need was identified locally. In San Juan and North Dakota, change efforts made participatory decision making and local goal definition central to their processes. These efforts, like those in Staples, Elk River, and Iowa, succeeded in part because the long-time residents of those communities pulled together their own plans for meeting needs and stood behind those plans. Change emanated from intrinsic problems rather than from an outsider's conception of "what you people need."

The need for local authorship and involvement is certainly not a novel observation. Many of us recognize its importance but grow frustrated by our inability to foster and maintain it. My second generalization for planning is one answer to this frustration: Take advantage of the sentiments aroused by opposition to externally imposed changes. The banding together of Iowa citizens to form PURE, the mobilization of the Elk River community, and the response of San Juan County, Utah, people to the threat of lawsuits reflect this phenomenon. The first two of these cases are especially encouraging because local citizens did not roll over to the demands of the state but rather took a constructive tack to prove that the small rural school has merits unattainable in large consolidated schools.

The fact remains, too, that the more successful efforts did not result from small groups of rural citizens going it alone. They used financial resources, management and "process" expertise, special legislative help, and the philosophical/ideological aid of many outside agencies and people (some of whom they opposed, in principle). Thus, I draw a third observation: We in rural schools are committed by necessity to a love-hate relationship with bigger, more influential outside agencies. Though we resist the kind of wholesale replanning of our schools witnessed in South Umpqua, ideas, practical services, and the firsthand experiences of our rural colleagues are available. Our greatest challenge as leaders is to see that the lines between our own plans and hopes for our schools and towns and the state and national plans and hopes for them do not, except in extreme cases, become battle lines. Each of us must stay as tough minded about the unique needs of our schools, yet as open-minded about new ways to meet them, as Dee Merrill, Babe Sampson, and Duane Lund did.

A fourth generalization modifies the third: Do not plan to adopt a program of change without altering it to fit the local agenda. Programs conceived by task forces at the district office, the state capital, or in Washington will seldom be bought lock-stock-and-barrel by local people. Fort Gay, South Umpqua, and the Mississippi Delta experiences should convince us all of that. We must remember Judge Nelson, the principal of the Delta school. The Teacher Corps aimed to "improve school climate and develop systems for educational personnel development." But what Judge Nelson needed, in the eyes of his teachers and community, was "three more classrooms." Though federal money, university aid and credits, and additional school personnel helped Nelson's school, they did not address the most critical concerns on the local agenda. As in South Umpqua and Fort Gay, local teacher and citizen groups grew to feel that they were not consulted or heard. Those projects ended with considerable hostility and frustration, which unfortunately eclipsed some real advances.

The politics of change occupy a large part of this volume, but we should not forget that many changes can and do occur outside the realm of political concerns. I have been repeatedly impressed by the instances of quiet adoption reported here. Thus the fifth generalization is that valuable progress can be piecemeal, involve little fuss, and require only moderate effort. We see such progress in the instances in which technical help, offered in the form of retraining, curriculum, hardware, or ongoing advice, is eagerly accepted by teachers, administrators, board members, and citizen groups. This progress often occurs outside the sometimes loud public debates about schools. The Maine Facilitator Center, the Texas Education Service Centers, Duane Lund's programs, and the North Dakota experience reflect elements of this process. It is even more evident in the controversial cases: Fort Gay teachers welcomed the retraining assistance offered; Vermont teachers and building principals drew sustenance from the Teachers' Center; and some teachers in the South Umpqua area gained significantly in equipment and versatility from the Experimental Schools program, in spite of their opposition to it.

Lincoln King and Babe Sampson best exemplify these five generalizations about the process of change. They combined local planning, outside resources and encouragement, flexible new ideas, and a small practical scope in their efforts. Introduced without fanfare, proposed first only as an idea that was adaptable to Gary, Texas, King's project grew with the energy and ideas of his students. It developed organically from the resources and interest of his community, rather than being thrust upon students and community as a fixed program to be instituted through an inflexible formula. Though the UND New School was controversial, Sampson's down-to-earth, sensible accommodation of some "open" practices created little trouble at all. Her commitment to slowly trying different practices, the access parents had to her and to her classroom, and her own sensitivity to her community's preferences made her efforts work.

Though the national mood, the availability of money, and the community's defensiveness toward outside forces undoubtedly influence efforts at school improvement, we can usually shape the manner in which a change is proposed. We can strive to see that positive changes are espoused by respected and trusted local leaders, that changes are seen as self-improvements rather than as knuckling under to the outside, that our school staffs receive a steady flow of new ideas and support, and that new ideas are calmly tested, altered if necessary, and proven serviceable to our constituents or discarded. Attempts at change that do not reasonably fit these specifications in a community are in all likelihood inappropriate to the community's rural school.

### Evaluating Outcomes: What Is the Change Worth?

Regardless of its origin, a change in a rural school causes teachers, students, parents, and many others to alter their daily routines. We all ultimately judge the worth of a new practice by what we see and hear about it in action. Particularly in small rural communities, that judgment is shared by most of the community. Because of the exceptional burden of rural school budgets on hard-pressed breadwinners, we often reduce the evaluation question to a matter of demonstrated return on dollars spent. As a rural school principal, I constantly face citizens who feel that some part of my school's staff or program is not "worth the powder to blow it to hell."

What lessons can we draw from these cases to help us make changes that our constituents will consider worth the money spent? First, we would be well advised to see that money is spent locally to the greatest extent possible. In Staples and Elk River, budgets bought expanded school services for a wider range of community members. New staff were hired and settled locally. Local curriculum development was financed over the purchase of packaged materials. Vocational training for students and retraining for adults were major emphases. Public facilities and services were developed in an effort to devote school funds and energies to the resurrection of the community. Taxpayers in Staples and Elk River could see the concrete benefits of "all that money" for themselves and their children, rather than discovering that it was being spent on "imports" and numbers of new administrators or consultants, as was the case in South Umpqua and Mississippi.

Second, we should note that changes that cost least in local tax dollars or were least ostentatious in their expenditures garnered most citizen acceptance. The efforts of Lincoln King, the housewives who started PURE, and the University of North Dakota required little additional funding by local communities. The success of these changes certainly lies mostly with the extraordinary people who pursued them, but it is significant that their low local costs made them less vulnerable to budgetary high jinks. Other successful efforts such as Shafto's Maine Facilitator Center, the Texas resource centers, and the San Juan district's process facilitators required heavy funding from supra-district sources but cost local citizens small amounts. Most important in these three cases is the fact that these funds bought "plain" services that had immediate goals and purposes. Local folks, again, could feel their investment was buying services they needed or wanted and nothing more.

Third, programs of change must be introduced so that the sense of local access to schools remains intact. Schemes for the wholesale reshaping of curriculum and teaching such as those in Oregon, West Virginia, and Mississippi threatened citizens' and staffs' feelings of control over their schools. Particularly when it is outside money paying for "carpet-bag" curriculum, teaching systems, and people, the folks in the community grow concerned that their schools are running away. The Fort Gay experience, like many outside-funded attempts to spread community control, should remind us to calculate not only the effects of money on our communities but also the effects of new voices and new pressure groups that arise with the introduction of change. The tensions created within social and political worlds by encouraging new interests within the community frequently have resulted in further tightening of traditional control. This backlash occurred in North Dakota and caused the demise of the Mountain Towns Teachers' Center.

Backlash can be reduced through a broad planning procedure, but citizen and staff sentiments must be monitored throughout implementation, and, most importantly, new practices must be adapted to local preferences in some manner. I include this point as my fourth "lesson": View change as a long process, as one that must move at the pace of rural life and earn the support of citizens and key school leaders if it is to endure. The South Umpqua and Mountain Towns staffs ignored this point, clinging to such immediate programmatic changes as MACOS and the "open classroom" when they might have salvaged more overall progress by compromising. In contrast, gradual adoptions of new practices, by fitting them piecemeal into accepted, timeworn patterns of management and school-community life, characterized King's, Sampson's, and Shafto's approaches.

Successfully intermingling a new practice with old ones requires a sensitivity to the history and importance of our small schools in their communities. If we ignore the influence of community sentiment, we will find our neighbors and perhaps our colleagues waiting out "that new program" until "things return to normal." We should be alert to signs of such benign neglect; it is part of the rural scene. I am reminded here of the farmer waiting under a hedgerow for the thunderstorm to pass so he can go back to raking his hay. As long as the farmer perceives the interruption to his daily routine as a negative one, as one that he cannot directly control, and as one that will pass, he is content to wait it out. Too many of our efforts at educational change, rural and urban, take on the characteristics of the thunderstorm and inspire the citizens of rural communities to do no more than wait them out.

The fact that citizens in South Umpqua, the Mississippi Delta, and Fort Gay eventually fell back into this passive posture in spite of federal funding makes me wonder whether the funding of one-time programs is a necessary or even desirable model for effective educational change. Vito Perrone's formulation of conditions critical to success in programs of rural educational reform provides an apt alternative: "Take more than enough time, and less than enough money." These are the conditions of my rural district; indeed, they are conditions faced by most rural people and educators. In my daily attempts to improve instruction, to provide support services to staff, to expand my school's curriculum to be more responsive to the community, I look for long-term, gradually integrated changes. To see that they happen, I constantly must remind myself that the amount of support from teachers, parents, students, and administrators for those changes will have a greater impact on the outcome than will one-shot budget allocations or staff development workshops. This also is the lesson of *Loblolly*, Elk River, San Juan, Edmore, and Staples.

### Personal Leadership: Who Is Making These Changes?

No rural story would be accurate without detailing the people behind it. The personal nature of rural school leadership makes that leadership the major factor in the success or failure of rural school change. Unlike heavily bureaucratic systems, the personal relationships and esteem established by a teacher, principal, superintendent, board member, or citizen leader will determine the extent to which he or she can effect progress.

In the case studies, most of the key actors in successful cases had roots in the communities they served. Babe Sampson and Duane Lund, to pick the most prominent, had lived in their communities for much of their adult lives and showed no indication of moving away. Their own life choices were votes, in a sense, cast for their communities and for the life-styles of rural North Dakota and Minnesota. This basic affirmation played a large role in moderating community opposition to Sampson's "consorting with Communist hippies" at the university and to Superintendent Lund's pursuit of nontraditional education and federal funds. Membership in the native community or tenured residence similarly fostered a level of acceptance and local confidence that made Kinney and Losure in Iowa and Merrill in Idaho unusually effective leaders.

It is also significant that these exemplary leaders were perceived by many of their constituents as competent and well meaning. Roots in the community alone were not enough to win the respect and trust of community members. To be successful a main actor needed to have demonstrated goodness in his or her actions, as Sampson did through years of instruction and care for the people of Edmore and Lund did through his service as teacher, counselor, and later fundraiser and fervent Staples advocate. By contrast, Fort Gay's superintendent, Sam Hubbard, though a man steeped in county ways and committed to life there, was constrained by a self-serving political system to support a status quo that ran contrary to important community interests. Such a person, from the viewpoint of the case author, stands little chance to harvest support for daring changes within the classroom, school, or district he or she leads.

A third characteristic of the effective main actors that perhaps overlaps other characteristics was an ability to establish a sense of partnership with their communities that broke down initial wariness. The Leadership Development Program recognized this fact, stipulating that participants must be established community members who would return home after the program. Bob Shafto built on his background as a Maine teacher, appealing to school staffs by speaking to them "from the teacher's room." Jan Christiansen managed rapid acceptance in San Juan County partly because her cultural and religious background and her teaching experience matched those of the citizens and staff with whom she worked. In a similar manner, Lincoln King's connection to Gary, Texas, through his wife's family, combined with his own good instincts with students and appreciation for the community's past, enabled him to fit more neatly into Gary and its high school than other outsiders might have. Community membership, nurtured through these individuals' willingness to mix in, to listen, and to make long-term commitments to the community's welfare, gave them access to local people.

One case author noted a fourth characteristic: Many leaders demonstrated a "person-intensive" personal style that led to community acceptance without compromising the leader's goals. Effective leaders demonstrated patience, persistence, an openness to include others in the process of change, and above all a willingness to work person to person with those who were to live with the changes. Successful leaders understood the importance of direct and regular communication, giving and taking within the local idiom while not dropping their ambitions for change. Their drive for improvement did not require instant gratification, it was not expressed through bureaucratic edicts, and their frustration with opposition did not flare into anger or polarize the community. Instead, they quietly persisted, finding "face-to-face" means of lubricating social and political structures along the lines of Merrill's and Deits's gradual mobilization of citizen support and Shafto's "front-end work." These three examples all required low-key personal contact over considerable periods of time and a desire to see change occur in individual instances, not in wide territorial swaths (as proved impossible in South Umpqua and Fort Gay).

A fifth factor influencing the success of some main actors was the stability of personnel around them, particularly the presence of benevolent administrators. In Edmore, where the population and school leadership was relatively permanent, the administration and board had a long-standing relationship with Babe Sampson, trusted her, and gave her leeway to experiment. In Vermont, a fluid population base and shifting staffs at both schools and the MTTC made it difficult, as Watt put it, to "win with principals." Key actors remained the same (and persisted toward their goals) in Gary, Staples, San Juan, and Maine. Where they did not, as in Mississippi and Fort Gay (where upgraded teachers left the county), progress came hard.

Finally, successful leaders shared a perspective on their work, their schools, and their communities that permitted them to see beyond the perimeters of common practice. They sought alternative visions for their community's schools and had the energy to find the means to put parts of those visions into practice. Lund, in his boundless imagination and ambition, was aggressive enough to seek training for himself and to establish contacts outside Staples. Sampson was willing to attend the New School, to share in its vision of strengthened rural school practice, and to carry that vision back to a traditional environment. Unlike Cox in South Umpqua or Watt and Steel in Vermont, Lund and Sampson achieved that rare blend of native community membership and transcommunity vision that seems indispensable to small-community change efforts.

Duane Lund provided a summary I cannot improve: "The shortcut to quality education is people, not programs. The important thing to do is to hire good people. Ideas are not enough." Whether or not the primary agents of change occupy positions of institutional leadership and power, our cases demonstrate they can have immense influence if they go about change in the proper manner. These varied case histories supply us with a corollary to Lund's axiom—the likelihood for successful change increases as the key actor acquires these six characteristics: (1) roots in and a commitment to live in the community, (2) a record of competent, well-meaning service, (3) comembership with school/community people, (4) a comfortable "person-intensive" work style, (5) stability of actors with whom he/she shares the stage, and (6) a realistic vision for better practices.

## And What Can We Do?

Reading these case histories has been like immersion in an anthology of adventure novelettes. Different plots, heroes, heroines, and settings barraged my mind, leaving me with tidbits of wisdom about the life around me. Those tidbits must be tied by each of us to our own work. For me, that process raises the question, "How have the experiences of school people in the cases reflected my own experiences, and how have these people coped with their problems in ways I have not?"

I am most impressed by the improvements that were made in spite of budgetary hurdles. The work of Lincoln King, of Babe Sampson, of the PURE leaders, and of schools using Bob Shafto's services required little if any funds beyond those already available for staff development and ordinary curricular purchases. Supra-district funding sources made it possible for small, out-of-the-way districts like Staples and Elk River to make radical strides with only minimal local costs. Though these sources might not exist for us in coming years, cooperative ventures on the model of Texas's Education Service Centers can continue to provide services to small systems with modest local funding. We must remember, too, that rural communities do not often take kindly to ostentatious programming changes. The large overhead costs of many programs should not be included in rural improvements. Expenditures must be modest and reflect the make-do character of most rural citizens' lives or they will spark accusations of wasteful, irrelevant practices.

I am continually reminded of the importance we have as leaders in our schools. Funding hurdles need not stop improvements, but only if we act and think resourcefully. We must commit ourselves to careful, continued analysis of our own schools' needs and to the dialogue with our constituents that this process involves. We must operate as brokers for useful and practicable educational activities. Our goal must be to look within our staffs and communities for the kinds of human resource that Lund, Deits, King, and many others tapped in making the progress that they made.

Further, we cannot afford to ignore the increasingly available network of professionals who can provide low-cost introduction to and training in practices that have worked elsewhere. We must demand of our state departments of education, our state diffusion networks, and federal agencies the small-scale, practical programs that do exist and are adaptable to our rural schools. And as we do this, we must bear in mind the lessons of South Umpqua, Fort Gay, and Mississippi: Consultation with parents and staff in the planning stages is imperative, and adoption of outside ideas must move slowly, must involve adaptation to local idiosyncrasies, and must address constituents' basic desires for upgrading what is already being done.

As school leaders, we are already beset by daily problems; the fact is that *we* need prompting and encouragement from those with whom we work and from outside sources. I could not help feeling jealous of the practical help and support provided teachers, principals, and superintendents by the Northwest Regional Lab, by the outreach of Vito Perrone's New School, by the Education Service Center, and by the Diffusion Network and Teacher Centers that finally succeeded in working in schools. The Leadership Development Program, though small, is structured to provide us the time and stimulation to refurbish ourselves professionally.

Most of the successes described in this volume resulted from the chemistry of active, respected school and community people and responsive middle-level agents like Shafto, Christiansen, and Perrone. We clearly need to develop a greater supply of both these ingredients, but we also need to know more about the chemistry of the relationship itself. Certainly, rural school leaders must willingly seek out new practices to meet the new demands on rural schools and communities. In addition, middle-level agents need to approach districts with flexibility and a sensitivity to the rural community's belief in its uniqueness and tradition. Services like those of San Juan's process facilitators can be most satisfactory in this regard because they do not preach specific products or philosophies but help districts move toward their own. Perrone and Shafto took a more didactic approach but permitted local schools to identify what they would need and to adopt only those practices they could endorse. The exciting curricula and novel and expanded school activities developed by individuals like Eliot Wigginton (Lincoln King's middle-level agent) and Duane Lund can be brought into our schools through publications, films, and case descriptions similar to this volume. What remains, once our professional organizations, education departments, and universities responsibly support these middle-level services, is for practitioners to use what is made available.

The experiences of this volume return again and again to two principles of rural change: change is most often a *personal* process and change requires *time.* Effective agents of change were skilled people who knew and were accepted by many of the citizens in the communities for which they worked. They listened to the expectations and limitations their neighbors placed on their schools; yet they clung to their own ambitions for their schools to grow into more effective educational environments. Growth of this kind, when witnessed by the rural eye, must be gradual to be supported. Our rural schools have served as community focal points longer than schools in nonrural communities; for the long-time residents of our districts, these symbols of community life will not be trifled with.

In the final analysis, teachers, principals, superintendents, and community leaders stand at the pivotal point in rural school change. We must tune ourselves to the changing needs of our children, who will find themselves in very different worlds than we did when we finished school. We must know and honor the traditional places our schools have occupied in our communities. And we must seek, in serving these sometimes differing ends, to learn how other schools and other communities have begun making their community schools resourceful deliverers of quality modern training. This volume and its many stories of such efforts should inspire and guide our work.

# 19
# Theme V:
# Accepting Rural Reality

*Paul Nachtigal*

Public policy with regard to rural education improvement has through the years been characterized by negativism. Theme I (rural schools are the problem) attempts to make rural schools into urban schools; Theme II (improving the "necessarily existent" small school) worked only with those that could not be consolidated; and Theme IV (education problems are generic) ignored their existence. Only Theme III, which died aborning, took a more positive stance, attempting to promote the strengths of smallness.

Neal R. Pierce, in an article written for the *Washington Post*, stated, "In history, the 1970's will be remembered as the decade of rural return."[1] With migration trends reversing (300,000 to 400,000 urbanites per year moving out of the city) attitudes and perceptions about rural America are changing. The negative descriptions of rural life—parochial, backward, conservative—are being replaced by more positive terms: more leisurely life-style, less crime, clean air. "In times past," Pierce continued, "the rural areas 'exported' their poor and ill educated to the cities. What they are now returning is quite different—affluent part-time commuters, young professionals, retired executives, mining engineers, resort managers, craftsmen, artists, unemployed idealists, and returning natives—even Southern blacks— who've decided they prefer life at home to the city." Rural life, which for years was destined to have the least currency in the marketplace of valued life-styles, is now rapidly moving up to take its place alongside urban and suburban living. Rural life is more and more seen as a choice of equal validity to living in the city, an option for those who prefer a different cultural milieu.

The time is right to move into Theme V of rural education improvement, accepting rural reality. The present study has concluded that rural communities differ from urban communities in a number of significant ways and that there exists a rich diversity among rural communities that adds to the complexity of developing public policy for rural America. We are only beginning to understand the implications of these differences for rural school improvement efforts. Our attempts at structuring a taxonomy of rural communities as a basis for public policy are primitive at best. It is clear that small rural communities have strengths and weaknesses that should be reflected in the operation of the schools serving those communities just as urban schooling should be tailored around the strengths and weaknesses of urban communities. The question, then, is: How do we get from a set of education policies and practices that view education as a generic endeavor to a set of policies and practices that value and accommodate rural small-town culture and rural small schools?

In asking for a more differentiated educational policy for rural education, we are fully aware of the difficulties in bringing that about. There appears to be even less flexibility in public policy now than there was when many of the programs in this study were initiated. The demand for accountability and equity in education appears to be moving education in the direction of more commonality and rigidity in the way schools operate. A reading of the case studies, however, indicates that the limits of rural education improvement have reached a point of diminishing returns under such an approach; further imposition of a common set of standards and processes will not see a corresponding improvement in education for rural youth. Accepting the reality of rural America will require a break in the 100-year tradition of one-best-system assumptions.

## Redefining Rural School Problems

The first step in moving toward a more differentiated policy of rural school improvement is to redefine the problems of rural education. This redefinition will require a shift in both who defines the problems and by what criteria.

Historically the problems of rural education have been defined by educational leaders of an urbanized profession. Ellwood P. Cubberly in 1914 was clearly speaking from that school of thought when he stated that rural schools were in a "state of arrested development . . . controlled largely by rural people, who, too often, do not realize either their own needs or the possibilities of rural education."[2] James B. Conant was reflecting the same set of assumptions forty-five years later in calling for large comprehensive high schools as the answer to the country's education problems, be they rural or urban. Public policy, both state and federal, has set about defining rural education's problems from a position far removed from the local community, using a set of standards much more applicable to large school systems than to small. In fact, many of the deficiencies of small schools relate to size and therefore cannot be eliminated by definition. If the school cannot get bigger, it cannot get better.

The case studies on Teacher Corps, Experimental Schools, and Urban/Rural are good examples of problems and strategy being decided primarily by program designers in Washington. In spite of the rhetoric for local involvement, deadlines imposed by program guidelines and the general stance of the people approving programs were such that local communities were involved only superficially at best. And, as we have pointed out in a preceding chapter, the solutions were generic. If better-trained teachers were the solution to urban education problems, they were also the answer to rural education's problems; and so the programs for improving teachers were very much the same for both. If comprehensive school reform was needed to improve schools in the cities and suburbs, it was also needed in rural areas; thus the strategies—new curricula, new teaching methods, new scheduling practices—were basically the same for both. If more community involvement would improve education in the cities, it would also improve education in rural communities; so the strategy of forming and funding school-community councils to shift some of the control from administration to teachers and communities was the same regardless of location.

The National Diffusion Network and the Leadership Development Program are examples of local participation in decisions about problem definition and strategy implementation leading to a high degree of success in the program. We are not saying that central agencies have no role in defining rural education problems; we are saying that the locus of control for making those decisions must be returned to the community, with outside agencies playing a facilitating role, not a dictating one. We are also saying that the criteria for deciding if a problem is in fact a problem be more firmly rooted in local conditions and not in a preconceived set of standards uniformly applied to all school systems regardless of size and location. Again, this does not mean that there may not be some minimum level of performance, nor a minimum level of program accessibility available to students wherever they live. Local communities should, however, have a say in what those levels might be and decide how they go about offering such an educational program.

The process of reflecting on local school problems, articulating these problems, considering possible solutions, and implementing what appears to be the best solution takes time and resources and usually happens as a result of a program initiative at the state or federal level, such as the Title IV-C innovation grants. Small rural schools seldom have the personnel to keep track of such programs, nor do they have the proposal-writing skills and grantsmanship to pursue such funds. Further, funding agencies, because of high administrative costs, are more likely to prefer funding a few large grants than great numbers of small grants.

The case studies are full of examples of problems arising between small rural schools and existing grant-making procedures. Often the amounts are too large, creating an artificial displacement that cannot be continued on local funding, as happened in the Experimental Schools effort. Or proposals written by local communities are not acceptable to the funding agent, as in Urban/Rural, where the subsequent rewriting by a higher education institution resulted in loss of validity with the local community. Or rural schools are relegated to being mere consumers of new developments, as has happened in NDN.

Efforts must be made to train individuals who work in education service agencies (the state education agency, intermediate service units, regional labs, or higher education institutions) to assist local schools in identifying and articulating their problems in such a way that they truly reflect community conditions, not some preconceived notions of problems as listed in a formal needs-assessment instrument. If rural education is to be improved, it will be because rural communities define their problems in ways that make sense to them.

## Reexamining Existing Public Policy

One of the major complaints of rural school people revolves around the ever increasing number of state and federal program mandates that must be carried out by a small, over-committed staff. Guidelines and accountability procedures designed primarily for larger systems not only cause an excessive amount of work, but in some cases, according to rural school administrators, just do not fit the reality of their schools and their communities. A major task for Theme V (accepting rural reality) involves reexamination of the plethora of legal statutes, school finance formulas, and credentialing and accreditation procedures—along with the growing array of equity mandates for women, minorities, and the handicapped—to see how appropriate and necessary they are for the various categories of rural communities. This reexamination will need to take place at both the state and national levels and by people who understand and identify with the concerns of rural communities. Determining the appropriateness of policy for rural communities/rural schools is as often based on value positions and points of view as on factual data and rational arguments. School consolidation, for instance, though meeting the test of rational arguments for "efficiency and effectiveness" as defined by those who view centralization as good, makes little sense to those who define efficient and effective education in terms of close community ties and maximum participation of all students in school activities. Analyzing and redressing the balance of educational policy in such a way as to be more favorable to rural communities will require the establishment of advocacy procedures to get the issues into the public forum and create the necessary political support.

In reexamining public policy, it would also be useful to look at the constraints that are built into the policymaking process. Compromise between program design and political salability is a reality of public policy formulation. Our cases would suggest (another hypothesis that needs testing) that the closer the policy formulation is to the scene of the action, the less distortion is likely to occur; both the program-design fit and political fit will be of sufficient fidelity to make the policy a useful one. Further, a broader constituency is involved in influencing policy as one moves from the local level to the state and national levels, and the necessity for compromise of program purposes is exacerbated accordingly. For instance, the notion of implementing a community empowerment strategy in Urban/Rural to take on the control of the education establishment was modified by political pressure to a parity strategy. The fact that the discretionary funds available to test such an idea came from the Education Professions Development Act required that the strategy be concerned only with teacher training, a complex field that even professionals have difficulty understanding and therefore not the best subject for fledgling community councils to deal with. Likewise, the Teacher Corps, which was originally to be education's version of the Peace Corps, has through the years responded to political compromise to the point that it is now one more inservice program and in Holmes County hardly discernible from the ongoing efforts of the university.

The cases also suggest ways that the federal government and large foundations can create policy that is useful to rural communities. National Diffusion Network, Title IV-C, and the Leadership Development Program are examples in which the necessary accountability structures were maintained while providing the necessary flexibility of design to fit local community needs. Regional educational laboratories could be useful vehicles for implementing such policy if they move away from large development efforts as a primary focus.

## Creating a New Responsiveness in Service Delivery Systems

Creating a new responsiveness in agencies providing services to rural schools may be particularly difficult because of the key role they have traditionally played in implementing a centralized school system. Colleges and universities have been responsible for teacher-training programs closely monitored by state certification standards. Such programs were considered to be so outdated in North Dakota that a new teacher training program, the New School for Behavioral Studies, was established to develop more appropriate teacher education programs, particularly for rural elementary school teachers. Schools of education that train teachers specifically for rural school assignments are rare and, where found, likely to train teachers to cope as best they can in a system more suited for larger schools rather than seeking a pedagogy and curriculum more in tune with the rural reality.

State education agencies are also likely to find it difficult to respond in a new way to rural schools. In spite of good intentions to be a service agency, their primary role is still one of regulation, enforcing the standards of a common school system. To view rural schools from a rural cultural perspective and to move from a traditional position that sees school consolidation as as primary strategy for rural school improvement will take more than a little reorientation. It is at the state and federal level that the major impetus for viewing education as a generic enterprise has originated. Where state department of education personnel are assigned specifically to work with the concerns and problems of small schools, their role appears to be as much one of helping small schools deal with program mandates from the top as one of advocating small/rural school concerns. As is evident in the Texas RESC story, even in intermediate units whose original mission was service to small rural schools, there is a tendency to take on an agenda determined at the state and federal level. As the major portion of the RESC's budget are state and federal dollars, state and federal programs receive high priority for implementation.

In the past, the operating guidelines of regional educational labs calling for the development of marketable packages have met with the same difficulties as other curriculum/school improvement programs. In failing to acknowledge the uniqueness of rural schools and rural communities, the multimillion-dollar development efforts have generally been "too much of the wrong thing." Reduced budgets and a return to a regional focus may force the labs to give up developing large national programs and focus instead on responding to local problems, which in most areas of the country include large numbers of rural schools.

This lack of responsiveness by service agencies is at least in part due to the dearth of information about the nature of rural communities and rural schools. It is also partly due to the fact that rural education issues have not been clearly articulated and placed before education services agencies. Lacking this direction, the agencies respond to pressures and problem definitions coming from the top. One step that would go far in improving the responsiveness of service agencies to rural schools would be to include in the finance formula for small schools additional increments to purchase services not available in the local community. Giving rural schools this buying power would encourage service agencies to be responsive to client needs rather than offering programs that they or some other agency feels the local school needs.

## Creating a Development Capacity Within Rural Education

The capacity to develop suitable programs for rural education is virtually nonexistent. Not because the people are not there; creative people are found in small as well as large schools. Large schools, however, have greater flexibility to free these individuals to engage in developmental work. And, as we have noted earlier, funding agencies are more inclined to fund the larger schools, as processing a few large grants is easier than administering a large number of small grants. Rural schools are therefore put into the position of being consumers of urban-developed programs. Textbook companies and other curriculum development efforts have also ignored the needs of rural schools. The small numbers involved compared to the urban market are perceived as limiting profitability. In addition, the widely accepted assumption that education is a generic endeavor, that rural schools are just smaller versions of large schools, leads to the conclusion that the curricula should be the same.

The case studies describe strategies that, if properly implemented, would go far in creating a development capacity in rural education. We are not suggesting the creation of rural education development centers; rather, we are suggesting strategies that should be a part of all agencies interested in improving rural education. Central to any school improvement program is people development—creating among those involved the new perspectives, skills, and understanding that will allow a program to move forward. The process of the Leadership Development Program that had participants working on real problems, visiting and working along with others in similar situations, proved to be very effective in nurturing the human resources needed to bring about educational change. Critical to such a strategy are a little money to buy the participants' time to develop their capabilities and sensitive program leadership to help participants think about the problems they wish to address and point them in the direction of helpful individuals and programs. Many of these ingredients were a part of the North Dakota New School Program. Teachers were released from their teaching assignments for a year, exposed to new ideas about teaching and learning, encouraged to think about how these new practices fit their own classroom situation, and given a chance to try them out in the presence of supportive assistance.

The Rural Futures Development Program of San Juan County was also useful in preparing the Native American minority of that area to deal with Anglo bureaucracy. Learning how to conduct needs assessments, analyze problems, consider the merits of alternative solutions (which they saw in action through visitation to other schools), and prepare well-reasoned recommendations empowered a population to influence local school policy as it had never done before.

Critical to any change effort is follow-up support, both technical and psychological. The teachers in North Dakota who brought change to their classroom and sustained that change were the ones who were part of the ongoing teacher-center network that serves the state. Fellows from the Leadership Development Program who continue to be a force for educational improvement in their communities have found ways to be part of a support network to which they can turn for help. The National Diffusion Network is responsible for establishing a similar network in Maine for both teachers and administrators.

There is a growing body of knowledge on networks—how they function, their usefulness, and what's needed to sustain them. Networking would appear to be a particularly useful strategy for rural education improvement where isolation weighs on school personnel who may be one of a kind in their community. The opportunity to share ideas and problems on a regular basis would contribute much to local capacity building.

A companion strategy to releasing people from day-to-day routines for personal and/or program development is to bring new ideas and assistance to small rural schools on a regular basis. We have noted earlier that how these ideas and assistance are brought in is as important as the substance of the ideas and assistance. Timing is very important; help is needed when it's needed, not before or after. The establishment of a basic level of trust between those providing and those receiving the assistance is essential. Establishing circuit riders in the mode of NDN state facilitators is one way to bring in this assistance; providing sabbaticals for talented rural teachers to serve as traveling "advisers" working in classrooms alongside the regular teacher while trying out new educational processes is another.

The preceding stories point repeatedly to two important elements in bringing about change in rural education: small amounts of money and long periods of time. These factors are also clearly a part of creating a development capacity in rural education. A field that has been so neglected for so long will not reemerge overnight. Care must be taken in whatever strategies are implemented to be sure that they contribute to local capacity building and not to a dependency on the state or regional agency. It is at the local school level where more suitable education programs for rural communities need to emerge.

## Developing Alternative Models for Small/Rural Schools

Because of size, density, and the nature of the rural social structure, small rural schools do not fit in a school system requiring large numbers of students for efficiency and operating in a mode of specialization more suited to urban society. In Theme I of rural school improvement efforts (the rural school is the problem) we saw the deliberate efforts of school reformers to give structure and organization to what was considered a haphazard process of education. Such an organizational structure is useful as a tool to help deal with reality, to provide order and make comprehensible that which is not, but when that organizational structure *becomes* reality, its usefulness ceases to exist. In accepting rural reality it becomes necessary to take a critical look at the present organization and conduct of schooling to see if changes need to be made to achieve a better fit between the education process and rural communities. We are not talking about going back to the one-room school, although as urban education problems seem more and more insurmountable, it is tempting, as many recent journalists have found, to search for answers in memories of one-room schools. What is needed is to develop some new models—an "intermediate technology" of education—that fall somewhere between the country school of days past and the urban-style school that has taken its place. Just what such a school would look like and how it would operate in different types of rural communities is difficult to imagine.

In beginning this task it is useful to consider Theme III (the strengths of smallness) to see what there is to build on and then add to those strengths more recent insights into the nature of rural communities that might have implications for education in rural America. Thus, the small scale of rural schools has the potential strengths of smaller classes with more individualized instruction and teachers who know their students as individuals, as well as the family background from which they come. Ideally, each student serves an important function in the ongoing life of the school and has a much greater chance for participating in all aspects of the educational program. Teachers have a sense of control over what and how they teach and more flexibility to capitalize on their individual strengths. Administrators and teachers are on relatively equal footing, and school board members are known as individuals, providing the opportunity for broad participation by all in policy formulation. Finally, there is a minimum amount of bureaucratic structure, which allows a higher percentage of the resources (financial and personal) to be devoted to the instructional process and less to "systems maintenance." And as "time on task" is one of the major factors of effective teaching, small schools have the potential for being even more efficient than large schools.

If small schools were to take full advantage of their flexibility and access to the world outside the classroom door, the learning tasks could be substantially more powerful than the currently used textbook replications. Studying history and learning to write by interviewing and capturing the information from the memories of senior citizens, as exemplified in the *Loblolly* and *Foxfire* publications, can make two traditionally dreary learning experiences come alive. Understanding the concepts of government by observing and participating in town meetings or sessions of the county commissioners can give real meaning to a civics course. Easily accessible to any rural school is a living laboratory for the study of biology and botany. Lumbering and mining activities provide examples of the problems of balancing access to needed resources with preserving the ecosystem. Space adjacent to schools is almost always available for use in the study of plants and animals. It is a strange perspective we have adopted when such reality is seen as "enrichment" rather than the real stuff of learning. Urban schools, because of logistics and inaccessibility of these resources, must simulate these learning experiences through textbooks and other learning aids. This need not be the case in rural schools.

Barker and Gump concluded in their book, *Big School, Small School*, "It may be easier to bring specialized and varied behavior settings to small schools than to raise the level of individual participation in large schools."[3] Providing these specialized and varied behavioral settings will require some different models of schooling, particularly for the smallest of rural schools. For instance, if schools were free from the constraints of our present organizational structure, specialists could be hired jointly by a number of districts. Using a block schedule—class periods of two hours or even half a day—would provide the required hours while cutting down on the time and cost of daily commuting on the part of the teachers.

Technology has long been heralded as holding the promise of expanding and enriching the curriculum of small rural schools. Educational television, amplified telephone, and microcomputers all promise to bring quality instruction to students, regardless of where they live. For various reasons —inadequate programming, insufficient teacher training, poor equipment, and unwillingness of teachers to change behavior—such promises have not yet been widely realized. Further study is needed to determine just why efforts to use technology have not met with greater success; it may be that the impersonal quality of technological instruction just does not quite fit what has traditionally been the human enterprise of rural schooling.

These are but a few of the possibilities for developing educational programs that are more suited for rural communities. By continuing to look at the inherent strengths of small rural communities rather than at the deficiencies of rural schools in terms of an essentially urban system, other ideas are sure to emerge. Developing a more differentiated public policy, which not only tolerates but supports these different approaches to schooling, is a chicken and egg problem. Without some notion of what rural schooling could look like, it is difficult to say what policy is needed. Without some flexibility of policy, it is difficult to develop the new models. The above recommendations are intended to provide some starting points on both fronts.

Much of the responsibility for moving ahead is on those working in rural education and those who live in rural communities. They cannot do it alone, however. Local people and rural educators must be linked with knowledgeable professionals in relationships of mutual trust and commitment. This implies the involvement of professional experts with local people over the long term and at each step of the developmental process.

It is also clear that state and federal intervention is at times necessary and, if done sensitively, can be useful. Without the threat of state-imposed standards, Elk River may not have been as aggressive in pursuing a quality education program. The fact that the state also provided the necessary funding for such a program made the intervention a positive one. It is also possible that the state could have imposed quality standards other than the usual course offering/teacher credential criteria and come up with equal or better results, perhaps for less money.

Without the threat of federal pressure, migrants and minority groups have not been well served in rural communities. For the Holmes counties of rural America, however, we have yet to discover ways to intervene that will result in significantly improved educational opportunities. Black control, when accompanied by white flight and loss of financial support for schools, is of limited value in achieving quality rural education in such communities.

Accepting the reality of rural America opens a whole array of possibilities not previously available. It opens the possibility that rural education could look and operate differently. It opens the possibility that inherent in size and sparsity are reasons for school finance formulas to provide more money for rural education. It opens the possibility that professionals can work in rural education at all levels—development, providing services, teaching and administration—without having to move to the cities to "get to the top" of the career ladder. It opens the possibility that rural children can receive a quality education designed specifically for their needs rather than a second-rate program defined by urban standards.

## Notes

1. Reprinted in the *Denver Post*, October 1, 1979, p. 16.

2. Ellwood P. Cubberly, *Rural Life and Education: A Study of the Rural-School Problem as a Phase of the Rural-Life Problem* (Boston: Houghton Mifflin, 1914).

3. Roger G. Barker and Paul V. Gump, *Big School, Small School* (Stanford, Calif.: Stanford University Press, 1964).

# Contributors

**Ralph Bohrson's** experience in rural education began when he was an English teacher in Aspen, Colorado, when it was a has-been mining town and not yet a major ski resort. As a member of the Colorado Department of Education he served as director of the Rocky Mountain Area Project for Small High Schools and later as coordinator of the five-state Western States Small Schools Project. As program officer for the Ford Foundation he was responsible for the foundation's rural-school improvement grants.

**James Branscome,** a native of the Blue Ridge Mountains of Virginia, has been a spokesman for the Appalachian region on a broad range of social issues. As a freelance journalist he has been a critic of longstanding economic and political policies that have contributed to Appalachia's problems. His articles have appeared in the *New York Times*, the *Mountain Eagle*, and the *Washington Post*. Mr. Branscome has served as director of the Southern Appalachian Leadership Training Program, a program for the development of local community leadership. He presently serves as bureau chief of the South for McGraw-Hill.

**Daniel Cromer** is an education practitioner and a former teacher, counselor, and principal in Georgia public schools. As a staff member of the Northeast Georgia Cooperative Education Service Agency in Athens, Georgia, he has worked with rural schools in educational planning and instructional improvement. He is currently assistant superintendent of Barrow County Schools in Winder, Georgia.

**Gordon Donaldson** is a supervising principal of a 7–12 high school that includes a vocational education center in Ellsworth, Maine. His teaching career has encompassed both urban and rural experience. His first teaching assignment was with the Pennsylvania Advancement School in Philadelphia, and he has since taught on North Haven Island off the coast of Maine. Mr. Donaldson served as a researcher for the New Hampshire voucher study funded by the National Institute of Education.

**Faith Dunne,** assistant professor in the Department of Education at Dartmouth College, is a researcher and writer on rural education. Her research interests include the vocational aspirations of rural women and giving better definition to the characteristics of small rural schools. Her writings have appeared in *Education in Rural America: A Reassessment of Conventional Wisdom* and *Rural Education in Urbanized Nations: Issues and Innovations* (both Westview Press). Ms. Dunne is a school board member in Hartland, Vermont.

**Thomas Gjelten** is a former teacher on North Haven Island in Penobscot Bay offshore from Rockland, Maine. While there he was instrumental in developing the federally funded North Haven Project for Career Development, which he then documented in the project publication, "Schooling In Isolated Communities." He has since done extensive writing for studies on rural education in this country and abroad. Mr. Gjelten has been a freelance reporter for National Public Radio and is currently working with the evaluation of California's School Improvement Program.

**Milbrey McLaughlin** is a researcher–policy analyst for the Rand Corporation, where she has worked on problems of evaluating large-scale social action programs. Ms. McLaughlin served as deputy project leader on a major national study of education change agents that examined four federal programs: the Elementary and Secondary Education Act (ESEA) Title III (Innovative Programs); ESEA Title VII (Bilingual Projects); Vocational Education Act, 1968 Amendments Part D (Exemplary Programs); and the Right to Read Program.

**Paul Nachtigal** began his career as superintendent of a small rural school (fifty-two students K–12) in the mountains of Colorado. He participated in the Rocky Mountain Area Project for Small High Schools and later was director of the Colorado portion of the Western States Small Schools Project. During ten years with the Ford Foundation he served as project monitor for twenty-five comprehensive school improvement projects and was later responsible for a study of that program, "A Foundation Goes to School." Mr. Nachtigal is currently with the Mid-continent Regional Educational Laboratory's Rural Education Project.

# Index